TORAH FROM HEAVEN

THE LITTMAN LIBRARY OF
JEWISH CIVILIZATION

Dedicated to the memory of
LOUIS THOMAS SIDNEY LITTMAN
*who founded the Littman Library for the love of God
and as an act of charity in memory of his father*
JOSEPH AARON LITTMAN
and to the memory of
ROBERT JOSEPH LITTMAN
who continued what his father Louis had begun

יהא זכרם ברוך

'*Get wisdom, get understanding:
Forsake her not and she shall preserve thee*'

PROV. 4: 5

*The Littman Library of Jewish Civilization is a registered UK charity
Registered charity no. 1000784*

TORAH FROM HEAVEN

◆

The Reconstruction of Faith

◆

NORMAN SOLOMON

London
The Littman Library of Jewish Civilization
in association with Liverpool University Press

The Littman Library of Jewish Civilization
Registered office: 4th floor, 7–10 Chandos Street, London W1G 9DQ

in association with Liverpool University Press
4 Cambridge Street, Liverpool L69 7ZU, UK
www.liverpooluniversitypress.co.uk/littman

Managing Editor: Connie Webber

Distributed in North America by
Oxford University Press Inc., 198 Madison Avenue,
New York, NY 10016, USA

Hardback reprinted 2012
First published in paperback 2018

Catalogue records for this book are available from the
British Library and the Library of Congress

ISBN 978–1–786940–85–8

Publishing co-ordinator: Janet Moth
Copy-editing: Lindsey Taylor-Guthartz
Proof-reading: Agnes Erdos
Index: Norman Solomon
Designed and typeset by Pete Russell, Faringdon, Oxon.

Printed and bound by CPI Group (UK) Ltd, Croydon, CR0 4YY

Preface

◆

THIS IS BOOK TWO of a trilogy that I do not intend to write. Book One would have been about theological matters, such as God and the afterlife; Book Three would be a reworking of the practical part of the Jewish religion, the system of halakhah (Torah-based law). Book Two, the present volume, is about the connection between the two: what sense can be made of the notion that God dictated words and laws, and that these were faithfully recorded for posterity by his servants, the prophets, and by their interpreters, the rabbis?

An analogous question arises for any religion that bases itself on a claim that God revealed his will through scripture, that the scripture has been preserved accurately, and that certain persons (rabbis, priests, imams) are entrusted with its interpretation. Though this book focuses on Judaism and draws most of its examples from that religious tradition, I hope it will be read by followers of other religions too; they will easily find analogies in their own religions, as well as analogies with the critiques to which all of us have been subjected and the responses that have been elicited.

Some might be surprised to see so many references to pagan, Christian, and Muslim thinkers in a book about Judaism. However, Jews were never isolated from surrounding cultures, nor were the surrounding cultures isolated from Judaism. Historical criticism of the Bible affected Christians as much as Jews; nor have Muslims, Sikhs, and Hindus remained unscathed by modern philosophies that challenge the perfection of sacred texts.

Readers with fundamentalist leanings may regard the book as controversial. If they reflect on their reading, I hope they will realize that what they are objecting to is not so much my opinions as the *facts* on which those opinions are based. It is futile to object to facts; the world is what it is, which is not always what we would like it to be or what our fathers told us; we must build our beliefs and philosophy on the evidence, not decide in advance what the facts are and then intransigently refuse to admit evidence that they are otherwise.

I aim to maintain a balance between the needs of the non-specialist, intelligent reader and the academic specialist. Mostly, I refer matters to their primary sources, though there are some exceptions, most notably in Chapter 8, 'The Original Torah', where I refer the reader to Emanuel Tov's authoritative summary of scholarship on the received biblical text rather than to the somewhat technical primary studies. Exhaustive scholarly references for every topic would fill several volumes; the sources indicated offer useful pointers for those who seek more specialized information.

The book ranges widely, crossing the boundaries of several disciplines. There are greater experts than myself in almost every topic covered, and I readily acknowledge my indebtedness to them as well as my own fallibility. I aim to describe the wood as a whole rather than the individual trees, though occasionally, for instance on the topic of rabbinic reasoning (Chapter 2), or with the concept of the 'Counter-Tradition' (Part II), I venture an original insight.

There is a fair amount of wry humour in the pages that follow; if you think something is meant to be amusing, it probably is; if you think I am writing with tongue in cheek, perhaps I am—I am not always sure myself. If you miss the humour you may still follow the argument, though you may misconstrue its tone (translators beware!).

Ultimately, the book is not so much an academic monograph as a personal reflection on a journey in which I have been engaged throughout my life. I believe others, especially in the Modern Orthodox community, have followed similar trajectories and have come to feel, as I have, somewhat let down by religious leaders whom they otherwise would like to respect; piety, learning, wisdom, and good judgement are not always found in partnership. Too often, I have felt I am engaging in battles which could and ought to have been decided a century or more ago.

Let me not raise hopes only to dash them. I cannot offer some final, triumphant solution to all the problems raised; the book must end on a *mezzo forte* rather than a clanging *fortissimo*. I shall be satisfied to have exposed the weaknesses of previously proposed solutions and to have cleared the way for a firmer path to be laid. Much work remains to be done if a defensible faith is to be articulated.

Acknowledgements

◆

I was certainly thinking of something along the lines of the present book when I arrived in Oxford in 1995, if not earlier, but the project only began to take form when I was invited to give the Sherman Lectures at Manchester University in April–May 2001; my thanks are due to the organizers and participants at that event not only for providing the stimulus but for the many helpful comments and suggestions I received at that time.

It is not possible to record the names of all the scholars, teachers, and students, from whose friendship and conversation I have benefitted; many are acknowledged by direct citation from their works, but there are others whose influence, though no less profound, is more difficult to document.

Apart from Chapter 20, a reworking of a review in the *Journal of Jewish Studies*, nothing in the book has previously appeared in print in similar form.

Translations are my own unless otherwise stated.

◆

My warmest thanks are due to Ludo Craddock and Connie Webber for their confidence and support and to Lindsey Taylor-Guthartz and all the team at the Littman Library for so expertly and enthusiastically guiding the project through the editorial process.

Above all, thanks are due to my wife, Hilary, whose encouragement, impatience to see the work completed, and numerous helpful suggestions have enabled me to bring it to some sort of conclusion. My four children, children of my first wife, Devora ל״ז, have all contributed in some measure through conversations we have had; my daughter Miriam read through much of the script and helped me avoid several philosophical errors.

And finally, *barukh sheheḥiyani vekiyemani vehigiani lazeman hazeh*, thanks to him 'who has kept me alive, preserved me, and enabled me to reach this day'!

Contents

◆

Note on Transliteration and Classical Sources

◆

THE TRANSLITERATION of Hebrew in this book follows the guidelines of the Littman Library, and reflects consideration of the type of book it is, in terms of its content, purpose, and readership. The system adopted therefore reflects a broad approach to transcription, rather than the narrower approaches found in the *Encyclopaedia Judaica* or other systems developed for text-based or linguistic studies. The aim has been to reflect the pronunciation prescribed for modern Hebrew, rather than the spelling or Hebrew word structure, and to do so using conventions that are generally familiar to the English-speaking reader.

In accordance with this approach, no attempt is made to indicate the distinctions between *alef* and *ayin*, *tet* and *taf*, *kaf* and *kuf*, *sin* and *samekh*, since these are not relevant to pronunciation; likewise, the *dagesh* is not indicated except where it affects pronunciation. Following the principle of using conventions familiar to the majority of readers, however, transcriptions that are well established have been retained even when they are not fully consistent with the transliteration system adopted. On similar grounds, the *tsadi* is rendered by 'tz' in such familiar words as barmitzvah. Likewise, the distinction between *het* and *khaf* has been retained, using *ḥ* for the former and *kh* for the latter; the associated forms are generally familiar to readers, even if the distinction is not actually borne out in pronunciation, and for the same reason the final *heh* is indicated too. As in Hebrew, no capital letters are used, except that an initial capital has been retained in transliterating titles of published works (for example, *Shulḥan arukh*).

Since no distinction is made between *alef* and *ayin*, they are indicated by an apostrophe only in intervocalic positions where a failure to do so could lead an English-speaking reader to pronounce the vowel-cluster as a diphthong—as, for example, in *ha'ir*—or otherwise mispronounce the word.

The *sheva na* is indicated by an *e*—*perikat ol, reshut*—except, again, when established convention dictates otherwise.

The *yod* is represented by *i* when it occurs as a vowel (*bereshit*), by *y* when it occurs as a consonant (*yesodot*), and by *yi* when it occurs as both (*yisra'el*).

Names have generally been left in their familiar forms, even when this is inconsistent with the overall system.

Translations of classical and Hebrew sources are predominantly mine; in cases where published translations have been used, these are documented in the notes.

ORIENTATION

GOD SAVED THE ISRAELITES from slavery in Egypt. Moses led them across the Red Sea, and they arrived at Mount Sinai (or Horeb), where God proclaimed the Ten Commandments to them from the heavens above, to the accompaniment of thunder and lightning.

That is what the Bible says.[1] But what on earth (or in heaven) does it mean? And how, why, when, and by whom were the Bible's words construed to signify that the whole Torah—meaning the five books from Genesis to Deuteronomy, together with a variety of interpretations and supplements— was revealed from heaven? How did *torah min hashamayim* ('Torah from Heaven') become the central doctrine of Judaism and, in modified form, of Christianity and Islam?

In general, what is 'sacred scripture'? How did such a concept develop? What problems do people lay themselves open to when they assert that certain books are inviolable sacred scripture? In the light of modern discoveries and changing moral perspectives, is there still any mileage in the idea of sacred, revealed scripture and tradition, and if so, how might such a notion be reinterpreted?

That is what this book is about, and I deal with it from within the context of Judaism. It is an important topic for 'believers' in any religion, but it is only one part of a bigger story. Related matters, without which the story is not really complete, include philosophical problems about the concepts of God and of revelation, and general questions arising out of the apparent divergence between scientific and religious world views. In this book I shall take for granted that 'God' and 'Revelation' *are* coherent concepts, and just ask what sense there is in linking them together.

Maybe side-stepping talk about God is nothing novel. Believers confidently declare *Allahu akbar*, 'God is great', or the equivalent in some other language, but when you start to talk to them about God what they actually say often seems incoherent and not at all like what the great theologians of their religion have taught. Many believers are quite intelligent, so evidently religion

[1] Exod. 1–20; Deut. 5.

makes some sort of sense to them, intellectual as well as emotional, even if they are confused about its fundamentals; the intellect, after all, has to take on some assumptions before it can get to work.

So let people by all means continue to assert that God is great and his Torah true, and I shall respond, 'Amen! Please calm down and be patient with me. I want to understand what you are telling me. One day perhaps we can talk about God, but let's start with something easier. What is Torah? Tell me as clearly as you can about the origin, meaning, and authority of the texts and traditions you hold sacred. Who first thought up the idea that a precise, written text had been dictated by God to Moses? Why did anybody believe him? How did it come about that people began to believe that the text now in our hands was perfect, free from error and redundancy, a comprehensive guide to life? When, how, and why did it come to be accepted by some Jews that not only the text of the Pentateuch, but the rabbis' interpretations, constituted the revealed Torah? How did a later generation of Jewish scholars come to believe that Torah incorporated, in addition, a mystical teaching, which has now generated its own literature?'

These are historical questions, and I shall address them on the basis of the available evidence.

But I cannot entirely avoid theology,[2] and I confess that this book has a theological agenda as well as an historical one, since it leads to recommendations as to how scripture and tradition might be regarded nowadays within the religious community which has adopted them. If I were just writing history I could try to present it in an objective, or at least an impersonal way. However, when theology is grafted on to history objectivity is compromised. Theology differs from philosophy, including the philosophy of religion, because it is done with a prior commitment to accepting the significance of a given vocabulary of discourse, a given way of talking. A statement made or a story told by a theologian is a statement made or a story told *with a commitment*. The commitment is to the privileged significance of certain texts within the community of the faithful (though not necessarily to any particular interpretation of those texts). The theologian, unlike the philosopher of religion, has made a prior commitment to a particular community (a 'Church'), and his/her reading of history and religion reflects that commitment.

---

[2] Peter Abelard (c.1079–1172) introduced the word to the Latin West and gave it a professional and technical meaning: 'reasoning about faith that proceeds in accordance with the principles of methodological doubt'.

Where I Come From

The purpose of this Orientation is to make clear where I come from—my standpoint, my commitment. I am not proposing 'frank confessions' about my private life; I am not proposing depth psychology or tense drama. But I do have a personal story that has shaped my reading of history and religion and that relates me to a specific religious community and to more than one culture. Without that personal story as background the history and theology I have constructed might be correct but would lack context and purpose. For instance, the fact that the earliest manuscripts of books of the Bible show variants from the received biblical text is not in itself problematic; it is a simple empirical fact. It only becomes a 'problem' for me and others like me because of the relationship we have with a society whose tradition claims that the extant biblical text reproduces precisely the text dictated by God to Moses in the Sinai desert somewhat over 3,000 years ago.

Any personal story is by definition unique. However, my story has much in common with the stories of many believers in all faiths who are unsure how to resolve the tension between the modern world view and the world view that arises from a plain reading of traditional religious texts. I shall tell the story in Jewish terms, because Judaism is my personal religious context. Parallel stories may be told by Christians, Muslims, Hindus, and others within the contexts of their own faith communities.

I shall tell the story in English, because that is my native language. English has been strongly moulded by Christian concepts, though many of these derive, through Bible translation and through Christian theology, from an ancient Hebrew culture. Yes, I am familiar with biblical Hebrew, and with rabbinic Hebrew and Aramaic, as well as with more recent Hebrew. But this does not mean that I think like an ancient Hebrew, a talmudic sage, a medieval rabbi, or a modern Israeli. My culture encompasses Bible, Talmud, and later rabbinics, but is not limited to them.

Texts are fixed, cultures are flexible and without clearly defined boundaries. I do not read the texts innocently, but with the 'baggage' of my whole culture. Historical criticism uses the resources of philology and archaeology to reconstruct the 'original' texts, contexts, and meanings. Perhaps, despite postmodernist denials, this is a coherent and achievable aim. But although the study of the ancient Near East has some relevance to the way I read texts, it does not determine how I read them in the religious context, for this is shaped primarily by the *reception* of the texts in my community. I do not, for instance, read 'An eye for an eye' (Exod. 21: 24) or 'You shall cut off her hand'

(Deut. 25: 12) literally, since rabbinic tradition understands these passages as indicating appropriate monetary compensation; but that is not to deny that such phrases may have been intended literally by those who first committed them to writing.

The Seduction of 'True Belief'

Children are vulnerable to intellectual as well as physical abuse from those into whose care they are entrusted. How are they to know whether the stories adults tell them about the world are true or false? Eager to learn who they are, what sort of world they inhabit, why this why that, they turn to those closest to them for information, guidance, reassurance.

They soon learn that some stories are enjoyable, but do not correspond to what actually happens. Snow White, Father Christmas, Harry Potter . . . 'Tell me another story!' They lap it up, but don't actually expect to meet Snow White, Father Christmas, or Harry Potter on the local bus, and if they do meet them—at Disneyland, for instance, or in the Christmas grotto, or in a movie —they know it's make-believe. Make-believe is fun, but you know it's make-believe, not for real.

Clear of the line on one side or the other you know where you are. But where precisely does the line fall, if indeed there is a sharp dividing line, between the real and the imaginary, between make-believe and actuality, fact and fantasy?

Are there fairies? Demons? Dragons? Angels? A devil? Souls independent of bodies? Spirits of the deceased?

Is there a God?

Is the world filled, or shaped, or given meaning, by a transcendent Presence, or an immanent divinity, by holiness, love, or whatever?

As a child I didn't hear much about Father Christmas, J. K. Rowling wasn't born yet so she hadn't created Harry Potter, and I don't think I ever regarded Snow White as anything but a pretty story (in those far-off days there was no Disneyland either). God was mentioned indifferently—'God bless you' if you sneezed, or 'God forgive you' if you had been really naughty—but didn't seem important in explaining events around me. I soon learned that if it thundered it was because clouds were crashing against one another; it never occurred to me that an angry deity was proclaiming something loud, nasty, but singularly inarticulate.

But there was something about musty books, about antiquity, about holy men, about the intensity and apparent integrity of the religious life, that fascinated me as I reached my early teens. As I was surrounded by none of these things in my rather secular, though firmly Jewish, home, they held for me the appeal of the exotic and the mysterious.

People asked, 'Do you believe in the Bible?' I decided I did. I hadn't actually read it; it was many years before I did, and even then there was much in it that I could not understand (and still don't).

So I started reading it. Before I got far with my reading it crossed my mind that there was something illogical about deciding to believe in a book I hadn't read. (Don't tell me I should have had faith, should have trusted God; it wasn't God who told me about His book in the first place; doubtless if He had I would have been swayed by His recommendation.) Maybe I also wondered how, having read neither in its entirety, I could decide that the Old Testament (I didn't know the expression 'Hebrew scriptures') was true and the New Testament false, and that other books I had heard of but not read at all, such as the Qur'an, were also false.

What Does It All Mean?

I also began to wonder what it meant, anyway, to say that the Bible was 'true'. It was certainly nothing like the propositions of geometry, which could be demonstrated and which, apparently, no one wanted to deny, or use as a 'test of faith'. Moreover, in geometry, it would not make much sense to assert as a general proposition 'Geometry is true' or 'Geometry is false'; one would say 'Pythagoras' theorem is true' or some other specific theorem was true or false as the case might be, rather than that the corpus of writing on geometry was either true or false as a totality.

It was also unlike geometry in another way, the importance of which became clearer to me as time went on. Propositions in geometry appear to have clear and definite meaning. People, other than philosophers, do not sit around and discuss questions like 'What does it mean to say that the square on the hypotenuse is equal to the squares on the other two sides?' Mathematicians might limit the application of the theorem to two-dimensional, plane geometry, but given that limitation there is no difficulty in understanding what the theorem means, and in applying it (within appropriate limits) in the real world.

Religious propositions are quite different. People discuss endlessly the *meaning* of verses of scripture or of key terms in religious discourse. Great and horrible wars have been fought over the correct interpretation of scripture, over who has the right to interpret scripture, or over the meaning of such basic terms as 'God'. This is in itself quite remarkable. If people don't have a clear grasp of what they are talking about, how can they be so certain that they are so right as to justify slaughtering people who disagree with them? And anyway, what justifies them in murdering or otherwise oppressing people who do not seek to harm them, merely because they happen to disagree on some intellectual topic?

The answer to this is that religious propositions are not simply academic hypotheses or intellectual statements. If somebody says 'AIDS is a divine punishment for promiscuity' or 'God dictated the Torah to Moses', he is raising an ensign rather than proposing a verifiable theory to account for certain phenomena. Clarity is less important than emotional commitment. Something similar happens in politics. 'All men are equal', or 'democracy is the most desirable form of government' are powerful slogans, but capable of infinite interpretations; they are clarion calls to commitment, not to clear thinking or empirical verification.

This is not to deny that scientific disputes can and do arouse personal rivalries and strong collective emotions. They can also get tied up with political or religious ideologies, as when the Nazis rejected 'Jewish science', the Soviets supported Lysenko, or the Catholic Church condemned Galileo. However, in all these cases the primary dispute was not about science but about ideology and authority.

At the time of my life of which I am speaking I knew nothing of all this. I naively thought that religious people were making truth claims that were capable of objective assessment, and that people of learning would be ready to discuss such claims dispassionately.

I tried hard to discover what the Bible was about. I was sent to Hebrew/ religion classes where I wasted several years, and then for a brief period had some teachers I could respect, not least among them the late Ephraim Wiesenberg, a fine scholar seeking refuge from wartime Hungary and condemned to spending six months in the mid-1940s clattering around my native city of Cardiff on an antiquated bicycle, teaching recalcitrant boys and girls the rudiments of Hebrew language and Jewish religion. But he certainly inspired me, and most of the Hebrew grammar I know was picked up in those brief months under his expert tutelage; only in later years did I come to appreciate his broader learning and wisdom.

Hebrew grammar is an indispensable key to understanding the Bible, but does not in itself tell you what anything means. Equipped with a modicum of Hebrew I would sit in the synagogue to which I was sent rather than taken, and tussle with the Hebrew text of the Torah reading. I obtained a copy to read at home, and supplemented it with the commentary of the great medieval exegete Rashi (1040–1105) and translations.

The easiest verse to translate was 'The Lord spoke to Moses saying'. But it was not the easiest to understand. I recall trying to imagine (*a*) what it would be like if you were Moses and the Lord spoke to you, and (*b*) what it would look like if you were watching Moses and the Lord spoke to him. I still don't know, and I am not sure that anybody else does, however glibly the words roll off their tongues, but at the time I took comfort in the thought that really wise, intelligent people, like chief rabbis or archbishops, understood such things. (They don't, but it took me a long time to figure that out, and even longer to admit it.)

Philosophical Beginnings

You cannot sit forever musing about the inexplicable, so I turned my attention elsewhere. There were at that time in Cardiff some Orthodox German Jewish refugees, followers of the school of Samson Raphael Hirsch. Unlike their east European co-religionists, including the learned local rabbi who guided some of my early steps in Talmud, these families seemed to have achieved a synthesis between religious tradition and modern thought. They introduced me, at the age of about 14, to rabbinic texts, notably the Mishnah, as well as to a form of religious observance which I found intellectually as well as emotionally satisfying, though my apparent 'religious mania' displeased my parents.

At the same time, I began reading philosophical and theological texts on my own, starting with Plato, and moving on to Augustine and Aquinas. The more christological aspects of Augustine and Aquinas wafted over me almost unnoticed; I suppose I regarded their christology with no more seriousness than their obviously antiquated scientific notions. What did appeal was what seemed at the time to be an intellectually coherent and profound account of God and the spiritual life, and this was perfectly easy to transpose into Judaism. With this background Maimonides' *Guide for the Perplexed* (in Friedländer's English) made easy enough reading, and the only thing that really perplexed me was why it was reputed to be such a difficult text to comprehend; it seemed to me far less obscure than Talmud, which was said to be easy by comparison.

In 1951 I entered St John's College, Cambridge on the strength of a narrowly missed music scholarship and decided to read Moral Sciences, as philosophy was still known at that time, for Part I of the tripos. Both Bertrand Russell and G. E. Moore had recently ceased teaching; Wittgenstein had died that April and his late, at the time unedited, scribblings, were already circulating among the cognoscenti, among whom I was not numbered. All three men were spoken of in awed tones. Logical positivism was still dominant, influenced by philosophers such as Ayer and Ryle, who taught that a proposition was meaningful only if empirically verifiable or deducible from empirical premises. I thought this was a stupid philosophy, more or less identical with ideas rejected by Sa'adiah in the tenth century; but as no one in Cambridge, at least no one in the philosophy faculty (I had no connection with theologians or medieval historians), knew the least thing about tenth-century philosophy, it seemed futile to attempt to discuss this with them.

I had spent a few weeks before going up to Cambridge at a Swiss summer school on philosophy, where I was introduced by Joseph Maria Bocheński OP not only to logical positivism but to a variety of 'continental' philosophies, including existentialism. It was salutary to realise that the disjunction be tween British and continental philosophy was so acute that Cambridge did not recognize 'continentals' as philosophers at all; if Heidegger, or Sartre (or later Foucault or Derrida) was to be studied at all, it was in a department of literature, not philosophy; even Hegel was regarded with circumspection. As late as 1992 Cambridge philosophers protested at the award to Jacques Derrida (1930–2004) of an honorary doctorate by their university, so presumably this remained the case at that time, and it was perhaps not such a bad thing.

Despite the limitations I thoroughly enjoyed my philosophical studies. I learned clarity of thought and the need constantly to question the way people use language, as well as a lot of useful things about ethics, logic, and experimental psychology. Two years was enough; I spent part of the summer vacation of 1953 at Gateshead Yeshiva, my mother said 'You need to do something useful', so I read music for Part II of the tripos.

Among the people who most influenced my religious development at Cambridge was Jacob J. Ross, then a graduate student;[3] Jack, as I knew him, was very knowledgeable in Talmud, and introduced me to the analysis of halakhic (legal) concepts as practised in the Lithuanian yeshivas. I was eventually to write my doctorate on this. At the time, it seemed to me that this method gave intellectual coherence to the provisions of the halakhah, and this bolstered my faith. On the other hand, I was sufficiently *au fait* with textual and historical criticism to worry whether such an approach was consistent with the 'real' meaning of the texts. But I was not yet ready to follow through my ideas, especially as the time had come to abandon the comfort of academe for the responsibilities of making a living and raising a family.

---

[3]   There is a reference to him in a footnote in Ch. 23; in Chs. 19 and 20 I shall have some comments to make on the work of his wife, Tamar.

I married into a family of Orthodox German Jews from a similar background to those I had known in Cardiff, and despite a brief flirtation with hasidism and a longer affair with Lithuanian yeshiva Judaism, German neo-Orthodoxy is the variety with which I feel most comfortable.

When I commenced my doctorate I anticipated that I would be able to demonstrate, through careful examination of the halakhic writings of Hayim Soloveitchik and his circle, the internal coherence and logical cogency of the halakhic 'system' (the system of Torah law). By the time I finished I knew that this was a fantasy. Halakhah is not, and could not possibly be, a 'system' in the deductive sense. In its detailed working out and application there is room for deductive reasoning, but the system as a whole is neither more nor less deductive than any other system of law.

Soloveitchik, and even more so his philosophically inclined grandson Joseph Dov (Joseph Ber) Soloveitchik, misrepresented halakhah by detaching it from its social and historical contexts. Joseph Dov in particular diminished Torah by equating it with halakhah. The motive for this will emerge in the course of the book (especially Chapter 18); to anticipate briefly, Joseph Dov, treating halakhah as a self-subsistent 'a priori' system, places it beyond the reach of history, 'rescuing' it from historical criticism, but at the expense of divorcing it from social reality.

Facing the Questions

But how seriously was I to take historical criticism? I knew something about it, since the synagogue I had attended in Cardiff used as its standard Torah text the *Pentateuch and Haftorahs* with commentary by the former Chief Rabbi Joseph H. Hertz; I shall examine this in more detail in Chapter 16. For all that Hertz denigrated 'Higher Critics' as 'Higher Antisemites' bent on discrediting the Bible, he was quite ready when it suited his purposes to invoke the findings of archaeology to 'prove' the truth of the Bible. His combative comments and Additional Notes made me aware of the challenges and opportunities confronting the believing Jew. He certainly did not shy away from the problems.

On the other hand, the men who were held up to me as masters of Torah erudition and paragons of saintliness—heads of yeshivas, for instance—refused to acknowledge any problems. 'Bible criticism', which they had heard of but not studied, was in their eyes a gentile plot to undermine the True Torah; one should not contaminate oneself by becoming familiar with it. 'Evolution'—again, something everybody had heard of but few if any understood—was 'just a theory', and since science was always changing whereas Torah was Absolute and Unchanging, there was no contest; Torah was the Absolute Criterion of Truth, and everything else had to be submitted to its scrutiny. Somebody, I forget who, even told me that if the Talmud was uncertain as to whether the earth was round or flat we should remain in doubt about it.

None of this was helpful, nor did it enhance my confidence in the men who adopted such obscurantist attitudes. At the time I assumed it was a consequence of the backwardness of central and eastern Europe, where many of them had been nurtured. However, it turned out that central and eastern Europe were not that backward, and that some at least of the leading rabbis, J. D. Soloveitchik among them, had studied in the Weimar years at German universities where they had undoubtedly become acquainted with contemporary scientific thought and biblical criticism. Not ignorance, but denial, underlay their attitude.

It was difficult to know how far this denial was conscious. When I was a young rabbi in my first pulpit, in Whitefield, Manchester, I had a colleague, whom I had met during my six weeks at Gateshead Yeshiva in 1953 and who, in private discussion, was quite ready to concede the possibility that Darwinian evolution might be reconciled with scripture. On some occasion we both took part in a public educational panel and I was taken aback when, in response to a question, he categorically denied the truth of the theory of organic evolution. Later, when I questioned him in private about his inconsistency, he replied that although evolution might be true, this could not be conceded in public since such an admission might mislead the young!

Denial is not always that blatant. Diversion, rather than outright denial, is the favoured strategy of the mainstream yeshivas.[4] If you can get your impressionable young students to devote their energy and enthusiasm to the minutiae of talmudic discussion they will not find time to worry themselves about science and evolution and historical criticism. If you can get them to exercise their consciences on small points of ritual law, to engage in earnest self-examination as to whether they have infringed some minor element of traditional ethical or ritual teaching, they will simply never start worrying about environmental issues, overpopulation, poverty in the developing world, and the like. This is not to suggest that the Torah has nothing to say on such matters, but rather that the yeshiva teachers do not see them as a priority for their students. They have reduced Torah to 'Yiddishkeit', i.e. 'being Jewish'; the emphasis is on those aspects of Torah which are distinctively Jewish rather than universal.

---

[4] By 'mainstream' I intend to exclude the so-called *ba'al teshuvah* yeshivas, where there is some pretence of addressing 'modern' problems.

It is possible to understand the persistence of this attitude today. Jews still tend to feel insecure, whether through collective memory of the Holocaust, through worries about the security of Israel, or simply because they see themselves as a minority under threat of cultural assimilation and with a consequent need to assert their distinctiveness. The feelings of insecurity are strongest among the religious, partly because traditional religious commitment is a minority preoccupation in society at large, and partly by a process of self-selection that leads people to assume a religious commitment precisely to compensate for their feelings of insecurity. Religion really does function, as Karl Marx observed, as the people's opiate.[5] However, the empirical fact that religion offers solace and reassurance in an uncertain world is irrelevant to whether its claims are true or false. Neither Marx's explanation of religious belief as originating in human desire nor the attempts of modern religious apologists to defend religion by establishing its psychological value to the believer or its social utility to the community has anything to do with the intrinsic truth or falsehood of religious truth claims. Plato, in the highly stratified society he designed in *The Republic*, was so well aware of the difference between truth and social utility that he proposed that appropriate myths—'noble lies'—be composed to dispose people to playing their required roles in society.[6]

Pulpit and Prejudice

My twenty-two years as a pulpit rabbi, in Manchester, Liverpool, and London, gave me some insight into the relationship between the pursuit of truth and the demands of running a religious establishment. Fresh from an academic background, I thought that my job was to impart information, to explain things to people, and that they would absorb what I told them and work it out for themselves in their own lives.

I soon found that this didn't work, at least not for the majority of people in the congregation. Partly my fault, since it took me a long time to learn to adjust a sermon or talk to the level of the congregation. One year, at Simhat Torah, I gathered the small children in a congregation and told them a simple story. A mother came up and thanked me: 'That was the first time I have understood what you were talking about', she said, bringing me down to size; and she was not an unintelligent woman.

So I learned that organized religion is neither the philosophy of the schools nor the Talmud of the rabbis but some sort of distillation from them,

---

[5] Marx, *Critique*, introd.   [6] Plato, *Republic*, 375–403.

mixed with ambient popular culture, and heavily dependent on language and customs passed down through family and congregation. Organized religion is a social phenomenon, not an intellectual enterprise. There is of course room within it for intellectual growth and expression for those able and so inclined, but the collective need that it satisfies is primarily emotional; there is a sense of fellowship, of shared history, language, and customs, a space within which the individual can find stability, whether on his/her own or in company with like-minded people, in an uncertain world. It is within the religious space, moreover, that the individual can pursue the elusive quality called 'spirituality'.

Organized religion inevitably suffers from the defects that afflict any large collective: the Roman Catholic Church is probably the world's largest social structure after the Republic of China, and even the Jewish religion, far smaller than Christianity or Islam, counts many more millions than the smallest nations.

This contrasts sharply with the situation at the beginning of a religion. Abraham had only his own somewhat dysfunctional family to worry about, Jesus a small group of disciples, Muhammad a fairly small number of loosely organized Arabian tribesmen. On the other hand, the Bible portrays Moses at the head of some millions of fractious Israelites (603,550 men, excluding women and children, according to Numbers 1: 46), and with a fairly complex administrative and judicial system in place. The description of Moses may well reflect conditions under the Israelite monarchy rather than those in the Sinai desert, but whatever the underlying reality, it is easy to see in the Bible's account of his career the problems that beset the leader of any large social group—problems of authority, of control, and of clarity and consistency in the message promoted.

As an official of the relatively modest organization of the United Synagogue—Britain's principal grouping of Orthodox Jewish congregations—I was inevitably caught up in the problems of authority, of control, and of clarity and consistency in promoting the message. This was not comfortable. I am happier searching for the truth than confidently telling people what it is. Nor do I relish the prospect of ordering other people's lives for them. But I recognized that I bore a responsibility to the organization that employed me, and my preaching and teaching were therefore broadly in line with their policies; I simply avoided, as far as possible, topics where my personal views were seriously at variance with those of the establishment.

It was not always a question of right and wrong; skewed priorities were more of a problem. I agree that it is necessary to remember the Holocaust, and more often than not I am ready to rally to the support of the State of Israel.

But I prefer to view the Holocaust in the broader context of the theology of suffering and the needs of Israel in a humanitarian rather than a tribal context, I object to religion being subordinated to political agendas, and I believe that the prime concerns of the Jewish religion are relationships with God and our fellow human beings, not the Holocaust and the State of Israel, nor even the ritual practices which I personally follow.

Interfaith Dialogue

At 50, with children having grown up and left home, I needed a change anyway, so I abandoned the pulpit and accepted an invitation to Birmingham to set up the Centre for the Study of Judaism and Jewish-Christian Relations at the Selly Oak Colleges. My contract was for five years, but I stayed for eleven and threw myself into academic work and interfaith relations.

I attended several international meetings of Jews, Christians, Muslims, occasionally 'Eastern' religions, and I learned a lot. For instance, a conference of Jews and Christians might open with Jews on one side of the table and Christians on the other and everyone being careful not to cause offence. By the end of the conference, two or three days later, two changes had taken place. First, there had been a growth of mutual confidence, even friendship, among participants, and it was not necessary to be so cautious. Second, several people had changed places, so that you ended up with traditionalists/fundamentalists, whether Jewish or Christian, on one side, and modernists/liberals, whether Jewish or Christian, on the other side. This led to the salutary realization that both faith communities faced similar problems in relating to the modern world. For instance, so far as Jews and Christians were concerned, we regarded the same Hebrew scriptures as sacred (though we may have interpreted them differently), and therefore needed to address the same problems about the historical and moral value of those scriptures, problems which are central to the theme of this book.

The social value of interfaith dialogue can scarcely be overestimated. The cultivation of mutual respect and dialogue with people of other religions or denominations leads to peaceful coexistence, whereas traditional religious triumphalism and separatism lead to confrontation and strife.

The theological value is also immense, for the presence of other 'believers' forces the theologian to question the assumptions he would make if all his/her contacts were confined to those of his/her own faith. Whether you believe that Moses came down the mountain with the Torah intact, that Jesus is a Person of the Trinity, or that Muhammad is the final, authentic Prophet of God, most people in the world do not share that belief. But it is quite easy to overlook this inconvenient circumstance if you remain confined within your own community, immersed in a sea of millions of like-minded believers. In the past you could pretend that your beliefs and practices were 'normal', since everyone with whom you came into contact shared them, but modern communications make it difficult to isolate yourself within a homogeneous environment; anyone who *does* cocoon themselves today is exercising a deliberate choice, opting for illusory safety rather than for truth.

Theology can now only usefully be done in the presence of the religious Other.

Dialogue presupposes a common language. Most often, interfaith dialogue is conducted in English or some other modern European language, though these are not the languages in which any of the great religious traditions was formed. The use of a common language implies some degree of shared culture through which the religious conversation is mediated; the shared culture is usually that of the liberal Enlightenment. Participants tend, as a result, to interpret their religious traditions in terms of this culture, emphasizing such aspects as universal justice, the desire for peace, respect for the freedom of the individual, and the equality of women. These interpretations are often suspect, different from what other representatives of that religion might say in church, synagogue, or mosque; they may be aspirations rather than accepted teaching, but this is all the more reason to encourage them.

The political background of dialogue is important too. Most dialogue takes place in states that are effectively (even if not constitutionally) secular. It is not possible to hold a dialogue of equals in a state governed by the law of any one religion, since this inevitably disadvantages adherents of other religions. The enforced disputations organized in the Middle Ages by the powerful Catholic Church did not allow non-Christians to participate as equals; even where permission was granted to 'speak freely' a participant would fear injurious consequences to himself and his community if he exercised that liberty. There was perhaps greater freedom in the *majalis*, or open debating sessions, that took place typically in the court of a caliph or emir in early Islamic times,[7] but even here prudence imposed severe limits on the freedom of expression of non-Muslims.

Academic Detachment?

From Birmingham I moved to Oxford. Teaching and research at a university are subject to constraints, but they are different from those of religious

---

[7]   Several studies of these meetings are collected in Lazarus-Yaffe et al. (eds.), *The Majlis*.

establishments or of interfaith dialogue. Probably the major distorting factor in the academic world is the constant pressure to publish, and to publish, moreover, in conformity with current academic fashion. However, since I was at a stage where I had no need to seek promotion I was largely free from this pressure.

I held a fellowship in Modern Jewish Thought at the Oxford Centre for Hebrew and Jewish Studies and this led me to reflect on what had happened in Jewish religious thinking in the centuries since the Renaissance. A vast amount of detailed research, some of it of excellent quality, had already been accomplished in this field, and much continues to appear. The past four hundred years have seen a transformation in Jewish thinking perhaps more radical than any that occurred in the past, yet the whole process can be summed up in one question: what has been the impact of modernity on Judaism?

The one question appears in many guises. What has been the impact of critical historical study of texts? Of the rise of science? Of the Enlightenment? Of Jewish emancipation? Of liberal democratic ideals, of secularism, of European nationalism? Of widespread disillusion with the belief in progress in the aftermath of twentieth-century wars and the Holocaust? Of changing gender relationships and sexual morals?

To my surprise, as I reflected on these issues from the point of view of religion, they resolved into one fundamental problem. Is what is claimed to be the Word of God really the Word of God, perfect and unchangeable for all time? Is there indeed a 'Torah from Heaven' in the sense in which our forebears understood this, an immutable text passed on through the generations with an authoritative interpretation, and now in the safe keeping of wise men able to apply its rules and regulations to every aspect of the altered world of today? Is Torah impervious to historical change?

Perhaps I should not have been so surprised. After all, modernity was brought about in Europe precisely by the questioning of traditional teaching, both written (scripture) and 'oral' (traditions of the Church). The humanist recovery and restoration of ancient texts and of the 'hermetic tradition' was itself a challenge to the assumption that the Bible was the repository of all truth; the application of philological, literary, and historical criticism to the text of the Bible (a process heavily indebted to medieval Jewish commentary) encouraged readings that diverged from those of the established Catholic Church, and led to speculation as to both the authenticity and the authority of the received scriptures. Without all this, there could have been no freedom of enquiry for the development of novel and radical philosophical, political, and social doctrines, and scientific advance would have been thwarted.

Clearly, no one will understand the evolution of modern Judaism, in all its shades of Orthodoxy, Reform, and secularity, unless they appreciate the challenges of modernity to Judaism's central doctrine, *torah min hashamayim* 'Torah from Heaven'.

Read on!

PART I

◆

REVELATION
Torah from Heaven: Growth of a Tradition

IN PART I, I ask 'What is Torah?' How was part of the literature of ancient Israel singled out as sacred? When did people begin to think that the text had been dictated by God to Moses? Why was the Pentateuch privileged over other parts of the Hebrew Bible? How accurately was the text preserved?

How did the rabbis interpret the Bible? What is the origin of the doctrine of 'Oral Torah', and what does Oral Torah consist of?

How were mystical doctrines, numerology, medieval philosophy, and science absorbed into interpretation of the text? Is there any limit to what the text of the Bible might be thought to contain?

And how have instances where the Bible or its interpreters seem to conflict with evidence from other sources been handled within the rabbinic tradition?

◆

ONE

HOLY BOOKS

The most important fact about ourselves: we are addressed
MEROLD WESTPHAL[1]

A FTER THE HEBREW SCRIPTURES, or Bible, the most important book in Judaism is the Mishnah, compiled in Palestine in the early third century CE. Mishnah lists 'one who says the Torah is not from heaven' among those who 'have no portion in the World to Come'.[2] The second-century sages whose views that statement represents evidently thought that to deny the doctrine of *torah min hashamayim* ('Torah from Heaven') was a very serious matter indeed.

But what does 'Torah from Heaven' mean? What is Torah? What is Heaven? What relationship between the two is conveyed by 'from'?

No one would dispute that the word 'Torah' has something to do with the Bible, so that will make a good starting point. Perhaps if we know what the Bible is we can begin to understand the term 'Torah'.

The Hebrew Bible as it has come down to us is a library rather than a book; it is the national literature of the ancient Hebrews, not a systematic treatise on theology or law.

How many books it contains depends on how you count them, and that in turn depends on how you classify them. They appear in modern printed Hebrew texts grouped and ordered as shown below:

Books of the Bible as in Modern Printed Hebrew Texts

1.   **Torah** (Pentateuch), consisting of:
     Genesis
     Exodus
     Leviticus
     Numbers
     Deuteronomy

---

[1]   *Levinas and Kierkegaard*, 2.
[2]   Mishnah *San.* 10: 1. 'Have a portion in the World to Come', i.e. eternal life, functions in rabbinic Judaism rather like 'is saved' functions in Christian writing.

2(*a*) **Former Prophets**, consisting of:
Joshua
Judges
1 and 2 Samuel
1 and 2 Kings

2(*b*) **Latter Prophets**, consisting of:
Isaiah
Jeremiah
Ezekiel
The Twelve ('Minor' Prophets: Hosea, Joel, Amos, Obadiah, Jonah,
Micah, Nahum, Habakkuk, Zephaniah, Haggai, Zechariah, Malachi)

3.   **Writings**, consisting of:
Psalms
Proverbs
Job
The Five Scrolls: Song of Songs, Ruth, Lamentations, Ecclesiastes, Esther
Daniel
Ezra
Nehemiah
1 and 2 Chronicles

This arrangement is broadly in line with the list preserved in the Babylonian Talmud,[3] though the order of the Latter Prophets is different, and some details such as the joining together of the Five Scrolls have been determined by later liturgical practice. Also, the division of Samuel, Kings, and Chronicles into two books each, and the separation of Ezra and Nehemiah, date only from the printed edition edited by Felix Pratensis, published at Venice in 1517–18.

A widely attested tradition asserts that there are twenty-four books.[4] Josephus, followed by some Church Fathers, states that there are twenty-two.[5] Perhaps the Jewish practice was influenced by the pattern set by the

---

[3] BT *BB* 13*b* establishes the tripartite division, and 14*b*–15*a* lays down the order of books. However, we cannot be certain of the 'original' reading in the Talmud, as copyists may have modified it in line with later practice, nor do we know how representative the talmudic discussion is of practice or opinion at the time.

[4] The tradition of twenty-four books is at least as early as the pseudepigraphic 2 Esdras (4 Ezra) 14: 44–6, composed about 100 CE, and is given in several midrashim, e.g. *Exod. Rabbah* 41: 6.

[5] Josephus Flavius, *Contra Apionem*, 1: 39–41; Origen, in Eusebius, *Ecclesiastical History*, 6: 25, 1 (Loeb edn. vol. ii), and Athanasius, *Festal Epistle*, 39. See below.

Alexandrian division of the *Odyssey* and *Iliad* of Homer into twenty-four books each, corresponding to the number of letters in the Greek alphabet; the twenty-two book division would in that case have been an adaptation of Greek practice to the number of letters in the Hebrew alphabet.[6]

Both Jeremiah (18: 18) and Ezekiel (7: 26) list prophet, priest, and sage as leaders of the people. The activities of these leaders correspond loosely to the three great divisions of scripture: law, originally administered by the priests, corresponds to Torah; prophecy (obviously) to the Prophets; the Writings, in particular Proverbs, Job, and Ecclesiastes, are concerned with wisdom, both practical and theoretical. However, Torah contains much beside law, 'Prophets' encompasses several historical works, and 'Writings' encompasses wisdom, poetry, and history.

Why are the five books (Pentateuch) comprising the Torah referred to as 'the Law', seeing they contain so much else? Perhaps it stems from the rescript of Artaxerxes I of Persia (465–424 BCE) authorizing Ezra to investigate the situation in Jerusalem 'according to the law [*dat*] of your God that is in your hand' (Ezra 7: 14); it remains an open question whether we should 'interpret the legal implementation of the Torah according to the known model of Persian imperial authorization', under which vassal states exercised internal jurisdiction.[7]

Later, the Jews of Alexandria may have felt that Torah was their equivalent to the constitution of a Greek city-state; for Philo of Alexandria (d. *c.*30 CE) it was perfectly natural to equate Torah with Law, for he and his fellow-Jews used it as their source of *politikoi nomoi* 'civic laws', applicable in the absence of specific royal decrees.[8]

The rabbinic traditions of the tripartite division[9] and of the placing of individual books are neither chronological nor genre-based; they derive from a sophisticated theology. Christian bibles ignore the tripartite division and place some books differently, reflecting their own theology. So, for instance, the rabbis wished to downgrade apocalyptic, so they argued that Daniel was not a prophet and they placed his book among the 'Writings';[10] Christians valued apocalyptic and so retained Daniel among the prophetic books.

---

[6] The suggestion is made by Epiphanius (315–403) in a passage reproduced in Leiman, *Canonization of Hebrew Scripture*, 43, from the Syriac version of the *Treatise on Weights and Measures*, 43–5. I have not checked the original text.

[7] Konrad Schmidt in Knoppers and Levinsohn (eds.), *The Pentateuch as Torah*, 37–8.

[8] Hecht et al., *Introduction to the History and Sources of Jewish Law*, 82–3.

[9] The tripartite and dual divisions will be discussed below.

[10] BT *Meg.* 3a states that Daniel was not a prophet. Whether this was because of a downgrading of apocalyptic is a matter for speculation. Gordis, *Kohelet*, 19, argued that

Neither the dates nor the processes by which the current selection of books was made and placed in order are known with certainty. Although Jews as well as Christians nowadays commonly talk about the 'canon' of scripture, the term 'canon' was introduced by the Church Father Athanasius (296–373) only in 367 CE,[11] and implies a way of looking at sacred writings and drawing boundaries around them that must have taken centuries to evolve. There is no exact equivalent in the rabbinic vocabulary of that period, though the rabbis had similar concerns about what was or was not an authentic record of revelation and dismissed other writings as *sefarim ḥitsonim*, 'outside books', that ought not to be read.

Josephus, in the first century CE, had a fairly clear concept of what was or was not authentic and hence authoritative. Only twenty-two books, he says, are *dikaiōs pepisteumena* ('justly accredited'), by which he means they were written by prophets under divine inspiration; however, 'from Artaxerxes to our own time the complete history has been written, but has not been deemed worthy of equal credit with the earlier records, because of the failure of the exact succession of the prophets'. Five (he continues) are the books of Moses, comprising law and history; thirteen were written by prophets, and cover the history from Moses to Artaxerxes; four consist of hymns and precepts.[12]

Decisions about where to draw the boundaries of the sacred, and about how to set the accepted books in order, depend on interpretation; they are guided by a broad theology rather than by the content of the individual books.[13]

Tradition articulates the theology. When the rabbis' predecessors set Genesis to Deuteronomy as a unit at the head of the scriptures and named it the Torah of Moses,[14] they were proclaiming that this set of books was pre-eminent within the tradition. The Torah of Moses, they were saying, was a unique revelation, and therefore the criterion for acceptance of any further claim to divine inspiration. Other books *might* be divinely inspired; but if, as

Daniel was placed in the Writings because of its kinship with wisdom literature, but this is unconvincing.

[11] *Festal Epistle*, 39: 4 (p. 552). I discuss the concept of 'canon' below.
[12] Josephus, *Contra Apionem*, 1: 39–41, p. 179. H. St J. Thackeray, in his introduction, surmises that the thirteen are Joshua, Judges with Ruth, Samuel, Kings, Chronicles, Ezra/Nehemiah, Esther, Job, Isaiah, Jeremiah with Lamentations, Ezekiel, Minor Prophets, Daniel; the four are Psalms, Song of Songs, Proverbs, and Ecclesiastes.
[13] Sarna, 'The Order of the Books', 407–13, argued that the order of the books originated with the order in which books were catalogued and shelved in the Palestinian schools. But he did not adequately explain *why* they were catalogued and shelved in that order.
[14] 'Torah of Moses' is a biblical phrase but, as we shall see, in its original setting it does not refer to the Five Books as a whole.

almost happened in the case of Ezekiel,[15] it could be demonstrated that a book was inconsistent with the Torah of Moses, it would be rejected on the grounds that it could not possibly have been inspired.

The Samaritans went even further; they accepted *only* the Torah of Moses as holy scripture.[16] Scholars have inferred from this that the other books were not accepted as scripture until after the Samaritan schism;[17] this is unconvincing, as it could equally well be the case that the Samaritans rejected as a matter of principle all writings other than the Torah of Moses even though these writings were already regarded as sacred by other Jews.

Rabbinic tradition regards the Prophets as having a higher degree of inspiration and therefore authority than the Writings; prophetic inspiration is qualitatively superior to inspiration through the 'Holy Spirit'. This explains the anomaly of including historical books like Judges and Kings among the Prophets, whereas other historical books, such as Chronicles, are classified as Writings. It is not the chronology of the books, nor even the nature of their content, that determines this classification, but the degree of inspiration attributed to them.

Within the tradition it is taken for granted that God dictated the Torah, that is, the books from Genesis to Deuteronomy, word by word to Moses. Yet the Torah itself makes no such claim; it normally refers to Moses in the third person, and it records his death and burial just as if it were a book composed long after the events it narrates.

Indeed, *no* biblical book lays claim to consist, *as a whole*, of words literally dictated by God, though several contain speech attributed to God. Whether such reports are intended as verbatim reports of God's words, or as attempts to capture the ineffable in human language, is rarely made clear.

However this may be, by the time rabbinic Judaism and Christianity began to form it was widely accepted that some books contained God's words, and others did not; Sundberg contends that in the first century CE scripture was simply a 'wide religious literature without definite bounds'.[18] The process by which the selection was made remains unclear; it seems to have been a process of rejection rather than of positive selection, and must have continued, in Jewish circles, until at least the fourth century.

---

[15] BT *Shab.* 13b; see below, p. 30.

[16] The Samaritan *Book of Joshua* is a 14th-c. work, so has no bearing on this discussion.

[17] Leiman, *Canonization of Hebrew Scripture*, 17.

[18] Sundberg, *Old Testament*, 102. See, in addition to the works of Leiman and Sundberg, Silver, *The Story of Scripture*, and, from a Christian perspective, with a critical review of the main theories, Barton, *Holy Writings, Sacred Text* and Sawyer, *Sacred Languages and Sacred Texts*.

The Hebrew canon excludes several books ('Apocrypha' *sefarim ḥitsonim* or 'outside books') that are included in the Septuagint, the ancient Greek Jewish version of scripture.[19] This seems to suggest that the Greek-speaking Jews of Alexandria regarded the apocryphal books, as they were later designated, as inspired scripture. However, there is no hard evidence to support this; Philo, whose knowledge of scripture was mainly if not entirely derived from the Greek, never cites any of them, and Josephus, though he frequently cites works such as the 'apocryphal' sections of Esther and 1 Maccabees, clearly excludes them from the twenty-two 'justly accredited' works. Since all our manuscripts of the Septuagint are Christian, it may well be the case that the 'extra' books were incorporated into the Septuagint only in the early Christian centuries.

Not that Christians were unanimous on the status of the apocryphal books. Melito of Sardis claimed, in a letter written *c.*170 to Onesimus, to have travelled to Palestine to check for himself which books were authentic scripture, and he produced a list that excluded the Apocrypha.[20] Though the Latin Vulgate includes apocrypha, Jerome himself (*c.*342–420) rejected the apocryphal books, with the possible exception of 1 Maccabees, as non-canonical,[21] and was opposed by Augustine (354–430). Jerome continued to cite them in his commentaries, notwithstanding his aspersions on their status.[22]

The churches retained the Septuagint tradition; only at the Reformation did the Reformed Churches decide to adopt the Hebrew canon and reject the Apocrypha. Even so, several Jewish writings extant in the period between the latest biblical books and the Mishnah, i.e. roughly 160 BCE to 210 CE, were rejected by many of the churches as well; some were preserved in more limited Christian circles, often on account of their apocalyptic content, and form the basis for collections of Pseudepigrapha.[23] Other Jewish writings of this period are known through literary references, and some have come to light since 1948 through the scrolls unearthed in caves near the Dead Sea.

We can infer from occasional remarks in rabbinic literature that the theological basis for retaining those books that remained in the Jewish canon was that they were (*a*) consistent with the Torah of Moses and (*b*) either composed by prophets under direct divine inspiration, or composed under guidance from the Holy Spirit.

[19] Strictly speaking, the Septuagint is the translation of the Torah, or Five Books of Moses; the other books that were eventually accepted as sacred were translated independently later.

[20] Eusebius, *Ecclesiastical History*, 4: 26 (Loeb edn., vol. i, p. 393).

[21] Jerome, *Preface to the Books of Samuel and Kings*, cited in Schaff and Wace, *The Nicene and Post-Nicene Fathers*, 6: 488 ff.   [22] Barton, *Holy Writings, Sacred Texts* 28.

[23] See Charlesworth, *The Old Testament Pseudepigrapha*.

No one knows how or why a consensus appears to have been reached that the canon was closed. Perhaps it was on account of the proliferation of books, not least Christian and sectarian works, for which sacred status was claimed but which the rabbinic sages considered heretical. Perhaps the statement attributed to the Babylonian Amemar (c.400 CE) that *hakham adif minavi* 'the sage is to be preferred over the prophet' gives us a clue; rabbinic Judaism regarded itself as heir to the prophetic tradition, but preferred to fulfil this role through study and interpretation and was mistrustful of the 'direct line' to God. In like vein, Amemar's Palestinian contemporary Avdimi (Eudymos) of Haifa said, 'From the day the Temple was destroyed prophecy was taken from the prophets and given to the sages.'[24] These remarks do not constitute a doctrinal position denying the possibility of prophecy after the close of the Bible; room was left for later Jewish authorities, for instance Moses Maimonides (Rambam, 1135–1204) and Abraham Abulafia (1240–c.1291), not only to affirm the possibility but actually to prescribe ways to achieve prophetic experience.[25]

What Is 'Torah'?

The Lord 'showed himself' to Abraham at the terebinth of Moreh (Gen. 12: 6–7); he revealed himself to the Israelites and proclaimed the Ten Commandments (Exod. 19 and 20). This is the biblical style of revelation; it is an *encounter with God*, rather than the *dictation of a book*.

So where did the idea of 'sacred text' come from? More precisely, when did people start to think that the Hebrew word *torah* designated a book or set of books dictated by God?

The plain sense of the books Genesis to Deuteronomy, collectively referred to as 'The Torah', reads like a story told later about events from the Creation to the death of Moses. Specific units, such as the Ten Commandments, are said to have been spoken by God (though the different versions in Exodus 20 and Deuteronomy 4 suggest that this is not a verbatim text), but not the books as a whole. Deuteronomy, for instance, tells a story *about* revelation, rather than

[24] Both sayings are in BT *BB* 12*a*.

[25] Maimonides described the requirements for prophethood in *Mishneh torah*, 'Yesodei hatorah' 7 and at greater length in the *Guide* ii. 32 f.; he considered receptivity to prophecy a natural faculty, though God would not necessarily communicate with someone who possessed the faculty. Abulafia was convinced that he had himself attained prophecy, and actually trained others in the 'prophetic kabbalah'; his techniques for attaining ecstasy, which he equates with mystical or prophetic experience, are described in Idel, *Mystical Experience*, 13–52. Several kabbalists claimed indirect personal revelation; see p. 54 below.

claiming to *be* revelation. It talks *about* Moses, in the third person, rather than purporting to be *by* or *through* him. Even Nahmanides (Ramban, 1194–1270), whose claims for the divine origin of the Torah are extravagant, felt called upon to explain why, if it was dictated as a whole to Moses, it did not open with the words 'The Lord spoke to Moses saying . . . '.[26]

The word *torah*, common throughout the Hebrew scriptures, derives from the root *yod-resh-heh*, which in the *kal* conjugation means to shoot (Exod. 19: 13), and in the *hifil* conjugation means to show, indicate, or teach (2 Kgs 12: 3; Ps. 27: 11). Among its several meanings[27] are the following:

1. A specific law or set of laws. For instance, Leviticus 6: 7–11 is headed *vezot torat haminhah* 'And this is the *torah* of the meal offering', meaning it is a set of rules for a particular procedure. In this sense, it can occur in the plural. Close to this is Ezekiel's use of *torah* to denote the set of instructions for construction of the future Temple: *vezot torat habayit* 'This is the *torah* of the House' (Ezek. 43: 12).

2. A specific ruling in response to a question. God instructs the prophet Haggai to 'ask the priests for a *torah*' i.e. a ruling, *she'al na et hakohanim torah* (Hag. 2: 11).

3. In Deuteronomy *torah*, or rather *hatorah* in the singular and with the definite article, refers to the literary unit under consideration, whether laws, narrative, exhortation, or liturgy; frequently, it is something written on a scroll (29: 20), perhaps entrusted to the safe keeping of the priests (31: 9). From the latter verse it is clear that *torah* refers neither to the Five Books of Moses as a whole nor even to the whole book of Deuteronomy. Quite consistent with this is 4: 44: 'And this is the Torah which Moses set before the Israelites', a verse chanted in the synagogue as the scroll containing the Five Books is raised;[28] Rashi, in his commentary, remarks that it refers to 'that which he was to set out after this', that is, the section of Deuteronomy comprised in our chapters 12–26.

4. Deuteronomy's use of *torah* continues in Joshua—'Take care to observe all the *torah* that my servant Moses commanded you' (Josh. 1: 7)—and in some of the historical books (1 Kgs 2: 3). It is not, of course, clear from the

[26] See below, Ch. 3, p. 55.

[27] On the use of *torah* in the Bible see Östborn, *Tōrā in the Old Testament*; M. Fishbane, 'Accusations of Adultery', 31–6, and his article 'Torah' (Heb).

[28] The expression 'by the mouth of God through the hand of Moses' (Num. 4: 37, 45; 9: 23; 10: 13) by which this is customarily followed refers to the numbering of the Levites and to the journeys of the Israelites, not to the Torah.

context that 'Torah of Moses' refers to the Five Books as a whole or to Deuteronomy as we know it; historically, neither is likely. But here, for the first time, there appears to be some concept of sacred, revealed literature; the reform of Josiah, incorporating the 'discovery' of a scroll (2 Kgs 22: 8), depends on it, even though the 'scroll of the covenant' (23: 2) that Hilkiah the High Priest found is not, in Kings, referred to Moses. Chronicles, however, frequently links *torah* to Moses, and presents the reformist kings as faithful to Moses' Torah. Likewise, Malachi and Ezra/Nehemiah refer to the 'Torah of Moses': 'Remember the Torah of my servant Moses' (Mal. 3: 22); 'And they found that it was written in the Torah that God commanded through Moses that Israelites should dwell in booths on the festival of the seventh month' (Neh. 8: 14). Evidently, by the time of the Babylonian exile and the Return the concept of *torah* as a sacred literary unit had taken hold, though we cannot be certain what it contained.

5. Many prophets use *torah* as a general word for the direction in life demanded by God—'You forget the *torah* of your God' (Hos. 4: 6). In this sense, *torah* could be translated as 'way' (akin to Chinese 'Tao'). Frequently, it is related to 'covenant'; *torah* is the way of life that is fitting within this close relationship (Hos. 8: 1).

6. Isaiah of Jerusalem uses *torah* in the sense of prophetic teaching or sacred oracle (Isa. 1: 10); *torah* in his famous phrase 'For from Zion shall go forth *torah*' (Isa. 2: 3) probably carries this meaning.

7. *Torah* in Psalms is used in almost all the previous senses, reflecting the diversity of composition of the book. Expressions such as *torat hashem temimah* 'God's *torah* is perfect' (Ps. 19: 8), or the richly mitzvah-oriented vocabulary of the 'Pharisaic' Psalm 119 in which the 'wonders of *torah*' are sought (Ps. 119: 18), do not necessarily refer to finished literary compositions or systems of law.

8. In the Wisdom books *torah* is identified as the personification of Wisdom (*sophia*), through whom kings reign (Prov. 8: 16), and who is possessed by God as the beginning of his way (Prov. 8: 22); there is the '*torah* of your mother' (Prov. 1: 8) as well as the '*torah* of the wise' (Prov. 13: 14). None of this presupposes an immutable sacred text transmitted from the days of Moses together with rules for its interpretation; the emphasis is on the living teacher and experience together with received wisdom, not on a set of canonical texts.

The 'Sacred Canon'

The concept of a sacred, revealed *canon*, incorporating literary texts that comprise the Torah revealed through Moses, is post-biblical. Jews, and Israelites before them, had *scriptures* from at least the fifth century BCE but they did not have a *canon*, in the sense of an approved list of holy books, until well into the Christian era.

The concept conflates several elements:

- The notion that some books are of special importance because they contain ancestral traditions of binding authority.

- The belief, clearly articulated in the Bible itself, that certain laws, instructions, or guidance were conveyed by God to a prophet, or in one case (the Ten Commandments) to the whole people.

- The idea, popular in apocalyptic writing, that inspired, 'secret' knowledge has been recorded in writing. Daniel, for instance, ponders upon a scroll (Jeremiah?) to discover that Jerusalem will lie desolate for seventy years (Dan. 9: 2).

All these elements reflect widespread attitudes to tradition and religion in the Hellenistic world, as well as in the ancient Near East.[29] Even the second, specific to Judaism since it refers to the biblical text, differs in content but not in form from other claims that laws or oracles had originated from some god.

In sum, the idea of a sacred canon establishes a boundary. That which falls within the boundary is authentic tradition, bearing the divine seal; that which lies beyond the boundary, for instance (from the Jewish perspective) the writings of gentiles or of heretical Jews, does not bear this seal, and is to be rejected.

Despite—or perhaps because of—the proliferation of writing by Jews of all sects right up to the rabbinic period, the sages intensified the boundary by attempting to ban the writing of books other than authenticated scripture. Even the Oral Tradition was not to be committed to writing, nor were laws, prayers, or midrashim. This extreme measure is stated in the name of Rabbi Yohanan (BT *Temurah* 14b): 'Those who commit *halakhot* to writing [are as if they] set fire to the Torah', and again in the name of his disciple and brother-in-law Resh Lakish. Even so, it is said of both of them that they read books of aggadah (non-legal material) on Shabat. They justified themselves by their interpretation of Psalm 119: 126: 'It is a time to act for the Lord, for they have violated your teaching'—better the Torah should be 'uprooted' [by commit-

[29] Hallo, 'Concept of Canonicity', 1–19; Sawyer, *Sacred Languages and Sacred Texts*, 59–75.

ting to writing that which should remain oral] than that it should be forgotten by Israel.[30] But if the ban on committing Oral Torah to writing was short-lived, that on books deemed heretical was not.

Why the Five Books Are Special

Archaeologists have unearthed Israelite epigraphic material dating at least as far back as the tenth century BCE. In 1979 an ostracon bearing roughly the text of the Priestly Blessing (Num. 6: 24–6) was discovered; it was dated approximately to the seventh century BCE and remains the oldest known biblical text.[31]

However, no manuscripts are known, whether of the Hebrew text of the Bible or of any ancient version, earlier than the third century BCE. By this time the 'Five Books of Moses' comprised a distinct unit known as the Torah, or the Torah of Moses. This is how the books were known to Philo and Josephus, and how they are cited in Apocrypha and Pseudepigrapha, in the Dead Sea Scrolls, and in the New Testament.

Were the five books written as a unit, on one scroll? Unlikely, since scrolls were generally much shorter. No text found among the Dead Sea Scrolls at Qumran appears to combine all five books, though 4QGen-Exod[a] and 4Qpaleo-Gen-Exod[1] combine Genesis and Exodus and 4QLev-Num[a] combines Leviticus and Numbers.[32] The Talmud forbids the public reading of *ḥumashim* (scrolls containing single books of the five), implying that the five books were to be written as one. However, this ruling is attributed to Rabbah and Rav Joseph, fourth-century CE Babylonians, and in any case acknowledges that the books were, in practice, being written on individual scrolls, even though it does not approve of this.[33]

The Hebrew term *sefer* 'book' in the Bible and early rabbinic writings normally denotes a scroll rather than a codex.[34] The codex (book of bound leaves) was invented in Pergamon in the third century BCE but was not perfected for some centuries; only much later was it adopted by Jews, who still retain the scroll form for copies of the Torah made for liturgical use. Some

---

[30] BT *Git.* 60a–b and *Tem.* 14b. The ruling against writing *halakhot* is attributed to 'the school of Rabbi Ishmael'.   [31] See below, p. 95.

[32] Tov, *Textual Criticism*, table 19 on p. 104. The Dead Sea Scrolls are discussed below, in Ch. 4, where their peculiar 'titles' are explained.   [33] BT *Git.* 60a.

[34] An anonymous *amora* in BT *Git.* 21b, commenting on Deut. 24: 3, suggests that, according to the majority of sages, *sefer* may refer to anything that contains *sefirat devarim* ('the recounting of words'). This is evidence of 4th-c. (or later) rabbinic wordplay rather than biblical usage.

scholars think that the term *kitvei hakodesh* ('holy writings'), occasionally used from the Mishnah onwards, refers to codices.[35]

The 'Book of the Torah' of Josiah's reform (2 Kgs 22, 23) was Deuteronomy, not necessarily in its finished form. At least from the time of Ezra and Nehemiah the other four books appear to be included; Nehemiah 8: 14–18 refers to Leviticus 23: 39–43, and Nehemiah 10: 30–40 spells out the oath of the penitent Judaeans in the course of which reference is made to numerous pentateuchal laws, including those in Numbers 15: 20 and 18: 8–20, though it is curious that they commit themselves (verse 32) to contributing a third of a shekel to the Temple funds rather than the half shekel of Exodus 30: 13. Chronicles likewise makes reference under the rubric 'Torah of Moses' to known passages drawn widely from the Pentateuch.

The division of the scriptures into three groups was made as early as the second century BCE. Ben Sira, who composed the apocryphal book Ecclesiasticus (Wisdom of Ben Sira) in approximately 180 BCE, wrote approvingly of 'the man who devotes himself to studying the law of the Most High, who investigates all the wisdom of the past, and spends his time studying the prophecies!'[36] His grandson, in the preface to the Greek translation he made in 132 BCE, is even more explicit: 'My grandfather . . . applied himself industriously to the study of the law, the prophets, and the other writings of our ancestors.'[37]

A twofold division into Torah and Prophets is also found. The pseudepigraphic Fourth Book of Maccabees refers to the 'Law and the Prophets', and clearly includes Daniel, Psalms, and Proverbs among the latter (4 Macc. 18: 10, 13–16). This simple division occurs in the Dead Sea Scrolls (1QS 1: 2–3); it is common in the New Testament (Matt. 5: 17; 7: 12; 11: 13; 22: 40; Luke 16: 16; John 1: 45; Rom. 3: 21), but only rarely used by the rabbis (Tosefta *Bava metsia* 11: 23).

Both divisions take for granted the priority of the Five Books over the rest of scripture. This priority is a fundamental doctrine of rabbinic Judaism. The Five Books came to be considered the only valid source for law, and the criterion for acceptance or rejection of other books; the Talmud tells of the first-century Hananiah ben Hezekiah ben Gurion who burned 300 barrels of oil in intense night-time study while preparing his successful defence of the book of Ezekiel against the charge that its contents contradicted the Torah of Moses.[38]

---

[35] For instance, Mishnah *Shab.* 16: 1. See Levy, *Fixing God's Torah*, 13.

[36] *Ecclesiasticus* 39: 1 (New English Bible).   [37] Ibid., preface.

[38] BT *Shab.* 13*b*. An alternative reason, the danger inherent in its supposed mystical revelations, is given in BT *Ḥag.* 13*a* for the proposed suppression of Ezekiel.

So it is reasonable to conclude that by the beginning of the rabbinic period the Pentateuch as a whole was regarded as the Torah of Moses, inviolable and sacrosanct. It did not necessarily follow that the text was dictated in its entirety by God to Moses, but this further assumption was soon made.

Philo on Moses and the Ancestral Books

The writings of Philo of Alexandria are better and more comprehensively preserved than those of any other philosophical exponent of Judaism in the Hellenistic world. In his second treatise on *The Life of Moses* he expounds at length Moses' excellence as philosopher-king, law-giver, high priest, and prophet. Through most of the treatise Philo writes as if these 'excellencies' were Moses' personal achievement. For instance: 'The next step needed was that the most suitable persons should be chosen as priests . . . Accordingly, he selected out of the whole number his brother as high priest on his merits and appointed his brother's sons as priests . . .'.[39] This makes it look as if the selection of the Aaronide priesthood was made on Moses' initiative. Likewise, the laws are presented as instituted by Moses. From this, one might conclude Philo believed that Moses was the original author of much of the content of 'his' Five Books, a position at odds with rabbinic doctrine as formulated a century or two later.

However, when Philo expounds Moses' fourth quality, that of prophet, a different picture emerges. Prophecy was necessary in order that through the providence of God Moses might discover what he could not grasp by reasoning.[40] All things written in the sacred books, says Philo, are oracles (*chrēsmoi*) delivered through him (*di'autou*—sc. Moses).[41] These 'oracles' fall into three categories:

- Those spoken by God himself with the prophet as his interpreter. Philo gives no instances of these, which are 'too great to be lauded by human lips', but appears to have in mind the bulk of legislation in the Five Books.[42]

- Those in which the prophet enquires and God replies and instructs. Philo gives four illustrations: the blasphemer (Lev. 24: 10–16); the man who gathered sticks on the sabbath (Num. 15: 32–6); the incident leading to the institution of the Second Passover (Num. 9: 6–12); and the inheritance of the daughters of Zelophehad (Num. 27: 1–11 and 36: 1–12).[43]

[39] Philo, *De Vita Mosis*, ii: 141–2.   [40] Ibid. 6.   [41] Ibid. 188.
[42] Ibid. 188, 189, 191.   [43] Ibid. 188, 190–245.

- Oracles 'delivered by the prophet himself under divine inspiration'.[44] These include Moses' address, extravagantly embellished by Philo, to the Israelites when they were about to cross the Red Sea; Moses' address (again reworked by Philo) to the people when the manna rained down; Moses' sabbath instructions concerning the manna; his oration at the incident of the Golden Calf; and his response to the rebellion of Korah.

Philo says nothing about the composition of the Five Books as a whole, certainly not that they constitute a sacred text literally dictated by God. They are part of 'ancestral tradition', and incorporate a record of divinely inspired oracles, but even the first and highest category of those oracles comes to us 'interpreted' by Moses, that is, expressed in Moses' words.

Philo's interpretation of the Bible is guided by his conviction that it contains all wisdom; since he regards Greek philosophy, or at least selected schools, as expressing wisdom, too, he has to interpret his Bible in a way that accords with Greek teaching. Similar interpretations were given by Alexandrian scholars in his time to Homer and Hesiod. It is probable that Philo was familiar with the methods by which Pythagoreans read numerology into the Greek classics, since he does the same sort of thing with the Bible, but the relationship of his allegorical interpretation with, for instance, that of the Stoics, is less clear.[45]

Contrary to what some scholars have claimed, Philo's categories of 'ancestral law' or of unwritten law (nomos agraphos) have nothing to do with the later rabbinic category of 'Oral Torah'; ancestral law is that which is written in scripture; 'unwritten law', of which he writes elsewhere, is basic morality, the 'law of the heart'.

Conclusion

By the time of the formation of rabbinic Judaism, Jews accepted that the Five Books (with the possible exception of the last eight verses) had been dictated by God to Moses. The precise status of other books was less clear, though a literary corpus not dissimilar to our present Hebrew Bible had been in existence for some time, and doubts remained about whether certain books, in particular Ezekiel, Ecclesiastes, Song of Songs, and Ruth were inspired, and hence 'canonical', at all. The process of canonization, or rather of *exclusion* from canonical status, was not a tidy one, formally undertaken and concluded at some 'Council of Jamnia' in the late first century CE, but extended over a period of several centuries.

[44] Philo, *De Vita Mosis*, ii: 188, 190, 246–87.
[45] Förster, 'The Exegesis of Homer'. See also below, Ch. 7, on Aristobulus.

TWO TORAHS?
Scripture and the Rabbis

T HE MISHNAH was completed in Galilee *c*.210 CE, under the direction of Judah Hanasi.[1] It articulated the programme of just one of several competing forms of Judaism at that time, but rapidly emerged as the formative text for the distinctive, 'rabbinic' Judaism that survived through the Middle Ages and into modern times. Similar material, together with comments, was gathered into a supplementary compilation, the Tosefta. Much of the content of Mishnah and Tosefta, together with cognate material, was reworked into a series of halakhic midrashim, or commentaries, on Exodus (*Mekhilta*), Leviticus (*Sifra*), Numbers and Deuteronomy (*Sifrei*). These, together with some works now lost, constitute the tannaitic writings, and the teachers whose views are recorded in them are referred to as *tana'im*, *ḥakhamim* (sages), or rabbis. Laws contained in these works were elaborated, applied in the rabbinic courts, and taught and discussed in schools in Roman Palestine, Persian Babylonia, and eventually other areas of Jewish settlement. The discussions, together with homiletic and other material, comprise the Talmud. The Talmud of the land of Israel, completed under Byzantine rule *c*.450 CE, is known as the Palestinian or Jerusalem Talmud (Talmud Yerushalmi); that of Babylonia, completed *c*.600 CE under Sassanian rule, is the Babylonian Talmud (Talmud Bavli).[2]

How did all these works come to be understood as belonging to 'Torah', and how was the concept of 'Torah from Heaven' modified in consequence?

Divine Revelation: The Story

Exodus 19–20 recounts dramatically how the Israelites, as the climax of their deliverance from Egypt, stood in the presence of God at Sinai and received the

---

[1] The earliest extant manuscripts, probably no earlier than the 8th c., have Babylonian vocalization imposed on a Palestinian substrate; see Yeivin, *A Collection of Mishnaic Geniza Fragments*. The earliest known fragment of rabbinic writing is an inscription in the Rehov Synagogue (near Beit She'an, Israel), probably 6th c.

[2] 'Completed' is a relative term, and dates approximate. Both Talmuds underwent extensive editorial revision in later centuries.

Ten Commandments from him to the accompaniment of thunder, lightning, and a smoking mountain; Deuteronomy 4: 4 and perhaps the theophany of Deuteronomy 33: 2 confirm that God spoke directly to the people. Yet both Exodus 20: 16–18 and Deuteronomy 4: 5 indicate that the people were over-awed, fearful of the voice of God, and begged Moses to act as intermediary. Exodus 24 has quite a different account of a covenant at Sinai, while Psalm 78, rhapsodizing about the Exodus, the plagues on Egypt, God's mercy, and the rebelliousness of Israel, makes no mention of Sinai at all.

What were the rabbis to make of these inconsistent accounts of what they did not doubt was the founding revelation at Sinai? Certainly, they took the words of Exodus 20: 22, 'for I spoke to you from the heavens', as bedrock historical fact. Torah, or at least the first two commandments,[3] came to the people direct 'from heaven', and the rest was received 'from heaven' by Moses and mediated by him to Israel.

But what did this mean? The actual phrase *torah min hashamayim* ('Torah from Heaven') in a doctrinal sense, and with reference to the Five Books, occurs for the first time in Mishnah *Sanhedrin* 10: 1: 'And these have no portion in the World to Come—one who says . . . the Torah is not from Heaven'. The Talmud comments:

'For he despises the word of the Lord and repudiates his commandment; that soul shall be cut off' (Num. 15: 31) . . . 'For he despises the word of the Lord'—this refers to one who says the Torah is not from heaven, even if he says that the whole Torah is from heaven except for one verse that the Holy One, blessed be He, did not say, but Moses said it on his own; 'For he despises the word of the Lord'—even if he says that the whole Torah is from heaven except for the inference from this [or that] *kal vahomer* or this [or that] *gezerah shavah*.[4]

This clearly presupposes the doctrine that the Torah was dictated to Moses by God, and that Moses transmitted not only the text but its correct interpreta-tion. It rules out notions such as Philo's that the Torah is a book which records oracles received by Moses, and in the formulation of which Moses played a part.

Elsewhere, the Talmud discusses whether the revelation took place all at once at Mount Sinai or was spread through the forty years in the desert,[5] and

---

[3] BT *Mak.* 24a; *Hor.* 8a.

[4] BT *San.* 99a. The *kal vahomer* is an inference based on an *a fortiori* argument; *gezerah shavah* is based on similarity of expression. See below, 'Rules of Interpretation', pp. 40–3.

[5] BT *Git.* 60a. Whether by 'all at once' Simon meant at Mount Sinai when the Ten Com-mandments were given or towards the end of the period in the desert is debatable, though the former seems the common understanding. Jacobs, *Structure and Form*, 38–9, denies that

whether the final eight verses describing the death of Moses were written down by him 'in tears' or added, at divine dictation, by Joshua; Simon bar Yohai, however, expostulated, 'Is it possible that the Torah would lack even one letter?'[6] Rashi and some later commentators suggest that the Talmud moots the possibility that Moses may have been responsible for arranging the revealed texts in order.[7]

The sages insisted on the authenticity of their textual interpretation; as this often depends on details of spelling and phraseology, they must have believed they were in possession of the precise text of the Pentateuch as received by Moses. Some of them held in addition that even such matters as the choice of script[8] (whether *ivri* or *ashuri*, that is, palaeo-Hebrew or Aramaic), paragraph spacing, and the *tagin* (ornamentation of letters), had been divinely ordained.[9]

Sets of rules for textual interpretation of the Five Books of Torah appear in texts from the third century onwards, bringing system to the interpretative practice of earlier rabbis. They are guided by three assumptions:

1. Scripture is free from error.

2. There is nothing redundant in scripture—every word, every nuance, yields novel information about the law, or is required by the structure of the Hebrew language.

3. Scripture is comprehensive, containing all that humans need to know, or at least all they need to know to conduct their lives in accordance with God's will; as it was put by the curiously named Ben Bag Bag, 'Turn it [the Torah], and turn it over again, for everything is in it'.[10] No one knows who Ben Bag Bag was, or what he meant by 'everything', and it was only in the post-talmudic period that the idea of the comprehensiveness of Torah was extended, by some, to mean that *all* knowledge was comprised within the Torah.

All three assumptions rest on the supposition that the text is a perfect transcription of God's words, right down to the details of its spelling and orthography.

anywhere in rabbinic literature is it claimed 'that God dictated to Moses at Sinai accounts of events yet to take place'; but this is surely just what Simon claims.

[6] BT *BB* 15a.
[7] Rashi on BT *Ḥul.* 101b s.v. *ela*, and Obadiah of Bertinoro in his commentary on Mishnah *Ḥul.* 7: 6. [8] BT *San.* 21b and *Zev.* 62a. [9] BT *Shab.* 103b; *Men.* 29b.
[10] Mishnah *Avot*, end of ch. 5; in *Avot derabi natan* 12: 11 the aphorism is attributed to Hillel. For alternative versions see Levy, *Fixing God's Torah*, 5, 6.

Mythic Accounts of Torah

The claim that the extant Torah constituted a divinely revealed and accurately transmitted text was certainly intended by the rabbis as a factual, historical claim. It denotes an event firmly located in time and space, involving real people and identifiable texts.

Other statements they made about the revelation of Torah are mythic in character; they tell us about the nature and values of Torah, not about history. The rabbis may not themselves have drawn a sharp line between the mythical and the historical, nor can we always assign a particular statement to one category or the other.

One group of stories portrays Moses as 'ascending'—whether to the summit of Sinai or to heaven—to receive the Torah as a gracious gift from God; they are linked by the opening formula *ki alah mosheh lamarom* 'When Moses ascended on high . . . '.[11]

'Heavenly ascent' stories were not new to Judaism or to the Graeco-Roman world. Elijah ascended to heaven in a fiery chariot (2 Kgs 2); the imperial cult which took hold in Rome in the time of Augustus allowed deceased emperors, subject to vote by the senate, to ascend to heaven and become gods (some achieved this notable feat while still alive); the *Sefer heikhalot* (Book of [the Heavenly] Palaces, also known as 3 Enoch), a Jewish mystical tract of the third or fourth century CE, describes how Enoch, who 'walked with God' (Gen. 5: 24), ascended to heaven and was transformed into the angel Metatron;[12] the somewhat earlier *Assumption of Moses* relates that Moses ascended to heaven at his death.[13]

Though the Enoch-Metatron theme was taken up in kabbalah, the rabbinic stories of Moses' ascent are different. There is no death, no transfiguration, no apotheosis, but a live mortal ascends to God's presence to receive the Torah:

Rabbi Joshua ben Levi said: When Moses went up on high, the ministering angels [protested] to the Holy One, blessed be He, What is one born of woman doing

---

[11] BT *Shab.* 88b; 89a; *San.* 111a–b; *Men.* 29b. Also *Midrash Rabbah: Gen.* 48; *Exod.* 40; *Num.* 19; *Deut.* 3 and *Midrash tanḥuma*, 'Kedoshim' 6, 'Ḥukat' 8, 'Ha'azinu' 3.   [12] *Enoch* 4.

[13] A more appropriate title for the extant work, as R. H. Charles observed in his 1897 edition, *The Assumption of Moses*, would be *The Testament of Moses*, since it does not cover Moses' ascent, which is presumably dealt with in a lost part or a separate work; as Charles points out, the *Stichometry* of Nicephorus refers to both a *Diatheke Mouseos* and an *Analepsis Mouseos*. James D. Purvis, in Nickelsburg, *Studies on the Testament of Moses*, 97, notes that the Samaritan scholar Markah refers to Moses' 'ascent' only to Mount Nebo, whereas the Jewish *Gedulat mosheh* has him ascend bodily to heaven.

among us? He replied, He has come to receive the Torah. They declared before Him, Do you really wish to deliver to flesh and blood a precious treasure that You have cherished since 974 generations before the world was created! ... Said the Holy One, blessed be He, to Moses, Give them answer! Lord of the Universe, replied Moses, I fear they will incinerate me with the breath of their mouths! Then [said God] take hold of My throne of glory and reply to them! ...

[Moses said:] Lord of the Universe! What is written in the Torah you are giving me? 'I am the Lord your God who brought you out of the land of Egypt.' [Did you angels] descend to Egypt? Were you slaves to Pharaoh? What do you want with the Torah? What else is written there? 'You shall have no other gods before me!' [Do you angels] live among the nations who worship idols? What else is written? 'Remember the sabbath day to keep it holy.' Do you ever work, that you should need rest? And what else? 'Do not take My name in vain!' Do you engage in commerce[, that you should need to swear oaths]? And what else? 'Honour your father and your mother.' Do you have fathers and mothers? And what else? 'Do not murder, Do not commit adultery, Do not steal.' Are you jealous of one another? Are you subject to evil impulses?[14]

When Joshua ben Levi told this story it was not in the context of history or doctrine, but rather to impress upon his hearers the *social* relevance of Torah; Torah is not designed for 'angels', i.e. people who withdraw from society to live holy lives, but for ordinary mortals who compete in the daily struggle for existence.

A subtheme of the story is the tradition of the pre-existent Torah, from '974 generations before the world was created', that is, a thousand generations including the twenty-six from Adam to Moses, for the Torah is 'that which He commanded for a thousand generations' or 'to the thousandth generation' (Ps. 105: 8). This is a Platonic understanding of Torah as perfect knowledge, the absolute Good. It echoes the language of biblical wisdom literature:

> The Lord created me the beginning of his works,
> before all else that he made, long ago.
> Alone I was fashioned in times long past,
> at the beginning, long before earth itself.
>
> PROV. 8: 22, 23, *New English Bible*

It becomes explicit in references in the pseudepigraphic *Book of Jubilees*, composed between 160–150 BCE, to the 'heavenly tablets' on which the law is inscribed (e.g. 3: 31).

---

[14] BT *Shab.* 88b–89a.

Both themes distance Torah from Christian doctrine. Moses is not a semi-divine being, let alone an 'incarnation' of the divine, but utterly mortal, and even so receives the Torah 'on high'; the Torah itself is eternal, prior to the creation, therefore not subject to change or 'completion' by some 'new covenant'.

Midrash tanḥuma[15] asks, 'On what was the Torah written before it was given? It could not have been written on silver and gold, as they did not exist before the world was created . . . [it was written] on the arm of the Holy One, blessed be He.' Clearly, this is homily, not history; myth, not memoir. Any 'translation' into the language of history, any resolution of the metaphor, would limit its resonances, its possibilities of meaning. It tells us:

• Torah is of God, and derives from his power (his 'arm') and being.

• The teachings of Torah are relevant at all times and places.

• Torah gives meaning and purpose to life in this world.

What it does *not* say is that:

• Torah as an actual document, naming names and detailing future events, existed prior to the time of creation.

• Torah is a metaphysical entity independent of human reality.

Both of these claims *were* actually made in later times, as we shall see, and the second is implied by the midrash of the pre-existent Torah. However, to interpret midrash as history is to misunderstand the nature of its discourse.

Other talmudic narratives highlight qualities of Torah, such as its joyfulness, the comfort it brings, its ability to liberate from distress and suffering, its role as the fulfilment of divine love.

The Written Torah and the Oral Torah

The rabbis taught: A heathen once came before Shammai and asked him, 'How many Torahs do you have?' He replied, 'Two, the Written and the Oral'. He said: 'I believe what you say about the Written, but not about the Oral. Convert me on condition that you teach me [only] the Written.' Shammai responded sharply and drove him away. He went to Hillel; [Hillel] accepted him as a convert. The first day he taught him, *Alef, bet, gimel, dalet*; the next day he reversed the order. [The convert]

---

[15] Parashat 'Vayelekh'. *Midrash tanḥuma* exists in several versions, and its composition is of uncertain date, but unlikely to be earlier than the 10th c. There is a parallel passage in another late midrash, *Midrash aseret hadibrot*.

protested, 'But yesterday you didn't say that!' He said, 'Did you not rely on me? Rely on me also with regard to the Oral [Torah]'.[16]

This story attributes the concept of the Dual Torah to Hillel and Shammai, early in the first century CE. Hillel and Shammai would surely have encouraged people to respect ancestral tradition, including the way they and other Pharisees interpreted scripture. But the notion of a 'Dual Torah' (Written and Oral) belongs to the narrator of the story, not to the historical Hillel and Shammai; absent from the Mishnah and earlier sources, it is a way to explain how the Mishnah and other rabbinic teachings related to the Torah of Moses.

As Joshua ben Levi (third century CE) put it: 'Scripture, Mishnah, Talmud, aggadah—whatever a diligent [vatik] student would [one day] teach in the presence of his master, was already imparted to Moses at Sinai.'[17] By his time, with the Mishnah recently published, interpretation and rabbinic teaching had become so extensive that the connection with the founding revelation at Sinai was becoming obscured; it had begun to look as if there were two distinct Torahs.

This situation is dramatized in a later legend which depicts Moses being projected forward in time and taking his seat in the school of Rabbi Akiva, where he was unable to comprehend the discussion; he was reassured only when Akiva responded to a question by declaring that the matter was *halakhah lemosheh misinai* (a law received by Moses at Sinai but not committed to writing).[18]

The idea that Moses received material additional to the Written Torah was not new. The opening chapter of the pseudepigraphic *Book of Jubilees* tells of a secret tradition revealed to Moses on Sinai in which he is shown all the events of history both past and future; perhaps Joshua ben Levi knew this or a similar legend and was recasting it in language better suited to rabbinic perceptions. The *Assumption of Moses* (1: 16) states that Moses handed secret books to Joshua. However, neither *Jubilees* nor the *Assumption* has anything to do with Oral Torah as understood by the rabbis. Likewise, Philo's references to *nomos agraphos* (unwritten law) are not to be identified with Oral Torah, but with the moral law, unwritten since it is already 'written' in the heart.

---

[16] BT *Shab.* 31a.

[17] JT *Pe'ah* 2: 4 (17a); compare BT *Ber.* 5a, in the name of Simon ben Lakish. A similar statement is attributed in BT *Meg.* 19b to Simon ben Lakish's brother-in-law, Rabbi Yohanan (Nappaha). All three were 3rd-c. Palestinians. Shamma Friedman has drawn my attention to the anonymous statement in Sifra on Lev. 26: 46 that the term *torot* indicates 'two Torahs', to which Rabbi Akiva replies that there are 'many Torahs'; a straw in the wind, perhaps, if authentic, but neither tanna uses the expressions 'written Torah' and 'oral Torah'.

[18] BT *Men.* 29b.

The rabbis devised stratagems to rescue the unity of Torah, that is, to show that what they were teaching was no departure from scripture, but its fulfilment. This parallels the way in which contemporary Christians tried to demonstrate that the 'New Testament' was the fulfilment of the 'Old', a process already under way in the Gospels' presentation of the life of Jesus as 'fulfilment' of the Hebrew scriptures, and implicit in Jesus' remark, 'I come not to destroy the Torah or the Prophets . . . but to fulfil them' (Matt. 5: 17). Jews and Christians, that is, were competing for the mantle of scriptural authority.

The rabbis supported their claim to scriptural authority in three ways:

First, they elaborated the concept of Oral Torah to explain how all they taught derived ultimately from the one divine revelation at Sinai: 'Moses received the Torah at Sinai, and handed it to Joshua'.[19] This idea may have developed from older claims, such as that in the opening chapter of *Jubilees*, that 'secret writings' had been entrusted to Moses; however, the Oral Torah envisaged by the rabbis was neither secret nor predictive, but on the contrary public and normative.

Then, material was reorganized in the form of scriptural commentary, giving rise to the classic works of the halakhic midrashim. These works (*Mekhilta, Sifra, Sifrei*) present rabbinic interpretation as the only rational and consistent way to read the Hebrew text.

Finally, the methodology of second-century sages such as Akiva and Ishmael in interpreting scripture was subjected to exacting scrutiny, and systems of hermeneutic such as the Thirteen Principles of Rabbi Ishmael were generated.[20] The purpose of these carefully formulated rules is to demonstrate that the interpretations of the rabbis are not arbitrary, but implicit in the biblical text.

Rules of Interpretation

Seven rules of interpretation are attributed to Hillel, thirteen to Rabbi Ishmael, and thirty-two to Rabbi Eliezer (Eleazar) the son of Rabbi Yosé the

[19] Mishnah *Avot* 1: 1. Parallels for the 'chain of tradition' in Greek and Roman succession lists and in Christian sources are discussed in Tropper, *Wisdom, Politics and Historiography*, chs. 6–8; the Jewish list defines both scholarly and doctrinal authority. 'We should envision the wider role of Hellenistic succession lists as setting the stage for the creation of rabbinic, Christian, and Gnostic successions' (ibid. 226).

[20] On the rules in general see Solomon, *The Talmud: A Selection*, introd., pp. xli–xlii, and Solomon, 'Evolution of Talmudic Reasoning'; on *kelal uferat* and *ribui umiut* see Solomon, 'Extensive and Restrictive Interpretation'.

Galilean.[21] Rabbi Ishmael's list features, under the heading 'Baraita of Rabbi Ishmael', as an introduction to *Sifra*, the halakhic midrash on Leviticus, presumably because *Sifra* itself is attributed to him, but this does not mean that he compiled it; all three lists are attempts to articulate the methods or 'system' of earlier sages, compiled by induction from reports of their scriptural interpretations. Efforts by modern scholars to relate the recorded teachings of, for instance, Ishmael and Akiva, to the principles formulated in their names, reveal wide discrepancies; Gary Porton, in an exhaustive review of the rabbinic corpus, found only six of the Thirteen Rules in any statement attributed to Rabbi Ishmael, while the use of twenty *unlisted* techniques was attributed to him.[22]

The thirteen 'rules' attributed to Rabbi Ishmael are:

1. *Kal vaḥomer* ('light and heavy' — *a fortiori* argument).

2. *Gezerah shavah* (similar wording in different contexts).

3. An example set out in one text or in two texts.

4. A general term followed by a specific (particular) term.

5. A specific term followed by a general term.

6. If a general term is followed by a specific term and then by [another] general term, follow the specific term.

7. A general term that needs a specific term [to clarify it], or a specific term that needs a general term [to clarify it].

8. If something was included in a general term, and then specified separately to teach something, it teaches us something not just about itself but about the whole general term.

9. If something was included in a general term, and then specified separately to demonstrate something similar, it alleviates the law, and does not make it more stringent.

10. If something was included in a general term, and then specified separately to demonstrate something dissimilar, it both alleviates the law [in some respect] and makes it more stringent [in another respect].

---

[21] Tosefta *San.*, end of ch. 7; *Baraita of Rabbi Ishmael*, end; *Avot derabi natan* 37: 10; Enelow, *Mishnat rabi eli'ezer*, edited MSS of the 32 rules of Rabbi Eliezer.

[22] Porton, *Traditions of Rabbi Ishmael*, vol. iv, table on pp. 201–3. For a more conventional view see Safrai et al., *Literature of the Sages*, 13–26.

11. If something was included in a general term, and then specified separately to provide an argument in a new matter, it cannot be reapplied to the general term unless scripture explicitly does so.

12. Something learned from its context, or from its ending.

13. Similarly, if two texts contradict each other, [the matter cannot be resolved until] until a third text comes to harmonize them.

It is the terminology rather than the content that is confusing. Take, for instance, rule 6. The Talmud applies this to Deuteronomy 14: 26,[23] which lays down how you should spend tithe money in Jerusalem: 'You shall spend the money on whatever your heart desires, on cattle, sheep, wine or strong drink, whatever you wish.' 'Whatever your heart desires' is a general term; cattle, sheep, wine, and strong drink are specific instances; 'whatever you wish' is again general. The rule says that we should 'follow the specific term'. Hence, the law is that the money may be spent on animal and plant foods but not, for example, on water or salt. There is still room for ambiguity—for example is fish brine food or water?—but the way of argument is clear.

Are these *logical* principles, as was argued by Adolf Schwarz over a century ago?[24] Apart from *kal vaḥomer* (*a fortiori* argument), certainly not; the rules are inductive, literary procedures, rather than methods of logical analysis. Saul Lieberman pointed to analogies with methods used by Alexandrian rhetoricians to interpret Homer and other Greek classics, while David Daube noted resemblances to ways in which Roman jurists interpreted the law.[25]

A clearer understanding of the purpose and function of the rules emerges when we consider the context in which they evolved. They serve two principal functions. First, they establish a one-to-one correspondence between the textual elements of the Torah and the propositions of law comprising the system of halakhah; this supports the rabbis' claim to be the authentic exponents of scripture. Second, in purely legal terms, they provide adequate justification for inferences to be made for the application of law from one situation to another.[26]

The Talmud (*Pesaḥim 66a; Nidah 19b*) enquires whether a suitably qualified scholar may apply a *gezerah shavah* on his own, i.e. whether without

[23] BT *Eruv.* 27b.

[24] Schwarz, *Der Hermeneutische Syllogismus.* For a different view, see the section on Mecklenburg in Ch. 14, below.

[25] Lieberman, *Hellenism in Jewish Palestine,* 47–82; Daube, 'Rabbinic Methods of Interpretation'.

[26] In Solomon, 'Evolution of Talmudic Reasoning', I have demonstrated formally how the rules can be reduced to these two categories.

a received tradition he may draw inferences for the law from parallel scriptural phrases. Medieval commentators ruled that this was not permissible other than where there was a tradition that the similarity was significant, though an *a fortiori* argument (*kal vaḥomer*) might be used even without a supporting tradition. With regard to the other rules, Rashi held that they could not be applied without a received tradition, but the Tosafists held that they could.[27] In practice, all except *kal vaḥomer* had fallen into disuse long before Rashi's time; even in the later layers of the Talmud the use of such rules is invariably attributed to earlier sages. Sa'adiah Gaon (882–942), moreover, held that the rules were '*descriptive*, not *productive*. That is to say, the ancient rabbis did not derive halakhah from the Bible using these rules; rather, these exegetical principles describe the Oral Law's relation to Scripture'.[28]

Interpretation *Against* the Plain Meaning

Rabbinic reading of scripture is not slavishly literal. 'You shall write them on the doorposts of your house' is read to mean 'affix to your doorpost a parchment scroll containing the appropriate words' (i.e. a *mezuzah*) rather than 'write the words directly on the doorpost'; 'an eye for an eye' (Exod. 21: 24) is understood to mean 'proportionate compensation', rather than physical retribution. This non-literal reading involves not *contradiction* of a biblical statement, but a reasonable understanding, in the light of common practice, of the 'plain sense' (which is not necessarily the *literal* sense) of scripture. Are there instances where interpretation actually *contradicts* the plain sense?

The statement *ein mikra yotse midei peshuto* 'scripture does not lose its plain meaning' occurs three times in the Babylonian Talmud, but what does it mean? Eliezer ben Hirkanos holds, against the majority, that arms may be borne on the sabbath, since they are an 'adornment' rather than a 'burden'. On what does he base this? On Psalm 45: 4: 'Gird your sword upon your thigh, O mighty one: your glory and your majesty.' But surely, asks Rav Kahana, that verse is a metaphor for words of Torah? Yes, he is told, but 'scripture does not lose its plain meaning'; that is, the *halakhic* interpretation (that arms may be considered an 'adornment' rather than a 'burden' in respect of the laws of the sabbath) follows the plain sense even though the *homiletic* interpretation (the true hero is the Torah hero who carries his words of Torah) may deviate from it.[29] In other instances the issue is whether, when a legitimate process of interpretation defines the context of a biblical phrase as other than the obvious

---

[27] BT *Shab.* 132a, Rashi s.v. *ela atya*; *Sukah* 31a, Rashi s.v. *lo makshinan*; Tosafot s.v. *veri*.

[28] Daniel Frank, *Search Scripture Well*, 24.   [29] BT *Shab.* 63a.

one, the obvious context retains its relevance for interpretation *side by side* with the new one.[30]

Even so, halakhic interpretation certainly does on occasion cut loose from the plain meaning. It is reported in the name of Rabbi Ishmael that 'In three places halakhah deviates from [the wording of] scripture', one of them being that halakhah permits ashes (*efer*) as well as earth (*afar*) to be used for the ceremony of the wife suspected of adultery (Numbers 5: 17). Rav Papa (fourth century), commenting on why the list is limited to three, makes the crucial distinction between a 'deviation' where halakhah merely *adds* to the provisions of scripture and those where it actually *contradicts* scripture; both, according to him, are possible.[31]

Arguably the most extreme case of halakhah overriding the plain meaning of scripture is that releasing the *agunah*, or 'chained woman', from a difficult situation. A woman may not remarry unless widowed or divorced. What if her husband is missing, but the normal complement of two independent, reliable, adult Jewish male witnesses is not available to confirm his death? On the basis of a case decided by Gamaliel I in the mid-first century CE the law was established that in such circumstances a woman might remarry on the testimony of a single witness, even by hearsay, or even on the testimony of a female or a slave.[32]

But does this really *contradict* the Bible, or only what the sages thought was its plain meaning? No modern Bible scholar, reading the relevant verses in their ancient literary contexts, would conclude that the requirement for two male witnesses applied across the board, or even that divorce was a male prerogative. The *agunah* situation, that is, arises not from scripture itself, since scripture could plausibly be interpreted in a manner that would not lead to such situations; it arises only from scripture *as interpreted by* the sages.

Even the expression 'The Court may make a provision that uproots the words of Torah'[33] is rather less radical than it sounds; it concerns adjustments within the system as developed by the rabbis, and is not a rejection in principle of Torah law. Such a rejection would be unthinkable to the rabbis. Yet the circumstances of their lives were so different from those in the biblical period that quite a lot of biblical legislation was either no longer applicable or, as we

---

[30] BT *Yev.* 11b, 24a.

[31] BT *Sot.* 16a: *bisheloshah mekomot halakhah okevet mikra* 'in three places halakhah deviates from scripture'. Rav Papa distinguishes between *okevet* 'deviates' and *okeret* 'uproots' or 'contradicts'.

[32] Mishnah *Yev.* 16: 7. The problematic nature of this decision may be gauged from the discussion in BT *Yev.* 87b–88a.   [33] BT *Yev.* 89b.

would put it today, conflicted with their moral intuitions. Two strategies are used to deal with these situations.

In some cases, a straightforward decision is made that the law is not applicable at this time. An obvious instance of this is Temple procedure, which cannot apply since there is no Temple. Likewise, the jubilee year (*yovel*) is said to be inoperative unless the twelve tribes of Israel are settled in their ancestral homelands, which is clearly not the case at this time. Less obvious are matters such as tithing and the sabbatical year, so there is considerable debate as to the extent to which they still apply, and the status (whether biblical or rabbinic) of such laws as do operate.

A second strategy is to define a biblical law in such a way as to render it inoperable in any real circumstances. This is how the rabbis deal with the 'law of the rebellious son', who according to Deuteronomy 21: 18–21 is to be hauled before the elders by his parents and stoned to death. Among the conditions attached to this law are: it can only operate within three months of the son's thirteenth birthday, and even then is subject to tests of physical maturity; formal prior warning is required; the son must steal from his father and with the proceeds purchase the requisite amounts of kosher meat and wine at bargain prices; he must consume the meat half-cooked and the wine mixed 'as gluttons mix it', greedily, not on his father's premises, in the company of good-for-nothings, and not at a religious feast; the voices of both parents must be indistinguishable, they must agree to bring him to justice, and neither must be blind, lame, or deaf; if the parents forgive him he is not put to death.[34] In other words, it isn't going to happen, but lessons can be learned from it.

The Bible mandates capital punishment for numerous offences, but the rabbis, whether under Roman or Persian jurisdiction, rarely if ever carried it out. This may have been because they lacked jurisdiction, but they certainly made a virtue of their reluctance:

Any Sanhedrin that executes a capital sentence once in seven years is known as a brutal [Sanhedrin]; Rabbi Eleazar ben Azariah says, Once in seventy years; Rabbi Tarfon and Rabbi Akiva say, Had we been in the Sanhedrin, no one would ever have been put to death. Rabban Simon ben Gamaliel commented, They would have increased bloodshed in Israel.[35]

The Talmud justifies Tarfon and Akiva:

'Rabbi Tarfon and Rabbi Akiva say, Had we been in the Sanhedrin, etc.' How could they have ensured this? Rabbi Yohanan and Rabbi Eleazar both said, They would

[34] Mishnah *San.* ch. 8; Maimonides, *Mishneh torah*, 'Hilkhot mamrim', 7.
[35] Mishnah *Mak.* 1: 10.

have asked, Did [the accused] kill a dying man or a sound one? If you claim he was
sound, perhaps the sword entered where [the victim] had already been pierced.[36]
How would they have handled a case involving sexual intercourse? Abbaye and Rava
both said, [They would have asked,] Did you see as kohl on a stick? How could the
[other rabbis] ever judge such a case? As Shmuel said, With adulterers, when they
appear to be committing adultery.[37]

That is, rabbis Tarfon and Akiva would have avoided passing a death sentence
by undermining the testimony of the prosecution witnesses. This stratagem
is in addition to the standard requirement of two independent adult witnesses
who have previously warned the defendant of the consequences of his action.

In sum, there is tension between the norms of biblical society as they
might appear from the plain text of the Bible, and those of a society governed
by the Torah as understood by the rabbis in late antiquity. Convinced that the
Torah as they taught it was identical with that received by Moses at Sinai, the
sages resorted to methods of interpretation which enabled them to read it as
unchanging and eternally relevant.

Conclusion

The sages of the talmudic period developed the concept of *torah min
hashamayim* in such a way as to incorporate both Oral Torah and Written
Torah. They elevated the Five Books of Moses above the rest of scripture as a
criterion for all subsequent revelation, accorded these books the status of
ultimate authority in all matters of halakhah, and absorbed both traditional
and innovative teachings into them through the 'Dual Torah' concept of an
Oral and Written Torah, received together at Sinai, bound together through
rules of exegesis, and faithfully transmitted to and through the sages
themselves and their predecessors back to Moses.

We must now enquire how this model of revelation was fleshed out in later
interpretations of Judaism; not until Chapter 6 will we be in a position to
specify what is included under the broad heading of Oral Torah.

[36] *Terefah*, literally 'torn'. This term is used of a human being or an animal which has a
disease or injury from which it will inevitably die.

[37] It is not necessary to witness in intimate detail—'as kohl on a stick'.

THREE

MYSTICS AND KABBALISTS

THE TALMUD, read on its own, may give an unbalanced impression of the range of Judaism during the period of its compilation; a student of Talmud may, for instance, conclude that Jews were indifferent or hostile to the visual arts, whereas archaeology has revealed the contrary.

Much of what was written, let alone spoken or taught, at that time has no doubt been lost, but enough remains to give some idea of what at least some groups of Jews were reading, hearing, and creating. The most important Jewish text was, of course, the Bible. Bible translation (especially into Aramaic), liturgy, and religious poetry were cultivated, and there was also an esoteric mystical tradition to which only sparing reference is made in the Talmud. Some of the sages may have sought to suppress mysticism, or to confine it within very limited circles, though later generations attributed much of it to rabbis such as Akiva and Simon bar Yohai, seeking to appropriate the magisterial status of such men for the 'secret' tradition. Should the esoteric tradition be viewed as part of rabbinic Judaism, an organic Jewish growth? Or should it rather be seen in its relationship with Hellenistic mystery religions and Gnosticism?

Whatever the origins, two features of the 'secret' teaching came to have a profound effect on Jewish understanding of the nature and content of Torah. One was the Gnostic emphasis on the redemptive power of esoteric knowledge, that is, knowledge acquired not by learning or empirical observation but by special divine revelation to chosen individuals. Jewish apocalyptic developed within this context, perhaps on the basis of Babylonian models,[1] and men belonging to apocalyptic circles put about the notion that a secret, superior Torah was revealed to Moses together with the public Written and Oral Torah. The idea that there was a body of knowledge that was both secret and important for redemption persisted into kabbalah and later Judaism.

[1] The earliest known apocalyptic works are the Babylonian Uruk Prophecy and Dynastic Prophecy. See Lambert, *Background of Jewish Apocalyptic*, and Grayson, 'Babylonian Origin of Apocalyptic Literature'.

A second feature is the notion that special enlightenment may be achieved by the favoured few. The mystical works known collectively as the *merkavah* ('chariot') or *heikhalot* ('palaces') treatises describe the journey of the adept through the seven heavens and among the angelic hosts.[2] These treatises give some insight into the mystical understanding of prophecy, and suggest that prophetic enlightenment including the mysteries of Torah is accessible to the gifted individual.

Song of Songs Rabbah, a sixth-century Palestinian work with later accretions, raises the theme of prophetic enlightenment to the national level. The revelation at Sinai is the 'marriage' of God and Israel, with Moses as 'best man' (*shoshvin*); for a moment, at Sinai, when God proclaimed 'I am the Lord your God' and 'You shall have no other gods before Me' the whole people participated in the ultimate revelation and experienced the ultimate 'mysteries'.

Early Jewish mysticism offers both a path to redemption, achieved through knowledge of divine mysteries, and a way of achieving personal enlightenment. These two aspects foreshadow what Abraham Abulafia referred to as theoretical and practical kabbalah. Modern scholars, led by Moshe Idel, likewise distinguish the 'theosophic-theurgic' and 'ecstatic' trends within kabbalah; do you use the secret knowledge of divine mystery to, so to speak, 'manipulate' the divinity towards redemption (theoretical, theurgic), or do you use that knowledge to transcend the material world, whether to perform magical transformations (practical) or to attain mystical ecstasy?[3]

The esoteric tradition extended the concept of Torah from Heaven in two ways. First, it meant that Torah was not just a law book supplemented with oral commentary, but concealed within itself a path to mystical experience. Second, although it accepted that the Sinai revelation was unique, it taught that revelation was not bound to a single event in Israelite history, but remained open as an ongoing experience in which the adept might share; Torah might be revealed to him direct, as a fulfilment or enhancement of the Sinai revelation.

Pythagoras, Numerology, and the Book of Creation

A distinctive twist was given to the notion of divinely revealed Torah by the *Sefer yetsirah* ('Book of Creation'), a mystical treatise of unknown origin, but

---

[2]   'Chariot' is the divine chariot described in Ezek. 1; 'palaces' derives from 1 Chron. 28: 18 and is first found with reference to *merkavah* mysticism at the end of Ben Sira 49: 8: 'Ezekiel saw a vision, and described the different orders of the chariot.'

[3]   See Idel, *Kabbalah: New Perspectives*.

which must have existed in some form by the sixth century, since it is cited by the poet Kallir.[4]

Sefer yetsirah is concerned with cosmology and cosmogony: what is the world and how was it created? According to Genesis God created the world by saying things, that is, by his 'word'. But what words? Genesis certainly gives the impression that God said things like 'Let there be light!' However, this naive reading does not satisfy the author of *Sefer yetsirah*. According to him, God created the world by means of the 'letters of Torah', that is, the twenty-two letters of the Hebrew alphabet, together with the ten numbers of the decimal system.

In Chapter 2 I mentioned the concept of the pre-existent Torah, perhaps an extension of Plato's theory of 'ideas', which constitute the ultimate eternal reality. *Sefer yetsirah* combines this with the Pythagorean metaphysic of number and the conception that reality is, at its deepest level, mathematical in nature. The author of *Sefer yetsirah* is attracted by the Pythagorean notion that everything proceeds from numbers and their relations, but he cannot remain satisfied with a system that leaves no room for Torah as the vehicle of God's creation.

Pythagoras' theory of the independent existence of numbers, and of their significance, was influential enough in the third century for the Sceptic philosopher Sextus Empiricus to devote substantial sections of his works to its refutation,[5] but he failed to stem the tide. Scepticism does not appeal to the imagination; magic numbers do. People prefer spurious certainty to rational doubt.

Numerology is quite distinct from number symbolism, a common feature of biblical and rabbinic discourse. Numbers 33: 9 states that at Elim there were twelve springs of water and seventy palms; these numbers obviously *symbolize* the twelve tribes and seventy elders, but the Bible is not attributing mysterious powers to the numerals themselves as numerologists do.

Sefer yetsirah's theory of the power and significance of individual alpha-numeric elements led to a conception of Torah as consisting of a precise, divinely ordered series of letters. This is radically different from the rabbis' understanding of Torah as a book of laws, and a far remove from the plain

---

[4]   According to *San.* 65b two 4th-c. rabbis, Hanina and Hoshaiah, used *hilkhot* (in some readings, *sefer*) *yetsirah* to create a 3-year-old calf, which they ate. The attribution of the story is unsafe, and identification with the extant book implausible. For an English translation of *Sefer yetsirah* see Blumenthal, *Understanding Jewish Mysticism*, 13–46.

[5]   Sextus Empiricus, *Outlines of Pyrrhonism* 3: 151–67 (pp. 428–39) and *Against Physicists* 2: 248–309 (pp. 330–63).

meaning of the biblical text; it tends to magic rather than to practical guidance in the conduct of life.

The trivial side of the notion was revived with the aid of digital computers by the authors of *The Bible Code*.[6] *The Bible Code* attempts to demonstrate that concealed within computer-generated arrays of the Hebrew letters of the Five Books of Moses is detailed information about future events such as Newton's discovery of the laws of gravitation and the assassination of Israel's Prime Minister Yitshak Rabin. Bizarre as this is, it is worryingly consistent with the world view of *Sefer yetsirah* and later kabbalah.[7]

However, a more serious side emerges when we ask what might have led the author of *Sefer yetsirah* to his fantastic cosmogony, bearing in mind that he lived in the sixth century (perhaps earlier), not the twenty-first. Very likely, he was adapting neo-Pythagorean ideas to a Jewish context. Not just numbers, he was saying, but letters, in other words Torah, constituted the essence of the created universe. That is, he was turning to any Pythagoreans who might have been listening and saying, 'You think the essence of the world is found in number alone. I do not doubt that numbers are important, but they are not the whole. The essence of the world is Torah, and the Torah itself consists of combinations of the twenty-two letters of the Hebrew alphabet. Hence, creation must proceed from all things that can be enumerated, both letters and numbers.'

A millennium and a half later this polemic sounds strange. In its time, however, it was a serious attempt to capture the thought widely expressed in rabbinic literature that the purpose of creation is established only through Torah; without Torah the world would be meaningless. It is a veiled attack on the pagan philosophies of late antiquity, suggesting the futility of any attempt to make sense of the world without Torah.

But this is not the way either rationalists or kabbalists read it. Rationalists like the author of the commentary on *Sefer yetsirah* attributed to Sa'adiah discovered within its pages the Ten Categories of Aristotle; kabbalists read into its allusive language all the speculations of later kabbalah, including the zoharic doctrine of *sefirot* (divine emanations, deriving from the word used for 'number'), and eventually the Lurianic doctrine of creation. Ingenuity did not

6 Drosnin, *Bible Code*. On the absurdity of the process see Levy, *Fixing God's Torah*, 167–73.

7 In Ch. 8 we will see that it is in any case impossible to determine with precision the 'correct' text on which such an exercise might be based. Nor does anyone appear to have explained on what basis the Bible coders ignore the spaces between letters. There is, despite this, a genuine issue of cryptography in the Bible; see M. Fishbane, *Biblical Interpretation*, 464.

always succeed in reconciling kabbalah with the actual received text of *Sefer yetsirah*, so the text was 'corrected' by such eminent rabbis as Isaac Luria (1534–72) in the sixteenth century and the Vilna Gaon in the eighteenth; it is now difficult to be sure what the original text was.

Mystical Significance of the *Mitsvot*

One might wonder what numerology, or 'letterology', has to do with the sort of things that both the Bible and the Talmud are more obviously concerned with, such as the *mitsvot*, or divine commandments.

Evidently, this troubled the pious Jews who rejected the rationalism of Maimonides and the philosophers, and consequently became embroiled in mystical speculations that were distant from the plain meaning of Torah. If the rational explanations Maimonides had assigned to the command-ments were unsatisfactory, then surely it was even less satisfactory to have no explanations at all. There were, indeed, those who engaged in the letter magic of 'practical kabbalah', through which they claimed to perform miracles, but this again was not a satisfactory substitute for the divine commandments which rabbinic Judaism regarded as the essence of Torah.

The word *kabalah* means 'tradition'; it was applied to esoteric teachings in thirteenth-century Spain in a spurious claim to antiquity and hence authority. Thirteenth-century kabbalists, particularly the school of Girona, addressed the question of the *mitsvot* with great seriousness. They extended the ideas of *Sefer yetsirah*, of the early thirteenth-century *Sefer habahir* and of the Zohar,[8] to generate a mystical interpretation of the *mitsvot*, and they came to perceive the *mitsvot* as parts, or 'limbs', of the divine essence.

The Zohar in particular stresses the 'one-ness' of God, Israel (i.e. the Jewish people), and Torah. Here are some typical statements:

Three levels are intertwined: the Holy One, blessed be He, the Torah, and Israel; each is on (two) levels, concealed and revealed.[9]

Whoever labours in Torah, it is as if he laboured on the palace of the Holy One, blessed be He, for the Torah is the exalted palace of the Holy One, blessed be He, and when a man labours in Torah the Holy One, blessed be He, stands there and listens to his voice.[10]

---

[8] The Zohar, the definitive work of the kabbalah of the *sefirot* (divine emanations), appears in the form of a commentary on the Pentateuch recording conversations in the names of Simon bar Yohai and his companions; scholarly consensus is that it was largely composed by Moses de León (1250–1305) in the last decade of the 13th c.

[9] Zohar iii. 73*a*. See Unterman, *Kabbalistic Tradition*, 36.   [10] Zohar ii. 200*a*.

When the angels above descend below they don the garments of this world, for if
they did not garb themselves in the manner of this world they could not exist here,
for the world could not endure them. If this is true of the angels, how much more is
it true of the Torah with which He created them and the whole world, and in virtue
of which they exist . . . therefore, the stories of the Torah are just the garment of the
Torah, and whoever thinks that garment is the Torah itself and not something else,
may his spirit expire and may he have no portion in the world to come![11]

Moshe Idel is of the opinion that possibly the Zohar, and certainly some
kabbalists, went so far as to *identify* the Torah with God.[12] It would be
impossible to demonstrate that *no* kabbalist went this far, but the Zohar is not
written in the sort of precise, scientific language that could ever justify the
claim that it identifies Torah with God; though it undoubtedly contains
statements which can superficially be read that way, it also speaks of Torah as
God's creation, and even relates 'conversations' between God and Torah,
which implies they are separate. Frequently, Torah is said to be the *Name* of
God: 'These ten words (the Ten Commandments) are the name of the Holy
One, blessed be He, and the whole Torah is one name, the real holy name of
the Holy One, blessed be He' (Zohar ii. 90b). It is not that the Zohar
contradicts itself, but rather that the language of the Zohar, as of mystics in
general, is not literal; it is the language of poetry and allusion, not of hard
doctrine. In just such a poetic sense the Zohar (iii. 93b) states, 'Israel and the
Holy One, blessed be He, are called one'; not that they are *identical* in a literal
sense, which would be nonsense, but rather, as the context indicates, that they
belong together 'as day and night'.

Whether or not Idel is correct, kabbalists certainly came to view the *mitsvot*
as constituting some sort of divine essence, and hence cosmically significant,
a view well articulated by Menahem of Recanati, Italy (*c*.1300). Recanati
writes:

I have found in the . . . that the ten *sefirot* are called the attributes of the Holy One,
blessed be He, and adhere to Him as a flame to burning coals and emanate from
Him and through them the world was created. . . . All wisdom is alluded to in the
Torah and there is nothing beyond it . . . each *mitsvah* hangs from a part of the
(heavenly) Chariot . . . the Holy One, blessed be He, is not something other than the
Torah, nor is the Torah outside Him . . .

. . . know then that the *mitsvot* of the Torah are divided into many, but all of them
derive from one Power, the Cause of Causes, may He be blessed; each *mitsvah* has a
deep root and concealed meaning, a meaning which cannot be discerned through
any other *mitsvah* . . .

---

[11]   They do not perceive the true meaning of Torah. Zohar iii. 152a.
[12]   Idel, 'Jacques Derrida', 112–16.

Whoever fulfils a *mitsvah* gives power to that *mitsvah* beyond the point where thought is exhausted and it is as if, so to speak, he were to confirm a portion of the Holy One, blessed be He, Himself.[13]

For Recanati and other kabbalists, therefore, the performance of the *mitsvah* is a theurgic act, justified not through its social utility or other 'natural' consequence but through its supernatural power in raising and restoring the creation to its Creator.

In this vein Recanati explains that the *mitsvot* connected with Passover relate to the cosmic process of redemption, in which God's attribute of mercy 'sweetens' the attribute of justice. For instance, the Passover lamb (corresponding to the attribute of mercy) must be eaten together with unleavened bread and bitter herbs (attribute of justice). Likewise, he groups together the prohibition of mixing milk and meat with other laws about mixtures, namely the prohibitions of sowing mixed seeds and of cross-breeding animals. These *mitsvot*, he says, are analogous to the prohibition of witchcraft, which mixes (i.e. confuses) the spiritual powers and thus controverts God's creation.

Contrary to the common view of mystics as antinomian, most kabbalists insisted on meticulous observance of the laws of Torah. Their mystical interpretations aimed to strengthen the law by deepening its significance, in contrast with Christian figurative or mystical interpretation, which was a form of 'spiritualization' aimed at replacing, or superseding, practical implementation of the law.

Prophets after the Bible

Several kabbalists professed to have received revelations themselves; occasionally they believed Elijah revealed himself to them and instructed them in the mysteries of Torah, a circumstance for which there is talmudic precedent.[14]

Others claimed more direct inspiration. In France and Germany in the twelfth and thirteenth centuries there were men from the Jewish pietist circles known as *perushim* ('those who withdraw [from society]') and *ḥasidim* ('pious ones'), who assumed or were accorded the title 'prophet'. They were apparently mystics of the *merkavah* tradition, and the title 'prophet' indicated that they had accomplished heavenly journeys and beheld deep mysteries.[15]

[13] Recanati, *Sefer ta'amei hamitsvot hashalem*, introd. 2, 3.
[14] For example, BT *Ta'an.* 22a.
[15] Scholem, *Ursprung*, 210 ff., (*Origins*, 239 ff.), with references.

Among them were Jacob of Marvège, who produced halakhic responsa that he alleged had been revealed to him from heaven through his dreams;[16] Ezra of Moncontour, referred to by the Tosafists as 'the prophet';[17] Isaac of Dampierre; Nehemiah ben Solomon; Troestlin of Erfurt; and Eleazar of Worms.

Few people after the thirteenth century laid claim to direct revelation, but Elijah continued to instruct the pious, and claims of *gilui eliyahu* (appearance of Elijah) are made to this day. In an intriguing variation on the theme, Joseph Karo (1488–1575) believed that the spirit of the Mishnah came to him and revealed mystical secrets, and he recorded these visions in the diary that, despite his best intentions, he failed to destroy before dying at the age of 89.[18]

The problem with all this for traditional Jewish teaching is not so much the implied renewal of prophecy as the risk that some would-be prophet might proclaim a law that added to or detracted from the Torah of Moses. Occasionally this has happened, as when the seventeenth-century prophet Nathan of Gaza endorsed the antinomian heresies of the pseudo-messiah Sabbatai Zevi. But by and large the danger has been contained, since the content of heavenly communications has been personal 'messages' that conform with halakhah, theosophical interpretations of scripture that have little or no bearing on halakhah, or quite ordinary halakhic clarifications and interpretations that can be rationally argued.

The prophetic tendency has strengthened the sense of renewal within Judaism, injecting additional vitality into tradition, but alarms those who regard movements of enthusiasm with circumspection.

Nahmanides (Ramban) the Mystic

Moses Nahmanides (1194–1270), known by his Hebrew acronym Ramban, achieved equal distinction as communal leader, halakhist, philosopher, poet, and Bible commentator. He hailed from Girona, in Catalonia, home of the major school of Spanish kabbalah; until about 1325, when the Zohar became more widely accepted, he was regarded as the leading kabbalist. His relationship with mainstream Spanish kabbalah is obscure, since his writings on the subject are mostly allusions rather than clear expositions.[19]

[16] Jacob of Marvège, *She'elot uteshuvot min hashamayim*.

[17] Tosafot on BT *Git.* 88a s.v. *vedilma*; *Shev.* 25a s.v. *rav*. Both citations 'revealed from heaven' are in fact standard talmudic arguments.

[18] The first complete edition of his diary, *Magid mesharim*, was published in Amsterdam in 1708. See Werblowsky, *Joseph Karo*.

[19] Scholem, *Ursprung*. Part IV (ch. 4) surveyed the kabbalistic outlook of Nahmanides and the Girona circle, and again in a series of Hebrew lectures, *The Kabbalah in Gerona*.

In his *Commentary on the Torah*, completed not long before his death, he combines the rational and mythic approaches. 'Our teacher Moses wrote this book together with the whole Torah at the dictation of the Holy One, blessed be He', he writes in the introduction to Genesis. Why, then, does the Torah not commence with the words 'The Lord spoke to Moses saying'? It is because the Torah preceded the creation of the world, written in black fire on white fire,[20] so that Moses was like a scribe copying an ancient scroll. There are fifty gates of understanding, and Moses received forty-nine of them. They cover knowledge of all that is in the world, all creatures, including humans, and the heavenly spheres. All this knowledge is indicated in the Torah, some expressly, some only through the numerical value of the letters or through their shapes; Solomon, the wisest of men, acquired his knowledge, even details of the medicinal properties of herbs, through the Torah in this way. We (i.e. kabbalists) have a reliable tradition, writes Nahmanides, that the whole Torah consists of Names of God, which may be assembled out of its letters in different ways, and that is why if even one letter is missing or wrong the scroll is invalid. In the original Torah, written in black fire on white fire, there were no spaces between the words, so that it could be read either purely as the Name(s), or in the split-up way in which we now read it to articulate the Torah and the commandments.

Conclusion

Kabbalists devised several ways to express the doctrine of *torah min hashamayim*. Common to all of them is the sense that Torah is not a 'mere' text dictated by God to Moses, as if it was something external to the godhead. Torah is a distillation of the divine essence; though the Infinite (*ein sof*) remains for ever beyond comprehension, Torah is itself, mysteriously, the accessible divine Presence.

Torah has not only *come from* Heaven, as a book might issue from the pen of an author at a specific time and place; it *radiates permanently* from heaven, creating a living bond between the human and the divine; prophecy in the forms in which it continues to be manifested confirms the revealed Torah and uncovers previously hidden depths within it.

[20] Nahmanides derives this idea from *S. of S. Rabbah* (Vilna) 5: 11, or perhaps from JT *Shek.* 6: 1, end (49*d*).

THE GREAT CHAIN OF BEING
Philosophers and Kabbalists

Philosophy is a fundamental human activity—even more fundamental than religion. It is an effort to inquire into the origin and
nature of everything we encounter, an inquiry that no individual
capable of reflection can avoid, but one that can be responded to
in a number of ways, some of which are religious.

R. BAINE HARRIS[1]

O NCE A RELIGION moves beyond the prophetic stage and tries to
explain itself, it tangles with philosophy; it is reassuring to have reason
on your side, though there is always the danger that it will turn round and
bite you. Sometimes, the religious will attempt to tame philosophy, to welcome it within the household of faith but downgrade it, as did the medieval
theologians, following Philo, when they called philosophy the 'handmaid of
theology', though the handmaid has a habit of coming back to dominate the
mistress.

Philosophy isn't there just when a theologian cites a philosopher openly,
as when Maimonides quotes Aristotle or Alexander of Aphrodisias. It is there
in attitudes, in turns of language, in ways of looking at things, in poetry, and
even in the thoughts of mystics who roundly deride philosophy as a waste
of time, an error, a heresy. Just as M. Jourdain, in Molière's *Le Bourgeois Gentil-
homme*, suddenly discovers he has been talking prose all his life unawares, a
mystic may one day 'discover' that his mantras and insights are the expression of a particular philosophy, and that far from transcending philosophy
he has simply been doing it rather badly. (Few mystics actually attain such
enlightenment; philosophers degenerate into mystics more readily than
mystics attain philosophical enlightenment.)

---

[1] Preface to L. E. Goodman (ed.), *Neoplatonism and Jewish Thought*, p. ix.

Platonists and Aristotelians

Today, at the press of a button, you can conjure onto your screen texts and translations of the works of Plato, Plotinus, and Aristotle, or enter a library and quickly locate critical, scholarly editions of the original Greek, with copious well-researched commentaries and an exhaustive secondary literature.

In the Middle Ages this was impossible. If, like Jewish philosophers in Muslim lands, you read Arabic, you might get access to an imperfect Arabic translation, perhaps with commentary, of some of the works attributed to Plato or Aristotle; these would be difficult to understand, for Arabic does not easily convey the sense of classical Greek, and the translation may in any case have been made from Syriac rather than from the original Greek. If, somewhat later, you lived in a Christian country and knew no Arabic, you might depend on an imperfect Hebrew translation of the imperfect Arabic, and perhaps you would attempt to translate that into Latin for the benefit of Christian scholars who were just beginning to rediscover classical wisdom. Cases are known of Latin translations made from Hebrew translations of Arabic translations of Syriac translations of Greek, a sure recipe for confusion.

In any event, the work that you thought was by Plato or Aristotle may not have been. The philosopher Plotinus (c.204–279), with his teacher Ammonius Saccas, is regarded as the founder of Neoplatonism; he had a considerable interest in the philosophies of Persia and India. A paraphrase of Books 4–6 of his *Enneads* was wrongly identified in the Middle Ages as *The Theology of Aristotle*;[2] this generated bewilderment as scholars attempted to harmonize the contradictions in 'Aristotle's' work. Another Neoplatonist, Proclus (c.412–485), an imaginative thinker who was convinced he had direct communion with the (pagan) gods, composed a work known as *Elements of Theology* of which an Arabic version was produced that somehow also got attributed to Aristotle; it was transmitted under the title *Kitab al-ḥayr al-maḥd* ('Book of the Pure Good'), and became known in the Latin West as Aristotle's *Liber de causis.*

The result of such chaos is that even a presumed Aristotelian like Maimonides was strongly influenced by certain aspects of Plotinus's philosophy, in particular his theory of emanations, his notion of the chain of being, and his contemplative ideal of the union with the Good through the exercise of pure intelligence. Nor was Maimonides uninfluenced by, even if he was

---

[2] Stern, in Altmann and Stern, *Isaac Israeli*, 95 ff., posits an earlier text, which he calls 'Ibn Hasdai's Neoplatonist', on which the fuller 'Theology of Aristotle' was based.

dismissive of, the work of overt Jewish Neoplatonists, such as Isaac Israeli and Solomon Ibn Gabirol.[3]

Plotinus himself detested Gnosticism as a 'barbarous, melodramatic, irrational, immoral, un-Greek, and insanely arrogant superstition',[4] so it is paradoxical that his teaching exercised its most pervasive influence in Judaism precisely on kabbalah, the nearest Jewish equivalent to Gnosticism. The paradox is deep; Plotinus believed neither in a personal God nor in the revelation of holy texts, yet his solution to the problem of the One and the Many in terms of emanations profoundly shaped kabbalistic understanding of God in his relationship to Torah, Israel, and the world.

But how could the contemplative ideal of the Neoplatonists be accommodated to the rabbinic ideal of the observance of the divine commandments? Could Torah be interpreted as 'philosophical soteriology', that is, as a way of being 'saved' through intellectual contemplation?

The transformation was accomplished by both philosophers and kabbalists. Jewish philosophers simply presented the *mitsvot* as preparation for closeness to God, in much the same way that their pagan forebears, including the Neoplatonists, had taught mathematics as a propaedeutic, or introductory course of learning that prepares the student for the ultimate study of philosophy. It was said that over the door of Plato's Academy in Athens was inscribed, 'Let no man ignorant of geometry enter here';[5] in like vein Maimonides dogmatized: 'And it seems to me that no one should walk in the garden (i.e. engage in the study of natural science and metaphysics) who has not filled his belly with bread and meat; and "bread and meat" is to know what is forbidden and permitted and such matters [in connection] with the other commandments.'[6]

The Ascent of the Soul

Proclus, following the Syrian Iamblichus (c.250–330), described the soul's ascent to the divine as a three-stage process of self-purification, illumination, and finally union with the One.[7] In the West, where Proclus's own writings were dismissed as pagan heresy, the Christian Pseudo-Dionysius reformu-

[3] His disapproval is expressed in a letter to Samuel Ibn Tibbon. Baneth, 'Maimonides as Translator', 178, notes that words for emanation occur approximately ninety times in the first two parts of the *Guide*.

[4] A. Hilary Armstrong, in *Encyclopaedia Britannica* (CD-ROM edn.). Armstrong edited the *Cambridge History of Later Greek and Early Medieval Philosophy*.

[5] Cited without source reference by Dunham, *Journey through Genius*, 28.

[6] Maimonides, *Mishneh torah*, 'Yesodei hatorah' 4: 13.

[7] Proclus Diadochus, *Commentary*, summarized in Altmann and Stern, *Isaac Israeli*, 185 ff.

lated the ascent as the threefold way of *via purgativa*, *via illuminativa*, and *via unitiva*, in which form it exercised a profound influence on Christian mysticism.

Proclus's ideas found fertile soil in the Islamic world, too. Al-Kindi and the radical Sufi Ikhwān al-Safa (Brethren of Sincerity) developed his ideas, and they were followed by the first Jewish Neoplatonic philosopher, the long-lived Egyptian-born Isaac ben Solomon Israeli (*c*.855–955), who found sufficient time to spare from his successful medical practice to elaborate Proclus's theory of the three stages of the soul's ascent, as well as to produce copious medical and philosophical writings.

How well did the three stages fit conventional Jewish teaching? For the philosophers, self-purification (*seauto katharsia*) meant liberating oneself from the material world. This led to an ascetic tendency that diverged from the more worldly rabbinic view; is this perhaps why Israeli never married?[8] 'Illumination' would not have been a problem, even though philosophers interpreted it somewhat differently from traditional rabbis. 'Union' was rather more difficult to accommodate to Judaism, for any notion of actual union with the divine was bound to raise questions of blasphemy; was it not presumptuous to obliterate or even minimize the absolute distance between creator and created? In addition, union implied the negation of personal individuality, and this was difficult to reconcile with the more traditional view of life after death as perpetuation of the individual soul. Israeli avoided both of these complications by describing union as the stage at which the soul became pure intellect, or spirit.[9]

Whether or not some Jewish philosophers or kabbalists actually envisage a *unio mystica*, in the sense of a total merging with the divine, remains a matter of scholarly contention. Gershom Scholem emphatically denied that such a concept existed in Judaism; his disciple Moshe Idel, on the other hand, emphatically affirms that it does. Idel, perhaps overlooking the Indian connection, argues that Plotinus's concept of mystical union may be traced through Numenius to Akiva and to Philo;[10] he divides Jewish *devekut*[11] terminology and the bodies of literature that arise from it into three groups:

[8] The Muslim historian Ibn Juljul stated that when asked whether he would like a child, Israeli replied: 'No, I have a much better thing in the *Book of Fevers*', meaning that his memory would survive better through his writing. Altmann and Stern, *Isaac Israeli*, p. xviii.

[9] Cf. Plotinus, *Enneads* vi.7.35 and iii.4.3. Altmann and Stern, *Isaac Israeli*, 188–9.

[10] Idel, *Kabbalah: New Perspectives*, 39.

[11] *Devekut* ('cleaving [to God]') is a term used by both philosophers and kabbalists to indicate the ultimate mystical attainment of closeness to the divine. It is derived from the biblical expression in Deut. 11: 22 and Josh. 22: 5.

1. Aristotelian, focusing on union between the intellect of the individual and that of the lowest of the superior intelligences—the 'Active Intellect'. This is found in Maimonides and to some extent in the ecstatic kabbalah.

2. Neoplatonic, focusing on the union of the human soul with its 'root', the universal soul, or even the godhead itself. This is found in philosophers such as Ibn Gabirol, from whom it moved to the kabbalah of Girona and ultimately to hasidism.

3. From the Hermetic corpus, Iamblichus and Proclus, comes the theurgic notion of 'bringing down' and 'manipulating' the divine; elements of this, though in combination with the other terminologies, are found among kabbalists of theurgic leanings such as Cordovero and, again, the hasidim.

The Descent and the 'Shells'

So much for the ascent, but what about the descent? How do lowly creatures emanate from the Creator who is, by definition, the source of all?

Israeli's scheme, if we omit his descriptions of the drama of fires and pure lights and darkness and shells through which the cosmos emerges, is represented in the diagram below. Each of the ten 'created' items is generated by the previous one.[12] The human soul is trapped in the embrace of the 'shells' and 'darkness' of the coarse material world of the senses; its destiny is therefore to pursue an upward path leading to union with the supernal light of wisdom.

Among kabbalists the system of emanations developed, in combination with notions from *Sefer yetsirah* and philosophical writing, into the zoharic system of the ten *sefirot*, and later into the highly complex Lurianic cosmology.[13]

Pseudo-Bahya[14] and other philosophers adopted Israeli's scheme almost exactly. Maimonides retained the general principle, but interpreted it in terms of a hierarchy of Intelligences associated with the heavenly spheres. For all of them, the essential concept was that a hierarchical chain of being extended from the Creator to the lowest matter of the universe, each item dependent for its being on the item immediately above, and ultimately on the uncreated

[12] The table is based on Stern's reconstruction of Israeli's *Book of Substances* in Altmann and Stern, *Isaac Israeli*, 79 ff.

[13] Idel, 'Jewish Kabbalah and Platonism', 319–51, has traced the relationship in admirable detail.

[14] Pseudo-Bahya lived *c*.1100. His principal work, *Kitab al-ma'ani al-nafs* ('On the Essence of the Soul'), was at one time erroneously attributed to Bahya ibn Pakuda; details of his life are unknown.

Isaac Israeli: Emanation of the Chain of Being

[God] generates primary matter and primary
form, i.e. absolute brilliance, perfect wisdom

Intellect (nous, in Plotinus's terminology)
(never affected by ignorance, since it is permanently
focused on wisdom from which it derives)
generates the Rational Soul (this can be ignorant,
since it focuses only on the superior Intellect, not on wisdom itself;
it therefore requires learning and memory)

Rational Soul generates Animal Soul
(lacks learning and understanding, but possesses faculties of
movement, sense-perception, and estimation)

Animal Soul generates Vegetative Soul
(growth and reproduction only)

Vegetative Soul generates the Corporeal Sphere

The Corporeal Sphere generates Fire

Fire generates Air

Air generates Water

Water generates Earth

Source: Altmann and Stern, *Isaac Israeli*, 159.

Creator, source of all being, identified with the ineffable One, or Good, of the philosophers.

The concept of the chain of being was uniquely satisfying as the intellectual mirror-image of the ordered, hierarchical societies of the medieval world. It was not necessarily static, as the classical Neoplatonists had presented it. A major contribution to the dynamism of the system was made by 'Avicebron', identified by Salomon Munk in the mid-nineteenth century as the Spanish Jewish poet and philosopher Solomon Ibn Gabirol (1021–c.1058). Ibn Gabirol, whose main philosophical work is extant as a whole only in Latin translation, under the title *Fons vitae* (*The Fountain of Life*),[15] laid great stress on the role of *will* in the process of emanation: 'form receives from will the power of holding on to matter';[16] this concept enabled philosophers to reconcile the biblical doctrine of Creation with Neoplatonic teaching on emanation, even though the classical Neoplatonists had envisaged an eternal, unchanging relationship of the One with the Many.[17]

Another Neoplatonic concept common to philosophers and kabbalists was the notion that the soul, weighed down by the material world, aspired 'upwards' to its divine source. Again, the social relevance is obvious.

Reasons for the *Mitsvot*

Philosophers and kabbalists agreed that the performance of the *mitsvot* was at least a preparatory step to this journey, and all that could be expected of the ordinary Jew. (Obey the king's laws and ask no questions.) All were agreed, moreover, that the next step, to be taken only by the more gifted, involved perfection of the intellect or understanding. To the Aristotelian Maimonides, perfection of the intellect involved, after the study of Torah, the study of the natural sciences and of metaphysics, which comprised the deeper truth of Torah.[18] To the kabbalists, perfection of the intellect involved, after the 'superficial' study of Torah, the study of *ḥokhmat ha'emet* 'The True Science', namely kabbalah, together with spiritual exercises.

This divergence is reflected in the way that rationalists and kabbalists interpret the *mitsvot*. Many scholars have argued that Maimonides rational-

---

[15] *Avencebrolis Fons Vitae ex Arabico in Latinum translatus.*

[16] *Forma suscepit a voluntate virtutem qua retinet materiam*; see Ibn Gabirol, *Avencebrolis Fons Vitae*, v. 39, 327, 24.

[17] McGinn, 'Ibn Gabirol', has traced the influence of Ibn Gabirol's innovation. See Heinemann, *Reasons for the Commandments*, for a general account.

[18] Maimonides, *Mishneh torah*, 'Yesodei hatorah' 2: 11 and 4: 13; id., *Guide*, introd. Maimonides' complex relationship with Neoplatonism is examined in Ivry, 'Maimonides and Neoplatonism'.

izes the commandments in terms of their ethical content. This is no more than a half-truth. He does indeed offer ethical justifications, but these are secondary to the primary purpose, which is the refinement of the intellect or spirit. As he makes perfectly clear in the final peroration of the *Guide for the Perplexed*, the ultimate aim of life is contemplation of the divine; this can be achieved in this world when one raises one's soul to the level of the Active Intellect; it will be achieved in the World to Come (life after death) when the soul is freed from the body.

The kabbalists are more radical in their interpretation of the commandments. They reject as superficial the social, moral, and ethical justifications offered by the rationalists, and view the *mitsvot* as a direct means to the comprehension and *control* of the divine realm. Torah, for them, has become both theosophy and theurgy; it is the key not only to the deeper understanding of God, but to the manipulation of aspects of divinity, of 'names of God'. Spiritual progress is dependent on identifying which *sefirah*, which aspect or attribute of the godhead, is active at a particular moment or in a particular situation, and acting (or praying) appropriately.

Conclusion

The absorption into Judaism of elements of Neoplatonic philosophy deepened still further the concept of Torah from Heaven. Both Written and Oral Torah, in the old sense, remain, and are eternally valid. They conceal a divine outpouring which the privileged few are called to explore to ever greater depths (or heights, depending on one's point of view) as their elevated souls aspire to the divine Source. Miraculously, through God's love for his creation, this divine outpouring has been made accessible to even the simplest Jew, for he or she can read Torah at its most basic level and observe its commandments and in this way elevate his or her soul to its maximum capacity.

MAIMONIDES
The 'Classical' Position

M OSES MAIMONIDES (1138–1204)—'Rambam', as he is usually known
from the acronym for his Hebrew name—figured in the last chapter as
a Neoplatonic mystic; this runs contrary to his conventional image as arch-
rationalist Aristotelian. There is no doubt, however, that he *was* a mystic, in
the sense in which students of religion (though not historians of Judaism)
normally use that term. Ben-Ami Scharfstein has noted that 'the usual
criterion for the mystic state is the certainty that one is undergoing the direct,
previously veiled touch of reality in itself'.[1] It is precisely this that Maimonides envisages when he represents the goal of human life as a state of
blissful contemplation on the divine reality.

Maimonides may have been a mystic, but he was certainly not a *kabbalist*.
In fact, he greatly despised what he knew of the Jewish esoteric tradition (the
term 'kabbalah' came into use only after his death); he contemptuously dismissed, for instance, the 'writers of amulets' for what he regarded as their
absurd interpretation and use of divine names.[2]

To Maimonides, the Sinai revelation was an historical event. The written
Torah was a text dictated word by word by God to Moses and supplemented
by an Oral Torah, likewise received from God by Moses. Oral and Written
Torah together formed an indivisible whole, entirely public and in conformity
with reason; if its profounder levels could only be approached by those with
exceptional aptitude and training, it was not because they were esoteric in a
mystical sense, but because behind their plain meaning lay philosophical
and scientific truths inaccessible to the uneducated, unintelligent public.
Maimonides was an intellectual elitist, not a crypto-kabbalist.

Revelation as History

What did he think were the *facts* about how Torah had been revealed? This is
not the same question as the much-debated one about whom he might have

---

[1] Scharfstein, *Mystical Experience*, I.   [2] *Guide* i. 61 and 62.

considered a denier or an unbeliever. He may, after all, have considered certain persons to be in error about the facts, though not therefore to be counted as deniers or unbelievers; for instance, if someone thought the paragraphs of a Torah scroll should be laid out in a different way from that endorsed by Maimonides as an authentic copy of what God had given Moses, he would be regarded as merely in error, not as questioning a principle of faith.

On the other hand, while the criteria of true belief Maimonides formulates in his *Commentary on the Mishnah* and in *Mishneh torah* articulate his understanding of the rabbis of the Talmud, they do not necessarily correspond to his personal belief as expounded in the *Guide for the Perplexed*.

The Oral Torah

In the introduction to his earliest major work, the *Commentary on the Mishnah*, Maimonides attempts a delineation of Oral Torah, which he is careful not to identify with any specific text, such as the Mishnah. The Mishnah, he says, has five constituents:

1. Elucidations, received through Moses, of scripture texts and commandments. For instance (he writes), God said to Moses 'Dwell in booths for seven days' (Lev. 23: 42); then he made known that the booth [*sukah*] was obligatory for males and not females, that sick people and those on a journey were not obliged to [dwell in] it, that the booth should be covered only with that which grows from the earth . . . that the space within should not be less than seven spans in length and width and that its height should be not less than ten spans. These detailed regulations belong to Oral Torah.

2. 'Laws of Moses from Sinai' (*halakhah lemosheh misinai*), that is, undisputed laws for which there is no basis in scripture.[3]

3. Laws derived by reasoning on the basis of scripture, and concerning which there may be a measure of disagreement.

4. Measures (*gezerot*) introduced from time to time by prophets or sages as a 'fence around the Torah', i.e. precautionary measures.

5. Customary law (*takanah*, *minhag*), including measures introduced by the sages for other than precautionary reasons.

Of these five categories, it is clear that in Maimonides' view only the first constitutes 'revelation' in the full sense of having been conveyed directly by

[3] See BT *Zev.* 110*b* for an illustration of the difference between this and *de'oraita*.

God to Moses; his list of 'laws of Moses from Sinai' includes enactments later than the time of Moses, while the final three categories are by definition not part of the original revelation. The Mishnah, that is, *encompasses* Oral Torah, but contains much additional material.

Torah and Dogma

In the same work, in the introduction to chapter 10 of tractate *Sanhedrin*, he elaborates his famous Thirteen Principles of the Faith. The eighth and ninth principles concern the text of the Torah, i.e. of the 'Five Books of Moses'. The eighth principle states that Moses made nothing up himself, but received the whole Torah from God; the ninth affirms that the extant text is a correct transcription of that received by Moses. Maimonides insists that every word of Torah, even apparent trivia such as 'Timna was the concubine of Elifaz' (Gen. 36: 12), is of equal sanctity, and that 'every single word of Torah has wisdom and wonders for those who understand it.'

In *Mishneh torah* he incorporates this principle into his legal code:

There are three deniers [*koferim*] of Torah. If someone says that the Torah is not from God, even one verse, even one word, if he says that Moses said it on his own initiative he is a denier of Torah. Likewise, one who denies its interpretation, that is, the Oral Torah, and like Zadok and Boethius contradicts those who transmit it [is a denier of Torah]. If anyone says that the Creator changed any of its commandments for another, and that it is no longer applicable even though it came from God, as the Muslims claim—all these three are deniers of Torah.[4]

As no law based on this principle could be implemented unless we knew just what the Torah comprised, Maimonides has to specify the correct text:

3. If a scroll is incorrect with regard to *malé* and *ḥaser*[5] it is possible to amend it and keep it as we have explained. But if [the scribe] made a mistake with the space between the sections and put a *setumah* in place of a *petuḥah*[6] or a *petuḥah* in place of a *setumah*, or if he left a space where there was no division between the sections or wrote in the normal way without leaving a space where there should be one, or if he changed the layout of the Songs, [the scroll] is invalid; the only way to repair it is by removing the whole of the sheet in which the error occurred.

4. As I have seen much error in these matters in all the scrolls I have viewed, and the Masoretes who compile information about *petuḥot* and *setumot* are divided about these matters according to the differences in the scrolls on which they rely, I have seen fit to set out here in writing all the sections of the Torah, the *petuḥot* and

---

[4] Maimonides, *Mishneh torah*, 'Hilkhot teshuvah' 3: 8.
[5] Full or defective spellings. See ch. 9.   [6] Closed or open paragraph. See ch. 9.

setumot and the patterns of the Songs, as a basis on which all the scrolls may be repaired and corrected. Now the scroll on which we have relied in these matters is the famous scroll in Egypt, which contains all twenty-four books and was [kept] in Jerusalem many years ago to correct [other] scrolls from. It is the one on which everyone relied, since Ben Asher had corrected it and worked on it meticulously for many years and corrected it several times as he copied it. It is the one on which I relied when I wrote my personal scroll of the Torah in accordance with the halakhah.[7]

Maimonides offers no evidence other than general consensus in justification of his preference for the Ben Asher Codex, subsequently known as the Aleppo Codex and now in the Ben-Zvi Institute, Jerusalem; it is unclear whether he commends the Codex generally, or only 'in these matters', i.e. spacing.[8] The Codex, completed in the tenth century, represents the culmination of the work of the Masoretes of Tiberias, whose aim was to establish a 'correct' biblical text; I shall discuss their work in Chapter 8.[9]

Much has been written on Maimonides' concept of prophecy, developed not only in his popular works, but at greater length and with greater subtlety in the *Guide for the Perplexed*. It has been suggested that he takes a more 'liberal' view in the *Guide* than in the popular works, but this appears to be incorrect. He argues strongly in the *Guide* that Moses' prophecy was like a direct conversation between people, unmediated, and hence is superior to all other prophecy and establishes the criterion for all other prophetic claims; by 'Moses' prophecy' he has in mind the revealed text of Torah, as he defined it elsewhere.

Conclusion: Maimonides the Minimalist

Maimonides' view of what constitutes Torah may be dubbed 'minimalist', though, as Marc Shapiro has observed, he exceeds some authorities in the claims he makes for the accuracy of textual tradition.[10] No one in the mainstream of rabbinic Judaism would have denied his basic contentions,

[7] Maimonides, *Mishneh torah*, 'Hilkhot sefer torah' 8: 3, 4.

[8] Copyists 'corrected' Maimonides' original divisions, so the printed versions depart from the Aleppo Codex. Penkower, 'Maimonides and the Aleppo Codex', has compared the Maimonides manuscripts and demonstrated the congruence of Maimonides' original section divisions with those of the Codex.

[9] In the 1860s S. Pinsker (cited in Dotan, *Ben Asher's Creed*, 13), followed by Graetz, *History of the Jews*, iii, ch. 7, p. 211, embarrassed the Orthodox by suggesting that Moses and Aaron Ben Asher were Karaites—how could their idol, Maimonides, possibly have endorsed the work of a heretic?—but Dotan has thoroughly refuted this suggestion.

[10] Shapiro, *Limits of Orthodox Theology*, 91–121.

though many would have exceeded them. The essential beliefs are (*a*) that
God dictated to Moses that text we now have, and (*b*) that Moses received, at
the same time, clarifications and supplements to that text which constitute
the Oral Torah, but fall far short of the contents of the Mishnah. He is less
dogmatic on the status of biblical books other than the Pentateuch. Others
would disagree with his claim that some of the profounder wisdom of Torah
may be recovered through the study of science and metaphysics; they would
agree that the Torah did possess profound meanings beyond the superficial
meaning of the text, but they would seek these meanings in halakhah and
kabbalah rather than in what they would regard as 'extraneous' science and
philosophy.

SIX

ORAL TORAH
What Does It Contain?

M<small>AIMONIDES</small>, we have just seen, was conservative in his definition of Oral Torah, restricting the term to a limited number of laws and rules articulated by the rabbis; he did not apply it to any written text, such as the Mishnah, nor to aggadah, the non-legal part of the rabbinic corpus.

The third-century Babylonian Shmuel said, 'One does not learn from *halakhot*, *agadot*, or *tosafot*, but only from Talmud.'[1] 'Talmud' does not denote a book of that name, for there was none in Shmuel's time (though there may have been by the time that his remark was redacted); it refers rather to the discussions that comprise the characteristic *activity* of Talmud. What Shmuel meant to say was: halakhic decisions cannot be based simply on statements made by *tana'im* (the sages of the Mishnah), but only on the results of the later discussions in the schools; moreover, not all material that is handed down is of binding authority.

If not all that is handed down is of binding authority, just where is the line to be drawn? We will see that later rabbis differed greatly from one another in the way they responded to this question.

Samuel ben Hofni (d. 1034), head of the academy of Sura in Babylonia, remarked that if the words of the sages contradict reason, we are not obliged to accept them; he therefore felt free to deny that the witch of Endor had brought the prophet Samuel back to life, even though the sages had taken the story in 1 Samuel 28 at its face value.[2] Samuel Hanagid of Granada (993–1055/6) wrote in his *Introduction to the Talmud*, largely based on Samuel ben Hofni's work:

Aggadah is whatever is stated in the Talmud on any topic other than a *mitsvah*. Nothing should be inferred from it other than what appears reasonable. You should know that whatever the rabbis upheld in a matter of halakhah with regard to a *mitsvah* [comes] from Moses our teacher (peace be upon him!), from the Almighty,

---

[1] JT *Pe'ah* 2: 5 (17a).
[2] Lewin, *Otsar hage'onim*, iv, Ḥag. pp. 2–5. See Berger, *Rabbinic Authority*, 164 n. 12.

and you should not add to it nor take away from it. However, the interpretation each one gave to verses of scripture according to what occurred to him or crossed his mind, we [accept] insofar as it appears reasonable, but we do not rely on the rest.[3]

Many medieval authorities, especially biblical commentators, were ready to express opinions contrary to those of the rabbis in non-halakhic matters, including biblical interpretation as well as science and history.

Does the Torah Teach Science?

Maimonides, in his medical and other scientific writing, ignores the Talmud and relies entirely on the science current in his own time. He seems to think that the sages themselves did likewise. Addressing his disciple Joseph ben Judah of Ceuta in the *Guide for the Perplexed* on the topic of the 'music of the spheres', denied by Aristotle but affirmed by the sages (and also by Pythagoras), he writes:

You should not find it blameworthy that the opinion of Aristotle disagrees with that of the *sages, may their memory be blessed*, as to this point . . . You know . . . that in these astronomical matters they preferred the opinion of the *sages of the nations of the world* to their own. For they explicitly say: *The sages of the nations of the world have vanquished.*[4] And this is correct. For everyone who argues in speculative matters does this according to the conclusions to which he was led by his speculation. Hence the conclusion that has been correctly demonstrated is to be believed.[5]

Later in the same work he gives perhaps the most extreme example of his readiness to abandon conventional rabbinic interpretation. Aristotle did not demonstrate the eternity of the universe, but had he done so convincingly Maimonides would have been ready to reinterpret the biblical story of creation in a figurative sense, just as he interpreted the Bible's many anthropomorphisms figuratively.[6]

Even in his halakhic work he occasionally disregards a ruling of the rabbis for some philosophical or scientific reason. For instance, he does not cite the talmudic ruling that a Jew should avoid litigation with a non-Jew in the period preceding 9 Av but should seek to engage in it in the month of Adar, presumably since the Talmud itself bases the decision on astrology and he dismisses astrology as nonsense.[7]

---

[3] Samuel Hanagid, *Introduction to the Talmud*, 46a.　　　　　　[4] BT *Pes.* 94b.

[5] Pines' translation of Maimonides, *Guide* ii. 8, vol. ii, p. 267. Pines' italics indicate Hebrew words in the Arabic original, not emphasis.　　　　　　[6] *Guide* ii. 25.

[7] BT *Ta'an.* 29b. Maimonides' obvious omission occurs in *Mishneh torah*, 'Hilkhot ta'anit' 5: 6. His objections to astrology will be discussed in Ch. 9.

The *ge'onim*[8] and classical commentators, such as the Provençals David Kimhi (Radak, *c.*1160–1235) and Gersonides (Ralbag, 1288–1344), readily departed from the sages' biblical interpretation in non-halakhic matters if their own speculations led them that way. For instance, the opening chapter of 1 Samuel describes the birth of Samuel in answer to Hannah's prayer. After Samuel was weaned, Hannah and her husband Elkanah brought him to the Tabernacle, and made sacrifice. 'And they slaughtered the ox, and they brought the child to Eli' (1 Sam. 1: 25). The Talmud weaves into this verse a convoluted story the nub of which is that the infant Samuel had sinned by issuing a ruling in the presence of his master Eli, thereby undermining Eli's authority.[9] Kimhi brushes aside this *derash*, as he disparagingly calls it:

And they brought the child. After they had slaughtered the ox as a sacrifice, Elkanah and Hannah [brought the child] into the House of the Lord to Eli to sit and learn from him, and so that [Eli] could train him in Torah and commandments. The *derash* is well known and need not be written; it is far-fetched.[10]

Medieval rationalists seem to have been particularly bothered by the extreme longevity of the antediluvians (Gen. 5). Maimonides restricted the longevity to the named individuals of that epoch, justifying the 'anomaly' with vague hints about nutrition, regimen, or just possibly miracle.[11] Moses Ibn Tibbon of Marseilles (late thirteenth century) went so far as to suggest that the high numbers, for example 969 for Methuselah, indicated not their lifespan but the duration of their dynasties and regimes;[12] Ibn Tibbon clearly did not recognize rabbinic interpretative tradition of non-legal biblical texts as Oral Torah, binding on the faithful.

The Torah of Kabbalists and Rationalists

Kabbalists, however, were reluctant to admit that *anything* in the rabbinic corpus, let alone the Bible, was 'far-fetched', speculative, or erroneous, preferring to find 'concealed meanings' where a statement appeared unreasonable. Moreover, aggadah was as significant to them as halakhah, if not more so. Kabbalists take it for granted that whatever is recorded in the name of the rabbis, not only in the Talmud but in midrashim, is 'Torah', whether Written,

---

[8] *Gaon* ('illustrious'; pl. *ge'onim*) was the title used by heads of the Babylonian academies from the 7th to 13th cc.   [9] BT *Ber.* 31b.

[10] David Kimhi (Radak) on 1 Sam. 1: 25.   [11] Maimonides, *Guide* ii. 47.

[12] Lasker, 'Longevity of the Ancients' (Heb.), 59, citing Moses Ibn Tibbon, *Ma'amar hataninim.*

Oral, or secret. Eventually the Zohar itself attained this exalted status; it was, after all, attributed to Simon bar Yohai.

The kabbalists of thirteenth-century Provence vigorously opposed the rationalistic biblical interpretations of Kimhi, Gersonides, and others; their opposition constitutes a major aspect of the centuries-long clash of Maimunists and anti-Maimunists. They began to appropriate the *agadot* to the esoteric system of the *sefirot*, or divine emanations. Azriel of Girona (1160–1238) studied in Provence under Isaac the Blind, and returned with this technique to his native city, where it was avidly taken up and reached its apogee in the Zohar.

The puzzling anecdotes and statements of the rabbis, the kabbalists maintained, were signs that might be read by the adept who held the key to decoding the deep mysteries of kabbalah, but which were concealed from the ignorant and the unworthy. Thus the image of God wearing tefillin (BT *Ber. 6a*) was 'decoded' by Azriel as the sacred narration of what God *really* 'wears', namely, the *sefirot*, the channels of emanation, the 'clothes' through which he is seen in the world.[13] In this way they sought to demonstrate that aggadah conveyed profound, 'literal' truth—God *really did* wear tefillin, of an exalted kind—the aggadah was no mere figure of speech. Such interpretation enabled kabbalists not only to defend tradition from its detractors, but to enter the space and to appropriate the authority of that tradition. Kabbalah, that is, had *become* Torah; the Written Torah, the Oral Torah, and the Secret Torah (kabbalah) were all three handed to Moses at Sinai.

Conclusion

No one, in the dispute between rationalists and kabbalists with regard to interpretation of Torah, questioned the integrity and authenticity of the biblical texts themselves, nor did either party doubt the existence of an Oral Torah complementing the Written. However, with regard to the *content* of Oral Torah there was deep disagreement.

At the rationalist extreme, Oral Torah consists of little more than basic halakhic interpretations and rules; other statements of the rabbis are to be treated with respect, but are subject to revision in the light of rational argument. What Moses received at Sinai was simply the written text of the Pentateuch together with the basic interpretations of halakhah. Some who are by no means kabbalists adopt a stronger position than this; the ninth-century *ge'onim* Amram and Natronai, for instance, basing themselves on an aggadic

[13] Azriel of Girona, *Commentary on the Aggadot*, 4–6. On Azriel's understanding of emanation see Scholem, *Origins*, 430–54.

statement attributed to Rav (early third century), held that the Targum, the Aramaic translation attributed to Onkelos, originated at Sinai.[14]

At the other extreme, kabbalists held that *all* the statements attributed to the rabbis in the Talmud and its associated writings, even apparently absurd *derashot*, were holy Torah, originating at Sinai; both halakhic and aggadic statements concealed mystical doctrines that constituted their real essence.

Even this position falls far short of the extravagant claims for Torah made by some later rabbis such as the Vilna Gaon who, as we shall see in Chapter 12, held that *all knowledge* including the details of everyone's life was implicit in the text of Torah.

Summary of Part I

◆

In this part we traced the evolution of the concept of 'Torah' to the end of the Middle Ages.

At the earliest stage Torah meant instruction or guidance in general, or a specific law or group of laws, not necessarily revealed by God. 'Moses' Torah', in later biblical usage, might refer to part or the whole of Deuteronomy.

By no later than the second century BCE, possibly much earlier, the term had come to denote the Pentateuch, or Five Books of Moses. If the Five Books are read in a plain manner they appear to contain a number of 'oracles', as Philo called them, in which the substance of divine instructions is recorded.

In the rabbinic period it was understood that the Five Books as a whole were dictated word for word by God to Moses.

When the tradition of interpretation had developed to the point at which there was a significant body of text supplementing and interpreting scripture, perhaps early in the third century CE, the concept of the Dual Torah—Oral and Written—emerged. God had not merely dictated the written text, but had entrusted supplementary material to Moses for oral transmission.

On account both of internal dissension and of challenges from rival groups, such as Christians, who laid claim to the authority of scripture, the rules of interpretation were formulated and incorporated into the body of Torah. The perfection, freedom from redundancy, and comprehensiveness of scripture came to be assumed.

In Chapter 8 we shall see how Masoretes and grammarians defined and

---

[14] This position is endorsed by several later authorities, including Joseph Karo (1488–1575) in *Beit yosef*, 'Oraḥ ḥayim' 285, even though it is against the plain sense of the Talmud (BT *Meg.* 3a), where it appears only as a rather forced defence of Rav's statement.

refined the biblical text, including its vocalization and the forms of letters. On the basis of their work the claim was made that one or other specific manuscript, for instance the Ben Asher Codex, was the definitive record of God's dictation to Moses.

Opinions varied as to the comprehensiveness of Torah. Does it contain simply narratives and revealed laws, or does it contain all knowledge, including prophecy as well as natural science?

Under Gnostic and Neoplatonist influence the doctrine of a 'secret Torah' emerges; kabbalists maintain that their esoteric doctrines were revealed to Moses as part, indeed the essence, of the Torah; philosophers, on the other hand, argue that a correct reading of Torah reveals that it rests upon, or at least is consistent with, the metaphysical system they regard as correct.

Which books emanated from Sinai? Just the Pentateuch? The Aramaic translation, and if so which version? An Oral Torah text, whether or not the extant Mishnah? The Zohar? Are those matters on which scripture is not explicit coded into the text, or implicit in its meaning?

Though there were constant and often acrimonious debates, no august council or committee was ever in a position to issue binding doctrinal definitions as had happened in the early church. Jews therefore faced the onset of modernity with a set of doctrines that were not rigidly defined. The core minimum was that the extant Torah was a more or less correct transcript of what God had dictated to Moses, and that the rabbinic tradition encapsulated its authentic interpretation, at least in matters of halakhah. Disagreement persisted as to the status of the esoteric tradition, and also as to the extent of the Torah's comprehensiveness.

In Part II we will examine criticisms to which even the minimum traditional claim has been subjected. Would it prove adequate to withstand the challenges of modernity, or would revisions and reformulations prove necessary?

PART II

◆

ATTACK

The Counter-Tradition: Hard Questions

To the faithful no question is a question;
to the sceptic, no answer is an answer.

IN PART I, I described the evolution of a tradition that ascribes directly to God the revelation of a basic text (the Written Torah) together with an explanatory and supplementary tradition (the Oral Torah). Some came to believe also that deeper, secret truths were revealed at the same time, forming the body of which the exoteric (open) Torah, both Written and Oral, is but the garment.

This rabbinic tradition evolved out of one of many varieties of Judaism that existed in the first century CE, perhaps out of just one of several trends among the Pharisees. Somehow, rabbinic Judaism as formulated in the school of Judah Hanasi in early third-century Galilee was the only one, of all the available brands of Judaism, to succeed in adapting itself to the conditions in which Jews were to live for the next two millennia.

The tradition was challenged at every point along its development, and its direction and expression were shaped by the ways it responded to the challenges. Nor were the challenges merely sporadic or unco-ordinated; they constitute a counter-tradition which may be traced back over two thousand years. Questions raised in the counter-tradition were not ignored within the tradition; tradition and counter-tradition differ not in the questions they ask, but in the answers they give to those questions.

The counter-tradition manifests itself in three settings. First, Jewish groups, for example Sadducees or Karaites, systematically rejected Pharisee and later Rabbanite claims to represent the authentic biblical tradition, claiming that prerogative for themselves.

Second, from beyond the Jewish fold, pagan philosophers, Zoroastrians, Christians, Gnostics, and Muslims posed questions, sometimes out of curiosity, often in order to discredit Judaism to their own advantage.

Finally, dissident Jews, such as Hiwi of Balkh or Spinoza, radically questioned the received traditions.

Problems originating in these sources overlap with doubts and reflections arising independently in the minds of 'the faithful' as they wrestle with apparent inconsistencies in the texts. External critique and internal organic development fuel one another.

The purpose of this part is to sketch the counter-tradition, to present its arguments as a coherent whole, and to observe how it affected the evolution of the tradition itself.

◆

SEVEN

THE COUNTER-TRADITION

For every action, there is an equal and opposite reaction.

NEWTON'S THIRD LAW

COUNTER-TRADITION begins within scripture; Job, for instance, may be read as a critique of the naive reward and punishment economy of Deuteronomy.

Fascinating as the internal dialectic of scripture undoubtedly is, I shall start with the Greek-speaking Jewish community of Ptolemaic Alexandria in the first two centuries BCE. There, Jews nurtured in the tradition of the Hebrew scriptures encountered and willingly adopted not only the Greek language but other aspects of Hellenistic culture and engaged in scientific and philosophical pursuits with their fellow citizens. Palestine itself lay within the Greek world, whether Ptolemaic or Seleucid, but the new interpretation of Judaism was forged in Alexandria rather than Jerusalem, which remained a cultural backwater for a long time.

The Alexandrians

Greek commentators on ancient poets such as Homer and Hesiod had long been troubled by inconsistencies in the material they studied, and by the attribution to gods and heroes of actions that were morally reprehensible. Plato openly accused Homer of error and recommended that his stories not be taught to the young, but Alexandrian scholars, especially the Stoics, defended Homer by refining the text, by filling gaps in the narrative so as to present their heroes in a more favourable light, and by allegorical and other radical forms of interpretation.[1] Small wonder that Jewish scholars engaged in similar interpretative practices with their own sacred texts, not just for defensive and conversionist purposes, but to make sense of narratives that had begun to appear incoherent or contrary to good morals.

Some Alexandrian Jews, like the classical historians with whose work they were familiar, worried about chronological problems in the sources, notably

---

[1] Lamberton, *Homer the Theologian*.

in the books we know as the Bible. For instance, in Genesis 15: 13 Abraham is told, 'Your offspring shall be strangers in a land not theirs, and they shall be enslaved and oppressed four hundred years', and this is confirmed by Exodus 12: 40: 'The length of time that the Israelites lived in Egypt was four hundred and thirty years'; yet the details supplied in Genesis and Exodus, such as the number of generations involved, suggest a much shorter period. The Septuagint, the Greek translation produced in Alexandria, overcomes the difficulty by counting the 430 years from the time of the promise to Abraham; it translates, 'And the time that the Israelites lived in Egypt *and other lands* was four hundred and thirty years.'[2]

Demetrius the Chronographer, who lived in Alexandria in the time of Ptolemy IV Philopator (221–204 BCE), has been described by Carl Holladay as 'perhaps the first Jewish author who systematically engages in biblical criticism'; however, the fragments that remain of Demetrius's work look very much as if he aimed at defending, not challenging, scriptural tradition.[3] We have no record of what he said about the length of the stay in Egypt, but his attempt to fit the births of Jacob's sons and daughter into the minimal period allowed by Genesis 29–30 was copied by Alexander Polyhistor and cited by the Christian Eusebius, 'the father of Church history', who became bishop of Caesarea in 314:[4]

Then after spending seven years there, he married two daughters of Laban, his maternal uncle, Leah and Rachel, when he was 84 years old. In seven more years, twelve children were born to him. In the tenth month of the eighth year, Reuben [was born]; and in the eighth month of the ninth year, Simon; and in the sixth month of the tenth year, Levi; and in the fourth month of the eleventh year, Judah. And since Rachel did not bear, she became envious of her sister, and gave her own handmaid [Bilhah] to Jacob as a concubine, who bore Dan in the fourth month of the eleventh year, and in the second month of the twelfth year, Naphtali. And Leah gave her own handmaid Zilpah to Jacob to concubine, at the same time as Bilhah conceived Naphtali, in the fifth month of the eleventh year, and he begot a son in the second month of the same year, whom Leah named Asher.

And in return for the mandrake apples which Reuben brought to Rachel, Leah again conceived, as did her handmaid Zilpah at the same time, in the third month of the twelfth year, and bore a son in the twelfth month of the same year, and gave him the name Issachar.

And again Leah bore another son in the tenth month of the thirteenth year, whose name was Zebulun; and in the eighth month of the fourteenth year, the same

² The rabbis in later times were aware of this 'translation', and concurred with the interpretation. See BT *Meg.* 9a.
³ Holladay, *Fragments*, iii. 53. Holladay transcribes and translates the extant fragments of Demetrius on pp. 51–92.   ⁴ Eusebius of Caesarea, *Praeparatio Evangelica* 9.21.11.

Leah bore a [daughter] named [Dinah]. And at the same time as Leah [conceived] a daughter, Dinah, Rachel also conceived in her womb, and in the eighth month of the fourteenth year she bore a son, who was named Joseph, so that in the seven years spent with Laban, twelve children were born.

Demetrius's attempts at harmonizing biblical chronology certainly influenced the rabbinic *Seder olam rabah* and subsequent midrashim.[5]

While Demetrius laboured with problems of internal biblical consistency, others were concerned with broader, philosophical issues:

It is time to hear what Aristobulus, who had partaken of Aristotle's philosophy in addition to that of his own country, declared concerning the passages in the Sacred Books which are currently understood to refer to limbs of God's body. This is that very man who is mentioned in the beginning of the Second Book of Maccabees: and in his writing addressed to King Ptolemy he too explains this principle.[6]

From the fragments of his work that have come down to us through Clement and Eusebius, it seems that Aristobulus may have been the first to articulate the allegorical interpretation of anthropomorphic expressions in the Bible that was developed by Philo and adopted by Jewish, Christian, and Muslim philosophers in the Middle Ages:

When, however, we had said enough in answer to the questions put before us, you also, O king, did further demand, why by our law there are intimations given of hands, and arm, and face, and feet, and walking, in the case of the Divine Power . . .

But I would entreat you to take the interpretations in a natural way, and to hold fast the fitting conception of God, and not to fall off into the idea of a fabulous anthropomorphic constitution.

For our lawgiver Moses, when he wishes to express his meaning in various ways, announces certain arrangements of nature and preparations for mighty deeds, by adopting phrases applicable to other things, I mean to things outward and visible . . .

First then the word 'hands' evidently has, even in our own case, a more general meaning. For when you as a king send out forces, wishing to accomplish some purpose, we say, The king has a mighty hand, and the hearers' thoughts are carried to the power which you possess.

Now this is what Moses also signifies in our Law, when he speaks thus : 'God brought thee forth out of Egypt with a mighty hand'; and again: 'I will put forth My

[5] See Milikowsky, 'Seder Olam', 231–41.

[6] Eusebius, *Praeparatio Evangelica* 8.10; Holladay, *Fragments*, iii. 134–5. If Clement and Eusebius correctly identified this Aristobulus as the recipient of the letter from Judas Maccabeus mentioned in 2 Macc. 1: 10, he was not only a member of a Jewish priestly family but the *didaskolos* 'teacher' of Ptolemy (probably Philometer VI); the letter was dispatched in the 148th Seleucid year, i.e. 164 BCE.

hand', saith God, 'and will smite the Egyptians.' Again in the account of the death of the cattle Moses says to Pharaoh: 'Behold, the hand of the Lord shall be upon thy cattle, and upon all that are in the fields a great death.' So that the 'hands' are understood of the power of God: for indeed it is easy to perceive that the whole strength of men and their active powers are in their hands.[7]

Aristobulus is sometimes said to have extended allegorical interpretation to the laws themselves, but I have not seen evidence of this.

Clement of Alexandria says that Aristobulus demonstrated the dependence of Greek philosophy on the Hebrews:

And by Aristobulus, who lived in the time of Ptolemy Philadelphus, who is mentioned by the composer of the epitome of the books of the Maccabees, there were abundant books to show that the Peripatetic philosophy was derived from the law of Moses and from the other prophets.[8]

The notion that all wisdom originated in revealed scripture ('Moses was the father of Greek philosophy and culture') is a stratagem for defending the primacy of scripture while remaining open to what appear to be independent sources of knowledge; we shall meet it again in Chapter 11 when we consider the Renaissance.

Sadducees and Pharisees

Most of the available material relating to the disputes of Pharisees and Sadducees comes to us through the hands of the victors, that is, the Pharisees themselves and their rabbinic followers, and reflects their point of view; we do not have Sadducee tracts to parallel the rabbinic account.

Both sides adduced scripture in support of their positions. Scripture specifies, for instance, that an offering of barley (the *omer*, or sheaf) should be brought on 'the day after the sabbath' (Lev. 23: 15); but did that mean, as the Pharisees taught, the day following the first day of Passover (since that might be referred to as 'the sabbath', being a day of rest), or did it mean Sunday, in which case not only the Omer offering itself but also the festival of Shavuot (Pentecost) would always fall on Sunday?[9]

---

[7] Eusebius, *Praeparatio Evangelica* 8.10. Cf. Holladay, *Fragments*, iii. 134–9.

[8] Clement of Alexandria, *Stromat* 5: 14: 97, p. 187. On the other hand Pseudo-Plutarch, in his essay written in approximately 200 CE on the life and poetry of Homer, claimed that Homer was the source of all philosophy, as well as of rhetoric and other human skills (cited in Förster, 'The Exegesis of Homer', 91).

[9] BT *Men.* 65a–66a. The common reading of the Mishnah in fact refers the dispute to 'Boethusians', probably followers of Simon b. Boethus who was appointed High Priest by Herod in 24 BCE (Josephus, *Antiquities* 15: 320); they were not theologically distinct from the

Some Pharisee/Sadducee disagreements hinge on legal argument independent of scriptural reading, as in the following (an obvious subtext is the disparagement of Greek culture):

Sadducees say: We criticize you, Pharisees, for you say that sacred scrolls defile the hands, but scrolls of Homer do not defile the hands!

Is that all you have to criticize of the Pharisees? asked Rabban Yohanan ben Zakkai. [Pharisees] also say that donkeys' bones are clean, yet the bones of Yohanan the High Priest are unclean![10]

[The Sadducees] replied, Uncleanness is in proportion to how much they are loved [by God]; this is so that a man should not fashion the bones of his father and mother into spoons.

[Yohanan] replied: Here likewise, sacred scrolls are unclean because they are so greatly loved [by God]; scrolls of Homer are not so loved, therefore they do not defile the hands.[11]

Other disagreements concern matters not explicit in scripture. Pharisees upheld belief in life after death, while Sadducees denied it;[12] perhaps Sadducees were not prepared to commit themselves like the Pharisees to a doctrine they regarded as a foreign import to Judaism.

Sadducees seriously challenged Pharisee latitude in biblical interpretation and Pharisee claims to an authentic extra-biblical tradition going back to Moses. The Pharisee reaction, sustained by the rabbis, was the development of systematic biblical exegesis to incorporate their teachings as the correct interpretation of scripture; eventually, the idea took root that the Written Torah was supplemented by an Oral Torah, also received at Sinai, that confirmed the sages' interpretations.

The Babylonian Talmud's report of the conflict of Pharisees and Sadducees concerning the day of the Omer shows how Sadducee questioning helped shape Pharisee and rabbinic development;[13] the report, redacted some centuries after the events it describes, incorporates earlier material, some of it known to us through *Sifra* and *Seder olam*.[14] Yohanan ben Zakkai argued with the 'Boethusians' as to whether the *atseret* festival (i.e. Shavuot, or Pentecost)

Sadducees. *The Book of Jubilees* and some of the Dead Sea Scrolls counted from the day after the sabbath *following* Passover.

[10] There could be an anti-Zoroastrian polemic here, too; the Zoroastrian *Vendidad* (5: 28, 35) states that the most polluting of all corpses is that of a priest, whereas that of a wicked man pollutes 'no more than a frog does whose venom is dried up, and that has been dead more than a year'.

[11] Mishnah *Yad.* 4: 6. Another example, concerning *tevul yom*, occurs in Mishnah *Par.* 3: 7.

[12] Josephus, *Antiquities*, 18: 1: 2 f.   [13] BT *Men.* 65a–66a.

[14] It is possible that the extant texts of *Seder olam* and *Sifra* were revised by copyists to accord with the Babylonian Talmud.

was always to be celebrated on a Sunday. In their defence, the Boethusians are (allegedly) unable to come up with any better argument than that Moses, who was well disposed to the Jewish people, would have wanted them to enjoy two days of celebration together, the sabbath and the festival. Yohanan has no difficulty in reducing this to absurdity: 'If Moses so loved the Jewish people why did he make them spend forty years in the desert?' Unfortunately, Yohanan himself fares little better at the hands of the *amora'im*, who reject his proof-text and those adduced by all but two of seven other *tana'im* cited.

The report may conceal a major issue of calendar determination; the Jerusalem Talmud sets it in the context of an alleged attempt by Boethusians to disrupt rabbinic determination of the calendar by subverting witnesses to the new moon.[15] Perhaps there is an echo here of resistance to rabbinic attempts to establish the luni-solar calendar.[16]

The talmudic discussion incorporates no more than elements of the original debate, but this is enough to make clear that the rabbis, in response to Sadducee (Boethusian) critique, expended much effort in developing biblical exegesis to support their own views. The counter-tradition, believed by the rabbis to derive from the Sadducees, has determined the shape of the Pharisee/rabbinic reaction.

Pagan Philosophical Critiques

Pagan critiques of Judaism in antiquity are well known;[17] they were not all as ill informed, ill intentioned, or scurrilous as those of Juvenal or Tacitus.[18] Indeed, in the fourth century BCE Hecataeus of Abdera had produced a more sympathetic account of Jews and Judaism,[19] though not as sympathetic as might appear from the pseudo-Hecataeus that Josephus mistook for the real thing.[20]

[15] JT *RH* 2: 1 (57d–58a).

[16] Both *Jubilees* (6: 23–8) and some Dead Sea Scrolls (4QMMT) commend a calculated solar calendar based on a 364-day year. On efforts at Qumran to co-ordinate the solar and lunar cycles see Ben-Dov, 'Initial Stages' and S. Stern, *Calendar and Community*.

[17] M. Stern, *Greek and Latin Authors*; Schäfer, *Judeophobia*; L. H. Feldman, *Jew and Gentile in the Ancient World*.

[18] Juvenal, *Satires* 14: 96–106; Tacitus, *Histories* 5: 5. Tertullian refers to Tacitus, precisely in connection with his remarks on Jews and Judaism, as *mendaciorum loquacissimus* (Tertullian, *Apology* 16: 3).

[19] Summarized in Diodorus Siculus (1st c. CE), *Bibliotheca historica* 60: 3, via the 9th-c. Photius, *Bibliotheca*, 224.

[20] Josephus, *Contra Apionem*, 1: 183–204. On Pseudo-Hecataeus see Bar-Kochva, *Pseudo-Hecataeus*.

Neither Juvenal nor Tacitus, so far as is known, bothered to engage in serious discussions with Jews. Others did. Many such conversations entered into Jewish legend. Rabbi Meir is said to have enjoyed the friendship of 'Avnimos Hagardi', perhaps to be identified with the Cynic Oenomaus of Gadara.[21] 'Rabbi', usually identified as Judah Hanasi but by Graetz as his grandson Judah Nesia, conversed with 'Antoninus', variously identified as Marcus Aurelius (Rapoport and Bodek), Septimius Severus (Graetz), Caracalla (Jost and Krochmal), Elegabalus (Cassel), and Lucius Verus (Frankel).[22]

Joshua ben Hananya is said to have debated with the Emperor Hadrian and with the 'elders of Athens';[23] and so great was his skill in debate with these and with Christian sectarians[24] that on his death the rabbis exclaimed: 'What will become of us now at the hands of the nonbelievers?'[25]

As Louis Ginzberg succinctly put it: 'Jewish folk-lore loved to personify the relations of Judaism with heathendom in the guise of conversations between Jewish sages and heathen potentates.'[26]

Unfortunately incongruities, anachronisms, and confusion characterize the rabbinic accounts of these meetings. Among the substantive topics that Hadrian is said to have discussed with Joshua ben Hananya are the creation of the world and resurrection.[27] An authentic contemporary account of a debate between any learned rabbi and a Roman philosopher, let alone the Emperor Hadrian, on either of those topics, would surely be interesting. But what are we to make of the following typical text in *Genesis Rabbah*, compiled long after the events to which it refers?

How did the Holy One, blessed be He, create his world? Rabbi Yohanan says, He took two bundles, one of fire and one of snow, and kneaded them together, and from them the world was created. Rabbi Hanina says four, for the four directions of heaven. Rabbi Hama bar Hanina says six, four for the four directions, one up and one down. Hadrian (may his bones rot!) asked Rabbi Joshua ben Hananya, How did the Holy One, blessed be He, create His world? He replied to him in accordance with Rabbi Hama bar Hanina. He said, Is that possible? He took him into a small

---

[21] *Gen. Rabbah* 65: 20, *Ruth Rabbah* 2: 13 and elsewhere. See Lieberman, 'How Much Greek in Jewish Palestine?', 129–30, and Daniel Sperber in *Encyclopaedia Judaica*, s.v. Oenomaus.

[22] Details from the *Jewish Encyclopedia* i. 656. Accounts of meetings between Rabbi and Antoninus occur in, *inter alia*, BT *San.* 91a–b, *AZ* 10b; JT *Meg.* 1: 11 (72b) and JT *AZ* 3: 2 (23b) go so far as to claim that Antoninus converted to Judaism.

[23] BT *Bekh.* 8b, *Ḥul.* 59b–60a. The sources are discussed or used in Lieberman, *Greek in Jewish Palestine*, 16–19; Finkelstein, *Akiba* (see index); Epstein, *Introduction*, 59–65. Podro, *The Last Pharisee* is an imaginative reconstruction.

[24] BT *Shab.* 152a, *Ḥag.* 5a–b.   [25] BT *Ḥag.* 5a; cf. Tosefta *Sot.* 15: 3.

[26] *Jewish Encyclopedia* i. 656.   [27] *Gen. Rabbah* 28: 3.

house and said to him, Stretch out your hand to East, to West, to North and to South. He said to him, This is how it happened before the Holy One, blessed be He.[28]

To the plain reader this is incoherent; to the kabbalist it suggests some profound mystery. But to nobody does it carry conviction as the authentic report of a second-century philosophical debate.

Still, there is little doubt that such debate took place, and that the Hellenistic Jewish intellectual tradition so powerfully represented by Philo and Josephus did not suddenly evaporate with the arrival of the Mishnah. Max Kadushin, a pioneer in the modern interpretation of aggadah, demonstrated the coherence of the rabbinic value system—'organic thinking', as he called it—as early as the 1930s. Jacob Neusner and his school have systematically articulated the thinking behind a large part of the classical rabbinic corpus; for instance, Neusner argues that *Genesis Rabbah*, taken as a whole, has 'a profoundly philosophical view of Israel's everyday and sanctified existence'.[29] Clearly, systematic thinking on philosophical issues persisted long after the eclipse of Alexandrian Jewry in 116–17 CE, even though no dedicated Jewish philosophical treatises are extant from this period (this may be an accident of what was preserved, copied, and escaped the destruction of the Great Library of Alexandria).

This Mishnah has more of the flavour of real debate:

They asked the elders in Rome, If He does not want idolatry, why does He not destroy it? They said to them, If they worshipped things that were not needed in the world, He would destroy them. But they worship the sun, moon, stars, and constellations. Should He destroy his world on account of fools? They said, If so, let Him destroy those things that are not needed in the world, and leave the things that are needed in the world. They said to them, But that would give support to the ones who worship those things, for they would say, You see they are gods, for they have not been destroyed.[30]

Stronger evidence comes from Christian sources, since Christians continued to use standard Hellenistic literary forms even when Jews (so far as we know) abandoned them. The main debating ground of Jews and Christians was scripture; Paul had declared of the Jews in this connection that 'even to this day when Moses is read, a veil covers their hearts', and Justin in his *Dialogue with Trypho*, written in the middle of the second century, constantly accuses the Jews of misinterpreting scripture. But Justin and his Jewish

[28] *Gen. Rabbah* 10: 3.
[29] Kadushin, *Organic Thinking*; Neusner, *Genesis Rabbah*. Neusner places the final redaction of *Gen. Rabbah* in the period when the Roman empire had become Christian.
[30] Mishnah *AZ* 4: 7.

interlocutor Trypho are philosophically competent too, and on the whole in agreement in their response to pagan philosophy.[31]

The common response of Judaism and Christianity to pagan critique is easily obscured by two features of the documents in which it is expressed:

- The Christian documents in which debates with Jews, real or imaginary, are recorded are primarily concerned with appropriating scripture in support of their claims; the Christian/Jewish battleground is scripture, not philosophy.

- The extant Jewish documents incorporate disjointed sayings rather than sustained philosophical discourse; the talmudic *sugya* is often tightly organized and carefully constructed, but its construction is governed by literary rather than philosophical concerns.

Another early Christian, the biblical scholar and apologist Origen of Caesarea (184–254), composed his *Contra Celsum* around 248. Paragraph by paragraph it answers the *Alēthēs Logos* ('The True Doctrine' or 'Discourse') written *c.*178 CE by the pagan philosopher Celsus, who attacked Judaism and especially Christianity as corruptions of the 'ancient doctrine which has existed from the beginning, which has always been maintained by the wisest nations and cities and wise men'.[32] As Celsus's original treatise has been lost Origen's work remains a principal source for the pagan intelligentsia's view of second-century Christianity and Judaism. Celsus had done some homework, if insufficient to justify his boast that he 'knew it all';[33] part of his critique argues the inconsistency of the Christian position in accepting the Jewish scriptures but being unfaithful to their obvious demands. Both Celsus and Origen frequently make references to conversations they had with learned Jews.

Galen of Pergamum, the great medical authority of antiquity, criticized Moses on the grounds that he ignored material causes and the need for demonstration, asking that everything be accepted on faith.[34]

---

[31] Justin Martyr, *Dialogue with Trypho*; Horner, *Listening to Trypho*; Rokeah, *Justin Martyr and the Jews*.

[32] Origen of Caesarea, *Origen contra Celsum* I: 14. There have been several attempts to reconstruct Celsus's original work, notably those of Bader, *Der alēthēs logos des Kelsos*, and Hoffman, *Celsus*.   [33] Origen of Caesarea, *Origen contra Celsum* I: 12.

[34] Galen, *De usu partium* xi. 14. Walzer, *Galen on Jews and Christians*, 9 and 80, presumably following Pfaff, 'Rufus aus Samaria', claims that the (questionably) Jewish physician Rufus of Samaria greatly influenced Galen's interpretation of Hippocrates; this is hardly consistent with Galen's own remark that Rufus's commentary took material from everyone, said nothing original, and praised the most outlandish statements by others (CMG 5.10.2.2, pp. 212, 293), as pointed out by Diller, 'Review', 231–2. See Smith, *The Hippocratic Tradition*.

Belief in miracles was often attacked by pagan philosophers. Cicero (106–43 BCE), a follower of the New Academy, cited with approval the Stoic Chrysippus who argued 'Nothing can happen without a cause; nothing actually happens that cannot happen; if that has happened which could have happened, then it should not be considered a portent; therefore there are no such things as portents.'[35] What he writes of 'portents' is equally detrimental to belief in miracles.

Celsus was less dogmatic; the miracles of the Bible were most improbable, but even if genuine they could hardly offset equally or better attested miracles of the pagan world, such as the healings of Asclepius.[36] He was more outspoken with regard to Jewish and Christian ways of talking about God. He ridiculed passages in the Bible which ascribe human feelings to God, such as words of anger towards the impious and threats against sinners, a criticism which as Borret remarks derives from Stoicism;[37] and he thought it absurd to say that God fashioned Adam with his hands (Gen. 2: 7), though admitting that 'the more reasonable Jews and Christians are ashamed of these things and try somehow to allegorize them'.[38]

Another traditional concept that clashed with philosophy was free will, though in this case philosophy merely aggravated an internal biblical conflict between the determinism implied by God's will and foreknowledge and the insistence on human freedom.

Jewish and Christian particularism, the conviction of enjoying the special favour of God, aroused pagan resentment. Celsus writes of Jews and Christians that they say:

[God] has even deserted the whole world and the motion of the heavens . . . to give attention to us alone; and He sends messengers to us alone and never stops sending them and seeking that we may be with Him forever . . . [Jews and Christians are] like worms who say: 'There is God first, and we are next after Him in rank since He has made us entirely like God, and all things have been put under us, earth, water, air, and stars; and all things exist for our benefit, and have been appointed to serve us.'[39]

Such criticism was not entirely unjust; Jews and Christians do think of themselves as God's elect, though they are not alone in this. Ben Zoma, when he saw crowds on the Temple Mount, declared 'Blessed be he who fathoms

[35] Cicero, *De divinatione* ii: xxviii.
[36] Origen of Caesarea, *Origen contra Celsum* 3: 24 (Chadwick, 142). The Talmud (*AZ 55a*) records a conversation between 'Zeno' and Rabbi Akiva in which the latter explains why miracles appear to occur at idolatrous shrines; this may be a response to Celsus's criticism.
[37] *Origène Contre Celse*, ii. 358–9; Book IV no. 71.
[38] Origen of Caesarea, *Origen contra Celsum* 4: 38 (Chadwick, 213).
[39] Ibid. 4: 23 (Chadwick, 199–200).

secrets;[40] blessed be He who created all these to serve me';[41] but this, like the Mishnah's statement 'Therefore one should always say, The world was created for me',[42] is a statement of humility before the boundless generosity of the Creator, and an acknowledgement of the responsibility that stems from this.

The criticism certainly struck home with the rabbis. The scepticism about miracles, for instance, is usually met head-on by assertion of the greatness and infinite power of the Creator. Miracles are multiplied and exaggerated, not played down. In a well-known passage in *Mekhilta*, familiar through its use in the Passover Haggadah, the rabbis outdo one another in numbering the plagues, hence miracles, in Egypt and on the Red Sea; Yosé the Galilean asserts that ten plagues were inflicted on the Egyptians in Egypt and fifty on the Red Sea, Eliezer increases this to forty plus 200, and Akiva to fifty plus 250.[43]

Occasionally, a more defensive position is taken:

Rabbi Yohanan said: The Holy One, blessed be He, laid down a condition for the Red Sea that it should part before Israel . . . Said Rabbi Jeremiah ben Eleazar, Not only with the Sea did the Holy One, blessed be He, lay down a condition, but with everything created in the Six Days . . . 'I commanded the Sea to part . . . I commanded heaven and earth to be silent before Moses . . . I commanded the sun and the moon to stop for Joshua . . . I commanded the ravens to feed Elijah . . . the fire not to consume Hananiah, Mishael, and Azariah . . . the lions not to harm Daniel . . . the heavens to open at the voice of Ezekiel . . . the fish to vomit Jonah . . . '[44]

Maimonides, in his endeavour to harmonize religion and philosophy, argued that to state that the parting of the Red Sea and the other miracles were 'conditions that God laid down for creation' was to acknowledge the rule of natural law; the exceptions were built in, so to speak, to the original law of nature, rather than being ad hoc interventions by God.[45] A more straightforward interpretation of the midrash would be to say that 'natural law' itself is God's creation, but that he retains the option of overriding it, and does so when required to save the faithful.

[40] This is the standard formula of blessing on seeing a multitude of people; God is praised for the diversity of humanity.
[41] BT *Ber.* 58a. In this second blessing Ben Zoma recognizes his dependence on the activities of all the people for clothing and sustenance. The chronology, or else the attribution, is suspect since Ben Zoma is unlikely to have been born at a time when pilgrims flocked to the Temple; Rashi's suggestion that he saw a great army on the Temple Mount is implausible.
[42] Mishnah *San.*, end of ch. 4.   [43] *Mekhilta*, 'Beshalah' 2: 6 on Exod. 14: 30.
[44] *Gen. Rabbah* 5: 5.   [45] Maimonides, *Guide* ii. 29.

On the nature of God there is ambivalence. On the one hand, innumerable rabbinic sayings attribute the most unlikely human activities to God; he dons tefillin,[46] he 'weeps in the inner houses',[47] he accompanies Israel into exile.[48] Many of these are so outrageous if taken literally that there can be little doubt that they were intended not to lay down doctrine but to stimulate the imagination and to give the faithful a lively sense of the presence of God. They respond to Christian notions of incarnation, as well as to the 'visibility' of pagan gods; it is as if they were to say, almost confirming Celsus's prejudice, 'God is more present to us than to you.'

Some sayings, on the other hand, deny material attributes and passions to God, or to the heavenly regions. For instance: 'Above [sc. in heaven] there is no sitting,[49] no envy, no "back of the neck,"[50] no tiredness.'[51]

Aristobulus and Philo interpreted the Bible figuratively in their project to harmonize Jewish and Greek concepts of God. This defensiveness is reflected in the Septuagint, the Greek translation of the Bible on which Philo was dependent—for instance, it translates 'And they saw the God of Israel' (Exod. 24: 10) as 'And they saw the place where the God of Israel stood'—but Philo is far more systematic and thorough. The Jewish Aramaic Targumim, or translations of scripture, continue the trend; Targum Onkelos, still printed in most Hebrew bibles, assiduously if not entirely consistently avoids gross anthropomorphisms.[52]

Yet again, we see action and reaction as Jews respond creatively to a counter-tradition, the Hellenistic philosophical critique of their beliefs.

Gnosticism

Both Judaism and Christianity found themselves in competition with various forms of dualistic belief. Babylonian Jews, during the period of formation of the Babylonian Talmud, lived under Sassanian rule where the dominant religion was Zoroastrianism. Orthodox Zoroastrians held that there were two powers; Good and Evil fight an unequal battle in which the former, easily identified with the Jewish or Christian God, is assured of triumph; humans, since they have free choice, are enlisted in the struggle, and they do this with both soul and body, not *against* the body, for the opposition between good and

---

[46] BT *Ber.* 6a.   [47] BT *Hag.* 5b.   [48] BT *Meg.* 29a.

[49] Rashi rejects the reading 'no sitting or standing'; perhaps he takes literally the idea of angels standing.

[50] Rashi, on the grounds that angels have faces on all sides.   [51] BT *Hag.* 15a.

[52] The extent to which Onkelos avoids anthropomorphisms has been debated at least since Nahmanides (*Commentary* on Gen. 46: 1) rejected Maimonides' claim (*Guide* i. 27) that Onkelos *consistently* avoids anthropomorphism.

evil is not the same as that between spirit and matter. The great appeal of dualism is that it accounts easily for the existence of evil in the world, whereas the absolute monotheism of Judaism, Christianity, and Islam has difficulty in reconciling the existence of evil with the goodness and omnipotence of the Creator, since there is no other power to be responsible for evil.

The prophet Mani (c.216–274), who had spent some time with the Jewish–Christian Elkasite sect, founded a religion that combined Zoroastrian dualism with elements of Gnosticism, Judaism, and Christianity; his dualism, unlike that of mainstream Zoroastrianism, is a cosmic dualism of soul (good) versus matter (bad). Manichaeism, in the face of opposition and persecution, gained a considerable following from the eastern reaches of the Sassanian empire in what is now Afghanistan to as far west as Rome; Augustine, who was to devote much of his philosophical effort to refuting Manichaeism, was for a time a convert, before returning to his mother's Christianity.

'Gnosticism' is a term devised by modern scholars to cover a range of philosophical and religious movements prevalent in the Roman Empire, especially around the second century CE. Gnostics (*gnosis* means 'knowledge') emphasized the redemptive power of esoteric knowledge, acquired by direct revelation. Gnosticism tends strongly to dualism, whether the contrast of body and spirit, or the belief in two ultimate Powers. Forms of Christian Gnosticism, ultimately declared heretical, included Docetism, according to which matter is essentially evil, and also Marcionism. Marcion held that the God of the Old Testament was an inferior and harsh creator demiurge, distinct indeed from his enemy, the devil, but also distinct from the supreme divinity, who manifested himself in Jesus and is a stranger to this world.[53]

So far as the 'counter-tradition' to Judaism is concerned, all these movements posed challenges to traditional teaching that were addressed by the rabbis who, like the mainstream church, perceived dualism as a major threat. It was countered in several ways:

- No opportunity is lost to declare the unity and incomparability of God, who has no 'equal'; that is, no one, such as some malevolent power, can be compared with him even negatively.

- Justice and mercy are seen as complementary aspects of God's relationship with his creation, not as opposing principles.

- As in the book of Job, Satan is portrayed not as God's independent

---

[53] Standard accounts of Gnosticism, such as Jonas, *The Gnostic Religion*, and Filoramo, *History of Gnosticism*, need to be supplemented by works such as those of Scholem and Idel which relate Gnosticism to early Jewish mysticism.

opponent but as his servant. Alternatively, he is reduced to an aspect of human psychology: 'Resh Lakish said: Satan, the evil inclination, and the Angel of Death are all the same thing.'[54]

- While modesty and frugality are praised, there is some opposition to the kind of asceticism that derives from regarding the material world as intrinsically evil. For instance, Bar Kappara (third century) suggests that the Nazirite is instructed to bring a sin offering on completion of his thirty-day naziriteship since 'he has sinned by depriving himself of wine; and if someone who merely deprived himself of wine is called a sinner, how much more so one who deprives himself of everything'.[55]

- God is perfect, and evil is the consequence of freely committed sin. Lamentations 3: 38, 'Do not both good and evil come from the Most High?', and Isaiah 45: 7, 'Who forms light and creates darkness; who makes peace and creates evil, I the Lord do all these', acknowledge that all things, both those that appear good to us and those that appear evil, come from the One God. God should therefore be praised not only when good things happen to us, but also when bad things happen; even on bereavement we praise God as righteous judge.[56]

- Rules were imposed to prevent the use in prayer of any expression that might be understood to acknowledge 'two powers', i.e. any hint of dualism.[57]

Later Developments

The criticisms of Judaism articulated in the ancient world are paralleled in criticisms voiced throughout the Middle Ages. This is true both of external and internal critiques.

The Sadducee rejection of extra-biblical tradition was paralleled some centuries later by the Karaite rejection of Oral Torah, including the Talmud, though a direct connection has not been established. Just as the Pharisees and early rabbis fought the Sadducees with ridicule, serious argument, and proof-texts, so do Sa'adiah and the Rabbanites in opposition to the Karaites pour scorn, give reasoned refutation, and attempt to regain the biblical high ground. Karaism, however, is far better documented than Sadduceeism, and

[54] BT *BB* 16a.

[55] BT *BK* 91b. The opinion cited in the name of Rav at the end of JT *Kid.* that 'a person will be held to judgement for whatever his eyes have seen but he did not eat' is often cited in this connection; however, the interpretation of this statement is problematic.

[56] Mishnah *Ber.* 9: 5; BT *Ber.* 60b.   [57] Mishnah *Ber.* 5: 3.

has persisted to the present, so we know how Karaite scholars such as Jacob al-Qirqisāni in the early tenth century heaped ridicule on talmudic homilies that referred to God in grossly anthropomorphic terms or otherwise struck them as absurd, as well as on inconsistencies in rabbinic law and scriptural exegesis.[58]

Christianity and eventually Islam displaced dualism as the dominant religious challenges to Judaism. In response, Jews asserted pure monotheism as against Christian trinitarianism, the perfection of the extant Torah as against Islam's new scripture, the Qur'an, and the eternal validity of Torah and its laws against both.

Gnostic ideas, with some modification, infiltrated esoteric mystical circles who maintained both the efficacy of their secret knowledge for the approach to God and the opposition of matter and spirit, body and soul. By the late Middle Ages kabbalists had thoroughly absorbed these notions, and reconciled themselves with traditional rabbinic Judaism by claiming that they had discovered the real, secret meaning behind the superficial texts of Bible and Talmud.

Pagan philosophers succumbed to persecution after the revived Academy was closed down by Justinian in 529, but many of their ideas persisted. Judaism, Christianity, and Islam were all recast in terms of current philosophies, whether Aristotelian, Platonist, or Neoplatonist. In all three religions this stimulated reactions, demands for a return to the 'pure, original' faith. In all three religions part of this reaction took the form of a resurgence of mysticism; in the case of Judaism, kabbalah emerged in the West and Sufi-like movements in the Islamic East.

Internal disputes, such as those of the Maimunists (followers of Maimonides' philosophical teachings) and anti-Maimunists, were acute, and many sought safety through meticulous adherence to halakhah and through simple faith in the plain meaning of biblical and rabbinic texts. When Maimonides classified as heretics people who believed that God had a body, Abraham ben David of Posquières (Ra'avad, c.1125–98) famously remarked 'Many greater and better men than he have walked in this way.'[59] Ra'avad (whose son, Isaac

---

[58] The commentaries of the 10th-c. Karaites Japheth ben Eli and Sahl ben Matsliah are discussed and documented in Daniel Frank, *Search Scripture Well*. Sa'adiah's critique of Karaism includes a lost *Refutation of Anan*, which may be identical with his partially extant polemical poem *Esa meshali*, ed. B. M. Lewin. Karaite responses include those of Salmon ben Yeruhim (Davidson (ed.), *Book of the Wars of the Lord*) and Mubashir ben Nasi Halevi of Baghdad (Zucker, *Critique*). See also Nemoy, 'Al-Qirqisāni's Account', and on Karaism in general, Polliack, *Karaite Judaism*.

[59] Abraham ben David of Posquières (Ra'avad) on Maimonides, *Mishneh torah*, 'Hilkhot teshuvah' 3:7.

the Blind, became a leading kabbalist) was probably not thinking of simple devout folk so much as of kabbalists, who drew their inspiration from works such as *Shiur komah*.[60] This early treatise, from the Merkavah tradition of Jewish mysticism, describes God's 'hidden glory', or the 'body of the Shekhinah', in grossly anthropomorphic terms; Maimonides declared that the book was the work of 'some Greek homilist' and ought to be destroyed as rank idolatry.[61] It gives a detailed description of the limbs of God in the figure of a man, with extraordinary measurements: the height of the Creator, for instance, is given as 236,000 parasangs.[62] Kabbalists, who are unsmilingly literal about such things, maintain that although God does not have an arm, leg, or whatever in the physical sense, he does possess limbs of a superior, spiritual kind, and that this is what the Bible is really talking about when it says things like 'The Lord raised his hand'; this is a defensive reaction to criticism levelled by philosophers, whether pagan or Jewish.

Conclusion

Judaism did not emerge in a vacuum, nor can all features of its mature teaching be explained as organic development from the biblical text. Much in the content as well as the precise articulation of rabbinic Judaism derives from its responses to criticism from within or without.

Not least of the defences developed against critics of tradition is the doctrine of the infallible, divinely revealed text; after all, if the text really was dictated by God it must contain perfect truth, and all criticisms fade away in its light even if we can't fathom how.

The text, then, is the criterion.

We must next enquire whether such a text can be identified.

[60] Twersky, *Rabad of Posquières*, 289, hints that Ra'avad may have had in mind some kabbalistic reference. On the place of *Shiur komah* in Merkavah mysticism see Scholem, *Major Trends*, 62–6.

[61] Responsum to R. Sa'adyah ben Berakhot, in Maimonides, *Maimonides' Responsa*, no. 4.

[62] That is, about 750,000 miles. This may be based on Psalm 147: 5, 'Great is our Lord, and mighty in power'; 'great' may be translated 'high', and the numerical value of 'and mighty in power' is 236! Scholem, *Major Trends*, 360 n. 86.

EIGHT

THE ORIGINAL TORAH

ENGLISH-SPEAKING CHRISTIANS commonly took the King James version of scripture to be the authoritative Word of God, the Roman Church for centuries regarded the Latin Vulgate of St Jerome as a divinely inspired, authoritative text, and the Eastern churches venerated the Greek Septuagint or the Old Slavonic. Among Jews, with the exception of the community of ancient Alexandria, the Hebrew text has always held sway; nowadays most Christians, too, acknowledge the primacy of the Hebrew.

That granted, we must still ask whether the Hebrew texts in our possession are accurate transmissions of the originals. Certainly, they are closer to the original than any Latin, Greek, or English versions; God did not speak to Moses in Latin, Greek, or English. But that does not mean they are perfect.

There is an even more fundamental question to ask. Was there ever such a thing as an 'original' text? Is such a concept at all applicable to the books of the Hebrew Bible?

Within the context of rabbinic Judaism there are further questions. Did the rabbis of the Talmud agree as to the precise text revealed to Moses on Sinai? Did anyone question the authenticity of the traditional text? How did the rabbis both then and later view such textual variants as they were aware of?

These are the questions to be addressed in this chapter.

How Texts Were Written

We need to know how Hebrew texts were written in earlier times, so we will need some technical jargon to be able to talk meaningfully about the sorts of variation that occur.

Biblical Hebrew was originally written in a script consisting of consonants only; there was no punctuation, and although in most known ancient manuscripts there are spaces or dots to separate one word from another, it is likely that the earliest texts simply ran all the consonants together.[1]

---

[1] Tov, *Textual Criticism*, 209.

Though there were no vowels as such, four consonants—silent *alef*, final *heh*, *yod*, and *vav*—could be used to indicate long vowels; of these, *yod* could be used for long 'i' or 'e' and *vav* for long 'o' or 'u'. Grammarians call these consonants *matres lectionis* ('mothers of reading'). The received biblical text is not consistent in its use of *matres lectionis*, and in early times there was great variation among scribes as to their use.

If a word contains *yod* or *vav* to indicate a vowel it is termed '*plene*' (full); in Hebrew *malé*. If the *yod* or *vav* is omitted from a position in which it is normally present the word is termed 'defective'; in Hebrew, *ḥaser*.

Modern printed versions of the Hebrew Bible incorporate with the consonantal text comprehensive vocalization, that is, the series of vowel signs and musical accents devised by the Masoretes (of whom more later) between 500 and 700 CE. However, halakhah decrees that Torah scrolls should be written in the conventional script, without vocalization, and that is the norm even today.

The 'conventional' script is called in Hebrew *ketav ashuri* 'Assyrian (= Aramaic) writing', or *ketav meruba* ('square writing'); modern printed Hebrew is derived from it. The rabbis, however, were aware of another script, which they called *ketav ivri* 'Hebrew writing', or *ketav rotsets*,[2] and which we now know as palaeo-Hebrew. They were not sure in which of these the original Torah was given to Moses, but held Ezra responsible for the change (or reversion) to the square writing.[3] Some scholars believe the two scripts existed side by side for centuries. Samaritans continued to use their own version of *ketav ivri*, and still do; there is evidence in the Dead Sea Scrolls of an archaizing attempt in other traditions, too, to reintroduce palaeo-Hebrew, especially for the divine names.

Palaeographers trace a gradual transition from proto-Canaanite script through Phoenician to palaeo-Hebrew and Samaritan; the Aramaic script, which displaced cuneiform for writing Assyrian, branched off the Canaanite tree a little after palaeo-Hebrew, and gave rise to the square Hebrew as well as Nabatean (whence Arabic), Syriac, and other scripts. So in fact *ketav ashuri* is not so much a 'new' script as a cousin to palaeo-Hebrew, deriving from the same stock.[4]

In some early forms of square Hebrew writing there are five letters,

[2] BT *San.* 21b–22a. The word probably means 'broken' or 'rugged'. Some (Tov, *Textual Criticism*, 218) believe it refers to proto-Hebrew rather than to the palaeo-Hebrew which developed from it, but I doubt that the rabbis would have made this distinction.

[3] JT *Meg.* 1: 9 (71b); BT *Shab.* 104a.

[4] See Naveh, *Early History of the Alphabet*. On p. 10 there is an excellent graphical illustration of the relationship between the various alphabetic scripts.

מנצפכ *mem, nun, tsadi, peh,* and *kaf,* that have dual forms םןץףך, rather like the difference between upper and lower case in English, except that the 'upper case' form occupies the final, not the initial, position in a word. These forms do not occur in all scribal traditions, and do not exist in palaeo-Hebrew, but the rabbis of the Talmud knew about them and debated whether they had originated at Sinai or had been introduced later by the prophets.[5] They were adopted by the Masoretes and have become the standard final forms of these letters.

Occasional scribal peculiarities, such as supralinear dots (*puncta extraordinaria*) and abnormally formed letters, feature in biblical manuscripts.

Among the earliest Egyptian documents is the Prisse Papyrus, dating from the Middle Kingdom, about 2000 BCE;[6] ancient Israelites, however, preferred to write on parchment scrolls made from animal skins. Nobody knows for certain when Jews first copied their scrolls onto papyrus or other writing materials (both leather and papyrus rolls were found among the Dead Sea Scrolls) and bound them into codices—'books' in the sense in which the term is understood today. The Masoretes certainly chose this form; they produced their model texts as codices rather than as scrolls. The codex form served to distinguish the vocalized copy of the Torah, unacceptable for liturgical use, from the unvocalized parchment scroll used in the synagogue; it was also much more convenient to use for study purposes, to refer to for corrections, and for the incorporation of the additional Masoretic apparatus of signs and notes.

The term 'Masoretic text', often symbolized by M, stands for texts based on the models provided by the Masoretes, and includes standard printed bibles as well as all current Torah scrolls.

Evidence of the Scrolls and the Ancient Versions

In 1979 two minute silver rolls, perhaps amulets, were found at Ketef Hinom, Jerusalem, inscribed with a Hebrew text close to but not identical to that of the Masoretic text of the Priestly Blessing (Num. 6: 24–6); they are written in the palaeo-Hebrew script. They are thought to date from about 600 BCE, and are the oldest known biblical writing.[7] This is several centuries later than the

[5] BT *Meg.* 2b; *Shab.* 104a. The actual term used for those who may have introduced the finals is *tsofim,* literally 'scouts'; Rashi interprets it as prophets.

[6] *The Instruction addressed to Kagemni* and *The Instruction of Ptahhotep* in Lichtheim, *Ancient Egyptian Literature,* i. 59–61, 61–80. A transcription and translation of *The Instruction of Ptahhotep* are available online at <http://www.digitalegypt.ucl.ac.uk/literature/ptahhotep.html>.

[7] Tov, *Textual Criticism,* 118, based on Barkai, 'Priestly Benediction' (Heb.).

presumed date of Moses, and later even than Isaiah of Jerusalem; anyone seeking to demonstrate that the Torah text now in our possession is identical to that of Moses will clearly have to make do without contemporary manuscript evidence!

In spring 1947 an Arab shepherd wandering near the Dead Sea a few miles south of Jericho threw a stone into a cave and heard it crash. When he climbed up to investigate he discovered jars containing ancient writings. The discovery and identification of what we now know as the Dead Sea Scrolls at Qumran and other caves in the Judean desert is one of the most dramatic events in twentieth-century archaeology, involving Israel's War of Independence, decades of bitter scholarly rivalry, and accusations of extortion, corruption, and the deliberate suppression of evidence. After half a century and the deaths of some of the leading protagonists the dust appears to have settled. The whole corpus is now readily accessible for study, and the significance of the discoveries becomes ever clearer; of prime significance is the unparalleled array of ancient biblical manuscripts.[8]

Before the discovery of the Dead Sea Scrolls the oldest known Hebrew biblical manuscript was a papyrus purchased from an Egyptian dealer in 1902 by W. L. Nash, and published by S. A. Cooke the following year; it contains the Ten Commandments in a mixed formulation of Exodus 20 and Deuteronomy 5, and the Shema (Deut. 6: 4–5), and was written about 100 BCE.[9] Apart from that, practically nothing was known that had been written before the ninth century CE, that is, at least a thousand years after the composition of the latest biblical books.

Even so, scholars had concluded by 1947 that at least three textual traditions existed: the Masoretic text, the Samaritan text of the Pentateuch, and the Vorlage, or presumed Hebrew original, of the Greek version made for the Jews of Egypt and known as the 'Septuagint', or translation of the seventy (LXX). These were sometimes known as the Babylonian, Samaritan, and Egyptian recensions respectively.[10]

The caves in the Judean desert have yielded manuscripts dating as far back as the middle of the third century BCE, well into Second Temple times, and before the probable date of composition of the latest books of the Hebrew Bible. All the books of the Hebrew Bible with the exception of Esther are represented, but most are mere fragments, and few comprise more than a tenth of a single book.

I once invited a young scholar to give a public lecture on some aspect of Scrolls research, and asked her for a snappy title. 'New light on 4QJer[b,d]', she

---

[8] For this and the related sections I am much indebted to Tov, *Textual Criticism*, where full bibliographical references will be found.   [9] Tov, *Textual Criticism*, 118.   [10] Ibid. 156.

proposed, and was rather taken aback when I expressed doubt that such a title would arouse the excitement of the general public. Scrolls addicts have their own jargon, which is not really difficult once you learn to unscramble it; '4QJer^{b,d}' is shorthand for 'fragments b and d in the scroll of Jeremiah found in the fourth cave at Qumran'. This, of course, would have been an even more off-putting title for a public lecture on what turned out to be a really exciting topic.

The Bible manuscripts found by the shores of the Dead Sea fall into three categories:

Proto-Masoretic texts. To this category belong almost all the texts written in palaeo-Hebrew script, as well as all the texts found at Masada. The rabbinic literature, the Aramaic Targumim, and some Greek translations (but not the Septuagint) clearly derive from texts of this tradition. The relative lack of variety in orthography suggests that the texts were copied with care, though there are significant differences among them and there is no one definitive 'Masoretic text'.

Pre-Samaritan texts. These are 'pre-' rather than 'proto-' Samaritan, since the later, distinctively Samaritan texts, carry emendations which reflect Samaritan theology, for instance references to the central status of Mount Gerizim. These references were not grafted onto the proto-Masoretic text, but onto a slightly different text which predates the Samaritan movement itself. The characteristics of this text in relation to the proto-Masoretic are harmonizing alterations, linguistic corrections, content differences, and linguistic differences.[11]

Texts written in the Qumran practice. These are thought to be texts copied by the Qumran covenanters themselves, whereas the proto-Masoretic and pre-Samaritan texts were imported by them. They show a distinctive orthography, rich in *matres lectionis,* and with a distinctive morphology, exhibited in forms such as lengthened independent pronouns (*hu*AH, *hi*AH, *atem*AH etc.) and lengthened pronominal suffixes for the second and third persons (*bam*AH, *bahem*AH, *malkam*AH).[12] The 'Qumran practice' is not a fourth textual tradition in addition to the three previously proposed; it is a particular way of copying the first two.

Scholars continue to debate whether any of the scrolls belong to the tradition of the Septuagint *Vorlage*; those listed as 4QJer^{b,d} and 4QSam^{a} may do,[13] but they are no more than fragments.

[11] Ibid. 84 ff.   [12] Ibid. 100, 107 ff.   [13] Ibid. 115, 116.

How careful were the ancient copyists to reproduce accurately the text before them? Tov writes: 'In the last century BCE and the first centuries CE, scribes were involved *mainly* in the transmission process, but prior to that most . . . considered themselves also to be petty collaborators in the creation of the books.'[14] Certainly, by the rabbinic period scribes were taking meticulous pains to preserve the sacred text. Rabbah bar bar Hana reported in the name of Yohanan (third century CE, Palestine) that the correctors of scrolls (*magihei sefarim*) in Jerusalem had been paid out of the Temple treasury.[15] A *baraita* cited in the Jerusalem Talmud reports in the name of Yohanan's disciple and colleague Simon ben Lakish that three Torah scrolls were kept in the Temple courtyard and that, in three instances, corrections were made according to the majority reading:

They found three Torah scrolls in the Temple courtyard: *maoni, zatutei,* and *hi*. In the first they found written 'The eternal God is your dwelling-place (*maon*)' (Deuteronomy 33: 27), but in two of them was written *me'onah*; they confirmed two and rejected one. In one they found written 'He sent the little ones (*zatutei*) of the Israelites' (Exodus 24: 5);[16] but in two was written 'and he sent young men (*na'arei*) of the Israelites'; they confirmed two and rejected one. In one they found *hi* written 9 times, and in two it was written 11 times; they confirmed two and rejected one.[17]

This late report indicates that the talmudic sages were aware of scribal variants and endorsed efforts to establish what they believed to be the correct text. The method, similar to that used by the copyists of the Dead Sea Scrolls, and invoked by later rabbis, is based on the halakhic principle of following the majority. This is not a scientific basis for the recovery of an original text, and indeed it is unclear how such a method could be applied outside the special circumstances in which it is reported, since it depends on the prior selection of approved texts by some unspecified method; who decided that the three scrolls in the Temple were the best available, and on what basis? Even if we have faith in the Temple authorities, how could we decide nowadays which are the authoritative scrolls, and how could we be sure that the correct reading was that of the majority? It is precisely this lack of conformity between scientific and halakhic procedure that underlay medieval debates about whether Talmud should have priority over Masorah or vice versa where the two came into conflict.[18]

---

[14] Tov, *Scribal Practices*, 25.   [15] BT *Ket.* 106a.

[16] This is one of the changes said to have been made by the authors of the Greek translation (BT *Meg.* 9a).

[17] JT *Ta'an.* 4: 2 (68a). Tov, *Textual Criticism*, 32; Talmon, 'The Three Scrolls of the Law'; Levy, *Fixing God's Torah*, 7 ff. Levy bases his analysis on the reworked version in the *c.*800 tractate *Soferim* 6: 4.   [18] See Levy, *Fixing God's Torah*, 145–7 on these debates.

David Rosental noted several instances where the sages, even where they determined that there was a 'correct' reading, based a *derashah* on the rejected reading. For instance, the Masoretic text of Exodus 21: 29, regarding an ox whose owner has been cautioned but fails to take adequate precautions, reads *velo yishmerenu ba'alav* 'and his owner did not guard him'. The Septuagint translates *kai mē aphanise auton*, 'and did not destroy him', which presupposes a reading of *yishmedenu* instead of *yishmerenu*. Rosental suggests that this is Rabbi Eliezer's justification for ruling 'the only [adequate] safeguard [against such an animal] is the knife'.[19]

However, although the rabbis were aware of scribal variants, and although they habitually solved problems in the Mishnah by resort to textual emendation, they never proposed textual emendation as a solution to difficulties with a biblical text. As Saul Lieberman observed:

The Rabbis never suggest the correction of the text of the Bible. In the entire rabbinic literature we never come across divergences of opinion regarding Biblical readings. It is therefore obvious that the textual corrections of Greek classics practised by Alexandrian grammarians have no parallel in the rabbinic exegesis of Scripture.[20]

Philip Alexander has proposed three reasons for the rabbis' abstention from textual emendation of the Bible:[21]

Tradition. Once the proto-Masoretic text had been accepted, perhaps in the circles from which the rabbis emerged, it was too authoritative to be modified in any way; even editorial scribal marks had to be preserved.

Apologetic. Since Jews, Christians, and Samaritans had accepted different text-traditions (Masoretic, Septuagint, Samaritan), the rabbis found it necessary to defend their position against rival claims.

Theological. The doctrine of the inviolability of scripture required a perfect, unalterable text, the 'blueprint' for Creation, as Rabbi Hoshaiah describes it in the opening chapter of *Genesis Rabbah*.

The Severus Scroll

The Talmud lavishes praise on the second-century Rabbi Meir for his skill as a scribe. When he told his teacher Ishmael ben Elisha what his profession was,

[19] Rosental, 'On the Sages' Treatment', 407; BT *BK* 45b. Rosental would presumably reject the attempts of Rabbah and Abbaye on 46a to harmonize the law with the current text.

[20] Lieberman, *Hellenism in Jewish Palestine*, 47.

[21] Alexander, 'Why No Textual Criticism in Rabbinic Midrash?', 175–90.

Ishmael addressed to him the words: 'My son, be careful in your work, for it is the work of heaven; if you omit or add even one letter you will destroy the world.'[22]

Meir was nothing if not conscientious—indeed, in opposition to his colleagues he maintained the rather nervous halakhic principle *ḥaishinan lemiuta*, 'we must be concerned about even a minority of instances'[23]—so we can safely assume that he would have exercised the utmost caution in scribal practice. In view of this it is rather surprising that the Midrash *Genesis Rabbah* should have noted three divergencies in Rabbi Meir's Torah scroll, including the spelling of the word אור *'or* 'light' (with an initial *alef*) rather than עור *'or* 'skin' (with an initial *ayin*) in Genesis 3: 21; in Meir's version the verse read 'God made Adam and Eve garments of light'.[24]

Some have identified Rabbi Meir's Torah scroll with the scroll that the eleventh-century Rabbi Moses Hadarshan[25] says was brought to Rome as booty in 70 CE and subsequently kept in the synagogue of Asverus (Severus?).[26] This scroll contained more than 30 divergencies from the subsequently established Masoretic text, few of them of great moment.

Genesis Rabbah, at any rate, refers to three divergencies. There is no indication in this midrash that Meir was regarded as heretical because he accepted a divergent reading; the reaction seems to be that his readings, far from being heretical, conveyed some deep mystery of the Torah.

Can the Original Text be Recovered?

Is 'original text of the Bible' a meaningful concept? Does some as yet unknown *Urtext* (foundational text) underlie the Masoretic, Septuagint, Samaritan, and other scribal traditions? If so, was the proto-Masoretic version any closer to it than the others? This is unlikely, since there are instances where the proto-Masoretic appears to be secondary to the Septuagint *Vorlage*.[27]

---

[22] BT *Eruv.* 13a.   [23] For instance, BT *Ḥul.* 6a.

[24] *Gen. Rabbah* 20: 28. The other two examples are in 9: 5 and 94: 8.

[25] *Bereshit rabati* on Gen. 45: 8 (Albeck edn., p. 209). See also Kimhi on Gen. 1: 31.

[26] Tov, *Textual Criticism*, 119 f., referring to Siegel, *The Severus Scroll*. Siegel relates four of the variants to orthographic peculiarities of the Isaiah scroll, arguing that the list of variants preserves an ancient tradition. In n. 8 on p. 160 he discusses whether 'Asverus' could be identified with either L. Septimius Severus (ruled 193–211) or Alexander Severus (ruled 222–35). Meir's scroll could not have been brought to Rome in 70 as he was not yet born.

[27] Ulrich, 'Jewish, Christian and Empirical Perspectives', 74, writes that the 'Massoretic edition of Jeremiah is demonstrably secondary to the earlier edition of that book in the Hebrew text of 4QJer^b, and the Greek translation of it in the Septuagint'.

Were different biblical books subject to different processes of development?[28] Was the concept of a 'book' more fluid in the biblical period, and is the notion of a fixed, sacrosanct text an anachronism?

These questions cannot be answered with certainty. It is clear, though, that the currently accepted Masoretic text, deriving as it does largely from the Ben Asher codex, cannot be the biblical *Urtext* from which all other versions have departed. Nor does it conform in all respects with the text(s) used by the rabbis. In numerous instances the Talmud itself bases a *derashah* (interpretation), sometimes one with halakhic consequences, on a text different from the received one. The thirteenth-century Tosafists noted this;[29] later, Rabbi Akiva Eger (1761–1837), a leading Orthodox talmudist and a vigorous opponent of historical criticism, listed over twenty such instances.[30] Eger's list is significant not for its originality but because it was made by a strongly traditionalist rabbi in the early nineteenth century.

How did a definitive Masoretic text ultimately emerge, seeing that already in ancient times there were divergent texts? Surely the copying process would result in the multiplication rather than the reduction of divergencies? The Temple scribes who corrected scrolls on the basis of majority readings, the rabbis who reported their activity, and the Masoretes all thought they were recovering the *Urtext* as received by Moses on Sinai, or through the prophets who had mediated the other books. But what actually happened was that, by a process of selection, alternative texts were gradually eliminated; whether what remained is what was there at the beginning is unproven.

The notion that scribes were engaged in the recovery and preservation of an authentic original text generated additional ambiguities. What were the writers of the Septuagint doing when, according to the talmudic account, they miraculously and independently introduced several deliberate mistranslations into the Greek, for instance translating *bayom hashevi'i* ('on the seventh day'—Genesis 2: 1) as 'on the sixth day'?[31] The *Letter of Aristeas*, to which the talmudic version must at some remove be indebted, says nothing of deliberate mistranslations, or of translators being isolated from one another to ensure accuracy; to the contrary, Ptolemy provides all their needs for a cooperative venture: 'So they set to work comparing their several results and

---

[28]   For a summary of scholarly opinion, see Tov, *Textual Criticism*, ch. 3B. George J. Brooke, 'Some Remarks on 4Q252', argues *contra* Ulrich and others who maintain that there is only one text tradition for Genesis, that 1QGen 'still needs to be aligned closely with that attested by LXX' (p. 25).

[29]   For example, Tosafot on BT *Shab.* 55*b* s.v. *ma'avirim*; *Nid.* 33*a* s.v. *vehanisa*.

[30]   Eger, *Gilyon hashas* on BT *Shab.* 55*b*.

[31]   BT *Meg.* 9*a–b*. Our extant Septuagint texts confirm this translation.

making them agree, and whatever they agreed upon was suitably copied out
. . . Everything they wanted was furnished for them on a lavish scale.'[32] So
evidently it was the rabbis themselves who introduced the notion of deliberate
mistranslation. Perhaps this was how they explained the divergencies between the Greek Bible used by the Jews of Alexandria and their own traditions, rather than on the basis of a Hebrew *Vorlage* which differed markedly
from their own received text.

What lay behind the *tikunei soferim* (scribal corrections),[33] *iturei soferim*
(scribal enhancements),[34] or *keri* and *ketiv* (instances where the text is written
one way but read in another way)?[35] Or what is the significance of para-textual
elements such as the *puncta extraordinaria*,[36] or the suspended letters[37] and
inverted letter *nun*,[38] all of which are noted in the Talmud, as well as the
details of spacing and layout? The traditional explanation in each case presupposes a fixed, received text; that is, the rabbis read these devices as ways of
reconciling the belief in a single authentic text with the actual circumstance of
divergent texts.

For instance, the dot over the final letter *heh* in the word *reḥokah* ('distant')
in Numbers 9: 10 is interpreted to modify the meaning of *reḥokah* 'distant' to
'not really distant, but beyond the threshold of the Temple courtyard'.[39] Dots
were used by the Greeks to indicate doubtful readings;[40] presumably they
were introduced by Hebrew copyists for the same purpose, in which case
this dot simply indicates a doubt as to whether the letter should be there, a

---

[32] *Letter of Aristeas*, 302–4; trans. in Charles, *Apocrypha and Pseudepigrapha*.

[33] Tov, *Textual Criticism*, 65, who cites *inter alia* the eleven instances listed in *Mekhilta* on
Exod. 15: 7.

[34] BT *Ned.* 37b. Nissim b. Reuben Gerondi (Ran, 14th c.) defines them as 'extra words
written to beautify the language', but Tov, *Textual Criticism*, 67, translates 'omissions of the
scribes'! The question seems to be whether, for instance in Gen. 18: 5, the *itur* consisted in the
addition of the word *aḥar* (Nissim b. Reuben) or the omission of the conjunctive *vav* (Tov).

[35] Talmudic references to *keri* and *ketiv* include: BT *Eruv.* 26a re 2 Kgs 20: 4; *Ned.* 37b–38a
lists several. The late tractate *Soferim* 6: 8 has a fairly comprehensive list.

[36] *Puncta extraordinaria* are dots traditionally placed above certain letters in the Torah;
Sifrei bamidbar 69 on Num. 9: 10 lists ten instances in the Torah. Talmudic references
include: BT *Ber.* 4a re Ps. 27: 13; BT *Pes.* 93b (= Mishnah *Pes.* 9: 2 = JT *Pes.* 9: 2 [36d]) re Num.
9: 10; BT *Naz.* 23a (= BT *Hor.* 10b) re Gen. 19: 33; BT *BM* 87a re Gen. 18: 9; BT *San.* 43b re
Deut. 29: 28; BT *Men.* 87b re Num. 29: 15; BT *Bekh.* 4a re Num. 3: 39. With the possible
exception of *Bekh.* 4a, all the attributions are tannaitic, most of them to R. Yose.

[37] BT *BB* 109b re Judg. 18: 30.

[38] BT *Shab.* 115b–116a re Num. 10: 35–6; they occur also in Ps. 107: 23–8 and according to
Rashi on Gen. 11: 32. Lieberman, *Hellenism in Jewish Palestine*, 38–43, traces the derivation of
the signs from the Alexandrian sigma and antisigma. The Talmud actually calls them
simaniyot—a Hebraized plural of the Greek *sēmeion*—not *nunin*.   [39] Mishnah *Pes.* 9: 2.

[40] Lieberman, *Hellenism in Jewish Palestine*, 43–6.

position reflected in a statement put in the mouth of Ezra, whose responsibility for the received form of the sacred text was acknowledged by the rabbis: 'Ezra said: If Elijah comes and asks me, "Why did you write this [word in your Torah]," I will say I have indicated it with dots. If he says, "What you have written is correct," I shall remove the dots.'[41]

On the whole, however, the rabbis preferred not to interpret supralinear dots as indicating doubt, since this would bring into question the authenticity of the received text. Instead, they interpreted them as a device to convey teachings of the Oral Torah. They assumed a single authentic text, containing *heh* with a supralinear dot; any text that actually omitted the dotted *heh* in the word *reḥokah* was incorrect. We can infer this from the statement attributed to Rabbi Isaac: 'The reading of the scribes, the scribal enhancements, the "read but do not write, and write but do not read [*keri* and *ketiv*]", are laws of Moses from Sinai.'[42]

The Masoretes

The nouns *masorah* and *masoret* mean 'tradition'. The men who, from about the sixth century CE, tried to write down and fix the correct way of reading the Torah are called 'Masoretes'. Musical accents, vocalization, punctuation, and other elements of the written apparatus of the Masorah postdate the Talmud, and are absent from the Dead Sea Scrolls. Fortunately, another of the great archaeological discoveries of modern times, the Cairo Geniza,[43] has produced a wealth of material, much of it dating from the creative period of Masorah, to supplement our understanding of the way the Masoretic text became fixed.

The rabbis debated whether *yesh em lamikra* or *yesh em lamasoret*,[44] that is, whether the traditional way of reading aloud (*mikra*) or the written consonantal text (*masoret*) had priority. If, for instance, a word read as a plural was spelled defectively, they would understand this as plural from the point of view of *mikra* (reading) but singular from the point of view of *masoret* (written text), and draw what they believed to be appropriate conclusions.

[41] *Avot derabi nathan* 34: 4.   [42] BT *Ned.* 37b.

[43] The *genizah*, or depository, of the Ben Ezra Synagogue in Old Cairo contained a hoard of manuscripts, many of them from the period of Fatimid rule in Egypt (969–1171), when the newly founded city of Cairo served as the political and administrative centre of the realm. Documents were obtained by European scholars as early as the 1840s, but the bulk of the material, consisting of about 140,000 items including 25,000 Hebrew Bible fragments, was shipped to Cambridge, England, in 1897 by Solomon Schechter, and is housed in the University Library as the Taylor-Schechter Collection. For more information, see <http://www.lib.cam.ac.uk/Taylor-Schechter/> and <www.genizah.org>.

[44] BT *San.* 4a. See also *Zev.* 37b.

Between 500 and 700 CE scholars in Southern Palestine, in Tiberias (Galilee), and in Babylonia devised vowel systems to preserve the traditional ways of reading in written form. Standard Hebrew vocalization derives from the Tiberian system, though Yemenite Jews preserved the Babylonian system; manuscripts of both of these as well as of the South Palestinian system have been recovered. The differences between the systems are not merely graphic, but reflect different phonology. No system yields a pronunciation which tallies consistently with earlier transliterations, such as the Septuagint rendering of names, or with the transliterations of the text in the *Hexapla*, a work by the Christian scholar Origen (185–254), which incorporates a Greek transliteration and translations with the Hebrew text.

What relationship was there between the Karaite movement and the development of the Masorah? The Karaites rejected rabbinic interpretation and law as a human fabrication and therefore an unwarranted, unauthoritative addition to scripture; such a position accords well with the scriptural focus of the Masoretes, and the appeal of Karaism may have been reinforced by this. Karaite treatises arguing new views of scriptural exegesis certainly stimulated renewed study of the Bible and Hebrew language among Rabbanites from the tenth century onwards.[45]

There were other factors. The establishment of an accurate Bible text was necessary to rebut Christian appropriation of scripture, to counter Christian and (from the seventh century) Muslim accusations of corruption of the text, and as a foundation for rabbinic exegesis. Moreover, the Karaite principle of *sola scriptura* ('by scripture alone') was in harmony with a counter-tradition extending back at least to the Sadducees of Second Temple times.

In Chapter 5 we referred to Maimonides' admiration for the accuracy and spacing of the Aleppo Codex. This codex, completed by the Masorete Aaron ben Asher *c.*925 CE, was written in a slightly modified Tiberian system. Somehow it made its way from Cairo, where Maimonides saw it, to Aleppo, Syria, where it was treasured by the community for several centuries—perhaps treasured too much, as they allowed only one page to be photographed, and of the original 380 pages only 294 now remain. These pages escaped the rioting mobs who set fire to the Aleppo Synagogue in 1948, and are now safely housed in Jerusalem in the library of the Ben-Zvi Institute.[46]

The Aleppo Codex contains both the *masora parva*, or lesser Masorah (Hebrew: *masorah ketanah*) and the *masora magna*, or greater Masorah (Hebrew: *masorah gedolah*). The former consists of notes for the correct reading and writing of the text, and is written in the side margins, adjoining the text to

[45] See above, Ch. 7 n. 58.   [46] Facsimile in Goshen-Gottstein, *The Aleppo Codex*.

which it refers; the latter consists of more extensive notes written in the upper or lower margins.

Partly through the advocacy of Maimonides the Aleppo Codex became the basis for the standard Masoretic text,[47] though today's Torah scrolls depart from it in minor ways.[48]

It was in this period of Masoretic activity that such compilations as the anonymous *Okhlah ve'okhlah* appeared. This treatise comprises about 400 lists of such things as pairs of unique phrases one of which begins with *el* and one with *al* (list 2); unique words ending with *vav* (list 33); pairs of words with final *heh* one of which is marked with *mapik* (internal dot) while the other is not (list 44).[49]

Another work devised to assist accurate recording and reproduction of the biblical text was Mishael ben Uzziel's Arabic *Kitāb al-Khilaf* ('Book of Differences'), a treatise on the differences between the Ben Asher and Ben Naftali Masoretic schools.

The Masoretes worked hard, worked meticulously, and worked over many centuries to establish a 'correct' biblical text. Ultimately, however, their achievement was the *creation*, rather than the recovery, of a standard text.

Rabbinic Responses to Textual Variation

Halakhah, as developed in the talmudic period and summed up in the *c.*800 treatise *Masekhet soferim*, lays great stress on attaining the maximum accuracy in writing biblical texts, especially in the copying of Torah scrolls. Textual variants are regarded as a misfortune, not as a rich historical resource, with the uncharacteristic exception of Rabbi Meir's 'garments of light',[50] though this instance is not mentioned in either Talmud and could be a late fabrication or perhaps merely homiletic.

Textual variants continued to surface despite the activities of the Masoretes. Though the variants were trivial from any normal literary point of view, they greatly worried the halakhists, since it is forbidden not only to read in public, but to retain uncorrected, a Torah scroll containing even the smallest error.

Meir ben Todros Halevi Abulafia (*c.*1170–1244), a leading authority in Toledo, engaged in research into the available manuscripts and composed his *Masoret seyag latorah* to bring some order into the confusion;[51] this work profoundly influenced *Kiryat sefer* of the Provençal scholar Menahem ben

---

[47] See above, p. 67.   [48] Tov, *Textual Criticism*, ch. 1, gives examples.
[49] Yeivin, *Introduction to the Tiberian Masorah*, 128–9.   [50] See above, p. 100.
[51] It was first printed in Florence in 1750 with numerous errors and omissions.

Solomon Meiri (d. c.1313) as well as later Masoretic research. Abulafia wrote a Torah scroll to serve as a master copy, and there are reports of scribes from Germany and Morocco visiting Toledo in order to copy it.

At about this time a rift surfaced between those who took a 'scientific' approach to textual variants, and arch-traditionalists who could not countenance any suggestion that the received Torah text was imperfect. The fault line more or less coincides with that between Maimunists and anti-Maimunists, that is, between rationalists and kabbalists.

On the rationalist side Abraham Ibn Ezra (1089–1164), in the introduction to his *Commentary on the Torah*, sketched five approaches to biblical interpretation. The fifth, his chosen way, regards plene and defective spellings as arbitrary variation without significance; people who base interpretations on them are indulging in mere homiletics, not serious elucidation of what the Bible means. David Kimhi, Profiat Duran (d. c.1414), and Isaac Abravanel (1437–1508) accepted the notion of early textual discrepancies and textual errors,[52] and they were followed by Elijah Levita ('Eliyahu Bahur', 1468/9–1549), the Hebrew philologist, grammarian, lexicographer, and teacher of many Christian humanists. Levita's approach, seen in his classic history *Masoret hamasoret*, tends to the historical-critical; he emphatically rejects, for instance, what he regards as a Karaite claim that the vowel signs and other Masoretic apparatus originated from Sinai.[53]

Rabbis with kabbalistic leanings refused to countenance the possibility of any imperfection or arbitrariness in the received biblical text. Mr Julian Abel of Manchester drew my attention to a comment by Rabbi Yedidiah Solomon of Norzi (1560–1626) in *Minḥat shai* on the word *umigvaot* ('and from the hills') in Numbers 23: 9. Noting that in some copies the word is plene and in others defective, Norzi opts for plene, adding that in the cases where there is a dispute in the Masorah both readings are correct, conveying deep mysteries. He then cites the Zohar, which asserts that one reading is to be found in the *metivta ila'a* ('high [earthly] academy') and the other in the *metivta derakia* ('academy of the sky', i.e. in heaven).[54] The Zohar was a very influential work,

[52] Levy, *Fixing God's Torah*, 144.

[53] Levita, *Masoret hamasoret*, third preface. The Protestant Louis Cappel (1585–1658), in his *Hoc est arcanum punctationis revelatum*, followed Levita in denying the antiquity of the vowels and accents. Johannes Buxtorf II, *Tractatus de punctorum vocalium*, cites Levita as unique among Jews and Christians for attributing the system of vocalization to 5th-c. Tiberians, and espousing what he regards as his father's cause against Cappel vigorously defends the traditional view of the antiquity of the Masoretic pointing.

[54] Zohar iii. 203b. Levy, *Fixing God's Torah*, 197 n. 13, points to the similarity of the Zohar's heavenly and earthly academy to the Islamic notion of the divine and earthly Qur'an. Both

since it was (and still is) widely believed to have been composed by the second-century Rabbi Simon bar Yohai. Few who read that statement would dare to suggest that any variant reading was erroneous; even variant readings come from Sinai and carry profound meanings!

David ben Solomon ibn Abi Zimra (1479–1573), known as Radbaz, a Spanish refugee, was official leader of the Jewish community of Egypt from 1517 to 1552, and for the rest of his life a leading figure in the land of Israel. He was an ardent defender of the authenticity of the received text, and several of his responsa deal with textual questions. Although a kabbalist himself, he refused to allow scribes to change from a defective to a plene spelling of the word *oto* in two places in the Torah in order to accord with an interpretation in the Zohar;[55] even so, he insisted that all variants were 'from Sinai'.

I noted earlier how the medieval Tosafists and, later, Rabbi Akiva Eger, worried about divergencies between the received text and that cited in the Talmud. With regard to plene and defective spellings the medieval Ashkenazi authorities simply threw up their hands in despair, and declared that we could no longer insist on a perfectly accurate Torah scroll since it was impossible to be certain of these spellings. Though the Sephardi Joseph Karo ruled, following the Talmud,[56] that 'if a mistake is found in a Torah scroll when it is being read [in public] another should be brought [in its place] and the reading resumed from that point', the Ashkenazi Moses Isserles (*c*.1520–72) glossed: 'This is only if it is a proper mistake, but another should not be brought out on account of plene and defective since our Torah scrolls are not so accurate that we could say that one is better than another.'[57]

The view codified by Isserles rests on a well-established tradition; it derives ultimately from the talmudic admission that 'we' are no longer expert in counting either the letters or the words of the Torah.[58] But neither the Talmud nor Isserles admits the possibility that the 'original' text was in any way indefinite; the Talmud simply concedes that we are not as good at counting letters and words as our ancestors were, and Isserles concedes further that our scribes cannot be relied upon to copy plene and defective spellings accurately. Both would concur that a precise text was received by

concepts derive indirectly from Plato's teaching on ideas. Norzi is discussed further below; see p. 108.

[55] Ibn Abi Zimra, *Responsa*, vol. iv, responsum 1172 (p. 101). Discussion and bibliography in Levy, *Fixing God's Torah*, ch. 2.

[56] R. Ammi, in BT *Ket.* 19*b*, rules that an uncorrected Torah scroll must not be retained for more than thirty days.

[57] Karo, *Beit yosef*, 'Yoreh de'ah' 279. His rulings are given in *Shulḥan arukh*, 'Oraḥ ḥayim' 143: 4 and 'Yoreh de'ah' 275: 2. [58] BT *Kid.* 30*a*.

Moses at Sinai, and that the text now in our hands is to most intents and purposes identical to it.

The first printed Hebrew Bible appeared in Spain, in about 1480. The introduction of printing, as well as general Renaissance interest in the recovery of authentic ancient texts, brought a new sense of urgency to establishing the 'correct' biblical text; for Jews, there was the added incentive of defence against Christian polemic, as we may see in a responsum by Judah Aryeh (Leone) of Modena (1571–1648).[59]

The second Rabbinic Bible was printed in 1524/5 under the editorship of Jacob ben Hayim ben Isaac Ibn Adonijah. In his editorial preface he takes issue with Kimhi, Profiat Duran, and Isaac Abravanel, the last-named of whom had, in his commentary on Jeremiah published in 1504, suggested that the prophet's lapses from correct Hebrew grammar and style had necessitated corrections which appear as *keri* and *ketiv*. Jacob accuses all three of ignoring the Talmud, and insists that all variants, including *keri* and *ketiv*, are 'from Sinai';[60] seeing that he ended his life as a Christian convert, this was perhaps an instance of 'the lady doth protest too much'.[61] His position was in any case exceeded by traditionalists such as Rabbi Judah Loew ben Bezalel of Prague (Maharal, 1525–1609), who insisted that not only variants, but even the vocalization, was 'from Sinai', and that the shapes of the vowels demonstrated the superiority of Ashkenazi pronunciation![62]

Yedidiah Solomon of Norzi devoted much of his life to textual research, travelling widely to compare manuscripts. His work, to which he gave the revealing title *Goder perets* ('Repairing the Breach'), was reprinted in Mantua in 1742–4 under the title *Minḥat shai*, by which name it still appears in most editions of *Mikraot gedolot* (the Rabbinic Bible). In his introduction Norzi laments the confusion into which the biblical text has fallen, and stresses the necessity of restoring each and every letter correctly, including plene and defective, since (as Nahmanides had claimed in the introduction to his own *Commentary on the Torah*) the Torah consists of the names of God, and one who reads from an incorrect scroll damages the Name of the King, as the Zohar states. This does not sound like heresy, but the whole introduction has been omitted from many editions of *Mikraot gedolot*, presumably because the printers were prevailed upon by heresy-hunting rabbis who thought it unsafe to allow the public any doubt as to the perfection of the received text.[63]

---

[59] Modena, *Ziknei yehudah*, responsum no. 115 on p. 165.

[60] Jacob's preface, early translated into Latin, appears anonymously in some modern *Mikraot gedolot* editions as *divrei hama'atik* ('words of the copyist').

[61] *Hamlet* III. ii. 242.   [62] Judah Loew ben Bezalel, *Tiferet yisra'el*, ch. 66.

[63] Levy, *Fixing God's Torah*, 32–3, translates a long section of the introduction into English.

Norzi did his best to restore the perfect text, but the situation worsened considerably in the nineteenth and twentieth centuries with the rise of textual criticism and the recovery by scholars and archaeologists of a vast wealth of material lost to earlier generations, not least the Dead Sea Scrolls. Many Jews have of course accommodated themselves to this situation, even welcomed it, but some among the Orthodox continue to reject the evidence and to engage in defensive manoeuvres. For instance, where *Genesis Rabbah* unabashedly recounted Rabbi Meir's divergencies from the generally accepted text,[64] Aaron Hyman, in his article on Meir,[65] assures the reader that—heaven forfend!—*Genesis Rabbah* does not mean to suggest that the scroll actually had a different Torah text from the 'received' one, only that it carried a marginal note interpreting the words in this manner. Hyman, an Orthodox rabbi of the early twentieth century, was of course responding defensively to the 'threat' of textual criticism; indeed, his encyclopedia of rabbinic biography is an erudite rejoinder to the historical revisions of the *wissenschaftliche* scholars, devotees of the 'science of Judaism'. That the compilers of *Genesis Rabbah* did not react in similar defensive mode suggests that they did not perceive the existence of variant readings as a threat.

Even the differences between Yemenite and other scrolls have proved difficult to accommodate; Rabbi Abdullah Sumak of Baghdad (1813–89) ruled that Yemenite scrolls were invalid. Baghdad-born Rabbi Ovadiah Yosef (b. 1920; Sephardi Chief Rabbi of Israel, 1972–83), on the contrary, has ruled that it is permissible for anyone, even a non-Yemenite, to read from a Yemenite scroll, despite the acknowledged differences from the Western Masorah.[66] But these are practical, ritual matters, carrying social consequences; the theological implications of an indefinable biblical text are not addressed.

An instructive controversy erupted between two Orthodox rabbis, Jehiel Jacob Weinberg (1884–1966) and Chaim Heller (1878–1960), in the 1930s. Weinberg, who studied under and worked closely with the Christian Masoretic scholar Paul Kahle in Germany,[67] was no lover of Higher Criticism, but was prepared, like David Hoffman (of whom more in Chapter 16 below), to accept that there were instances of non-halakhic Targumim and minor

[64] Above, p. 100.
[65] Hyman, *History* (Heb.), iii. 876. Mr Julian Abel of Manchester drew my attention to Norzi's remark in *Minhat shai* on Gen. 1: 31 that Rabbi Meir's 'readings' were merely midrashic glosses. See also Epstein cited by Albeck in his edn. of *Bereshit rabati* on Gen. 45: 8, p. 209). [66] Levy, *Fixing God's Torah*, 37–8 and references.
[67] Kahle (1875–1965) collaborated with Kittel in revising the *Biblia Hebraica* (see below); in 1938, suspected of pro-Jewish sympathies, he moved with his family to Oxford, but returned to Germany after the war.

variants from the Masoretic texts which were not merely copyists' errors. Heller, who published a number of works on Targum, Peshitta, Septuagint, and the Samaritan Pentateuch, refused to budge from the dogma of the authenticity of the received Masoretic text, only to have his works denounced by Weinberg as entirely unscholarly.

Weinberg's own defensiveness surfaced shortly after the discovery in the Cairo Geniza in 1930 of a Targum manuscript which, contrary to the talmudic rendering of the root *b-'-r* in Exodus 22: 4 as 'consume',[68] translated it as 'kindle', implying a non-Masoretic vocalization of בעירה *b'yrh* in the same verse. Weinberg, claiming that his motives were scholarly not dogmatic, insisted that either the Aramaic was to be translated differently or else that it was a mere copyist's error.[69]

Modern Editions of the Bible

Most modern editions of the Hebrew text are simply more or less accurate copies of the standard 'received' text. This is true even of the beautiful new 'revised and augmented' edition of *Mikraot gedolot* (the Rabbinic Bible) in process of publication by Bar Ilan University under the direction of Menahem Cohen; the Bible text and Masorah apparatus are (where extant) those of the Aleppo Codex.[70]

There are, however, some critical editions of note. The most popular (it is also the cheapest, most convenient, and most complete) is the *Biblia Hebraica* (known as BH), of which the first edition was that of Rudolf Kittel, Leipzig 1905; this was based on the second Rabbinic Bible of Ibn Adonijah. There have been many revisions, notably the third (Stuttgart 1929–37), jointly edited by Kittel and Paul Kahle (hence BHK), based on the Leningrad (St Petersburg) Codex B19A; later editions incorporated some Qumran variants. Next came the *Biblia Hebraica Stuttgartiensis* (BHS), edited by W. Rudolph and K. Elliger in 1967–77, still based on the Leningrad Codex but incorporating an enhanced critical apparatus.

However, all these are essentially editions of the *Masoretic* text which, as we have seen, represents only one of three known scribal traditions. The edition under production by the Hebrew University Bible Project in Jerusalem is far broader in concept, though it abstains from conjectural emendation and does not take a position on the comparative value of readings. The first

[68] BT *BK* 2b.   [69] Shapiro, *Between the Yeshiva World and Modern Orthodoxy*, 164–71.
[70] *Mikraot gedolot haketer*. At the time of writing, volumes have appeared on Genesis, Exodus, Joshua, Judges, Samuel, Kings, Isaiah, Ezekiel, and Psalms.

volumes (Isaiah) appeared in 1975 and 1981, under the direction of the late M. H. Goshen-Gottstein, but the vast project remains incomplete.

Conclusion

The evidence of the imperfection of the Masoretic text is unambiguous, and has been considerably reinforced in the past two centuries. The standard Masoretic text, in so far as there is a standard, cannot be relied upon as the 'original' text of the Bible, even if we are prepared to grant validity to such a concept. There are no contemporary manuscripts for any biblical book, and in most cases, none for several centuries after the book was composed. By the time manuscripts appear, competing scribal traditions have already been established.

Attempts at denial, unsupported assertions that a minuscule selection of variant readings was 'dictated at Sinai', absurd kabbalistic claims about alternative 'readings in the sky', are dishonest and merely exacerbate the problem. It must be accepted that the traditional dogma of a literally revealed and perfectly transmitted text is untenable in the light of the evidence; the received text is the somewhat arbitrary end result of a long process of redaction.

This is a perfectly normal process of formation for any ancient text,[71] but how significant is it for Jewish theology to accept that the Bible, too, was formed in this way?

On the positive side, it is clear that the Bible, in much the form we know it, has been around for at least 2,000 years. Manuscripts of some books, notably the five incorporated in the Torah scroll, exhibit little variation in substance, much as they vary in spelling and orthography. Discrepancies are neither as radical as alleged by some Muslims nor as tendentious as was once claimed by Christians.

For the theologian, in any case, the significant fact is the reception, rather than the early literary history of the books; for Jews, this means that a theology has to be built on the way the rabbis read the texts they regarded as sacred, rather than on reconstructions of 'original texts'.

The halakhist is troubled because his problem is a practical one: how to implement a rule that insists on 'perfect' transcription of the text. For practical purposes there is no reason to deny the halakhist the indulgence of working on the basis of a myth, namely that what has come to be accepted as the Torah text really is the Torah text of 'Moses on Sinai'. After all, it would be

---

[71] See, for instance, the account of the fixation of the Sumerian/Babylonian Epic of Gilgamesh in Tigay, *Empirical Models for Biblical Criticism*.

confusing if people were allowed, as allegedly the historian Graetz did on an occasion when reading the prophetic lesson at the London Great Synagogue,[72] to make emendations as they saw fit, even on the basis of manuscript evidence.

But for general theological purposes the difference between plene and defective is not significant; God still reigns in his heaven and people ought to be good to one another.

Even the more striking textual variations are distinctly less troubling to the theologian than the contradictions and other problems to be addressed in the next chapter.

[72] I heard this anecdote from the late Louis Jacobs, but have not found documentary evidence.

NINE

CONTRADICTIONS, MORAL PROBLEMS, FACTUAL ERRORS

Every scientific truth goes through three stages. First, people say it conflicts with the Bible. Next, they say it has been discovered before. Lastly, they say they have always believed it.

Attributed to LOUIS AGASSIZ

EVER SINCE THE BIBLE was first read friends as well as foes have noticed that it appears to contradict itself every now and then. Glaring examples would be the numerous ways in which the laws for priests and sacrifices in the final chapters of Ezekiel differ from those in Leviticus, or the statement in Deuteronomy 15: 4, 'for there will be no needy among you', which conflicts with another verse in the same chapter, 'for the poor shall not cease from the land' (15: 11).

Friends as well as foes have recognized, too, that some passages in the Bible are morally questionable. Not only is the behaviour attributed to people represented as holy sometimes subject to reproach—how, for instance, could Moses order the cold-blooded slaughter of presumably innocent captive women and male children? (Num. 31: 4–7)—but some terrible acts are attributed to God himself.

With the passage of time, moreover, many of the historical and scientific statements made by the rabbis as well as the Bible have been challenged.

If the Torah is perfect as claimed, it should be free from contradictions, moral lapses, and factual errors. In strict logic, if it contains even one real contradiction, one moral lapse, or one factual error, it cannot as a totality be the Word of God, though some of it might be.

Strict logic, however, is difficult to apply. Nobody can be quite sure, if there appears to be a contradiction, moral lapse, or factual error, that there is not some 'explanation' that would make it come right. Just as in science logic decrees that one contrary experimental result is sufficient to overthrow a theory, but scientific practice recognizes that it would be rash to abandon an apparently good theory until there was a convincing build-up of evidence, so in religion one learns to live with the occasional problem and is not seriously challenged until the scale of evidence has become formidable.

We will look at some examples of questions that have been raised to challenge traditional Jewish belief in the authenticity of the Bible as the Word of God or in the rabbis' interpretation of it. We need not be unduly troubled by a mere handful of 'difficult' cases, but if the evidence is strong some theological revision will be called for.

The Reconciling Hermeneutic

Apparent contradictions in scripture have often been welcomed by rabbis as an opportunity to demonstrate the power of hermeneutic; they do not see them as a challenge to faith. In this vein Rabbi Manasseh ben Israel (1604–57) compiled a book in which, chapter by chapter, he reconciled contradictions throughout the Bible, including the two mentioned above.[1]

Up to a point this is perfectly reasonable. Since language does not allow you to say everything simultaneously, nor to define precisely all the conditions attaching to a statement or law, it is more than likely that any extended piece of writing, especially legislation, will need interpretation to smooth out apparent contradictions, errors, omissions, and superfluous repetitions.

If, for instance, Deuteronomy 15: 18 says you shall dedicate (sanctify) your firstborn animals to God, and Leviticus 27: 26 says you should not, it is not unreasonable to suggest, as the halakhic midrash does,[2] that two types of 'dedication' are involved: the status of the animal as firstborn may not be changed, i.e. the animal may not be dedicated as a sacrifice on the altar, but its *value* may be dedicated to the Temple treasury. On the assumption that Holy Writ is consistent this is a perfectly reasonable interpretation, in harmony with the plain meaning of both texts. A modern critic might question the assumption that laws in Deuteronomy need be consistent with those of Leviticus, since they derive from different sources, but this would run contrary to the traditional view of Torah as a perfect unity reflecting the unity of the One who gave it.

Sometimes things get more complicated. For instance, one verse says 'Eat unleavened bread for seven days' (Exod. 12: 15) and another says 'Eat unleavened bread for six days' (Deut. 16: 8). By applying one of the Thirteen Principles attributed to Rabbi Ishmael we infer that just as eating unleavened bread is optional on the seventh day (the one 'omitted' in the second verse), it

---

[1] Manasseh ben Israel, *The Conciliator*. The Ezekiel/Leviticus contradiction is Ezekiel Question 12, pp. 221–3 in part 2; the poverty contradiction is Question 178, pp. 283–84 in part 1.

[2] *Sifra*, 'Beḥukotai' 29a; *Sifrei devarim*, 'Re'eh', no. 124; BT *Arakh.* 29a.

is optional throughout the seven; it is mandatory to eat unleavened bread only on the first night of Passover, since this is specified in another verse (Exod. 22: 18).[3]

This may be confusing, but it does bear some relation to the context. More disturbing for ancient as well as modern readers is the tendency to degenerate into a sort of verbal mechanics that ignores the context. This happens most clearly when a text invokes the technique of *im eino inyan* 'if it cannot be applied to . . . '. This technique is based on the most questionable assumption of rabbinic exegesis, i.e. the assumption that no word in scripture is superfluous. The corollary of this is that if something *is* stated, apparently unnecessarily, and cannot yield anything novel in its own context, it has to be applied in another context; twice, the Babylonian Talmud speaks of *eruv parashiyot*, 'mixing of sections', though just why the Torah should mix unrelated topics is not explained.[4]

The halakhic midrash *Sifra* on Leviticus 19: 6 illustrates the former technique. *Sifra* comments on the words '[The peace-offering] may be eaten on the day you offer it or on the following day': 'If this [restriction] cannot be applied to eating, apply it to slaughtering; it means that the sacrifice must be slaughtered with the intention of eating it that day or the following day.' That is, the requirement to consume the offering that day or the following day could be derived from another verse, so to state it here is superfluous; therefore, this verse must be applied to something other than what its plain sense dictates, namely to the *intention* of the slaughterer.

Such methods of interpretation aroused criticism from within the Jewish fold as well as from outside, but from the perspective of the rabbis the 'reconciling hermeneutic' transformed apparent defects of scripture (inconsistency, incompleteness) into a virtue of the 'Dual Torah' system. The Oral Torah is seen to be the *necessary* complement to the Written; it is vital for the interpretation of scripture, and to draw out from scripture its implicit laws, handed by God to Moses and, so to speak, coded into the text of the Written Torah. Written and Oral Torah are shown to constitute a seamless whole.

Clearly, the reconciling hermeneutic bypasses the question of source analysis. The rabbis by no means overlooked the contradictions and superfluous duplications which in recent centuries have led scholars to believe that the Bible was compiled from a variety of sources. On the contrary, the rabbis were well aware of them. They responded not by dismantling the text, but consistently with their basic assumption that the Torah text was inerrant, free

[3] *Mekhilta* on Exod. 12: 18; *Pes.* 120a. The Thirteen Principles are discussed above, Ch. 2.

[4] *BK* 107a (see Tosafot), *San.* 2b.

from redundancy, and comprehensive. If you had asked them on what they based this assumption they would have answered, as fundamentalist Jews do today, that it followed from the basic premise that God and his Torah were perfect; there, on the unforgiving bedrock of faith, argument ceases.

Interpreting Aggadah

The reconciling hermeneutic, in its strictest form, is particularly suited to the exposition of halakhah; it is applied most powerfully and consistently in *Sifra*, the halakhic midrash on Leviticus.

Aggadah presents somewhat different problems, but even so the assumptions that scripture is inerrant, free from redundancy, and comprehensive are upheld.

Several situations generate aggadic interpretation:

Contradictions must be resolved. Moses' father-in-law is differently named in several passages. Solution—he was given seven names to indicate seven aspects of his character.[5]

Lacunae need to be filled in. The Torah states regarding Moses, 'he buried him in a valley in Moab' (Deut. 34: 6), but it does not state *who* buried him. Answer—God himself buried Moses.[6]

Apparently **superfluous repetition**, for instance of the story of Abraham's servant's mission to find a wife for Isaac (Gen. 24), **needs to be shown to have a purpose**. There is a general answer—see how great was our father Abraham, that the minutest details of his servant's dealings are recorded in holy writ! And there are specific answers, arising from the difference between the first description of Eliezer's doings and the account Eliezer himself gave in the house of Bethuel. (The identification of Abraham's servant as Eliezer is another instance of the rabbis filling in a lacuna.)

Heroes, such as David, **must be defended** from the charge of moral or halakhic lapses. 'He who says David sins is in error . . .'. He did not actually sin with Bathsheba; at the time he slept with her she was, technically, divorced from her husband Uriah, since 'Whoever goes out to war for the house of David writes his wife a [conditional] divorce.'[7]

Villains, such as Laban and Esau, **are painted even blacker** than the text demands; when Esau kissed his long-absent brother (Gen. 33: 5), some say

[5] *Mekhilta* on Exod. 18: 1.   [6] BT *Sot.* 13b–14a.   [7] BT *Shab.* 56a.

that despite his hostility he was overcome by emotion, but others say that he tried to bite him.[8]

The Bible, taken at face value, contradicts some established theological principles, for instance by referring to God in **anthropomorphic terms**; such language is treated as symbolic or metaphorical.

There are **theological lacunae**, for instance the absence of any clear doctrine of life after death; the Talmud, not for a moment doubting the doctrine, conducts a lengthy if inconclusive search for proof-texts.[9]

There are **theological puzzles**, such as the use of different names for God. Thus Hannah is observed to be the first to use the name *tsevaot*, for she appealed to God as Lord of Hosts (*tsevaot* 'multitudes') to grant her just one child from that multitude.[10] More generally, the name spelled YHVH is used of God in his attribute of mercy, while Elohim is used of him in his attribute of justice. He wanted to create the world in strict justice, hence Genesis 1 uses only the name Elohim; but he saw that it could only survive if justice was tempered with mercy, hence both names are used together in Genesis 2–3.

Other problems suggest to modern scholars that the text of the Bible has been derived from multiple sources, not always satisfactorily combined. For instance, Deuteronomy 10: 6–9 interrupts the narrative in which Moses, in the first person, describes his ascent of Sinai to receive the replacement tablets of the Ten Commandments; one can skip from verse 5 to verse 10 perfectly smoothly. The intervening verses, related in the third person, refer to some journeys of the Israelites in an order contrary to that of Numbers 33: 31–7, and to the death of Aaron, which they locate at Moserah, contrary to Numbers 20: 22–9 and 33: 38, where it is stated that he died at Mount Hor; before returning to the narrative, verses follow on the elevation of the Levites.

In response, the Jerusalem Talmud proposes that Aaron died at Mount Hor; however, the Israelites eulogized him not there but at Moserah, and since it is such a great act of kindness to deliver a fitting eulogy, scripture regards it as if he had died there. However, this does not explain how the Israelites *got* to Moserah, which according to Numbers is a full eight journeys *after* Mount Hor. To explain this, the Jerusalem Talmud invents a minor civil war that led the Israelites back in their tracks and, solving some other scriptural mysteries, conveniently disposed of five Benjaminite, four Levite, and a few other clans.[11]

---

[8] *Gen. Rabbah* 78: 12. There is a pun here on the roots *n-sh-q* 'kiss' and *n-sh-k* 'bite'.
[9] BT *San.* 90b–92b.   [10] BT *Ber.* 31b.   [11] JT *Yoma* 1: 1 (38b).

Rashi swallows the story whole, possibly from a different source, but Abraham Ibn Ezra, who hints that it falls somewhere between the implausible and the preposterous, evades the difficulty by proposing that, despite the similarity of names in Numbers and Deuteronomy, the locations referred to are not the same. No medieval commentator would openly propose divergent literary sources.

The two versions of the creation story are perhaps the most striking instance of the many duplicated stories in the Bible. Philo, well before the rabbinic period, explained that the first creation was the creation of 'ideas' (in the Platonic sense), that is, the perfect, changeless, intelligible world; the second creation was the casting of those ideas in physical form, in the imperfect world of change.[12]

But although Philo drew attention to the duplication, and the rabbis to the change of divine names, it was to be many centuries before anyone generalized from this and sought a theory to explain and relate the many instances of duplication associated with a change of divine name. A Provençal author and translator, Kalonymus ben Kalonymus (d. 1348), addressed a polemic to Joseph Ibn Kaspi (1270–1340); after criticizing Ibn Kaspi's *Sefer hasod* (also known as *Tirat hakesef*), he adds, *inter alia*:

But, dear brother, I am greatly confused by a matter I have noticed recently in Genesis and which can hardly be there for no purpose, though I have not seen or heard to this day that anyone paid attention to it. The confusion is this. From the beginning of Genesis to the end of rest [Gen. 2: 4] the only divine name used is Elohim. From there onwards to *veha'adam yada* [Gen. 4: 1] it is YHVH-Elohim, and from there to *Eleh toldot no'ah* [Gen. 6: 9] it is YHVH only and in the story of the flood Elohim only. This cannot be fortuitous, but in my opinion he who gave us the Torah hints here at important secrets, but they are a mystery to me and I do not understand.[13]

Another Provençal, the poet and philosopher Yedaiah of Béziers (Bedersi or Bedershi, 1270–1340), stung by the ban on the philosophers of Provence instigated under the leadership of Solomon ben Adret (Rashba, 1235–1310) of Barcelona, composed a lengthy 'apology' in response.[14] After a grovelling exordium several pages long he attempts to reassure Rashba that despite

---

[12] Philo, *Questions on Genesis*.

[13] Kalonymus' polemic was edited by Perles and published in Munich in 1879. I have translated the extract cited in the *Entsiklopediyah mikra'it*, viii. 710.

[14] The *hitnatselut* (apology) is reproduced as no. 418 in the first volume of Solomon b. Adret's *Responsa*. Halkin, 'Yedaiah Bedershi's Apology', describes the ban as 'the triumph of the antirationalist group over the forces which it designated as alien and hostile to the faith and the tradition' (p. 184).

interpreting biblical characters figuratively (for example, Abraham is spirit, and Sarah matter), his countrymen have complete faith in the patriarchs who are the foundation of Judaism. Nor is it new, continues Bedersi, that they interpret aggadic passages figuratively. What sense otherwise, he asks, are we to make of such *agadot* as that in which Rabbi Bena'a is said to have been admitted by Eliezer to Abraham's grave, where he found Abraham resting his head in Sarah's bosom and Sarah examining his hair?[15] The figurative interpretation of the *agadot* is not a denial of the truth of the biblical narrative. Bedersi's defence of the philosophical interpretation of aggadah indicates that the traditional reading was proving troublesome, and not only to the philosophers.

Historical and Archaeological Problems

In Chapter 7 we referred to Demetrius the Chronographer's attempts to make sense of the chronology of the patriarchal narratives. The Septuagint provides further evidence of the efforts of Alexandrian Jews to construct a coherent history not only of the patriarchs and the Exodus, but of the kings of Judah and Israel; yet the extant Greek text suffers as much from internal inconsistencies as the Hebrew Kings and Chronicles.[16]

There is no evidence that the rabbis of the Talmud were familiar with any *external* historical source which might have cast doubt on the biblical story. The earlier written languages of the Near East, such as Sumerian, Egyptian, and Akkadian, were largely forgotten by their time, and though something of Egyptian antiquity might have been gleaned from Greek literature they would be unlikely to know this or if they did to take it seriously.

With post-biblical history the situation is somewhat different. Their reading of events is often in stark contrast to that of historians whose works must have been familiar to some of them. The Hanukah story, for instance, is told in a way which has little in common with the accounts in 1 and 2 Maccabees, once characterized by scholars as, respectively, Sadducee and Pharisee interpretations of events; Judah the Maccabee is ignored, and a completely novel story of the miracle of the oil becomes the central feature.[17]

Scientific archaeology was of course unknown to the sages, even though some ancient sites were identified. It is open to speculation whether the following was stimulated by the observation of fossils or simply by the legends of other nations:

---

[15] BT *BB* 58a.

[16] The details may be followed in ch. 8 and appendix E of Galil, *Chronology*.

[17] *Megilat ta'anit*, cited in BT *Shab.* 21b.

Rabbi Simon says: It is not written here 'Let there be evening' but 'And it was evening'. From here [we learn] that there was an order of times before this. Rabbi Abbahu says: It teaches us that the Holy One, blessed be He, created worlds and destroyed them, until He created these; He said 'This gives me pleasure; those do not give me pleasure'.[18]

Questions of the sort that arose from the eighteenth century onwards when archaeologists unearthed new evidence about the course of events in the ancient Near East could not have been posed in the rabbinic period.

Rabbinic statements on historical matters were rarely subjected to scientific criticism by Jews before the sixteenth century, when Azariah de' Rossi (c.1511–1578) produced his *Sefer me'irat einayim*, in which he utilized classical and Christian sources as well as Philo and Josephus to 'correct' the rabbinic histories. Like other humanist scholars—Mercator, for instance, whose *Chronologia* appeared in 1568/9—he is anxious to demonstrate his conformity with tradition, and perhaps naively expects his conservative colleagues to go along with him. In chapter 20 Azariah examines the rabbinic tract *Seder olam*, attributed to the second-century Rabbi Yose, and certain other works the texts of which he suspects are corrupt. Skilfully applying humanist techniques of textual criticism, he suggests that *Seder olam* was composed after the Talmud, that sections of the Zohar are much later than Simon bar Yohai and stylistically inappropriate to him, and that there are interpolations in the texts of Josephus and Josippon.[19] On the other hand, he cannot accept the notion that the *tikunei soferim* represent real changes to the biblical text,[20] but argues instead that the passages in the Talmud referring to them are interpolations, or else individual opinions expressed in an unfortunate manner; either way, he says, it would be respectful to the sages to disregard such statements.

In chapter 22 he embarks on historical revision. The rabbis describe a meeting of Simon the High Priest with Alexander of Macedon.[21] Drawing on sources including Philo and Josephus, Azariah demonstrates that this is impossible, since the two were separated by more than 150 years. This leads him into a discussion some chapters long on the basic chronology of Jewish tradition, including the determination of *anno mundi* (years from the Creation) on which the Jewish reckoning of years is based. In the course of this discussion he puts his finger on the major flaw in early Jewish chron-

[18] *Gen. Rabbah* 3:7.

[19] He incorrectly refers to Josippon as 'the Hebrew Josephus'; it is now known to be a 10th-c. compilation deriving much of its information from Latin versions of Josephus.

[20] See above, p. 102.

[21] De' Rossi's references are confused; the story occurs in BT *Yoma* 69a, *Lev. Rabbah* 13:5 (194) and *Midrash tehilim* on Ps. 18.

ology, including *Seder olam*, namely an underestimate by almost 180 years of the period of Persian rule, and hence of the duration of the Second Temple.

The reaction to Azariah was harsh. The book was printed in November 1573, and by April of the following year a group of Venetian rabbis headed by Samuel Judah Katzenellenbogen issued a manifesto stipulating that no Jew possess or read the book without permission from the sages of his city; when Azariah made some minor changes to his text the ban was lifted.[22] Karo[23] and later Maharal[24] nevertheless called for the book to be burned.

A generation or so later Judah Aryeh of Modena published, under a pseudonym and with a 'refutation' in his real name, *Kol sakhal* ('The Voice of a Fool'),[25] a more radical critique of rabbinic culture than Azariah's, and certainly indebted to the latter.[26] By this time the Middle Ages were ceding to modernity, Uriel da Costa (1585–1640) had twice been expelled from the community for denying the immortality of the soul and for contending that all extant religions were man-made, Spinoza (1632–77) had arrived on the scene, history was emancipated from theology, and the first steps had been taken in modern historical criticism of the Bible.

Moral Issues

Pre-Socratic philosophers articulated moral criticism of sacred texts; the Ionian poet Xenophanes (560–478 BCE) criticized Hesiod and Homer for having 'attributed to the gods all that is shameful and disgraceful among men—theft, fornication, and deception'.[27] Plato, devising an educational programme for his model city, gave an honoured place to 'music', including the art of poetry; but, like Xenophanes, he rejected much of the poetry of Homer and others on the grounds that it portrayed the lives of the gods in such a way that they might be taken as role models for unjust and immoral behaviour.[28] Subsequent debate between the Academy, which upheld Plato's scepticism towards Homer and the gods, and the Stoa, which sought to uphold 'tradition', is reflected not only in philosophical attacks on the Hebrew scriptures and Christianity, but in the Jewish and Christian defences which, ironically, resemble arguments advanced by Stoics in defence of the pagan *status quo*.

[22] De' Rossi, *Light of the Eyes*, p. xliii.
[23] Weinberg, introducing De' Rossi, *Light of the Eyes*, p. xxi, notes doubts as to the authenticity of the ban alleged to have been issued posthumously in Karo's name.
[24] Judah Loew b. Bezalel, *Be'er hagolah*, 6.   [25] Fishman, *Shaking the Pillars of Exile*.
[26] Ibid. 167.   [27] Cited by Sextus Empiricus, *Against Physicists* 9: 193 (p. 98).
[28] Plato, *Republic* from 377. See also *Republic* 522a; *Timaeus* 26e; *Gorgias* 527a. For a full assessment of Plato's attitude to myth see Brisson, *Plato the Myth Maker*.

The pagan philosopher Celsus, discussed in Chapter 7, likewise attacked the Bible, both because it attributed wicked deeds to many of its supposed heroes[29] and because it attributed character deficiencies to God, such as acting with passion.[30]

Modern readers of the Bible are often scandalized by passages which run counter to current moral consensus. Why, for instance, did God command that whole nations should be exterminated? How could Moses, days after God had proclaimed 'Thou shalt not murder', call on his brother Levites to slaughter brother, neighbour, and kin (Exod. 32: 27)? How can death sentences or excision be meted out so copiously for a host of offences,[31] many of them apparently trivial, such as preparing incense according to the formula prescribed for use in the sanctuary (Exod. 30: 33)?

Not every society has the same moral scruples. Ancient Romans, who were fond of slaughtering their enemies wholesale in battle, might not have baulked at what modern readers of the Bible regard as atrocities perpetrated in the name of God by the ancient Israelites; nor would the Crusaders under their hero Tancred, celebrated in Tasso's *Gerusalemme liberata*, when (having already killed the Jews) they systematically slaughtered all the Muslim men, women, and children they had confined in the al-Aksa Mosque of Jerusalem and sang hymns of joy to God over the bodies of the 'infidel'. Religious terrorists even today might regard the zealous, idol-smashing Israelites as model heroes.

Nevertheless, such matters did not go unremarked in the ancient world. Even in the Middle Ages, when it was more difficult to express one's views freely, Hiwi of Balkh, Afghanistan, a sceptical ninth-century Jewish pamphleteer, scandalized the faithful by '200 Questions' on the morality as well as the consistency and rationality of scripture, though the evidence that he produced an expurgated edition of the Bible for schools that omitted 'offensive' materials, such as stories of God acting dishonestly, is weak. Hiwi's original is lost, but Israel Davidson pieced together about a quarter of the questions from quotations that appear in the extant fragments of Sa'adiah's refutation, in the commentaries of Abraham Ibn Ezra, and in other works, some of them by Karaites.[32] Ibn Ezra seems particularly incensed by Hiwi's

---

[29] For example, Origen of Caesarea, *Origen contra Celsum* 4: 45 ff. (Chadwick, 220 ff.).

[30] For example, ibid. 4: 71 ff. (Chadwick, 240 ff.).

[31] The meaning of 'he shall be cut off from his people', sometimes rendered by terms such as 'excommunication', is unclear, but it is certainly something nasty.

[32] Davidson, *Saadia's Polemic*; Schechter, 'Geniza Specimens'; Soloweitschik and Rubascheff, *History of Biblical Criticism* (Heb.), 27.

rationalization of biblical miracles, such as when he suggests that Moses got the Israelites across the Red Sea because, unlike the Egyptians, he knew the shallow places (Exod. 14: 27), or that Moses' face was frighteningly pale, rather than shining, because he had not eaten bread for forty days (Exod. 34: 29);[33] but Hiwi was certainly concerned about moral and theological issues and contradictions too, such as why should the blood of animals be acceptable to God as an atonement, why is God represented as eating and as accepting bribes, or whether 2 Samuel 24: 7 contradicts 1 Chronicles 21: 5.[34]

Yet again, though, we discover that the criticisms which surface in the counter-tradition are echoed within the rabbinic tradition; several of Hiwi's questions reflect midrashic statements,[35] though he evidently found the answers unsatisfactory. Typically, the problems appear in the rabbinic sources not as critical arguments but as constructive interpretation, and numerous strategies are employed to sidestep the 'difficulties' of the texts.[36]

Obvious examples of the rabbis' sensitivity to moral critique include the refining of the law of the rebellious son (Deut. 21: 18–21) to the point where the conditions for its application were so outlandish that it was possible to deny that it had ever been applied,[37] and the boast of rabbis Akiva and Tarfon that if they had been in the Sanhedrin no one would ever have been judicially executed.[38]

By today's standards much rabbinic legislation is discriminatory. The Mishnah rules: 'If a Jew's ox gore the ox of a gentile he is exempt; if a gentile's ox gore a Jew's ox he must pay full compensation, whether the ox is *tam* or *muad*'.[39] The Tosefta adds, 'If a gentile's ox gore the ox of another gentile, then even if both parties agree to be judged by Jewish law, he must pay full damages, since for gentiles there is no difference between *tam* and *muad*.'[40] This appears to be straightforward discrimination against non-Jews, though

---

[33] Ibn Ezra, *Commentary* on Exod. 14: 27; 34: 29. Other examples are in Ibn Ezra on Exod. 16: 13, and his *Long Commentary* on Gen. 1: 1; 3: 9.

[34] Davidson, *Saadia's Polemic*, pp. 24–5, questions 14, 24, and 33.

[35] Other criticisms are found in the Pahlavi *Shikand Gûmânîk Vijâr*, a 9th-c. Zoroastrian critique of Islam, Judaism, and Christianity. Davidson, *Saadia's Polemic*, 80–2, reproduces E. E. West's translation from *The Sacred Books of the East*, vol. xxiv (Oxford, 1885, now available online); see also Neusner, 'Zoroastrian Critique'.

[36] See Solomon, 'Reading Intolerant Texts', and Lesser, '"It Is Difficult to Understand"'.

[37] BT *San.* 45b–46a, 68b–72a. The statement that the law never operated and never would operate is made on 71a, but contradicted by R. Jonathan who says, 'I saw it, and I sat upon his grave'—probably a homiletic statement, as Jonathan did not live at a time when such jurisdiction existed.   [38] Mishnah *Mak.* 1: 10.

[39] Mishnah *BK* 4: 3. *Tam* (an ox not known to be dangerous) normally pays half-compensation; *muad* 'warned', (i.e. established as dangerous) pays full compensation.

[40] Tosefta *BK* 4: 2.

perhaps, as argued by Bernard Jackson, it is the discriminatory consequence of applying defendants' law, in this case the Roman *actio de pauperie*, which does not differentiate between *tam* and *muad*.[41]

The rabbis were clearly uncomfortable with such rulings. The Babylonian Talmud reports that two Roman soldiers were despatched to study Torah under the sages, presumably with a view to making sure it was acceptable to the government of the day; when they departed they pronounced themselves satisfied with everything except the Mishnah ruling just cited.[42] The parallel in the Jerusalem Talmud identifies Rabban Gamaliel (presumably Gamaliel II) as the recipient of the delegation, and says that he thereupon decreed that anything stolen (wrongfully obtained?) from a gentile was forbidden, and a desecration of the divine Name.[43] The story may reflect actual Roman criticism of discriminatory legislation, or may be apocryphal; either way it indicates qualms of rabbinic conscience in the face of a seeming injustice demanded by the Torah. The same Gamaliel expressed satisfaction when he found a pretext to emancipate his slave,[44] and rejected a proposal to limit the proprietary rights of wives: 'We are embarrassed by the previous [restrictions], but you propose to add new ones!';[45] in both instances he may have felt that Roman practice was morally preferable.

Some moral objections came to the fore only in recent times. For instance, the Torah repeatedly inculcates the virtue of *kana'ut* (zeal) against idolatry, as in Deuteronomy 12: 3. The positive side of this is the devotion to God, and consequently to justice and compassion, that it demands. Compassion, however, is explicitly denied to 'idolaters', that is, people whose worship is focused on images. Whatever views one may have about the historical circumstances in which scripture first appeared, it runs counter to the moral convictions of most people today that they should be guided by such verses in their own relationships with, say, Hindus or Buddhists whose worship is focused through idols.

Only very recently have people begun to think of 'racism' as reprehensible. What we now reject as racist attitudes were normal in the pre-modern world and are assumed in scripture. Genesis 9: 25 declares that the 'sons of Ham'

---

[41] Jackson, 'On the Problem of Roman Influence', 168 ff. Jackson's suggestion does not suffice to explain the exemption of the Jew whose ox gores the ox of a gentile. On the extent of rabbinic jurisdiction under Roman occupation see M. Goodman, *State and Society in Roman Galilee* and Oppenheimer, 'Jewish Penal Authority'.

[42] BT *BK* 38a. Novak, *Natural Law*, sees the rabbinic response as arising from an apparent contradiction between their perception of natural law, rooted in Torah, and the specific provisions of statutory Jewish law. Jackson, 'Review', disputes this.   [43] JT *BK* 4: 3 (4b).

[44] BT *BK* 74b; cf. Rabbi Eliezer's emancipating his slave to make up a quorum for prayer (BT *Ber.* 47b and *Git.* 38b).   [45] Mishnah *Ket.* 8: 1.

(black people) are to be slaves to the 'sons of Shem', and was frequently cited by Christians as a proof-text against the abolition of slavery or in support of the apartheid system of South Africa.[46]

Also contrary to Enlightenment notions of equality is the privileged status afforded to *kohanim* (priests), Levites, Israelites, males, and free men. Biblical legislation offers *protection* to foreigners, females, and slaves, not equal status.

Scientific Inaccuracy

Scientific inaccuracy starts with the flat-earth account of Genesis, outmoded already in ancient Greece; Aristotle, drawing on still earlier work, advanced three proofs that the earth was a sphere.[47] Ptolemy (90–168), whose cosmology dominated the Middle Ages, held that the spherical earth was surrounded by invisible spheres carrying the sun, moon, planets, and stars.

The early rabbis are vague on such matters. The Mishnah rules that a human statue with a ball in its hand must be assumed to be an idol,[48] and the Jerusalem Talmud comments:

'A ball', because the world is made like a ball. Rabbi Jonah said: When Alexander of Macedon wanted to ascend he went up, and up, and up, until he saw the world like a ball and the sea like a dish; that is why they sculpt him with a ball in his hand. Then picture him with a dish in his hand? He ruled over the earth only, but the Holy One, blessed be He, rules also over the sea and the dry land.[49]

Some think this means that Rabbi Jonah acknowledged that the world was a sphere, though a plain reading indicates that he was thinking of only the dry land as a sphere, partly submerged in a flat ocean. A debate cited in the names of the second-century rabbis Eliezer and Joshua as to whether the earth was created starting with the middle or the edges quite clearly assumes a flat earth,[50] as do other talmudic passages.[51]

Other rabbis held divergent views. Since the close of the Talmud rabbis have interpreted Genesis 1 in terms first of Ptolemaic astronomy, then Copernican, and more recently in terms of 'big bang' cosmology. Some have disdained the attempt to harmonize scripture with science and have focused instead on reading mystical doctrines into the Genesis text; this is ironic

---

[46] On Jewish attitudes see Schorsch, *Jews and Blacks*, ch. 6.

[47] Aristotle, *De caelo* 2.13, pp. 297b–298a.   [48] Mishnah *AZ* 3: 1.

[49] JT *AZ* 3: 1 (42c). The passage is cited in *Num. Rabbah* 13: 14. For an interpretation of this passage see my article 'Judaism and Natural Science'.

[50] BT *Yoma* 54b.   [51] Notably BT *Pes.* 94a and *Ḥag.* 12b–13a.

since, in its ancient world context, Genesis 1 is probably as de-mythologizing as one can get, as it pointedly omits and effectively denies the existence of anything but God and the 'natural' world. The interpretation of Genesis through the ages carries self-delusion to unprecedented heights; the best one can say is that the convolutions of the interpreters indicate that they are aware of a serious discrepancy between text and reality.

Several scientific errors occur in the classical rabbinic texts.[52] Here is a selection.

Where does rain come from? Rabbi Eliezer stated correctly that it originated as vapour rising from the ocean; Rabbi Joshua vigorously retorted that it was sent down from heaven, and that even though scripture states 'a mist arose from the earth' (Gen. 2: 6), the clouds that gave rise to this mist were merely a receptacle for rain from above.[53] An anonymous teacher states, 'There is a cubicle in the sky from which rain comes.'[54]

The third-century Babylonian *amora* Shmuel laid claim to extensive knowledge of medicine and astronomy. He had a reputation for eye salves,[55] and asserted that he had remedies for all bad eating habits except three.[56] He boasted, 'The paths of heaven are as familiar to me as the streets of Nehardea',[57] but as he left no pharmacopoeia, no star atlas, nor a map of Nehardea, it is impossible to assess any of these claims. Shmuel's calculation of the *tekufah*—the average period between solstice and equinox, or precisely a quarter of the solar year—is 91 days and 7 hours.[58] This coincides with the length of the Julian year, and is inaccurate; hence the Jewish festivals now occur on average almost two weeks later in the year than their relationship with the seasons requires. A more accurate figure, of 91 days 7 hours 28 minutes 51.34 seconds, is attributed by Jewish scholars from about the tenth century to Shmuel's contemporary Adda bar Ahava; this value is close to that given by Hipparchus in the second century BCE, but it is not mentioned in the Talmud, and the link with Adda bar Ahava is spurious.[59]

The sages evidently believed, like other people in their time, in spon-

---

[52] Cf. Lieberman, *Hellenism in Jewish Palestine*, 180–93, drawing on work of Lewysohn, Preuss, and Löw (see bibliography).   [53] BT *Ta'an.* 9b.

[54] BT *Ta'an.* 8b.   [55] BT *Shab.* 108b.

[56] BT *BM* 113b. Several authors have written that Shmuel claimed to have remedies for all *maladies* except three; one can only assume they ignored the context of the remark.

[57] BT *Ber.* 58b.   [58] BT *Eruv.* 56a. The attribution to Shmuel may be questioned.

[59] W. H. Feldman, *Rabbinic Mathematics and Astronomy*, 74–6. Maimonides, *Mishneh torah*, 'Hilkhot kidush haḥodesh' 9 and 10 explains both calculations of the *tekufah*. The attribution of the more accurate figure to Adda bar Ahava may well be an attempt to claim a Jewish origin for Hipparchus's calculation. On calendrical calculations see also E. Frank, *Talmudic and Rabbinical Chronology*, and S. Stern, *Calendar and Community*.

taneous generation. Lice were said not to 'be fruitful and multiply', implying that they did not reproduce themselves, but were generated spontaneously from sweat or dirt; fleas, on the other hand, were fruitful and multiplied.[60] Likewise, the Mishnah,[61] in the context of creatures in the process of formation, refers to a mouse, 'half flesh and half earth', that was widely believed in the ancient world to demonstrate abiogenesis;[62] and an anonymous *baraita* rounds off its catalogue of transformations by stating that after seven years (in the grave) the human spine turns into a serpent—that is, if its owner had failed to bow down at the thanksgiving blessing.[63] The rabbis denied that mushrooms derived nourishment from the soil,[64] or that bees played any part in the production of honey other than extracting it from plants (whereas in fact they mix it with their saliva).[65] Several of these matters have halakhic consequences.

On the other hand, they occasionally use observation to establish a correct conclusion, such as that hair grows from the roots, not the tip.[66]

The Bible states that the Sea of Solomon (a large basin for ablutions) was 10 cubits in diameter and 30 cubits round (1 Kgs 7: 23). The rabbis do not take this as an approximation, but use it as the basis for a precise calculation of how many times the volume of a *mikveh* the Sea contained.[67] The values $\pi = 3$ and $\sqrt{2} = 1.4$ are standard in rabbinic calculation, the Mishnah for instance stating, 'What must the circumference be if it opens to (i.e. has a diameter of) a span? If it is round, three spans, and if it is square four spans, since the square is a quarter more than the round.'[68] This was intended to be a precise relationship, otherwise it could not have been used as the basis for leniencies as well as stringencies in the law. It was not challenged until the Middle Ages, when Jews such as Abraham bar Hiyya were serious mathematicians. Halakhic problems remain.

Can a halakhah be changed if it transpires that it was based on erroneous scientific understanding? A striking example of this occurs in connection with blood typing. The Talmud, contrary to Galen who thought that females

---

[60] BT *Shab.* 107b. Aristotle, *De generatione animalium*, held that oysters, mussels, mosquitoes, flies, and some plants were spontaneously generated. Pliny adds more species, and Sextus Empiricus, *Outlines of Pyrrhonism*, 40–4, cites the variety of modes of generation as a cause of contrariety in sense-impression. The 4th-c. Christian Lactantius pointed to abiogenesis as nature's demonstration of the possibility of the virgin birth! Even Pasteur, in the 19th c., did not finally lay abiogenesis to rest.   [61] Mishnah *Ḥul.* 9: 6.

[62] Cf. Ovid, *Metamorphoses* 1: 423 ff; Pliny, *Natural History* 9: 84, 179.   [63] BT *BK* 16a.

[64] BT *Ber.* 40b.   [65] BT *Bekh.* 7b.   [66] BT *Nazir* 39a–b.   [67] BT *Eruv.* 14b.

[68] Mishnah *Ohol.* 12: 6. 'A quarter more than the round' means a quarter of the larger figure, the size of the square; we would say 'a third more', referring to the smaller figure, the size of the circle.

merely provided a nurturing environment for the male seed,[69] unequivocally states that blood is 'from the mother':

There are three partners in [the generation of] a person, the Holy One, blessed be He, his father, and his mother. His father generates the seed of whiteness, out of which [are formed] bones, sinews, nails, the [soft matter of the] brain in his head, and the white of the eye. His mother generates the red seed, out of which [are formed] skin, flesh and hair, blood,[70] and the dark part of the eye. The Holy One, blessed be He, puts in him *ruah* and *neshamah*,[71] and facial appearance, and the seeing of the eye, the hearing of the ear, the speech of the mouth, the movement of the legs, and discernment and understanding. When his time comes to depart from the world, the Holy One, blessed be He, takes His portion, and leaves to his mother and father their portion.[72]

A Sephardi Chief Rabbi of Israel, Rabbi Ben-Zion Uzziel (1880–1953), ruled on this basis that blood typing could not be used as a means of ascertaining paternity, since 'any scientific examination is nullified by this trustworthy tradition of our sages all of whose words were spoken by divine inspiration'.[73] His Ashkenazi counterpart, Chief Rabbi Herzog, strongly differed. In a letter dated 1954 he wrote:

How unfortunate it is that while science is progressively conquering worlds and discovering all sorts of secrets, although it too errs at times, we bury our heads in the sand like that well-known bird and look no further with regard to scientific matters that concern our Holy Torah.[74]

Herzog's sentiments follow a long tradition. Azariah de' Rossi, reflecting earlier comments such as that of Maimonides regarding the mathematics of the sages,[75] wrote:

Our sages, blessed be their memory, treated such scientific subjects as astronomy and cosmology from a completely human perspective; each sage addressed those subjects according to his intellectual ability or else by means of the knowledge he had acquired from the recognized scholars of whatsoever nationality. Prophetic inspiration did not aid their endeavour in any way. With their good will, we may therefore give a hearing to the later sages who wrote against them and evaluate the disputants according to our intellectual capacity . . . the superiority of the ancient over the modern consists in matters that are dependent on prophecy since he would

[69] Galen, *On the Natural Faculties* I: 6, 11 and 2: 3, 83.
[70] 'Blood' is absent from the standard Vilna text, but the Vilna Gaon and other commentators insert it and it is present in the Munich manuscript.
[71] These two words, meaning respectively 'wind' and 'breath', carry also the ideas of 'spirit' and 'soul' respectively.   [72] BT *Nid.* 31a.
[73] *Sha'arei uzi'el*, ii. 40: 18.   [74] Cited in Frimer, 'Jewish Law and Science', 42–4.
[75] Maimonides, *Guide* iii. 14 (p. 459 of Pines' translation).

have been closer in time to those who were prophetically inspired; the modern, on the other hand, is in a more advantageous position in matters which stem from speculative thinking and empirical investigation.[76]

Others were more defensive. Azariah's Polish contemporary Solomon Luria (1510–74), for instance, held that the sages were right but that nature had changed since their time. He writes: 'There is an ancient ban of excommunication on those who rely on the cures prescribed in the Talmud. [This is so that we should] not bring the sages into disrepute, for [people] do not know that there are differences in place and in time.'[77]

It may be argued that errors of this kind are no worse than those found in other religious traditions, and are typical of their era. That is true, but it is not the point. If the Bible and the rabbis were merely reporting what they had been told, directly or indirectly, by God, it ought to have been *better* than other religious traditions or purely human science, and to have withstood the test of time, which it manifestly has not. Of course it is of little intrinsic importance that the festivals fall on average about eleven days later in the solar year than they should; but if, as has been claimed, the calculation of the calendar is a divine science by which Israel is distinguished from the nations,[78] it ought at least to be accurate.

Fantasy, Arbitrariness, Superstition

One man's superstition is another man's deep spiritual conviction; what to one is arbitrary or absurd is to another necessary and profound. Few things in Judaism are more beautiful and meaningful than the sabbath, and its profound teachings on human dignity and equality and on the blessings of creation are a gift to humankind, yet Plutarch dismissed it as an idle superstition. Or maybe this is not quite fair. What Plutarch actually wrote was: 'But the Jews, because it was the sabbath day, sat in their places immovable, while the enemy were planting ladders and capturing the defences, and they did not get up, but remained there, fast bound in the toils of superstition as in one great net.'[79] So perhaps Plutarch condemned only those Jews who did not foresee the rabbinic halakhah that self-defence is mandatory on the sabbath!

Celsus seems to have been aware of Jewish as well as Christian responses to accusations that their stories were absurd: 'The more reasonable Jews

[76] De' Rossi, *Light of the Eyes*, 268–9.   [77] Luria, *Yam shel shelomoh* on Ḥulin 8, no. 12.
[78] BT *Shab.* 75a, commenting on Deut. 4: 6, as often interpreted; Rashi, curiously, thinks the pre-eminence of Israel arises from their ability to forecast the weather!
[79] Plutarch, *Moralia: On Superstition*, 169C (p. 481).

and Christians are ashamed of these things and try somehow to allegorize them.'[80] Perhaps he was thinking of Aristobulus or Philo.

Post-talmudic rabbis, many of whom practised medicine, relied on Hippocrates, Galen, and their successors for their professional skills rather than on the medical recommendations scattered through the Talmud. The halakhic rulings of Abaye, head of the academy of Pumbedita in the early fourth century, fill the pages of the Babylonian Talmud and are regarded with veneration, even though there were only six instances in which his view prevailed over that of his rival, Rava;[81] the same cannot be said for his folk-medicine remedies and dietary advice, introduced by the phrase 'Mother told me . . .'.[82]

Demons, possession, and the evil eye—notably absent from the Hebrew scriptures—figure commonly in rabbinic literature. Numerous Hebrew amulets and incantation bowls from the first to fifth centuries CE were recovered in the twentieth century and studied by archaeologists; many of them were written by non-Jews evidently hoping to capture the efficacy of the 'Jewish magic' which was held in high repute in late antiquity.[83] Two-headed monsters, stones that shine by night, the 'rock of the nail', and a variety of amulets are among the items that link rabbinic folklore with the surrounding world.[84]

The power of the stars to influence people's lives is taken for granted. Two rabbis, Hanina and Yohanan, debated whether Israel (the Jewish people) was subject to the stars; Hanina said yes, Yohanan said no.[85] Either way, astrology was accepted as a valid science; the only issue was whether Israelites were protected from its influence.

Despite this, Maimonides wrote a forthright letter to the rabbis of Marseilles denouncing astrology as a pseudo-science; he claimed that he had carried out empirical tests on various astrological theories, and that astrology was nonsense.[86] In his *Mishneh torah* he formulated a more general rejection of pseudo-sciences:

[80] Origen of Caesarea, *Origen contra Celsum* 4: 38 (Chadwick, 213), apropos of the story of God fashioning Adam allegedly with his hands.   [81] BT *BM* 22*b*.

[82] BT *Shab.* 134*a*, *Kid.* 31*b*, and parallels. There is a large collection of magical 'cures', mostly not attributed to Abaye's foster-mother, in *Git.* 68*b* ff., though she has one on 67*b* and another on 70*a*. See Kottek, '*Amra li em*'.

[83] Naveh and Shaked, *Amulets and Magic Bowls*; Naveh, *On Sherd and Papyrus*; Neusner, Frerichs, and Flesher (eds.), *Religion, Science and Magic*; Schäfer, 'Jewish Magic Literature'; Schiffman and Swartz, *Hebrew and Aramaic Incantation Texts*; Trachtenberg, *Jewish Magic and Superstition*.   [84] See Sperber, *Magic and Folklore*.

[85] BT *Shab.* 156*a*; Bar-Ilan, *Astrology* (Heb.).

[86] Maimonides, *Igerot harambam*, ii, pp. 478–90. Shailat (p. 466) notes that the letter was written in Hebrew as the rabbis of Provence did not know Arabic, and that it is dated 11 Tishrei in the Seleucid year that is the equivalent of AM 4955 (1194/5) or 4956 (1195/6).

And all these matters [*sc.* astrology, necromancy, etc.] are falsehood and deceit, by means of which idolatrous priests in ancient times misled the people of the nations to follow them. It is not fitting that [the people of] Israel, who are wise and learned, should be attracted by such nonsense or entertain the possibility that there is any benefit in it; as it is said, 'Surely there is no divination in Jacob, and no augury in Israel' (Numbers 23: 23), and 'Those nations whose place you are taking listen to soothsayers and augurs, but the Lord your God does not permit you to do this' (Deuteronomy 18: 14). Whoever believes in such things, or anything like them, and thinks that they are true, though the Torah forbade them, is a fool, an ignoramus, and in the category of women and children whose comprehension is imperfect. But wise people, of perfect understanding, know through convincing proofs that all these things which the Torah forbade are not wisdom, but empty nonsense which attracts the ignorant and on account of which they abandon all the paths of truth; that is why the Torah states, in prohibiting this nonsense, 'You shall be perfect with the Lord your God' (Deuteronomy 18: 13).[87]

Jews who preceded Maimonides in his rejection of astrology included Bahya ibn Pakuda (eleventh century)[88] and, half-heartedly, Judah Halevi (*c.*1075–1141),[89] but this enlightened view convinced few scholars at the time and had virtually no impact on popular belief. As late as the eighteenth century the Vilna Gaon sharply criticized Maimonides for denying the existence of demons;[90] even today reactionary Orthodox leaders endorse such beliefs, including astrology, on the grounds that they were accepted by the rabbis of the Talmud.

Conclusion

In this chapter we have seen how the Bible was subjected to criticism, both benign and hostile, in the ancient world, and how such criticism affected the expression of Judaism. The major responses of the rabbis to criticism were the development of the 'reconciling hermeneutic' and the concept of the Oral Torah. These responses generated further criticisms, and additional problems were raised over the centuries by the progress of science and changing moral perspectives. Internal disputes, such as those of the Maimunists and

---

[87] Maimonides, *Mishneh torah*, 'Hilkhot avodah zarah' 11: 16. He argues the case against astrology at great length in the *Letter to the Congregation of Marseilles*, stressing that astrology was not a Greek science, but part of the religion of Chaldeans, Egyptians, and Canaanites; see Maimonides, *Letters of Maimonides*, trans. Leon D. Stitskin, 113–29.

[88] Langermann, 'Maimonides' Repudiation of Astrology', reviews precedents as well as Christian and Islamic parallels. See also A. Marx, 'Correspondence between the Rabbis'.

[89] In *Kuzari* 4: 9 he rejects astrology as it does not yield firm results and is not a revealed science.   [90] Elijah of Vilna, *Be'ur hagra*, n. 13 on *Shulḥan arukh*, 'Yoreh de'ah' 179.

anti-Maimunists, represent different approaches to the resolution of conflict; the former are prepared to accept external evidence and to abandon non-halakhic elements in the Talmud, whereas for the latter the priority is to uphold the authority of the rabbis in all matters, if necessary rejecting external evidence or interpreting the rabbis in mystical terms.

The problems raised in this chapter are serious enough, but worse was to come in the early modern period. We turn now to historical criticism of the Bible, which threatened to overturn the foundations of both Judaism and Christianity.

THE RISE OF
HISTORICAL CRITICISM

HISTORICAL CRITICISM applies to the Bible the same investigative
techniques as to any other ancient writing; with the rise of archaeology
and the recovery of ancient languages and literatures it has become increasingly dependent on sources of information external to the Bible itself. The
traditional Jew or Christian, however, accords the Bible a status quite unlike
that of other literature. The historian reads the text one way, according to its
historical context; the priest or rabbi reads another way, within the context of
his tradition.

Only in the modern world did it become clear that the two ways of reading were not compatible, and that historical study of the text of the Bible lay
beyond the realm of theology. In this chapter we investigate how the two
approaches diverged.

Issues of interpretation were always divisive, since every faith community
is convinced of the absolute correctness of its own interpretative tradition.
Christians, from the earliest times, accused Jews of misinterpreting scripture
(as Jews accused them), but they did not, as a rule, accuse them of falsifying
the text, since they too subscribed to the integrity and authenticity of a text
they regarded as sacred. Both Jews and Christians made every effort to ensure
that their texts and translations were accurate.

Accusations of falsifying the text were, however, made by Muslims,
following earlier aspersions cast by pagans, some Christians, and Samaritans
on the work of Ezra.[1] Though they declared Moses was a true prophet and the
Torah was true, Muslims accused both Jews and Christians of changes (*tabdil*)
and forgeries (*tahrif*) in the text, since in several instances it conflicts with
Qur'an or Hadith. 'The' Torah, that is, the one received from God by Moses,
was certainly true, but the actual scriptures possessed by Jews and Christians
were not the *true* Torah. By no means all Muslims took, or take, this line; some
claim merely that Jews and Christians *misinterpret* the Torah and the Gospels.

---

[1] Lazarus-Yaffe, *Intertwined Worlds*, 50–74.

An eleventh-century Spanish Jewish scholar, perhaps Samuel Hanagid, was alleged to have published some criticism of the Qur'an.[2] Whether in reply or retaliation, or simply out of pique at Samuel's prominence, the Muslim scholar and polemicist Ibn Hazm of Córdoba (994–1064), who had known Samuel as a young man, composed a vitriolic attack on Judaism. In this and other tracts Ibn Hazm touches on Jews and Judaism and develops the accusation that Jews and Christians have corrupted the text of the Bible; he identifies the principal forger as Ezra.[3] Few of his aspersions on the text would impress the modern reader, and he is not always well informed. However, the book must have made a lasting impression not only on Muslims but also on Jews, since Solomon ben Adret found it necessary to respond to it over two centuries later in Christian Spain,[4] and Simon ben Tsemah Duran (Tashbats, 1361–1444) responded even later than that.[5]

Clearly, then, Jews in the West in the late Middle Ages were no strangers to attacks on the integrity of the biblical text. Sometimes they themselves challenged the traditions of authorship, along the lines of the opinion mooted in the Talmud that the last eight verses of the Pentateuch, recording the death of Moses, were added (under divine dictation) by Joshua.[6] Moses ben Samuel Hakohen Gikatilla, a contemporary of Rashi (late eleventh century) in Muslim Spain, is cited as claiming that the final part of Isaiah was from the hand of a later prophet, and that the author of Psalm 106: 47 lived in Babylon.[7] Abraham Ibn Ezra endorsed the late composition of Isaiah 40–66 and hinted at the non-Mosaic authorship of various pentateuchal verses,[8] though he roundly castigated the grammarian Isaac ibn Yashush of Toledo (d. 1056) for daring to suggest that the list of the kings of Edom in Genesis 36: 31–9 had

[2] Scholars are divided on this. Abbas suggested that the criticism was the work of Samuel's son, Joseph; Stroumsa that it was a fabrication of Ibn Hazm, and the arguments refuted were those of the Muslim heresiarch Ibn al-Rawandi; Fierro that it was the work of an unknown Jewish sceptic; Brann that Ibn Hazm constructed a typological figure embodying a spectrum of beliefs offensive to Muslims. For references see Adang, *Muslim Writers on Judaism*, 59–69.

[3] The text was analysed by Perlmann, 'Eleventh-Century Andalusian Authors'. Adang, *Muslim Writers on Judaism*, 237–48, discusses Ibn Hazm's allegations in detail.

[4] Solomon ben Adret, *Ma'amar al yishma'el* ('Treatise against an Ishmaelite'), in Perles, *R. Salomo b. Abraham b. Adereth.*

[5] Martin Jacobs has been working on Duran's *Keshet umagen*, MS Oxford, Bodleiana 151; publication is awaited.   [6] See above, Ch. 2.

[7] His commentaries are lost. Citations of his work by other authors are collected in Poznański, *Mose b. Samuel hakohen Ibn Chiquitilla.*

[8] Ibn Ezra on Gen. 12: 6; Deut. 1: 2 and 34: 6. Spinoza, *Tractatus Theologico-Politicus* VIII, leans heavily on Ibn Ezra.

been composed in the days of King Jehoshaphat, some centuries after Moses.[9] Ibn Ezra was understandably reticent on the matter, but his hints were deciphered; his commentary directly influenced Spinoza[10] and the early modern textual and historical criticism of Isaac de la Peyrère, Uriel d'Acosta, Thomas Hobbes, Jean Astruc, and others.

Less well known are the historical speculations of some Jewish commentators in the Rhineland in the twelfth and thirteenth centuries. Israel Ta-Shma drew attention to an anonymous commentary on Psalms inserted in a Rashi manuscript which carries a colophon dated 1285; the author, ignoring the superscriptions on the Psalms, gives historical dating for individual psalms, placing many of them long after the time of King David. Ta-Shma concludes that at a later period this approach was rejected by Ashkenazim.[11]

The Beginnings of Biblical Criticism

The questioning of traditional assumptions by a small number of medieval Jewish scholars was a marginal phenomenon, vigorously opposed by the mainstream religious leadership. Only in early modern times, with the secularization of knowledge and the weakening of clerical control, was it possible for such radical notions to be taken seriously.

Among those who questioned traditional attitudes to scripture and authority in the seventeenth century were several who hailed from families who had been forced converts from Judaism to Christianity in Spain and Portugal; they included Uriel d'Acosta, Isaac de la Peyrère (1596–1676), and Baruch Spinoza. If, like a member of a Converso family, you are brought up in a religion you are taught to question, and then you revert to what you think is your 'proper' religion but doesn't turn out to be quite what you thought it was, the habit of questioning persists.

But the roots of historical criticism in Christian Europe lay elsewhere, in Renaissance and humanist culture, in the rediscovery of a world of wisdom and vitality that lay outside the dominant Christian tradition. Independence of thought leads to the questioning of conventional teaching, and fascination with ancient texts sharpens the critical skills of the scholar. If the newly acquired knowledge of Greek and the availability of authentic manuscripts of

---

[9] Ibn Ezra on Gen. 36: 31 says that Ibn Yashush's book should be burned. See Fishman, *Shaking the Pillars of Exile*, 204 n. 63, and her references to 'certain Byzantine Jewish scholars recorded in ninth-century sources'.

[10] Spinoza, *Tractatus Theologico-Politicus* VII and VIII.

[11] Ta-Shma, 'An Anonymous Critical Commentary' (Heb.), and id., 'Note on Biblical Criticism' (Heb.).

works by Plato and Aristotle force you to question the medieval scholastics'
interpretations, it is natural to question both the Vulgate translation of the
Bible and the way the church interprets it. Renaissance scholars were first
concerned with Greek and the New Testament, but it was not long before they
turned to Jewish scholars such as Elijah Levita and Obadiah Sforno (*c*.1470–
1550) for guidance in Hebrew, and they soon began to subject the Hebrew text
of the Bible to literary and historical analysis in the same way they had already
dealt with the Greek and Latin classics and the New Testament. Christian
'Hebraism' was part of this process; the new independent understanding of
the Hebrew scriptures was independent of church tradition, but heavily
dependent on the achievement of medieval Jewish grammarians and Bible
commentators such as Rashi, Abraham Ibn Ezra, and David Kimhi.

Douglas Knight has described how the Council of Trent (1545–8) formulated the concept of an oral tradition, a *traditio oralis*, in the context of church
teaching. The rejection of this notion was a cornerstone of the Reformation's
sola scriptura programme; *sola scriptura* meant that only scripture was authoritative, that is, the word of the Bible, and not the 'oral tradition' of the church.
But *sola scriptura* demands careful examination of the text, and this yields
surprises.

Knight describes Richard Simon (1638–1712) as 'the pioneer of historico-
critical biblical research and . . . the precursor of the tradito-historical investigation of the Old Testament'.[12] 'The book of Genesis, for example, can be
Holy Scripture without being the literary product of Moses . . . With Simon
the basic idea of tradition and transmission gains central significance . . .
What caused Simon to propound this idea? . . . the realization that the
Tridentine *traditio oralis* was relevant also for the biblical period . . . biblical
research must be concerned with the history of the Old Testament as
literature.'[13]

Simon was familiar with the Jewish idea of Oral Torah; he certainly studied
with Jews and is said to have considered with his friend Jonah Salvador, an
Italian Jew, a project to translate the Talmud. Guy G. Stroumsa, having drawn
attention to the influence on Simon of Judah Aryeh of Modena's *Historia de'
riti hebraici*, observes:

Simon's attitude towards the Karaites is ambivalent. On the one hand, their rejection of the Talmud seems close to Jesus's rejection of most rabbinical traditions . . .
In that sense, he feels closer to the Karaites than to the Rabbanites. On the other
hand, Catholics and Rabbanites have in common the respect for tradition (of the

---

[12] Simon wrote a *Histoire critique du Vieux Testament*.
[13] Knight, *Rediscovering the Traditions of Israel*, 44–50.

rabbis or of the fathers). For both, the text of the Bible is not self-explanatory, and can be properly understood only with the help of tradition . . . he addresses letters for a Protestant friend, Frémond d'Ablancourt: 'Mon cher Caraïte', and signs them 'Le Rabbahniste'.[14]

Once you have started to read the Bible independently of tradition, whether the tradition of the rabbis or the tradition of the church, you may easily derive from it a theology at variance with that of the tradition. Theology then becomes an independent discipline, potentially in conflict with the rabbis or the church. As Henning Graf Reventlow notes, biblical theology as an independent discipline was a natural consequence of the Protestant call for *sola scriptura* and its abandonment of church tradition. Johann Philipp Gabler articulated the requirements for a biblical theology independent of church tradition in his inaugural lecture at Altdorf in 1787:

True biblical theology treats in an historical manner of what the sacred scriptures perceive of divine things; dogmatic theology, on the other hand, treats in a didactic manner of what a particular theologian . . . philosophizes rationally on divine matters.[15]

For Christians, an independent 'Old Testament theology' necessitated an independent 'New Testament theology', and problems arose of the relationship between Old and New Testament theologies and of the relationship of both with systematic, or dogmatic, theology.

The development of independent biblical studies brought home to Jews how different the world outlook of the Bible was from that of the rabbis. Symptomatic of the dissonance between Bible and rabbinic tradition was the low place accorded to Bible studies in the traditional yeshivas; the Talmud, rather than the Bible, reflected the realities of Jewish life in central and eastern Europe. Traditional rabbis such as Elijah of Vilna (the Vilna Gaon, 1720–97) who encouraged Bible studies did not conceive them as a discipline independent of rabbinic tradition; to the contrary, their understanding of Bible rested on a firm foundation of rabbinic sources. But very soon, in the West, new Jewish theologies appeared which were driven more by contemporary philosophies than by rabbinic texts, and were in some cases hostile to the rabbinic tradition; we shall meet some of them in Chapter 17.

---

[14] Stroumsa, 'Jewish Myth and Ritual', 28.

[15] J. P. Gabler, as cited in Reventlow, *Problems of Old Testament Theology*, 3–4. The title of Gabler's lecture was a lecture in itself: *Oratio de justo discrimine theologiae biblicae et dogmaticae regundisque recte utrius finibus* 'On the Correct Distinction between Dogmatic and Biblical Theology and the Right Definition of their Goals'.

Deists and Sceptics

What most people understand by 'scepticism' nowadays is a philosophy of doubt, mainly directed *against* religion. The term derives from the Greek verb *skeptomai*, a neutral word that simply means 'to inquire', and should be opposed to 'dogmatism' rather than to 'religion'. Only since the Enlightenment has 'scepticism' come to mean primarily religious disbelief.[16]

Scepticism as a formal movement is traced back to Pyrrhon of Elis (*c.*360–272 BCE). Pyrrhon travelled with Alexander the Great, and saw in the fakirs of India an example of happiness flowing from indifference to circumstances. He concluded that man must suspend judgement (he must practise *epochē*— a term famously revived by the phenomenologist Edmund Husserl) on the reliability of sense perceptions and simply live according to appearances. The closest biblical analogue is Ecclesiastes, possibly composed under Pyrrhonist influence.

Sextus Empiricus (third century CE) was one of the last of the ancient Sceptics; he left two works, *Outlines of Pyrrhonism* (*Hypotyposeis*) and *Adversus mathematicos*, that were rediscovered in the Renaissance and strongly influenced the development of modern scepticism. He argued that people who thought that they could know reality were constantly disturbed and frustrated; if they would suspend judgement and live according to appearances, customs, and natural inclinations, they would find peace of mind (*ataraxia* 'imperturbability'). This attitude appealed greatly to scholars who suffered through the wearisome and insoluble theological controversies of the Reformation; you could suspend judgement on all but the clearest issues, and adjust yourself to life under the dominant church even when it did not command intellectual assent.

If you doubt the reliability of human reason you can either suspend judgement with regard to the truth, as the Pyrrhonists recommended, adapting yourself to life with doubt, or you can declare reason inadequate and make a leap of faith. Augustine, in his *Contra academicos*, and later the Muslim philosopher al-Ghazali (1058–1111) and the Jewish Judah Halevi, were 'sceptics' in this latter sense; reason, though a God-given faculty, was inadequate either to establish or refute religious truth, which could only be acquired through the 'mystery' of faith.

The attitude of enquiry stirred by the revival of Scepticism encouraged people to question traditional assumptions about the origin and nature of the biblical text. More specifically, it paved the way for the growth of Deism, that

[16] On early modern scepticism see Popkin, *History of Scepticism*.

is, belief in the existence of a Creator and in moral standards, but rejection of
the idea that God has revealed his precise will.

Reventlow stressed the significance for biblical criticism of theological
developments in England between the Reformation and the Enlightenment,
and especially of the impact of Deism;[17] in a penetrating chapter on Thomas
Hobbes (1588–1679) he demonstrated the intricate and peculiar relationship
in England between political authority, theology, and biblical interpretation.

Edward Herbert, Lord Cherbury (1582–1648) was a pioneer of English
Deism; theologically, he stood between the Cambridge Platonists and the
Latitudinarians. In his tract *De veritate* he aims to rebut the arguments of
the Sceptics. 'Truth exists', he boldly declaims.[18] Though it has little to do with
textual criticism, his formulation of what he calls (borrowing Stoic terminology) *notitiae communes circa religionem*, or common ideas on religion, points
to a new way of understanding the authority of scripture, not for its dogma
and rules, but as confirmation of the religious fundamentals on which all
reasonable people might agree. Herbert recognizes five *notitiae*: that there is a
supreme being; that worship is due to this being; that the essence of religion
is morality; evil deeds should be expiated through repentance; there are
reward and punishment after this life. This 'natural religion', or ethical
rationalism, is, for Herbert as it would be for Spinoza, the criterion by which
one should judge what in scripture might be regarded as the Word of God.[19]

In the eighteenth-century Enlightenment the more aggressive Deism and
anti-religious scepticism of Voltaire and other *philosophes* led to scathing
attacks on the morality of scripture as well as on its internal inconsistency.

The Bible as Literature

A line runs from Azariah de' Rossi (see Chapter 9) to Johann Gottfried
Herder (1744–1803). De' Rossi headed the final chapter of his *Imrei binah*
'On the poems composed in the holy tongue'.[20] He rambles from references
to Aristotle's *Poetics* to Jerome, to a range of Jewish authorities from Philo to
Abravanel, to his personal conversations with the Provenzali brothers of
Mantua, and throws in for good measure a poem composed for his own
epitaph. But he also throws new light on the nature of biblical poetry, in
particular on the characteristic feature of balanced clauses (parallelism).

De' Rossi's work was noticed by Christian scholars. Johannes Buxtorf II
(1599–1664) translated the chapter into Latin, and Robert Lowth (1710–87),

---

[17] Reventlow, *Authority of the Bible*.
[18] Herbert, *De Veritate*, 75; Popkin, *History of Scepticism*, 154 ff.
[19] I elaborate on Spinoza's view in Ch. 17.   [20] De' Rossi, *Light of the Eyes*, 710–21.

who from 1741 was Professor of Poetry at Oxford, and subsequently bishop first of Oxford and then of London, further developed its ideas in his *De Sacra Poesi Hebraeorum* (*Lectures on the Sacred Poetry of the Hebrews*, 1753), reviewed by Moses Mendelssohn in 1757 and 1761.[21]

But such matters were the preserve of a few scholars who perhaps thought they could evade textual and historical criticism of scripture or unfavourable comparisons with the newly rediscovered literature of Greece and Rome by drawing attention to the Bible's superb literary qualities. It took the poet Johann Gottfried Herder, one of the architects of the German Romantic movement, to popularize the notion that the Bible might be admired in its own right as literature. This was an age when historical criticism on the one hand was undermining faith in the Bible, and unquestioning orthodoxy on the other was refusing to face the consequences of new scholarship. Herder, in *Vom Geist der ebräischen Poesie* (*On the Spirit of Hebrew Poetry*, 1782/3), offered a fresh approach, delighting in a full, intuitive appreciation of the humanity of the Hebrew scripture and the richness of its literary quality; the Hebrew Bible was requisitioned for the Romantic movement, and in turn gained prestige as being in harmony with the spirit of the age.

From History to Myth

David Friedrich Strauss (1808–74) was expelled from the University of Tübingen following the publication, in 1835, of his *Leben Jesu kritisch bearbeitet*, in which he sought to prove that the gospel histories constituted a collection of myths which enshrined a non-supernatural historical truth; his dogmatic review, *Die christliche Glaubenslehre*, appeared in 1840/1. In *Der alte und der neue Glaube* (1872) he tried to prove that Christianity as a system of religious belief was dead, and that a new faith must be constructed on the basis of contemporary art and science.

The opening sentence of Strauss's preface to the first edition of the *Leben Jesu* is instructive:

It appeared to the author of this work . . . that it was time to substitute a new mode of considering the life of Jesus, in the place of the antiquated systems of super-naturalism and naturalism . . .

The new point of view . . . is the mythical . . .

The most learned and acute theologians of the present day fail in the main requirement for such a work . . . the internal liberation of the feelings and intellect from certain religious and dogmatical presuppositions . . .

---

[21] Altmann, *Moses Mendelssohn*, 410–12. Mendelssohn actually sent Lowth a copy of his review, and later on his *Be'ur* commentary on Exodus; he cites Lowth in the *Be'ur* on Gen. 4: 23.

The supernatural birth of Christ, his miracles, his resurrection and ascension, remain eternal truths, whatever doubts may be cast on their reality as historical facts.[22]

Jews who worried about the historical accuracy of the Hebrew scriptures were not slow to apply the lesson. Abraham Geiger (1810–74), who was certainly influenced by Strauss,[23] declared that 'the Bible, that collection of mostly so beautiful and exalted—perhaps the most exalted—human books, as a divine work must . . . go'.[24] Geiger himself made an immense contribution to unravelling the history of the biblical text and its reception in Jewish tradition. The words with which he opens the introduction to his major work on the topic—'Die Bibel ist das Buch der Welt' ('The Bible is the world's book')—immediately tell us that, wonderful and influential as the book is, it is a human compilation;[25] reading further, we discover that not only has its text been modified in transmission, often to suit sectarian purposes, but that its interpretation has been mediated for Jews through the rabbinic tradition, and for Christians through a variety of imperfect translations. Kaufmann Kohler (1843–1926), an erstwhile admirer of Samson Raphael Hirsch but subsequently a major leader of Reform Judaism and from 1903 President of Hebrew Union College, promoted similar ideas in America.

The Galician *maskil* Joshua Heschel Schorr (1818–85) was the first to propagate biblical criticism in the Hebrew language, in his journal *Heḥaluts* which commenced publication in 1852. But the Orthodox remained committed to the literal doctrine of *torah min hashamayim*, upholding both the inerrancy of scripture and the authenticity of traditional interpretation.

Source Theory

The Bible occasionally cites sources. Numbers 21: 14 refers to a 'book of the wars of the Lord'. The book of Kings several times makes reference to 'the book of the chronicles of the kings of Judah' and 'the book of the chronicles of the kings of Israel'. Chronicles does likewise. Altogether, twenty-four extra-biblical sources are cited in the Bible.[26]

---

[22] D. F. Strauss, *Life of Jesus*, pp. li, lii.   [23] S. Heschel, *Abraham Geiger*.

[24] Geiger made the remark in the course of a letter he wrote to J. Derenbourg; the relevant part of the letter is translated in D. H. Frank, Leaman, and Manekin (eds.), *Jewish Philosophy Reader*, 376. Meyer, *Response to Modernity*, 416 n. 16, notes some of Geiger's references to Strauss, but observes that 'a meeting of the two men late in their lives (1868) produced mutual dissatisfaction'.   [25] Geiger, *Urschrift und Übersetzungen der Bibel*, 1.

[26] Leiman, *Canonization of Hebrew Scripture*, 17–18. 'The book of the chronicles of the kings of Judah' is referred to in 1 Kgs 14: 29; 15: 7, 23; 22: 46; 2 Kgs 8: 23; 12: 20; 14: 18; 15: 6, 36; 16: 19; 20: 20; 21: 17, 25; 23: 28; 24: 5, and 'the book of the chronicles of the kings of Israel'

This would not be a problem if not for the doctrine of *torah min hashama-yim*, if that is taken to mean that scripture was dictated by God, who surely does not need to cite human sources. Still, the citations, or references, might be on a par with reports of speech. Abraham, Moses, and other biblical characters were no doubt free to speak as they wished, not in accordance with a pre-ordained script; inclusion of their words in the Torah might be understood as, so to speak, the authoritative, divine stamp of approval on the inclusion of those words in holy writ. Likewise, when the Talmud quoted Rabbi Joshua's view that the last eight verses of the Torah were added by Joshua, it was not suggesting that Joshua made the verses up, but that God had dictated them to him rather than to Moses.[27]

Ibn Yashush and Ibn Ezra, however, seem to imply something else, namely that someone (they do not specify who) had added verses to the received text at a much later stage. Ibn Ezra is coy about this, and unfortunately only parts of Ibn Yashush's grammatical works are extant and not his original commentary.

By the time Christians became seriously involved in the discussion they had already established that the classical texts of Greece and Rome had been corrupted, and had begun to countenance the possibility that interpolations had occurred in the New Testament. Consequently, they were able to move from the notion of an occasional interpolation to the idea that the text of the Hebrew Bible had a history, and that parts of it may have been compiled out of earlier documentary sources. In this way it became possible to formulate a theory about those sources and to speculate as to what they were.

Henning Bernhard Witter (1683–1715) is credited with the development of the first documentary hypothesis. In 1711 he published a new Latin translation of Genesis 1–18 under a three-line title commencing with the words *Jura Israelitarum in Palaestinam terram Chananeam commentatione in Genesin.* He makes skilful use of Jewish sources, from Philo and Josephus to Talmud and midrash, as well as Rashi, Ibn Ezra, Maimonides, and Obadiah of Bertinoro; no newcomer to rabbinics, he had in 1703 published a Latin translation of a section of Maimonides' *Mishneh torah* dealing with the Jewish festivals. There is not much 'documentary hypothesis' in *Jura Israelitarum* apart from the argument, set out in section 22 of the Prolegomena, that several sections of the Pentateuch were clearly not written by Moses, since (as

is mentioned in 1 Kgs 14: 19; 15: 31; 16: 5, 14; 20: 27; 22: 39; 2 Kgs 1: 18; 10: 34; 13: 8, 12; 14: 15, 28; 15: 11, 15, 21, 26, 31.

[27] BT *BB* 15a. Doubt is expressed there as to whether it was Rabbi Joshua or Rabbi Nehemiah who held this opinion.

was observed by Nahmanides),[28] Moses is spoken of in the third person as having written sections of it. He adduces some fifteen biblical references in support of this,[29] but only the pentateuchal verses appear to be relevant. The argument does not go significantly beyond Spinoza's line of reasoning in *Tractatus Theologico-Politicus* VIII, and is in many respects less well developed.

Sir Isaac Newton (1642–1726) is not generally noticed in histories of biblical criticism, yet the opening chapter of his *Observations upon the Prophecies of Daniel, and the Apocalypse of St. John*, published posthumously in 1733, is a systematic account of what he calls the 'Compilers of the Books of the Old Testament' in which he draws attention to the documents from which the Bible was compiled and concludes *inter alia* that Genesis could not have been written before the reign of Saul.[30]

Jean Astruc (1684–1766) was a French physician famous for his treatises on midwifery and venereal diseases and also for a work on the fistula of the anus. He did not know Witter's work, but like him devised a lengthy title for his researches; his *Conjectures sur les mémoires originaux dont il paroit que Moyse s'est servi pour composer le livre de la Genese* was first published in Brussels in 1753, and went through many editions. The name Astruc was common among the Jews of southern France, and though Jean's father was a Huguenot preacher he may have been of Jewish extraction. Unlike Witter, Astruc shows little familiarity with Jewish Bible commentary, nor does he appear to doubt Moses' authorship of the Pentateuch. He argues that Moses composed Genesis and the first two chapters of Exodus on the basis of more ancient documents, sections of which he incorporated without any change, which is why several narratives are duplicated in part or whole, and why different names of God occur in them. He thinks Moses sorted a dozen documents into four groups, which he names A, B, C, and D. In the second part of the book he sets out a French translation of Genesis to Exodus 2 in columns, so that sections belonging to A start on the left of the page, those belonging to B further to the right, and so on. Part 3 is a commentary explaining why each passage is aligned in its chosen column. There is probably no connection between Astruc's plan to 'décomposer la Genese'[31] and his fellow-countryman Jacques Derrida's programme some centuries later to 'déconstruire' everything.

Johann Gottfried Eichhorn (1752–1827) is said to have been the first

[28] See above, pp. 25 and 55.

[29] Exod. 17: 14; 24: 4, 7; 33: 1, 2; 34: 27; Num. 33: 2; Deut. 31: 9, 22; Josh. 1: 8, 31; 10: 13; 2 Chron. 35: 14; 2 Kgs. 22: 2

[30] This was Abraham Ibn Ezra's 'secret of the twelve', the very point on which he criticized Ibn Yashush.   [31] Astruc, *Conjectures*, 17.

person to write a general introduction to the Bible, whether because he preferred a short title or because, unlike Astruc, he had pursued his research beyond Genesis. His influential and popular three-volume *Einleitung in das Alte Testament* (1780–3) exerted great influence on the biblical studies of Moses Mendelssohn and his circle, especially the Galician-born grammarian and lexicographer Judah Leib Ben-Ze'ev (1764–1811).

Wilhelm M. L. de Wette (not to be confused with Witter) put forward in 1805 the predominant modern view that Deuteronomy, or at least its nucleus, had been composed only shortly before its 'discovery' in the time of Josiah (2 Kgs 22: 8). Among his students at the University of Berlin was Leopold Zunz (1794–1886), founder of the Wissenschaft des Judentums ('Science of Judaism'). In his seminal work on Jewish preaching Zunz assigned late dates to several psalms and Ezekiel and suggested that the Hebrew canon was not completed until shortly before 70 CE;[32] in later life he affirmed de Wette's hypothesis on Deuteronomy.

Marcus Moritz Kalisch (1828–1885), a graduate of both the University of Berlin and its Rabbinical Seminary, served from 1848 to 1853 as secretary to Chief Rabbi Nathan Adler in London. He then took a post as tutor to the Rothschilds, in which capacity he felt free to commit to writing his some-what radical views on biblical scholarship, anticipating the source theory of Wellhausen in his commentary on Leviticus.

'Classical' source theory emerged from the work of Karl Heinrich Graf (1815–69) and Julius Wellhausen (1844–1918). Graf argued that the Priestly Code, i.e. the source which includes Leviticus, which had until then been considered the earliest source of the Pentateuch, was actually the latest of the pentateuchal sources. Wellhausen posited four sources: Jahwist (J), Elohist (E), Deuteronomy (D), Priestly Code (P); he dated the Priestly Code to the period after the Babylonian Exile, and Deuteronomy with its legal code to shortly before the Exile.[33] Since Wellhausen's time considerable modifica-tions have been made to the theory; there is no single, agreed documentary hypothesis today, though the basic principles have been accepted by biblical scholars.

Archaeology

Scientific archaeology emerged in the nineteenth century. Jean François Champollion (1790–1832), founder of modern scientific Egyptology, de-

---

[32] Zunz, *Die gottesdienstlichen Vorträge*.

[33] For major works of these authors, see Kalisch, *Historical and Critical Commentary*; Graf, *Die geschichtlichen Buecher*; and Wellhausen, *Die Composition des Hexateuchs*.

ciphered the Rosetta Stone around 1824. Friedrich, son of the German theologian Franz Delitzsch, developed Assyriology late in the century, and the
historical and cultural context of the Bible became increasingly clear.

Increased knowledge of the languages of the ancient Near East led to
improved understanding of the vocabulary, grammar, and styles of the Hebrew scriptures; literary and historical criticism threw light on the dates of
composition, authorship, and original function of the various types of writing that constitute the Bible. More speculative are tradition criticism, which
attempts to trace the development of the oral traditions that preceded written
texts; redaction criticism, which studies how the documents were assembled
by their final authors and editors; and form criticism, initiated in the
twentieth century by Rudolf Bultmann and Martin Dibelius, which classifies
the written material according to the preliterary forms, such as parable or
hymn. Other fashions in criticism come and go with the reputations of the
professors who devise them.

Higher Criticism = Higher Antisemitism?

Orthodox Jews often justify their refusal to come to terms with historical
criticism by the equation, promoted by the Conservative Solomon Schechter,
'Higher Criticism equals Higher Antisemitism.' This is not a good excuse
for ignoring the evidence, but neither is it mere fantasy. Biblical criticism,
especially in Germany, often did lend itself to antisemitism. This was because
a historical perspective on the Bible led Christians to separate not only Bible
and theology, but Old Testament and New Testament theology, a position
that became clear in Georg Lorenz Bauer's *Biblische Theologie des Alten und
Neuen Testaments*.[34] What was the relationship between the two 'Testaments'?
Protestant theologians desperately strove to demonstrate the superiority of
the New over the Old; it is as if they wondered, if the New was not superior to
the Old, what was the point of Christianity?

Among the worst works to address this problem was P. de Lagarde's *Die
Religion der Zukunft* (1878). Romantic German nationalism combined with
Protestant apologetics to lead him to call for a 'new German religion composed of authentic Christianity and the noble elements of the German soul,
but purified of all un-German vices, such as the Old Testament'.

Things were to get still worse. Houston Stewart Chamberlain (1855–1927),
a British-born Germanophile political philosopher who spent most of his
life in Germany, was a devoted admirer of Richard Wagner and married the

---

[34] (Leipzig, 1796–1802). This section is indebted to Reventlow, *Problems of Old Testament
Theology*, 28–43.

latter's only daughter; he defended Germany's military efforts and aims during the First World War, received the German Military Cross in 1915, and became naturalized the following year. In 1899 he published a work,[35] drawing on the race theories of Count Gobineau, in which he argued the superiority of the Nordic race and of 'Indo-European' religion, that is, the New Testament, over 'the religion of the Jews', that is, the Old Testament. Christianity, he claims, arose from two roots: Jewish historical–chronistic faith and Indo-European symbolic and metaphysical mythology. For all that, Chamberlain does not devalue Judaism outright; he acknowledges, unlike some of his followers, that Jesus was a Jew, though he has his doubts about Paul, whose mysticism and idea of redemption are so Indo-European that he might even be called anti-Jewish. The Nazis loved Chamberlain, but he should not be blamed for all their perversions.[36]

Arguments of this kind, and constant harping on the superiority of the 'gospel of love' over the 'religion of law', were characteristic of Protestant theology, especially in Germany, until well after the Second World War, and have by no means disappeared, though there have been notable efforts to develop forms of Christian theology that are free of antisemitism; at Budapest in August 1984 the Lutheran Church formally repudiated the antisemitic diatribes composed late in life by its founder Martin Luther (1483–1546).

However, the abuse of scholarship by some Christian theologians is not our concern. There have certainly been 'Higher Critics' who were 'Higher Antisemites', but the discipline of criticism cannot be abandoned on that account. If Friedrich Delitzsch,[37] for instance, abused his great discoveries in Mesopotamia to downgrade the Hebrew scriptures by stressing their historical unreliability and the low character of their 'national God', that is unfortunate and will undermine his scholarly reputation. But the archaeology of Mesopotamia still stands, and Delitzsch's work on ancient languages remains foundational; the questions it raises cannot be shrugged aside by casting personal aspersions on an individual scholar.

Conclusion

By the dawn of the twentieth century biblical scholarship had advanced to the point where the old reconciling hermeneutic was no longer plausible; traditional Jews and Christians were challenged not so much by each other's

[35] Chamberlain, *Grundlagen des XIX. Jahrhunderts.*
[36] On the re-imaging of Jesus under the Nazis, see S. Heschel, *The Aryan Jesus.*
[37] Delitzsch, *Die grosse Täuschung.*

competing ideologies, or by a foreign ideology such as Islam, as by the findings of apparently objective scientific research that they were free to verify for themselves. Three possibilities faced them. They could abandon the specific claims of their faith and become deists, agnostics, or outright atheists; they could adopt a fideistic approach, and simply assert that the certainties of faith were greater than those of reason; or they could, like the Protestant D. F. Strauss or the Jew Abraham Geiger, construct new theologies that did not depend on the accuracy of the Bible's record of events.

Summary of Part II

◆

Questioning and criticism of the biblical and rabbinic tradition have persisted since biblical times. The principal targets for criticism have been:

- The claim to authoritative extra-biblical tradition (the 'Oral Torah')
- Philosophical criticisms of anthropomorphism, *creatio ex nihilo*, miracles, and freedom of the will
- Doubts as to the authenticity of the received biblical text
- Contradictions within the Bible
- Historical inaccuracy
- Moral issues
- Scientific error
- Fantasy and arbitrariness
- Superstition

Hard questions arise in all these fields. That faith in Torah has survived is due not just to conservatism but to the fact that at all times tradition has engaged with at least some of these questions to great effect; modes of interpretation, notably the 'reconciling hermeneutic', have been developed to counter the difficulties.

Yet in modern times the system has come under renewed pressure, and the traditional reconciling hermeneutic appears less plausible. In the next part we will examine some of the strategies that have been devised to defend Torah in the modern world.

PART III

◆

DEFENDERS OF
THE FAITH

Repairing the Breach: In Defence of Tradition

H OW DID TRADITIONALISTS in modern times respond to the questions in Part II, especially the development of historical criticism?

In Chapter 11 I clarify what it was that they felt they ought to defend.

Chapters 12 to 16 offer a series of thumbnail sketches of Jewish Bible commentators from the eighteenth century onwards, with special attention to their responses to historical and textual criticism.

◆

ELEVEN

DEFENDERS OF THE FAITH

DEFENDERS OF THE FAITH have always been in demand, for there was never any lack of detractors from without and doubters from within. However, what had to be defended in one age or in one society was not the same as what called for defence in another. In pre-modern Christian or Muslim societies, for instance, no one was called upon to defend Judaism from a charge that it incited people to violence against idolaters; such violence was thought entirely proper.

What Must be Defended

In modern times, defenders of traditional Judaism have mostly been concerned with three doctrines that have repeatedly come under attack.

The first is the doctrine of the integrity of the *written* text of the Torah, the belief that the received text of the Pentateuch was dictated to Moses and texts of the other books of the Hebrew Bible were composed under divine inspiration and preserved unchanged. That is, no book has any 'history' beyond the circumstances of its first being set down.

The second is that the Oral and Written Torah together form an indissoluble unity. This is important because it provides the basis for the authority of the rabbinic tradition. This doctrine does not allow for an independent 'biblical theology', since the only authentic way to read scripture is as it is interpreted by the Oral Torah preserved by the rabbis; any attack on the rabbis, like those mounted in earlier times by Sadducees and Karaites, is *ipso facto* an attack on scripture since the two are inseparable. This mirrors the situation within the Roman Catholic Church; when Luther called for *sola scriptura*, the right to read scripture independently of church tradition, he was challenging papal authority, since that authority rested on the claim that the church's tradition as to the meaning of scripture was authentic and binding.

But men such as Azariah de' Rossi and Judah Aryeh of Modena who, in the early modern period, questioned rabbinic interpretation and aggadah were neither Sadducees nor Karaites, nor even hostile in principle to rabbinic tradition. In reaction to the doubts they raised, conservative rabbis such as Judah Loew of Prague and Samuel Edels (1555–1631) pioneered an apologetic literature, defending the rabbis of the Talmud against charges of fantasy and irrationality.

The third conviction is that the Torah is infinitely superior to any merely human fabrication; since it accurately records what God said, it must be perfect both morally and intellectually. Numerous biblical passages do indeed appear morally objectionable to the uninitiated, such as the account of the behaviour of the 'model' King David; others, like Genesis' account of creation, appear to contradict science, or even to contradict each other. But these are handled by the traditional 'reconciling hermeneutic' already described.[1] Numerous medieval scholars laboured to reinterpret the words of Genesis so that they should not conflict with the science of the time, while the exposition of Torah by reconciling apparent internal contradictions lies at the very heart of talmudic exegesis.

All three problems are facets of one major issue, the relationship between revelation and other sources of knowledge. The conflict was aggravated in the modern period by the development of (*a*) ethical philosophies and social teachings derived from sources other than the Bible and its dependent literature, (*b*) a more confident and better-founded natural science, and (*c*) the application of new literary techniques to scripture.

Ancient Wisdom Restored: The Renaissance

Azariah de' Rossi and Judah Aryeh of Modena did not present themselves as innovators, but as restorers of ancient teaching that had become corrupted during the ages. Likewise, the scholars who had powered the Renaissance rarely challenged the teachings of the church head on; many, perhaps the majority, were faithful churchmen. Most often, they portrayed themselves as restoring the *prisca philosophia*, the first, original wisdom that had become obscured in the course of the ages. Ideas that nowadays, with the hindsight of history, we regard as new, were presented as ancient teaching that had been lost or obscured. Nobody can tell when or to what extent any of these scholars genuinely believed he was rediscovering ancient wisdom, or when he was using the pretext of 'rediscovery' to cover his promotion of non-establishment views; among both Jews and Christians it was dangerous, in early modern times, to set yourself up as an innovator.

In 1463 Marsilio Ficino, at the behest of his patron Cosimo de' Medici, made a Latin translation of a Greek manuscript of the *Corpus Hermeticum*,

---

[1] The defence of David described on p. 116 above is an example.

brought to Florence by a Macedonian monk; the recovery of these writings, mistakenly believed to emanate from ancient Egypt but in fact a product of second- and third-century Greek writers, strengthened the belief that 'true' knowledge had been in the possession of the ancients and had been preserved in secret by the favoured few. The idea that a secret doctrine, purer than and superior to the public teachings of the church, had been handed down among initiates, was bolstered by Christian interest in kabbalah.

The temper of Renaissance scholarship was well summarized by Dame Frances Yates:

The great forward movements of the Renaissance all derive their vigour, their emotional impulse, from looking backwards. The cyclic view of time as a perpetual movement from pristine golden ages of purity and truth through successive brazen and iron ages still held sway and the search for truth was thus of necessity a search for the early, the ancient, the original gold from which the baser metals of the present and the immediate past were corrupt degenerations.[2]

Even the innovations of Renaissance music, with its rich and unprecedented polyphony, were presented by Jewish as well as Christian scholars as 'recovery' of the music of King David[3]—a spurious claim, since no one then or now has the faintest idea what David's music was like, though we can be certain that in the absence of a system of notation it would not have been possible to devise the counterpoint of Palestrina or even of Salomone de' Rossi.

In 1614 the French classical scholar Isaac Casaubon, then living in England, correctly dated the hermetic corpus, though incorrectly identifying it as a Christian forgery.[4] Even so, late in the same century, the great Isaac Newton, creator of a radically new physics and cosmology, could confide to his notebook, 'So then the first religion was the most rational of all others till the nations corrupted it', and convince himself that he was merely restoring knowledge that had once been in the possession of humankind.[5]

John Maynard Keynes wrote of Newton that he was 'the last of the magicians', 'Copernicus and Faustus in one':[6]

[2] Yates, *Giordano Bruno*, 1.

[3] This is the theme of Judah Aryeh of Modena's introduction to Salomone de' Rossi's *Hashirim asher lishelomoh*.

[4] Casaubon, *De rebus sacris et ecclesiasticis*; Yates, *Giordano Bruno*, ch. 21.

[5] Cited in White, *Isaac Newton*, 106, from Yahuda MS 41, fos. 6–7, in the Jewish National and University Library, Jerusalem.

[6] Keynes, 'Newton the Man', 27, 34. Keynes perhaps underestimated Copernicus' own Faust-like attributes.

Why do I call him a magician? Because he looked on the whole universe and all that is in it as a riddle, as a secret which could be read by applying pure thought to certain evidence, certain mystic clues which God had laid about the world to allow a sort of philosopher's treasure hunt to the esoteric brotherhood. He believed that these clues were to be found partly in the evidence of the heavens and in the constitution of elements (and that is what gives the false suggestion of his being an experimental natural philosopher), but also partly in certain papers and traditions handed down by the brethren in an unbroken chain back to the original cryptic revelation in Babylonia. He regarded the universe as a cryptogram set by the Almighty—just as he himself wrapt the discovery of the calculus in a cryptogram when he communicated with Leibniz. By pure thought, by concentration of mind, the riddle, he believed, would be revealed to the initiate.

He did read the riddle of the heavens. And he believed that by the same powers of his introspective imagination he would read the riddle of the Godhead, the riddle of past and future events divinely fore-ordained, the riddle of the elements and their constitution from an undifferentiated first matter, the riddle of health and of immortality.[7]

Newton's attitude astonishes the modern reader, and was perhaps already outmoded in intellectual circles even in his own time, which is one reason he took pains to conceal it. But it was a common enough attitude in traditional religious circles, and remains widespread among fundamentalists who believe that all knowledge is contained in the scriptures. Indeed, this line of defence—that divine revelation through scripture is the source of all knowledge—had been developed as early as the second century BCE by Aristobulus, as we saw in Chapter 7; similar ideas recur frequently in the traditional Bible commentaries we shall review.

Jewish Bible Commentary Rekindled

Often, recovery of 'ancient wisdom' raised questions as to the reliability of traditional texts and histories, since the evidence of classical antiquity did not always tally with traditional religious claims. The successful recovery and critical restoration of classical texts stimulated scholars to apply similar techniques to their sacred texts. Research on the Hebrew Scriptures was heavily dependent on medieval Jewish commentators, especially Rashi, Abraham Ibn Ezra, and David Kimhi, whose works were translated into Latin; unsurprisingly, the results often conflicted with the Latin Vulgate accepted as authoritative by the Roman Church, since this was closer to the Septuagint tradition.

As well as problems of translation, historical questions arose when the evidence of classical sources ran counter to scripture or to traditional inter-

[7] Keynes, 'Newton the Man', 29.

pretation. In Chapter 9 we described how Azariah de' Rossi and Judah Aryeh of Modena pursued such questions in a Jewish context, and how Azariah excited the wrath and furiously defensive outpourings of Judah Loew (Maharal) of Prague. The difference between medieval and modern rationality becomes clear when we look at the arguments Maharal marshals, in a work on the excellence of the Torah and its commandments, in defence of the doctrine that Torah is 'from Heaven':[8]

- All ('even the philosophers') agree that the world is orderly, and therefore the product of an orderly Creator. An orderly Creator would certainly set orderly principles for human behaviour, and that is what we find in the Torah; therefore, Torah is from Heaven.

- Whatever the Creator made fits perfectly its intended function or purpose. But human intellect is perfect only potentially; its perfection is actualized only through Torah; therefore, Torah is from Heaven.

- Creation was for the sake of man, who is its highest being, and the only one possessed of free will. His connection with the First Cause is established only when he voluntarily submits his behaviour to its wisdom, and that necessitates that the First Cause convey its will to him, for to act on the basis of his own understanding would not effect a connection. Therefore, it is necessary that there should be Torah from Heaven.

- Even the philosophers agree that man can only progress from potential to actual through the agency of the Active Intellect, which they identify with an angel; however, it is not the Active Intellect, but the Creator himself, who performs this function through the medium of Torah.

The 'rationality' of Maharal's arguments is typically medieval (its roots are of course traceable to ancient Greece). A rational world is one that conforms to the patterns that have been implanted in the human mind by the all-wise Creator; reason tells us what the world is like, and fallible though our use of reason is, since it is corrupted by our moral failings, it is a better guide to reality than observation based on the physical senses. Historical evidence, and eventually scientific evidence, radically undermined this kind of rationality.

There were other reactions, more veiled than that of Maharal. Two Spanish (Ladino) Bible commentaries targeted the new criticism indirectly, simply by attempting to demonstrate the perfection of tradition. Manasseh ben Israel's *Conciliador*, the first part of which was published in Spanish in Amsterdam in 1632, attempted to reconcile apparent biblical contradictions on the basis not

---

[8] Judah Loew ben Bezalel, *Tiferet yisra'el*, ch. 16.

only of traditional sources but of the new learning and discoveries of his time. The encyclopaedic *Me'am lo'ez*, commenced by Jacob Culi (d. 1732) and completed after his death by Isaac Magreso and Isaac Behor Arguiti, was first published in 1733, and has remained popular in Hebrew and English versions; more comprehensive, but narrower in outlook than Manasseh's work, it confines itself to traditional sources.

These works, both aimed at a popular readership, inaugurated a new and fertile epoch in Jewish Bible commentary. Both depend on a 'reconciling hermeneutic'; they start from the assumption that scripture and tradition are free from contradiction, and interpret in such a way as to make the apparent contradictions vanish. This often leads them to adopt interpretations that go against the plain sense of the words, a price they are ready to pay since they believe that a forced interpretation is preferable to the admission that a sacred text might be wrong.

The 'reconciling hermeneutic' of the traditionalists no doubt annoyed Manasseh's young pupil Baruch Spinoza in Amsterdam, as he must have found it maddeningly implausible; several times, in his *Tractatus Theologico-Politicus*, Spinoza inveighs against people, not sparing Maimonides himself, whom he accuses of twisting the meaning of scripture to demonstrate its consistency or to accommodate their own philosophies.[9] Spinoza rejected the reconciling hermeneutic in favour of a more rational, critical, and historical approach to scripture, and was in turn rejected (for the time being) by the Jewish community, but the questions that he posed drove the agenda of much subsequent apologetics and Bible commentary.

Conclusion

In the seventeenth and eighteenth centuries a new sense of intellectual freedom emerged in Christian Europe, if in limited circles, mainly non-Catholic. Newton may have genuinely believed that he was 'recovering ancient wisdom', but few of the scientists who followed him were under such illusions. Philosophers from Descartes onwards, even when they justified their conclusions as being in accordance with church teaching, were openly innovative and ready and even anxious to distance themselves from medieval 'obscurantism'.

The extent to which Jews were affected by, and participated in, such developments has been the subject of excellent studies by David Ruderman and others;[10] no one can any longer claim that European Jews as a whole were

[9] See, for instance, his rejection of Maimonides' argument in *Tractatus Theologico-Politicus* VII.   [10] Ruderman, *Jewish Thought and Scientific Discovery*.

'isolated within the ghetto' at the onset of modernity. By the middle of the eighteenth century the stage had been set for a full-scale confrontation between Jewish tradition and modernity. In the coming chapters we will see how the main lines of response emerged, how the concept of 'revealed Torah' was reinterpreted, and how Bible commentary functioned as a vehicle for articulating reactions to the conflict.

TWELVE

THE TRANSFORMATION OF JUDAISM

Interpretation, Interpretation Interpretation

European Jews reached the end of the eighteenth century committed to quite different forms of faith from those with which they began it. The Enlightenment undoubtedly played a role in effecting the change, though its direct impact was largely confined to the intelligentsia in the West. Rather more influential were movements of religious renewal, for these penetrated deeper into eighteenth-century society than Enlightenment. Movements of religious enthusiasm, from Methodism in England to the charismatic sects of the Ukraine, captured the popular imagination throughout the continent; the Counter-Reformation was well under way, spearheaded by the educational reforms of the Jesuits, with their emphasis on learning, spiritual formation, and correct doctrine; and there were movements of retrenchment and renewal within the Orthodox churches too.

All these trends affected Jews, and are clearly discernible in the lives of the three eighteenth-century Jewish leaders who, between them, dominated Jewish religious thought until well into the twentieth century. Their lives overlapped for more than thirty years, but they never met. They spoke mutually intelligible dialects of Yiddish and professed allegiance to the same Torah, but they did not read it the same way; their cultural differences exceeded their linguistic ones. Each was firmly rooted in his local Jewish culture, and stood out from his surroundings in terms of personal genius and influence rather than radical originality; and each regional Jewish culture resonated with the local Christian culture. The big question was not did you *believe* in Torah, but how did you *interpret* it?

Israel ben Eliezer (1700–60), more commonly known as the Ba'al Shem Tov, was an itinerant preacher and charismatic healer; according to the standard hagiography *In Praise of the Besht*, it was only in his thirties that he chose to reveal himself to close disciples as a profound scholar and mystic. Born to aged parents in Podolia (Polish-occupied Ukraine), he not only absorbed traditional Jewish teaching but came under the influence of Christian charismatics such as the Filippovtsy and the Dukhobors.[1] He eventually settled in Medzhybizh (Volhynia, Ukraine), where he attracted a circle of ardent followers, some of them men of considerable learning, who formed the first generation of hasidic rebbes, or masters. His teachings are known mainly through the work of his disciple Jacob Joseph Katz of Polonnoye (Pulnoye) (d. 1782), author of the first published hasidic work, *Toledot ya'akov yosef*.[2]

Elijah ben Solomon Zalman, 'the Vilna Gaon' (1720–99), was born in Selets, now in Belarus, to a family of talmudic scholars; he settled in Vilna (Vilnius) around 1745. Like the Jesuits who had established an academy in 1568 which became the University of Vilna in 1579,[3] he mistrusted religious enthusiasm but valued devotion, detachment from worldly concerns, and especially learning, which in his case meant the learning of rabbinic Judaism, from Bible to Talmud to kabbalah. Again, like the Jesuits, he was not over-awed by 'authorities', even those endorsed by the (rabbinic) establishment.

Moses Mendelssohn of Dessau, Saxony-Anhalt (1729–86), arrived in Berlin in 1743, already well versed in traditional Jewish studies but eager to soak up the new learning of the Enlightenment. He eked out a miserable living as tutor to a wealthy Jewish family, and studied mathematics, philosophy, and languages privately, since German universities did not admit Jews. A traditional Jew attempting to come to terms with the Prussian Enlightenment, he was constantly hampered by the need to defend his fellow-Jews against false charges and attempts at conversion.

If the three did not meet, or even correspond, there were indirect conduits for ideas. Students, merchants, and 'economic migrants' wandered throughout the Pale of Settlement and to the West. Solomon Dubno (1738–1813), for instance, exposed to hasidism in his native Volhynia, collaborated with Mendelssohn in Berlin, and then moved on to Vilna, where he associated with the circle of the Gaon yet continued to promote Mendelssohn's *Be'ur*, to which he had contributed.[4] Baruch of Shklov (Baruch 'Schick', c.1740–1812) left Belarus to study medicine in England; later, in Berlin, he published a Hebrew work on anatomy and he eventually settled in Vilna, where he

[1] Eliach, 'Russian Dissenting Sects'.
[2] For a reconstruction of the life of Israel Ba'al Shem Tov, see Rosman, *Quest*.
[3] The Commission of National Education took control of the Academy in 1773 after the suppression of the Jesuits.   [4] On Mendelssohn's *Be'ur* see below, pp. 167–70.

associated with the circle of the Gaon, at whose behest he produced more Hebrew scientific works, including a translation of Euclid.[5]

Spinoza, Leibniz, and Wolf had raised important issues of interpretation (what is the right way to read any text?), and these were developed and articulated by Johann Martin Chladenius (1710–59)—probably the first to develop hermeneutics as a 'science'—and later by Friedrich Schleiermacher.[6] Mendelssohn was himself a significant figure in Romantic hermeneutics, but it is unlikely that either of the other Jewish leaders had direct knowledge of such matters. Nevertheless, all three were deeply concerned with hermeneutic problems; each interpreted Bible and rabbinic tradition in a distinctive way, and each inspired a characteristic form of Bible commentary.

In eastern and central Europe the hasidic movement, for which the Ba'al Shem Tov was the inspirational figure, continued the tradition of kabbalistic commentators such as the sixteenth-century Moses Alshekh (c.1498–1593), Isaiah Horovitz (Shelah, ?1565–1630), and Hayim ben Moses Attar (Or Hahayim, 1696–1743). The hasidic commentaries, for the most part confined to the Pentateuch, combined Lurianic kabbalah with hasidic homily; notable instances are the posthumously published *Mei hashilo'ah* of Mordecai Joseph Leiner of Izbica (1792–1854),[7] and the *Sefat emet* of Judah Aryeh Leib Alter (1847–1905), the Gerer Rebbe.[8] Critical and historical questions are ignored; the whole tradition—that is, those texts admitted by the hasidim as belonging within the tradition—is interpreted synchronically, as if all had been revealed simultaneously at Sinai. The hasidic masters were less concerned with philology than with weaving the words into homilies and expounding hasidic doctrine.

A second stream issued from the north, and was channelled by Elijah of Vilna. His aim was to demonstrate the perfection, comprehensiveness, and consistency of Written and Oral Torah taken as a single entity. The *mitnagedim* ('opponents'), as the Gaon's followers are known, appear at first sight to ignore historical criticism of the Bible just as the hasidim do, but the appearance is misleading; if they are motivated to demonstrate the perfection of

---

[5] That despite his 'Enlightenment' training Baruch remained an arch-conservative is demonstrated by his vitriolic attack on Azariah de' Rossi in his *Keneh hamidah* on trigonometry.

[6] Chladenius, a professor of theology, was reluctant to apply the didactic and cognitively oriented procedures he had developed for interpretation of texts to the Bible: 'The Holy Scripture is a divine writing, to which indeed many rules [apply] as to human books, but some, which are useful here, cannot be applied' (*Einleitung*, no. 189, p. 106).

[7] First published 1860. See Faierstein, *All is in the Hands of Heaven*.

[8] Ger, or Gur, is Gora Kalwaria, about 30 km south-east of Warsaw, Poland. For an English selection from his commentary see Green, *Language of Truth*.

Written and Oral Torah, this is because they are acutely aware of the critical Enlightenment stance. Homiletics features in their works, but halakhah is also prominent, to a greater extent than with the hasidim.

In the west, Moses Mendelssohn was the dominant figure in acclimatizing Judaism to modern culture; the Bible is for him not only a source of moral inspiration but a work of incomparable aesthetic value. Though he stimulated an interest in scientific biblical studies that eventually led to some accommodation with historical criticism, Mendelssohn's own defensive stance did not permit him to engage in radical speculation.

Elijah, the 'Vilna Gaon' (1720–1799)

Elijah ben Solomon Zalman, the 'Vilna Gaon',[9] is said to have delivered a homily in the synagogue of Vilna at the age of 6½; by the age of 8 he had outstripped all available tutors. Subsequently, he studied mainly on his own, 'untrammelled' by the conventional methods of talmudic education of his day.

After his marriage and some early travels in Poland and Germany he settled in Vilna, where he remained until his death. He was maintained through a family bequest and through a pension allocated him by the community board.

It was said that to shut out distraction he would close the windows of his room by day and study by candlelight and in winter he studied in an unheated room, placing his feet in cold water to prevent himself from falling asleep.[10] His sons, who could not have known this unless they took turns to spy, claimed that he did not sleep more than two hours a day and never for more than half an hour at a time.

He did not hold any formal position, nor head a yeshiva, but from the 1760s a circle of aspiring disciples gathered around him.

On his abortive journey to the Holy Land Elijah dispatched to his family, who were intended to follow, a spiritual testament. He gave instructions for the education of his daughters and admonished them to refrain from taking oaths, cursing, being deceitful, or quarrelling. He considered empty talk and gossip great sins and counselled making few visits, even to the synagogue; better to pray at home, alone, in order to avoid idle talk and envy, and not to covet wealth and honour, because 'it is certain that all this world is vanity'.

[9] 'Gaon' ('illustrious') was the formal title of the heads of the Babylonian academies following the close of the Talmud. It remains common as an honorific, but only Elijah is known as 'the Gaon' par excellence.

[10] Israel of Shklov, introd. to Elijah of Vilna, Pe'at hashulḥan.

He opposed philosophical study, seeing it as a threat to faith and tradition; even Maimonides and Isserles were not spared his wrath for having been 'led astray by accursed philosophy'.[11]

He vehemently opposed hasidism.[12] Among the aspects he objected to were (a) giving precedence to kabbalah over halakhic studies, (b) liturgical innovations and the introduction of new customs reminiscent of the Sabbatian heresy, (c) the creation of a new group that would lead to a split in the community, (d) disdain for Torah study, resulting from hasidic stress on the love of God and the service of God in joy as distinct from and superior to Torah study, and (e) the emphasis on the immanence rather than the transcendence of God. Minor differences included the question of what status to accord the Lurianic kabbalah; Elijah respected it, but did not regard it as authoritative.

The objections were backed up with bans and book burnings. In 1796 Elijah wrote, 'I will remain vigilant; it is the duty of every believing Jew to repudiate and pursue [the hasidim] with all manner of afflictions and subdue them, because they have sin in their hearts and are like a sore on the body of Israel.'

Over seventy works and commentaries are attributed to him, though it is said that after the age of 40 he ceased writing himself as he could not keep pace with his own thought processes. As none of his works was published in his lifetime we are dependent on his sons and a select group of disciples for the form in which most of them saw the light; several were not written by him, but compiled on the basis of lecture notes.[13]

Maskilim (followers of the Enlightenment), who admired some aspects of his work, gave the impression that he disdained kabbalah. This is manifestly untrue, a misinterpretation either of his opposition to the hasidim or of his sometimes radical emendations of kabbalistic texts. In Talmud as in kabbalah he revised texts in the light of his conviction that all rabbinic teaching, including halakhah, aggadah, and kabbalah, was mutually consistent; Etkes's remark that 'he did not dare to emend the existing reading unless the revision was based on many good arguments'[14] is a disingenuous way of acknowledging the lack of manuscript support.

One of his most carefully written works is his commentary on the *Sifra ditsniuta*, a section of the Zohar which he regarded as summing up kabbalistic teaching in much the same way that the Mishnah sums up halakhah; he believed kabbalah equally with halakhah originated at Sinai. In chapter 5 he

---

[11] *Be'ur hagra* on *Shulḥan arukh*, 'Yoreh de'ah' 179: 6 and 246: 4.
[12] Etkes, *Gaon of Vilna*, chs. 3–5, covers the dispute comprehensively.
[13] Ibid. 20.   [14] Ibid. 17.

articulates his outlook on the eternity and comprehensiveness of Torah:

In sum, everything that was, is, and will be throughout time is included in the Torah from 'In the beginning . . . ' (Genesis 1: 1) to ' . . . before the eyes of all Israel' (Deuteronomy 34: 12). And not only the general principles, but even the details of each species and of each human individual, whatever happens to him from the day of his birth until his end, and all his transmigrations, all in full detail. Likewise, [details of] every species of animal and living being, as well as of every plant and mineral . . . whatever happened to the Patriarchs and Moses and all Israel in each generation, for undoubtedly the sparks of all of them are reincarnated throughout the generations . . . and all their deeds from Adam to the end of the Torah are [re-enacted] in each generation, as is known to those who understand [these things]. All this is included in the portions from 'In the beginning . . . ' to Noah and summed up in the opening chapter to 'in creating had made' (Genesis 2: 3).[15]

His disciple Hayim of Volozhin (1749–1821) wrote an introduction to the work emphasizing the Gaon's respect for the Zohar and the works of Isaac Luria, and offering many personal glimpses into Elijah's life. The master, he avers, believed himself to be in communication with Simon bar Yohai (traditionally regarded as author of the Zohar) and Isaac Luria, and to have received offers from many *magidim* (supernatural spiritual mentors) to guide him in Torah, but he consistently refused such offers of help and insisted on discovering the deep truths of Torah through his own effort, guided by God alone. Hayim writes that Elijah suspected that the supernatural agencies had become contaminated; Etkes suggests that this was a reaction to the rise of the Frankist movement.[16]

Elijah is alleged to have acquainted himself with astronomy, mathematics, and geography in order better to understand Torah; a disciple wrote in his name that 'To the degree that a man is lacking in knowledge and secular sciences he will lack one hundredfold in the wisdom of the Torah.'[17] This casts some doubt on Hayim of Volozhin's assertion that 'he never strayed beyond his four cubits', i.e. beyond the texts of Torah.[18] However, his interest in sciences, including medicine, was constrained by the fact that he derived all his secular knowledge from Hebrew sources, most of which had been compiled during the Middle Ages.

Such science as he adduces in his commentaries is decidedly medieval; he routinely reads the theory of four elements, earth, water, air, and fire into biblical texts. He can perhaps be forgiven for that—Dalton did not propound

---

[15] Elijah of Vilna, *Sifra ditsniuta*, 34a (205). The work was first published posthumously, in 1820/1, by Elijah's grandson, Jacob Moses of Slonim, on the basis of an autograph.

[16] Etkes, *The Gaon of Vilna*, 29.

[17] Introd. to Baruch of Shklov's *Euclid*.   [18] Introd. to *Sifra ditsniuta*.

his atomic theory until after the Gaon's death, and more time passed before it was generally accepted. Newtonian celestial mechanics, on the other hand, dominated eighteenth-century thought, so the reader may well be astonished that the Gaon, in his reading of Genesis,[19] ignores Newton and even Ptolemy, and reverts to early rabbinic sources that describe the earth as resting on a vast ocean through which the sun descends at night, and the sky as surmounted by further quantities of blue water, 'unknown', he remarks, 'to gentile scientists'!

Occasionally he makes some observation which indicates awareness of a source outside rabbinic tradition; for instance, in a marginal note on Babylonian Talmud, *Sukah* 51b he corrects 'Alexander of Macedon' to 'Trajan', perhaps having inferred from Josephus, whose work he desired translated into Hebrew, or from the Hebrew *Josippon*, that Alexander would not fit the context.

He paid great attention to Hebrew grammar, drawing on the work of Elijah Levita, whom he follows in rejecting the Sinaitic origin of the vowel signs and other Masoretic apparatus,[20] and composed his own handbook on grammar. He also greatly valued music and said that 'most of the cantillation of the Torah, the secrets of the levitical songs, and the secrets of the *Tikunei hazohar*, cannot be understood without it'.[21] It is often claimed that he wrote books on geography, geometry, and astronomy. However, the alleged geography book is merely a commentary on Joshua 15–19 and some other biblical passages; the work on geometry, eventually published under the title *Ayil meshulash*, consists merely of notes he apparently jotted down for his own use; no work on astronomy has been found.

We do not know much about his music, but his grammar is adapted to his peculiar notion of Torah as a coded, literal revelation. So he insists that *shemot nirdafim* (apparent homonyms) each have distinct, consistent shades of meaning; a list of homonyms with references to where they are explained in his work is appended to his *Barak hashahar*.[22] For example, on Genesis 1 he explains that *bara* 'created' refers not to *creatio ex nihilo* but to the formation of the thing in its essence; *yatsar* 'formed' refers to the formation of essential

---

[19] *Aderet eliyahu* on Gen. 1.
[20] See above, Ch. 8.   [21] Israel of Shklov, introd. to Elijah's *Pe'at hashulhan*.
[22] Solomon Ze'ev Herr compiled a list of homonyms from the works of the Gaon and Malbim (Meir Leibush ben Jehiel Michel Weiser, 1809–79) under the title *Likutei shoshanim*. It would be interesting to know whether either the Gaon or Herr was aware of the publication of *Yeriot shelomoh*, a massive study by Salomon Pappenheim (1740–1814) of Hebrew synonyms, of which the first part was published in 1784, but the remaining two in 1811 and 1831, well after the Gaon's death.

properties; *asah* 'made' refers to the formation of accidental characteristics. He seems unaware of the Aristotelian provenance of such concepts as essence and accident, though had he known, he would most likely have claimed that Aristotle lifted these concepts from a lost Jewish source.

His refusal to accept that there are true homonyms, and that the meanings of words are flexible, is contrary to Abraham Ibn Ezra's express contention on Numbers (10: 35; 12: 6; 23: 7) that the language of prophecy repeats the same thought in different words as a literary device for emphasis, a point of view strongly argued by the great Hebrew grammarian Jonah Ibn Janah in the eleventh century; but the Gaon clearly disapproved of Ibn Ezra on this point, and would have approved even less of de' Rossi's and Mendelssohn's veneration of the literary qualities of scripture. It is difficult to know what he made of the definition of *itur soferim* offered by the medieval commentator Nissim of Girona (Ran, 1310–75?) as 'extra words that were written to beautify the language; they are called *itur* (adornment) since they adorn the language'.[23]

Hebrew grammar, for the Gaon, is a disciplined science that aims to decode a system of divinely ordained signs, each of which has a precise and consistent meaning; it is a world apart from the flexible, context-sensitive, and historically aware analysis of the language to be pursued by, for instance, Samuele Davide Luzzatto (see Chapter 13) early in the following century.

Elijah does not lack aesthetic sensitivity; he exhibits it clearly in other contexts, such as the performance of the *mitsvot*. It is rather that he believes that to treat God's word as 'mere' literature is somehow to demean it, to fail to appreciate how it differs from any merely human artefact. A similar thought is expressed in the Talmud, where we read:

> If anyone recites a verse of the Song of Songs as if it were a [mere] song, or recites a verse of scripture at a feast at an inappropriate time, he brings evil to the world, for the Torah girds sackcloth, stands before the Holy One, blessed be He, and declares, 'Lord of the Universe, your children have treated me as a lyre on which scoffers make music.'[24]

He uses his grammatical knowledge to advantage in his Bible commentaries, of which that on Proverbs remains popular. His commentaries on most of the Bible were published posthumously under the title *Aderet eliyahu*, and that on the Pentateuch appears in many rabbinic bibles. In *Aderet eliyahu* he not only applies his theory of homonyms, but strives to explain narratives in terms of zoharic kabbalah. Number relations of all kinds were important

---

[23] Nissim of Girona on BT *Ned.* 37*b*. On the world-view of Rabenu Nissim see Harvey, 'The Halakhic Philosophy of the Ran' (Heb.).   [24] BT *San.* 101*a*.

to him; *Aderet eliyahu* on the portion 'Ha'azinu' provides an extraordinary demonstration of his ingenuity in this method of interpretation.

An Orthodox apologist, Isidore Grunfeld, aptly wrote of him:

Elijah, the Gaon of Vilna, foresaw the danger which lay ahead, and made a special point of stressing again and again the unity of the Written and Oral Law and of drawing the attention of his disciples to the fact that what is known as *derashot ḥazal*, the halachic expositions of our sages, is inherent and latent in the written text of the Torah and can be logically deduced and made manifest from its wording, grammatical structure and phraseology.[25]

This is understated, since Elijah claimed that far more than that halakhah was 'latent in the written text of the Torah', but it correctly pinpoints his aim of defending Torah against 'the danger which lay ahead', and which in fact already threatened—the questioning of the integrity of the Torah text as divine revelation.

Grunfeld also understates the reforming aspect of the Gaon's intellectual activities. As the Gaon saw things, he was labouring to restore the 'original' Torah. This involved much textual criticism and revision, if not of the Bible itself, of almost every other literary source of Judaism. That is why so much of his output consists of marginal notes, textual adjustments, and of tracing teachings to their earliest sources, demonstrating (as he believed) that all that was authentic in Judaism was latent in the Torah. In halakhah, it required not only the adjusting of texts, but the revision of commonly accepted decisions. For instance, as against the consensus of Ashkenazi authorities he attempted to institute the daily recital of the priestly blessing; this failed in Vilna, but like other rulings of his was implemented by his disciples in Palestine and has profoundly influenced liturgical usage in modern Israel.

Elijah's way of life and devotion to learning set the stamp on the Lithuanian *mitnaged* culture, which attained its pinnacle of expression in the nineteenth century in the yeshivas of Volozhin, Mir, and other centres. Paradoxically, he was also venerated by the secular Lithuanian maskilim, mostly yeshiva-educated; they disdained his religious beliefs, but saw him as a pioneer in broadening the range of Jewish interests, in the scientific study of Hebrew culture, and as an ally in opposition to hasidic superstition and obscurantism.[26]

[25] I. Grunfeld, introd. to Isaac Levy's translation of S. R. Hirsch, *Commentary on Genesis*, ix. Grunfeld refers to *Aderet eliyahu*, to the Gaon's comments on Prov. 2: 3 and 8: 9, and to *Revid hazahav* by the Gaon's disciple Dov Ber ben Yehudah L. Trivish; I have not checked the references.

[26] The historiography of 'the Gaon as maskil' is amply dealt with in Etkes, *The Gaon of Vilna*, ch. 2.

Moses Mendelssohn (1729–1786)

Mendelssohn, grandfather of the composer Felix Mendelssohn-Bartholdy, was an ardent advocate of Jewish civil rights and vigorously discouraged Jewish separatism; he intervened successfully through influential friends in several European states to ameliorate anti-Jewish legislation and wrote extensively on the theme of Jewish emancipation. He urged his fellow Jews to speak High German rather than Yiddish and to assimilate, so far as their religion would permit, into German culture and society:

Adapt yourselves to the morals and the constitution of the land to which you have been removed, but hold fast to the religion of your fathers too . . . I cannot see how those born into the house of Jacob can in any conscientious manner disencumber themselves of the law.[27]

Partly to this end, but also to improve knowledge of Hebrew, he composed the *Be'ur*, of which more below. Likewise, he encouraged the setting up of the Jewish Free School in Berlin in 1781, in which secular subjects, French, and German were taught, as well as traditional Talmud and Bible.

In a letter he wrote in 1770 to J. D. Michaelis, Mendelssohn mentioned the publication of a translation of Psalms into German which was to act as a counterbalance to the translations and commentaries written in the spirit of Christianity. The Psalms translation was not published until 1783, by which time headway had been made with Mendelssohn's great project, the *Be'ur* (Hebrew for 'commentary'), on the whole Bible. This comprised Hebrew text, a German translation (in Hebrew letters), and a Hebrew commentary; in many editions it is accompanied by Targum (Aramaic translation) and Rashi's commentary, in their original languages. It follows the tradition of Rashi, Rashbam, and Abraham Ibn Ezra in its scientific approach to Hebrew philology, and its emphasis on the literary and aesthetic qualities of the text fitted well with the contemporary German Romanticism of men such as Herder and Gunkel, to which Mendelssohn's own aesthetic philosophy contributed. Mendelssohn was largely responsible for the composition of the *Be'ur* on the opening section of Genesis, on Exodus, and on much of the beginning and end of Deuteronomy, but the boundaries between his work and that of his collaborators are not sharp; Dubno, for instance, was responsible for most of the grammatical notes even on sections where Mendelssohn had contributed the main commentary.[28]

[27] Mendelssohn, *Jerusalem*, 133. See Kochan, *Jewish Renaissance*, 68–9.
[28] Sandler, *Mendelssohn's Edition of the Pentateuch*, 98.

The *Be'ur* does not engage in historical criticism, perhaps because Mendelssohn felt that such speculations would be controversial and detract from the main purpose of the work; his successors, however, particularly those aligned with the Reform Judaism which was formally constituted only after his lifetime, very soon attuned themselves to the new critical trends.

Despite the fairly conventional nature of its content the initial, partial publication annoyed some traditional rabbis, notably Raphael Kohen of Altona and Ezekiel Landau of Prague. Threats of excommunication were bandied about but not implemented, and the unpleasantness frightened Solomon Dubno into resigning his collaboration with Mendelssohn (other explanations have been suggested); however, the project was completed with the assistance of Naphtali Herz Wessely, Naphtali Herz Homberg, and Aron Jaroslaw. It was so successful in the West that it ran through numerous editions and a French Jew could reflect in 1905 that 'At this day the Perush of Rashi and the Biur of Mendelssohn are the favorite commentaries of Orthodox Jews.'[29] A century later, however, Orthodox Jews still cherish Rashi but they have abandoned Mendelssohn to liberals, for whom he has been superseded by more modern commentators, and to antiquarians.

Mendelssohn was a knowledgeable and intelligent man, and in 1763 beat Immanuel Kant, by five years his senior, for first prize in a contest set by the Prussian Royal Academy of Sciences for an essay on evidence in the metaphysical sciences. He was certainly not unaware of developments in biblical criticism, such as those we described in Chapter 10. But, as Soloweitschik and Rubascheff observed:

The prime concern of [Mendelssohn] and his disciples was to strip away the layers of midrash and aggadah which the scriptural books had attracted to themselves, and to return to Rashbam, to Ibn Ezra, and to Radak . . . the translation and the *Be'ur* appeared only after the publication of the works of Astruc and Eichhorn, and after a generation of researchers had gathered around Eichhorn, but their influence on the translation and the *Be'ur* was very limited. Mendelssohn does not mention Astruc at all, but he cites Eichhorn's *Introduction* favourably, though he permits himself to cite only matters to do with different translations [but not source criticism].[30]

Just occasionally the *Be'ur* makes some reference to classical literature. For instance, on the words 'Tubal-Cain's sister was Na'amah' (Gen. 4: 22) it comments:

A midrash of our rabbis of blessed memory [states that] she was the very beautiful woman after whom the 'sons of the gods' strayed . . . Others say she was the wife of

---

[29] Liber, *Rashi*.
[30] Soloweitschik and Rubascheff, *History of Biblical Criticism* (Heb.), 125–6.

Shemadon and the mother of Ashmodai, and through her the *shedim*[31] were born
. . . There is a vestige of this in the vanities of the nations, for the poems of the
Greeks refer to the demon or god who rules over iron and bronze work as Vulcan,
which is close to Tubal-Cain, and his sister and wife is Venus, who rules over all that
is pleasant and desirable and [over] love, and she was very beautiful as is known to
those who read their books.

There is, however, little attempt to assess the significance of such references,
though links with classical and even Indian literature had been made by
several Christian scholars and must have been known to Mendelssohn.

Occasionally there is some note or comment of a philosophical or
apologetic nature. For instance, the rabbis base on 'Do not seethe a kid in its
mother's milk' (Exod. 23: 19; 34: 26; Deut. 14: 31) the rules prohibiting the
cooking together of meat and milk, as well as the use and consumption of the
product;[32] Mendelssohn's rather lame comment on the verse is 'We do not
understand why the Holy One, blessed be He, forbade meat in milk, for God
gave us many commandments without revealing their reason, and it is
sufficient that we should know that they were commanded by Him, may He
be blessed, and since we have taken on ourselves the yoke of His kingdom we
are obliged to keep His will; the benefit lies in their performance, not in
knowing their causes.'

More striking is Mendelssohn's excursion into aesthetics. He introduces
the Song at the Red Sea (Exod. 15) with an extended and impassioned essay on
the virtues of biblical poetry. Rhyme and metre, he declares, are attractive to
the ear and lend themselves to musical setting; however, the need to comply
with the rules forces writers to compromise meaning. Biblical poetry, in
contrast to other poetry including later Hebrew, eschews such artificial rules,
and is based entirely on short, meaningful phrases which powerfully and
accurately convey the intended meaning, and are combined into balancing
groups of two, three, or four; together with the wonderful but now lost music
of biblical times this was an ideal medium for the divine message.[33] He cites
with approval chapter 60 of Azariah de' Rossi's *Imrei binah*, discussed in
Chapter 9, and concludes by outlining his motives for including such a
lengthy essay, contrary to the general brevity of his commentary. He has not
found an adequate statement on these matters among the commentators, but
now finds it necessary since 'the young of our people' admire so greatly the art
of poetry as practised by other nations, and he is consumed with jealousy on

[31] Demons. Ashmodai was king of the demons; the names Ashmodai and Shemadon are
derived from the Hebrew root *sh-m-d* 'destroy'.   [32] BT Ḥul. 113b–114.

[33] Mendelssohn here marries his own aesthetic philosophy to the prosody of his
predecessors.

behalf of the holy scriptures which, as poetry, are as high above the creations of other nations as the heavens are above the earth.

Mendelssohn's aesthetic was the most enduring and influential aspect of his philosophy, and is central to his religious thought. Klaus-Werner Segreff comments that in the face of the prevailing attitude that 'The Creator takes no pleasure in the Beautiful', Mendelssohn argued that (*a*) beauty is the index of human mortality and (*b*) beauty is the index of human freedom.[34] Though the Creator himself is beyond sensual pleasure, aesthetic perfection leads us to him. Mendelssohn's demonstration of the beauty of biblical language is fundamental to his theology.

The detailed notes in the *Be'ur* on Exodus 15 do not develop this theme, but are mostly devoted to matters of grammar and vocabulary, and rely heavily on the commentaries of Rashi, Ibn Ezra, and Ramban. From time to time, though, he notes that a particular usage is poetic, for instance the final *vav* in *yekhasyumu* (Exod. 15: 5).[35]

Herder's famous essay *Vom Geist der ebräischen Poesie* created quite a stir when it appeared in 1782 about a year after the *Be'ur* on Exodus, and was undoubtedly influenced by Mendelssohn; Altmann claimed that 'Herder's attitude to Mendelssohn in his early period came close to being that of a disciple.'[36]

Torah—Mystical Code, or Source of Values?

Elijah of Vilna and Moses Mendelssohn espoused diametrically opposed concepts of what Torah is.

For the Gaon, the written text of Torah is a code dictated by God, in which every letter, every mark, even the traditional cantillation, encodes layer upon layer of information; the whole world and its history and all of science are contained in it, as are the minutiae of the *mitsvot* that alone can enable the faithful to negotiate the hazards and temptations of this world. Its contents are teased out in the Oral Torah, likewise revealed at Sinai, which includes both halakhah and kabbalah. The sciences of the nations are but remnants of what Israel has lost in its understanding of Torah; science, history, and all knowledge are subsidiary to Torah, and ultimately contained within it. Like Newton,[37] Elijah regarded the universe very much as 'a cryptogram set by the Almighty'; but his decoding efforts were focused on Jewish holy writings and

---

[34] Segreff, *Moses Mendelssohn*, 30.

[35] It is unclear how much of the philological material in the commentary on Exodus was composed by Solomon Dubno. See Altmann, *Moses Mendelssohn*, 405.

[36] Altmann, *Moses Mendelssohn*, 73, citing Haym, *Herder*.   [37] See p. 154 above.

did not lead him to original investigation of nature or to challenge received wisdom beyond the restricted sphere of halakhah.

For Mendelssohn the Torah is no mystical code, but a literary work of beauty and majesty, articulating Israel's relationship with her God as a model of the relationship of human and divine. It is not a code for decryption, but a source of values, whose essence lies in its ethical and moral teaching; those of its laws that are not primarily ethical and moral are not universal, but constitute the 'revealed legislation' of the polity of Israel. The Oral Torah is simply the extension and application of Torah by the rabbis; Mendelssohn's attitude to Talmud is ambivalent. His stance on kabbalah, in so far as he takes any interest in it at all, is negative; he certainly does not consider it an integral part of Torah. As the literary heritage of ancient Israel the Torah is not the repository of scientific information; God revealed laws, not science; philosophical truths, not religious dogma.

THIRTEEN

MENDELSSOHN'S INFLUENCE

MENDELSSOHN'S INFLUENCE on subsequent Jewish Bible commentary was profound, both on those who tried to emulate his achievement
and on those who reacted against it. Here we consider the work of some of his
avowed followers.

Isaac Samuel Reggio (1784–1855)

Among his most ardent admirers was Isaac Samuel Reggio of Gorizia,[1] a
town in northern Italy (then within the Austro-Hungarian empire) on the
border of what is now Slovenia. Reggio is sometimes known as Yashar, the
Hebrew acronym of his name, meaning 'upright'; his major Hebrew work,
Hatorah vehafilosofiyah ('Torah and Philosophy'), published in Vienna in
1827, follows Mendelssohn's path in reconciling faith and reason.

In 1818 the publisher Holzinger of Vienna published a 'manifesto' an-
nouncing Reggio's proposed Italian translation of the Pentateuch; it comprised introductory material and some sample pages. The full title, retained
when the complete work appeared in 1821, reveals his agenda: 'The Law of
God translated into Italian, illustrated with a new commentary aiming to
elucidate the literal meaning of the sacred text, and preceded by a preface
which demonstrates rationally the divinity of the Holy Law of Moses.'[2] On
the opening page Reggio pays tribute to Mendelssohn's example, and in the
Hebrew introduction he stresses that Italian is no less suitable a language
than German for expressing the profundity and beauty of scripture, hence it is
appropriate that Italian readers should have their own translation.

Reggio discharges his promise to 'demonstrate rationally the divinity of
the Holy Law of Moses' in a long Hebrew essay that follows, entitled 'Torah

[1] See Malkiel, 'New Light'.

[2] *La Legge di Dio tradotta in lingua Italiana, illustrate con un nuovo commento tendente a
dilucidare il senso litterale del sacro testo e proceduta da una prefazione che dimonstra
ragionamente la divinità della Santa Legge di Moise.*

min hashamayim'; he vigorously defends the theory that every letter, even the 'large and small' letters,[3] of the Pentateuch was revealed at Sinai. This defence is needed, says Reggio, because 'as time has passed and people have become confused . . . the evil inclination has prevailed . . . the plague of unbelief [apikorsut] has spread through the inhabitants of the earth.' He defends the authenticity of the received text with six arguments, based on:

- The time the Torah was given

- The language in which it is composed

- Its character

- The chain of tradition

- The godliness of those who walk in its ways

- The rightness of its content.

The first argument simply takes for granted that the Torah was given in the year 2448 from Creation (approximately 1312 BCE). Proper writing had not been invented at that time, he states, even though the Egyptians had hieroglyphics that we are mostly unable to decipher; the Chinese also lacked an alphabet.

Reggio was unfortunate in his timing, as Champollion published his decipherment of Egyptian in the 1820s, and it became evident that Egyptian *did* include alphabetic signs.[4] But even granted Reggio's premise, that the Torah was the first work written in alphabetic characters, one would need a great leap of faith to conclude (*a*) that it must have come from heaven and (*b*) that the precise text as now written, including the 'large and small letters', had been perfectly transmitted.

S. D. Luzzatto (see below), a precocious 19 at the time, was more percipient. He wrote a letter to Reggio on 19 May 1819 citing a vast range of classical authors as evidence that alphabetic writing existed before the time of Moses, and in particular that the Egyptians possessed an alphabetic script as well as hieroglyphics. He argues that (*a*) our lack of knowledge is no proof that writing did not exist, (*b*) traditional Jewish sources do not claim that writing originated with Moses, and (*c*) even if Reggio were correct that writing did not exist before Moses it would be better not to pursue the matter, since critics

---

[3] Letters that the Masoretic tradition requires written larger or smaller than usual. See above, p. 102, on orthographic textual variants.

[4] G. F. Grotefend had won a bet with his drinking companions by deciphering some proper names in the alphabetic cuneiform script, and this was first reported 2 Sept. 1802; however, alphabetic cuneiform belongs to the Achaemenid period, far later than Moses.

would take this as evidence that (as Spinoza had claimed) the Torah had been written later.[5]

The correspondence blossomed into friendship and Reggio, who founded the rabbinic academy at Padua, got his young friend a job there.

Reggio's 'arguments' are not very convincing, but they do demonstrate what people were worrying about at the time. One suspects that after reading Reggio they would have continued to worry. Before many years had elapsed Reggio himself was at odds with the Orthodox establishment, including his father, and eventually accepted the need for textual emendation, if not of the Pentateuch, of other biblical books.[6]

Samuele Davide Luzzatto (1800–1865)

Samuele Davide Luzzatto has become known by his Hebrew acronym Shadal, which does not mean anything useful like 'upright'. Like his mentor Reggio, Luzzatto battled against those who 'deny' Torah, i.e. who deny that the extant text of the Pentateuch is exactly that received by Moses; like Reggio, he occasionally proposed minor emendations of other biblical books.

Luzzatto's ground-breaking work in Hebrew grammar and philology, building on the foundations laid by a wide range of Jewish grammarians including Levita, is of lasting value, and his observations on the history of the systems of accentuation and pointing are percipient, though he is occasionally led astray by the conviction that Hebrew is derived from Aramaic.[7]

The work on which he appears to have lavished most attention is his commentary on Isaiah.[8] He states that he completed it on 13 Adar I in 5592 (1832), but the complete translation was not published until 1867, some time after his death. The requirements for the aspiring biblical commentator are set out in the introduction, composed in 1845:

1. Belief in a Creator, distinct from the world, who created by an act of will, contrary to the false philosophy of Spinoza, who misinterpreted the sources.

2. Belief in reward and punishment.

[5] The letter is in *Igerot shadal*, 31–5. The correspondence is discussed in Vargon, 'Controversy'. Vargon's title is misleading; the controversy is about the origin of writing, not about when the Pentateuch was written.

[6] Letter V of *Igerot yashar*, his collection of exegetical, philosophical, and historical treatises in the form of letters to a friend.   [7] Luzzatto, *Prolegomena* and *Grammatica*.

[8] Luzzatto, *Il profeta Isaia*. An introductory note explains that Luzzatto himself published (i.e. supervised publication of) the work up to p. 432, and the remainder was supervised by his sons. There are 648 pages in all; ch. 38 begins on p. 432.

3. Belief in the supernatural, for instance the miracle of the manna, and that God may convey information to human beings. If you do not believe in the supernatural you will be led to the conclusion that the Torah was composed much later than the events it records, and that the stories it contains were garbled in transmission.

4. Love of truth. The commentator must want to know what scripture really means, unlike those who use it to justify their philosophy or even to justify accepted Torah beliefs; Rashi and Rashbam did not hesitate to establish the correct meaning even when this did not coincide with the halakhah.

5. The commentator must be able to distance himself from his own time and place and imagine himself in the time and place of scripture.

6. He must be immersed in the Hebrew language, for if other languages dominate his thought, his understanding of Hebrew will be confused.

7. He must attend to the musical signs, for these were inserted as an aid to understanding by the sages of the Second Temple period.

8. He must be sensitive to the nuances of Hebrew poetry, rather than to Greek and Latin. 'My father was a carpenter and never read Homer or Virgil, but he read the Bible every day. He entered into the thought of our father Jacob, who said "I wait for Thy salvation, O Lord" (Gen. 49: 18). But Mendelssohn, who studied in depth the poetry of the nations, failed to comprehend that Hebrew poetry is completely free of metre; he was led astray by Rabbi Azariah, author of *Me'or einayim*, and went even beyond his opinion that the poems of our ancestors had balance, if not of metrical quantity like the poems of Greece and Rome, at least of the number of words. This is completely wrong, as I demonstrated in *Orient* early in 1840.'

9. He should note that the Targumim (Aramaic translations) and the interpretations of the rabbis are not always intended as literal translation.

10. The text of the Pentateuch has been transmitted with complete accuracy. However, there may be occasional lapses in transmission of other books, since these were not copied so painstakingly.

Luzzatto asks the reader not to be surprised if he cites non-Jewish commentators, for 'Some 80 years ago unbelief swept through Protestant circles in Germany . . . "rationalism" led them to compose lying and denying commentaries . . . I have to save my students from their errors, and show that the good things [to be found in these commentaries] are taken from our sources, but their own comments are rubbish.'

This last paragraph could almost find a place in the famous *Syllabus* listing eighty of the 'principal errors of our times' attached to the encyclical *Quanta Cura* issued on 8 December 1864 by Pope Pius IX. Reactionary Jews were as frightened of Risorgimento liberalism as reactionary Catholics were, and Orthodox Jews reacted to German Jewish Reform as Roman Catholics reacted to Protestant theologians.

Despite his obvious debt to Mendelssohn, Luzzatto did not think that Judaism was a 'religion of reason'; he inveighs against what he calls Mendelssohn's 'Atticism'. Yet he did not close his eyes to the new biblical scholarship. He makes liberal use of Septuagint, Vulgate, and Peshitta, and is by no means dismissive of 'Protestant' innovations. On Isaiah 40: 9, for instance, he cites with approval the Anglican Bishop Lowth's (highly questionable) observation that in ancient times women were entrusted with bringing good news, hence the feminine *mevaseret* ('herald', 'announcer'). On Isaiah 33: 7, on the other hand, he rejects Lowth's proposed insertion of a letter *yod* to make the word *er'elam* a regular plural, and proposes instead that *er'el* is a collective noun for 'hero', hence the plural verb.[9] Maybe he prefers English to German Protestants; they were less overtly antisemitic. At any rate, his rejection of such proposals of Lowth and others is no more robust or less courteous than his rejection of Ibn Ezra's suggestion that the chapters of Isaiah from 40 onwards are from another hand, or of innumerable instances of disagreement with traditional commentators.

He is far more scathing in his condemnation of kabbalah. In the French introduction to his lively *Dialogues on Kabbalah* published in 1852 but written a quarter of a century earlier, he writes of 'the dangerous effects that kabbalistic fanaticism, under the name of hasidism, enemy of all culture, still today produces among our northern brethren', and of the abuse made by 'kabbalistic texts, of attributing to the Doctors of Mishnah and Talmud doctrines opposed to their teachings, on the identity of Creator and created, and on the plurality of God'. He thinks that 'the most famous and orthodox contemporary Jewish scholars' will agree with his main thesis, concerning the age of the Zohar, and he feels that he has a religious as well as scientific duty to publish.[10]

His strongest ire is reserved for Spinoza, and in particular for the *Tractatus Theologico-Politicus*: 'To Luzzatto, who believed in the Mosaic authorship of

[9] The difference in translation is slight; whereas Lowth would have 'The mighty ones cry without' Luzzatto would have 'Their mighty ones (heroes) cry without'. The Kittel–Kahle Hebrew Bible indicates manuscript evidence supporting Lowth's suggestion.

[10] Luzzatto, *Dialogues sur la kabbale*. The dialogues themselves are in Hebrew. There is a fine analysis of the debate surrounding this work in Guetta, 'The Last Debate'.

the Pentateuch, the authenticity of the Bible, the historicity of the revelation, the actuality of miracles, and the veracity of the prophets as the corner-
stones of the Jewish faith, Spinoza's position in these matters was absolutely
untenable.'[11]

He is, however, ready to make concessions to scientific advances and,
unlike Elijah of Vilna, does not expect the Torah to provide information on the
natural sciences:

The cosmogony of Moses is not and ought not to be a tractate of physics, geology, or
natural science for it would have been incomprehensible to mankind during many
generations and would have been more harmful than beneficial to their religious
and moral education. However, that cosmogonic narrative itself in describing the
sun, moon, and stars set in the sky to shine upon the earth teaches us the unity of
the world machine.[12]

Reggio and Luzzatto alike make liberal use of non-Jewish historical
sources in their commentaries. Though aware of developments in textual and
historical criticism, they reject source criticism and remain reluctant to
make textual emendations, especially to the five books of Torah; this caution
allowed them to see themselves as within the Orthodox 'camp', even though
their use of extraneous sources and their rejection of kabbalah proved
disconcerting to their 'northern brethren'.

Luzzatto was acutely aware of the accusations of moral deficiency levelled
against the Bible and rabbinic tradition. In an essay presented to his father-in-
law, Raphael Baruch Segre, in 1842, and published some twenty years later, he
argues that the Torah rests on three foundations: compassion, divine providence (reward and punishment), and the election of Israel.[13] He cites several
instances of Torah laws that instil compassion; some are obvious, such as 'Do
not muzzle the ox when he threshes' (Deut. 25: 4), others less so, such as
opening the Exodus code (Exod. 21) with laws on slavery, which Luzzatto
interprets as an instance of compassion, since the Hebrew laws of slavery
mitigate the practice of that inherently cruel institution of antiquity. He then
has to fit the commands to exterminate the Canaanites and to 'borrow' from
the Egyptians into his scheme, somewhat dubiously putting the two on an
equal moral footing. After citing Francis Bacon on Providence and noting that
earthquakes and plagues are undoubtedly commanded by God, he concludes:

[11] Rosenbloom, *Luzzatto's Ethico-Psychological Interpretation*, 38.
[12] Ibid. 71, from *Discorsi morali agli studenti Israeliti*, 103; cf. his commentary on
Genesis, p. 2.
[13] The essay, *Yesodei hatorah* ('Foundations of the Torah'), is translated in Rosenbloom,
Luzzatto's Ethico-Psychological Interpretation, 147–204.

I am not here to defend God. It suffices that I have proved clearly that God's command to the Israelites, whether concerning the borrowing of the valuables from the Egyptians or with regard to the extermination of the inhabitants of Canaan, did not leave upon them an immoral impression, but, on the contrary, was useful to strengthen their belief in Providence, reward and punishment.[14]

Nor am I here to defend Luzzatto. But I like his readiness to acknowledge and face openly problems, raised already in ancient times, that other comment-ators on Bible and tradition prefer to conceal or deny.

Heinrich Graetz (1817–1891)

Abraham Geiger, who identified fully with the Jewish Reform movement, was certainly among those influenced by Mendelssohn's circle, and perhaps even more by the exegete and grammarian Wolf Heidenheim (1757–1832). He illustrates how the Mendelssohnian approach led, in German Reform circles, to a readiness to accept the results of historical critical research; in Chapter 10 we cited his assertion that 'the Bible, that collection of mostly so beautiful and exalted—perhaps the most exalted—human books, as a divine work must . . . go'. In contrast Heinrich Graetz, the 'father of Jewish historio-graphy', remained cautious, especially with regard to the authorship of the Pentateuch, though this did not save him from the ire of his one-time mentor, S. R. Hirsch.

Graetz wrote commentaries on Song of Songs (Leipzig, 1871), Ecclesiastes (Vienna, 1871), and Psalms (Breslau, 1881–3), and published in addition numerous biblical studies in which his historical-critical approach, often taking him far from traditional exegesis, is clear; for instance, he argued that there were two Hoseas and three Zechariahs and he interpreted Ecclesiastes as a political satire directed against Herod. His views on biblical history may also be gleaned from the opening two volumes of his monumental *History of the Jews*, the first covering the period to the death of Solomon, and the second to the death of Judas Maccabeus; these were published in 1874–6, several years after volumes 3–10 had appeared, as he did not feel that he could produce a satisfactory history of Israel without visiting Palestine, which he did in 1872.[15] The visit enabled him to get his geography approximately right but, like Zacharias Frankel and others associated with the 'positive-historical' school of Judaism in nineteenth-century Germany, Graetz was too traditional in his approach to the Pentateuch to rewrite the earliest history of Israel; where he parted company from the Orthodox was in his rejection of the

[14] Rosenbloom, *Luzzatto's Ethico-Psychological Interpretation*, 175.
[15] The visit had ideological as well as scientific aims (Michael, *Heinrich Graetz*, 124–9).

rabbinic revision of that history, but for this there was ample precedent in the writings of Azariah de' Rossi and others.[16]

Umberto Cassuto (1883–1951)

Umberto (Moses David) Cassuto was ordained in Florence at the Collegio Rabbinico Italiano, founded by Reggio and Luzzatto, and succeeded Samuel Hirsch Margulies as its head and as rabbi of Florence in 1922. Three years later he resigned to become professor of Hebrew language and literature at the University of Florence, and in 1933 received a similar appointment at the University of Rome, where he catalogued the Hebrew manuscripts in the Vatican Library. In 1939, in consequence of the enactment of racial laws in Italy, he accepted an invitation to fill the chair of Bible Studies at the Hebrew University, a position in which he remained for the rest of his life.

Like David Hoffman, of whom we shall speak later, he appreciated the scholarly basis of Higher Criticism but rejected the Graf–Wellhausen documentary hypothesis.[17] Unlike Hoffman, he proposed an alternative critical theory, that an oral tradition of epic poetry, something like the Homeric tradition, provided raw material that was subsequently woven into the unitary and artistic texts of the Pentateuch. His expositions, strongly geared to revealing the plain sense in historical context, make full use of comparative literary and linguistic material, not least of Ugaritic studies (the scribal library at Ras Shamra was discovered only in 1929), which he used to throw light on the literary structure and vocabulary of the Bible.

Cassuto built both upon his native Italian Jewish tradition, through Reggio and Luzzatto, and on the tradition of German Jewish scholarship imported by Margulies. Even so, he was impelled by the evidence to adopt a view of scriptural origins far removed from the naïve tradition of a text literally dictated by God with an accompanying commentary. Had he remained in the rabbinate he might have come under pressure to abandon such a view, but as a scholar he evidently felt free to seek the truth wherever it might be found.

[16] See Chs. 9 and 11 above.

[17] His critique of the documentary hypothesis on Genesis was first published in 1934 in Italian as *La questione della Genesi*; the English translation was made from the Hebrew version of 1944/9. See the Bibliography for details of English translations of his works. He was also the chief editor of the Hebrew biblical encyclopedia, *Entsiklopediyah mikra'it*, and took an active role in its planning and the preparation of its first volumes.

FOURTEEN

INDEPENDENTS

THE THREE COMMENTATORS discussed in this chapter all attempted to defend the traditional view of Torah from Heaven against criticisms raised by historical research; each developed a highly personal style and method which it would be simplistic to characterize either as Mendelssohnian or as 'in the steps of the Vilna Gaon'. All three were certainly responding to the issues raised by Mendelssohn; Mecklenburg had some knowledge of the Gaon's writings and the other two would certainly have been aware of his reputation, though direct influence is less likely.

Jacob Tsevi Mecklenburg (1785–1865)

Jacob Tsevi Mecklenburg[1] was born in Inowrocław, a spa town that won prizes in 2005 and 2006 in the Polish National Ecological Contest, but was under Prussian occupation in Mecklenburg's day. In 1831, following the failure of a business venture, he accepted a call to serve as rabbi of Koenigsberg, where he remained until his death. He was a redoubtable opponent of Reform; since his sparring partner was the Reform leader Joseph Lewin Saalschütz (1801–63), a pioneer in what was known as 'Hebrew archaeology', Mecklenburg would not have been allowed to remain in ignorance of historical criticism.

Koenigsberg lies on the Baltic coast, at that time in East Prussia but now, as Kaliningrad, a Russian enclave sandwiched between Poland and Lithuania. It was a centre of the Haskalah (Jewish Enlightenment), a place where Jews were very much involved in general culture including university studies, notwithstanding limits on what was officially open to them. The *éminence* of Koenigsberg was the philosopher Immanuel Kant (1724–1804), who had several Jewish students and followers, such as Markus Herz, Lazarus Bendavid, and Salomon Maimon.[2] A Hebrew language association was founded

---

[1] The name was commonly spelled Meklenburg; I have adopted the current spelling of Mecklenburg.

[2] Graupe, *Rise of Modern Judaism*, devotes a chapter to Kant's influence on German Judaism.

in Koenigsberg by followers of Mendelssohn, Hebrew printers vied with one another, and the first three volumes of the cultural Hebrew journal *Hame'asef*, founded by Mendelssohn's pupils and subsequently renowned as 'the first organ of the Haskalah', made their appearance in Koenigsberg in 1784–6; discussions among Jewish intellectuals there must have been lively.

The Prussian authorities disliked innovations other than those they themselves imposed on the community; while on the one hand they satisfied the Orthodox by now and then prohibiting the setting up of Reformist institutions, on the other hand they dismayed them by attempting to regulate marriages. On one occasion Mecklenburg, obliged by the authorities to perform a marriage ceremony for a couple who 'did not behave in the spirit of Torah', is alleged to have said *kedat friedrich hagadol* ('according to the law of Frederick the Great') in place of the standard formula *kedat mosheh veyisra'el* ('according the law of Moses and Israel').[3]

Mecklenburg's major work was a commentary on the Pentateuch, called appropriately *Haketav vehakabalah* ('Writing and Tradition'), in which he sought to demonstrate conformity between the oral tradition and the written law. It was first published in Leipzig in 1839, and reprinted twice during the author's lifetime with additions, together with a German translation by Jonah Kossman of the scriptural text, based on Mecklenburg's commentary. In 1880 Abraham Berliner published a new and improved edition at Frankfurt am Main and this, through facsimiles, has become the standard text.

There can be little doubt that Mecklenburg's work was stimulated by Mendelssohn's *Be'ur*, though he does not cite Mendelssohn directly. *Haketav vehakabalah* is essentially an Orthodox *reaction* to the *Be'ur*, aimed at supplanting it; where Mendelssohn aimed at elucidation of the biblical text *per se*, Mecklenburg sets as his prime objective the demonstration of the correctness of traditional interpretation. He is defending rabbinic tradition against its Jewish detractors rather than, like Mendelssohn, defending the Bible against Protestant historical criticism and antisemitism, though he is concerned with that too. He significantly subtitles his work 'Commentary on the Five Parts of the Torah, explaining the verses of scripture according to the plain sense [in such a way as] to unite them with the Oral Torah'.[4]

His introductory essay to the work is a prose-poem in high-flown biblical Hebrew, entitled 'Ma'amar hatorah', meaning 'Essay *by* the Torah' rather than 'Essay *on* the Torah'. It opens with the words: 'It seemed good to me to set these words in the mouth of the Torah, as if she were to raise the words upon

---

[3] Halahmi, *Sages* (Heb.), 299.

[4] *Be'ur al ḥamishah ḥumshei torah hamefaresh et hamikraot bederekh hapeshat le'aḥdam im hatorah shebe'al peh.*

her lips and make her voice publicly heard to declare to people why her written words are so very few that they cannot be explained without that which is handed from mouth to ear by the sages of each generation, and why all was not written clearly in the divine Torah.' The general idea is that it would be unseemly for Torah to indulge in complicated disquisitions; she has said clearly what she means, and those who know her, viz. the sages who through received tradition are close to her, understand what she means and how that is precisely conveyed through her words.

Much that could not decently be put into the mouth of the Torah herself is expressed in lengthy footnotes. Of particular interest is note 4, on the thirteen exegetical principles,[5] which he observes are referred to in the Talmud as *simanim* (signs). He writes (the German equivalents are his):

There are two sorts of sign, the *siman moda'i*[6] and the *siman zikhroni*. The *siman moda'i* (*Merkmal*—sign, mark, characteristic) is when the sign is embodied in that which is signified, as the signs by which a lost object, a corpse, or an unobserved piece of meat [are recognized], for the sign tells us that that which is signified is connected with the person who gives the sign. The *siman zikhroni* (*Denkmal*— monument, memorial) is when the sign is not embodied in that which is signified, but they are two separate things, but only in our thoughts have they become neighbours to one another . . . so that as soon as one is revealed to us we are stimulated to mention the second which is connected to it.

Mecklenburg argues that the thirteen exegetical principles are of the former type, *simanim moda'im*. That is, they are not merely mnemonics which work by arbitrary association of the signifier with the signified, but are contained within the text in an essential fashion. For instance, the words 'his blood is upon him' occur in Leviticus 20: 9 in connection with one who curses his mother or father, and in Leviticus 20: 17 the same expression, in the plural, is used in connection with wizards and sorcerers. When the Talmud infers from this that just as wizards and sorcerers must be put to death by stoning, so must one who curses his mother or father be put to death by stoning,[7] this is not a mere mnemonic; it is a demonstration that the phrase *damav bo* 'his blood is upon him' actually *means* stoning. In this way, it may be seen that the Oral Torah is actually implicit in the Written; they are as one.

As Grunfeld puts it,

Following the teaching of the Vilna Gaon, Rabbi Yaakov Zevi Mecklenburg sums up his view in the following sentence . . . 'Apart from our faith in the truth of the Oral

---

[5] These are listed above, p. 41.

[6] This curious expression is derived from R. Eleazar's exposition of Prov. 7: 4 in BT *Eruv.* 54b.   [7] BT *San.* 66a.

Law we are in duty bound not to rest in our studies until we have understood the complete inner unity of the Written and Oral Law, so that there is in our mind and conviction, not the slightest difference between the truth of the *derash* [interpretation] and that of the *peshat* [plain meaning].'[8]

Mecklenburg often cites the Vilna Gaon; for instance, his comment on Genesis 1: 1 that (contrary to Rashi) the word *reshit* carries an absolute rather than a relative sense paraphrases a comment in *Aderet eliyahu*. And like the Gaon, he assumes that similar Hebrew words are not optional alternatives, but that each has a precise, definable meaning. The Berliner edition of his commentary incorporates, near its beginning, a useful index of almost a thousand words with references to where they are defined in the commentary.

On the other hand, though he shares the Gaon's dedication to Hebrew grammar, his grammar is that of nineteenth-century scholarship rather than medieval philology. In this he is indebted to Wolf Heidenheim. Heidenheim had edited and commented upon Ibn Ezra's *Moznayim*,[9] written his own grammar, and produced meticulous editions of prayer books and a critical edition of the Pentateuch; he strongly influenced Abraham Geiger.

Mecklenburg insists on precise translation, which he frequently gives in German (in Hebrew characters). He occasionally refers to the Syriac, for which he appears to be dependent on Heidenheim.

Amos Frisch[10] has argued that Mecklenburg adopted a special, defensive position with regard to the alleged sins of the patriarchs, going beyond traditional apologetic. Mecklenburg is concerned not just to defend the personal reputations of the patriarchs, who he assumes were exemplary characters; he believes that, even if they had sinned, the Torah would not wish to make this known, since the purpose of Torah is to present the patriarchs as examples for emulation. Mecklenburg therefore consistently defends the behaviour of the patriarchs and matriarchs even when it is criticized by the rabbis. A test case, in which Frisch contrasts Mecklenburg's approach with that of Samson Raphael Hirsch, is the story of the rape of Dinah (Gen. 34). Hirsch unequivocally condemns the behaviour of Jacob's sons in slaughtering the inhabitants of Shechem; he puts in the mouth of Jacob the words, 'Our reputation, our name, our honour, which was as clear as crystal you have besmirched . . . And just as you have dealt unjustly so have you dealt

[8] I. Grunfeld, in Hirsch, *Commentary on Genesis*, p. x.   [9] (Offenbach, 1791).
[10] Frisch, 'R. Jacob Mecklenburg's Method'. On Mecklenburg see also Druck, 'The Gaon'; E. Breuer, 'Between Haskalah and Orthodoxy'; Ben-Menahem, 'Two Letters' (Heb.), lists editions of *Haketav vehakabalah*.
[11] Isaac Levy's translation of S. R. Hirsch, *Commentary on Genesis* on Gen. 34: 25, p. 523.

unwisely.'[11] Mecklenburg, to the contrary, and against the Targum and Rashi, draws on midrash to embellish the story, alleging that the men of Shechem regretted their circumcision and were planning to slaughter Jacob's sons, who then acted in legitimate self-defence. In this instance Mecklenburg's obvious desire to defend the Torah and its heroes as perfect has to some extent exceeded his zeal to demonstrate the unity of Written and Oral Torah, since (like the late midrash he cites) he rejects the mainstream rabbis' questioning of the morality of Jacob and his sons. The truth seems to be, as Frisch observes, that 'he believed it dangerous for his contemporaries to understand the narratives in Torah as imputing sin to its great figures'.[12]

In Chapter 9 we cited the pagan philosopher Celsus's critique of the way the Bible attributes moral deficiencies to its heroes; the same critique is frequently voiced by Muslim theologians on the basis of the common Islamic teaching that a true prophet never commits any evil deed. The predominant Jewish view, to the contrary, is that God communicates through fallible human beings.[13] It is strange that Mecklenburg should adopt what is in effect a heterodox theology on this.

Mecklenburg frequently cites the Zohar, under the title of *Mekhilta derabi shimon ben yoḥai*, and occasionally cites sections of it, such as the *Raya mehemna*, by name. For instance, on Genesis 15: 15, when Abraham is promised 'thou shalt go to thy fathers in peace', Mecklenburg cites both these works to prove that Abraham's father, Terah, and all the family, repented, so that Abraham might literally 'go to his fathers' (in Paradise). He uses the Zohar as a midrash, to fill gaps in the story or to get a precise definition for a word, but not, as the Gaon and Lurianic kabbalists use it, to read theosophic mysteries into the biblical text.

Samson Raphael Hirsch (1808–1888)

Hirsch is best known as a leader of the neo-Orthodox reaction against Reform in Germany. His first pulpit was in Oldenburg, where he introduced a regular German sermon, a male choir, and improved decorum, and omitted the Kol Nidrei prayer on Yom Kippur for fear that its abnegation of certain vows might be misinterpreted by gentiles as evidence of Jewish dishonesty. From 1841 he was rabbi in Emden and in 1846 he became chief rabbi of Moravia, then an Austrian province.

---

[12] Frisch, 'R. Jacob Mecklenburg's Method', 114.

[13] For instance, in BT *Sot.* 47a Elisha is openly censured for his harsh treatment of the 42 children who mocked him and for his treatment of Gehazi.

In 1851 he accepted a call from the Rothschild-backed *Israelitische Religionsgesellschaft* in Frankfurt am Main,[14] and devoted himself to creating a model Orthodox community in which traditional Torah and contemporary culture could coexist.[15] In the wake of the 1848 revolution the civil authorities were well disposed to religious conservatives and approved his appointment as a rabbi to the exclusively Orthodox group within the Frankfurt congregation.[16] Later, he disputed with another Orthodox rabbi, Seligman Baer Bamberger (1807–78) of Würzburg, whether it was possible for Orthodox Jews to identify themselves, in integrity, with the larger Jewish community, which was predominantly reformist; in 1876, under the Prussian-dominated regime, the Hirsch community seceded from the main Frankfurt community and became a legally separate *Austrittsgemeinde*.[17]

Hirsch thought of Judaism in universal terms, with a world mission to be consummated in the time of the messiah. In Letters 8 and 9 of his *Nineteen Letters* (1836) he stresses how the foundation of Israel's (i.e. Jewish) nationhood is Torah, not land: 'land, prosperity, and the institutions of statehood were put at Yisrael's disposal not as goals in themselves but as means for the fulfilment of the Torah', and conditionally on that fulfilment.[18] Hirsch emphasized biblical texts as the foundation of education; though accepting Talmud as the definitive statement of Judaism he did not, in his published writings, engage in talmudic dialectics, and was ambivalent toward Jewish mysticism. Israel's mission in exile was to disseminate 'pure humanity' among the nations.

He adopted as a slogan the expression *torah im derekh erets* ('Torah with the way of the land'); this derives from the remark attributed to Gamaliel III that 'It is good to combine learning Torah with the way of the land [*derekh erets*], for labouring on both leads [man] from sin.'[19] As used by Hirsch the phrase echoes the Protestant theologian Friedrich Schleiermacher's reconciliation of Christianity with culture,[20] and accords with the attitude of his own teacher,

---

[14] The late Manfred Lehmann stated of Wilhelm Carl ('Willy') Rothschild (1828–1901), 'Hirsch staunchly took his small group of faithful and formed an independent congregation with its own synagogue, school, etc. Providentially, the Baron was there to fund him lavishly.' (<http://www.manfredlehmann.com/sieg442.html>). See Liberles, *Religious Conflict*, 89.

[15] Liberles, *Religious Conflict*, 108–12. Liberles is at pains to stress that Reform was not so dominant nor Orthodoxy as weakened as is often claimed; on pp. 94–5 he thoroughly discredits Hirsch's claim that a mere 'eleven men' had founded the Orthodox community.

[16] Liberles, *Religious Conflict*, 93.

[17] Much of the correspondence is in S. R. Hirsch, *Collected Writings*, vi. 153–317.

[18] S. R. Hirsch, *Nineteen Letters*, Letter 8, p. 116.   [19] Mishnah *Avot* 2: 2.

[20] Schleiermacher, *On Religion*, written in 1799, presents a view of a living union of religion and culture. Hirsch rejected Schleiermacher's subjectivism; his emphasis on law

Isaac Bernays (1792–1849), Chief Rabbi of Hamburg;[21] a Jew should combine the best of the ambient culture with his own religious tradition, differing from a non-Jew primarily in undiminished adherence to halakhah.

What Gamaliel meant is open to debate, but Hirsch's interpretation would probably have alarmed him. It is also difficult to see how Hirsch's accommodation in practice as well as in theory with what he regarded as the best of the ambient culture accords with his emphasis on the *selbstbegreifend* interpretation of Torah, that is, the interpretation of Torah entirely within its own terms.

Claims have been made for the influence of Herder, Fichte, Hegel, and even Schelling on Hirsch, though they are vigorously denied by some of his followers.[22] Such claims are hard to substantiate, as he rarely cites the sources of his ideas, preferring to 'discover' them in some biblical or rabbinic text. Certainly, his concept of the nation, its 'one spirit', its language, and its destiny, shares much with that of Hegel and Herder,[23] as does his openly expressed admiration for ancient Greece: 'The Hellenistic spirit creates civilized, gentle, joyful, and free men.'[24]

Kant's (unacknowledged) influence is more pervasive, and is evident in two ways: the general tone of his ethical writing lays great stress on the concept of duty, and his interpretation of the commandments focuses on their ethical significance in a way that reflects Kant's use of the concept of God as the basis for ethics. For Hirsch, ethics, rather than spirituality, is the mark of the divine, and ethics is the essence of Torah law. Unlike Kant, however, Hirsch believed in revelation—Torah from Sinai—in a perfectly traditional sense; for Hirsch, God is the eternal, living, commanding source of ethics, not a metaphysical presupposition invoked to underpin ethics.

Like Mendelssohn, Hirsch denied that Judaism had dogmas, and he also emphatically denied that it had a 'theology'.[25] 'Judaism knows 613 commandments, but no commandments of faith. Those truths that form the basis of Judaism it reveals as facts, and it proclaims them for all who are able to perceive the truth . . . the Torah . . . is . . . a fact, just like heaven and earth.'[26]

rather than faith ('La loi und nicht la foi ist das Stichwort des Judentums') may be directed against Schleiermacher (Rosenbloom, *Tradition*, 215).

[21] Bernays left very little in writing; he denied authorship of an essay called *Der biblische Orient* which was attributed to him.

[22] For instance by Joseph Elias, in S. R. Hirsch, *Nineteen Letters*, 22.

[23] Rosenbloom, *Tradition*, 152 ff.

[24] S. R. Hirsch, 'Hellenism and Judaism', 202. Hirsch sees the virtues of Hellenism as individualistic; they must be subordinated to the social and spiritual values of 'Shem', i.e. Judaism.   [25] *Collected Writings*, i. 198–9 (*Gesammelte Schriften*, i. 88 ff.).

[26] *Nineteen Letters*, Letter 15, p. 200.

It is difficult to see how this statement is a whit less dogmatic than the statement that Jesus is the Son of God, or that Muhammad is God's messenger and the Qur'an is true. It is said that when the bodily assumption of Mary was proclaimed by Pius XII on 1 November 1950 in the bull *Munificentissimus Deus*, a rabbi ventured to his Catholic friend that such an absurdity was perhaps a step too far. 'But', retorted the priest, 'you surely believe, as the Bible states, that Elijah ascended to heaven in a fiery chariot?' 'How can you compare?', replied the rabbi. 'That really happened!' One man's dogma, it seems, is another's plain fact.[27]

What does Hirsch mean when he denies that Torah statements about God and revelation are 'commandments of faith' (Maimonides certainly categorizes them as such) and do not constitute a 'theology'? Surely rational talk about God and revelation is precisely what theology is and rational, even systematic, talk about revelation is precisely what Hirsch does in his exploration of the *mitsvot*. Most likely he designed such statements to distance himself from Christian and Reform Jewish speculation on the nature of God, a topic he felt it was futile to pursue and lacked relevance to the life of the ordinary worshipper. Many professed theologians might share this attitude, but would not deny in consequence that they were theologians; even bad theology is theology.

It is precisely his dogmatic belief in the divine origin of the whole Torah including rabbinic law that set him apart from Reform. He not only rejected historical criticism as a matter of principle, but attempted to refute it on its own grounds; his harsh and none-too-scholarly critique of the work of his erstwhile disciple Heinrich Graetz in *Jeschurun*, the monthly journal he founded to promote his ideas, demonstrates the souring of his relationship with the great historian.[28]

In 1855, in the very first issue of *Jeschurun*, he wrote:

The Written Law abandons itself if we deny the Oral Law . . . the Written Law seeks to be celebrated only in a company of men who are permeated by the living breath of the Oral Law, which is Divine like the Written Word; and in this way the Written Law itself makes it clear that its very being depends on the existence of the Oral Law. Indeed, it is not the Oral Law which has to seek the guarantee of its authenticity in the Written Law; on the contrary, it is the Written Law which has to look for its warrant in the Oral tradition.

[27] Not so much a joke; a web search retrieved a page from the *Catholic Encyclopaedia* actually headed 'The Fact of the Assumption'! On 'theology', see above, p. 2.

[28] Hirsch's critiques of Graetz and of Zacharias Frankel are included in his *Collected Writings*, vol. v.

When we raise aloft this Torah, the revelation of which we celebrate on Shavuoth, we jubilantly proclaim *vezot hatorah*, etc. ['and this is the Torah'], that it is still the same Torah which Moses brought to Israel 'through the mouth of God, through the hand of Moses'—the same Torah, pure and unadulterated. When we live and die in the conviction that this precious heritage has been preserved pure and genuine amidst all the tempests and vicissitudes of a history of more than three thousand years, or when we rely for the earthly welfare and heavenly salvation of ourselves and our children on the truth of this Torah, what guarantee have we for all this other than the tradition of our fathers? Yea, the selfsame fathers, who, together with the Written Law, handed down to us the Oral Law also. If our fathers have deceived us with the one, how could they be trustworthy with the other? Indeed, there is no evidence or guarantee for the truth and reality of a historic fact, save our trust in tradition. All sorts of documents and monuments, all kinds of internal and external circumstances may lead you to the conclusion that it is probable, or almost certain that such and such an event did really happen; but who tells you that what you consider probable or even certain has really happened? Or that the very documents from which you draw your conclusion are not in reality forged? ... The fact remains however, that Jewish tradition—a phenomenon unique in its kind—refers us back to itself only; and that it refuses any documentation by the Written Torah which, after all, is only handed down by that oral tradition and presupposes it everywhere.[29]

Many years later, in his commentary on Exodus 21: 2, he argued that 'to the unprejudiced mind, nothing can show so strikingly the truth of the traditional oral-law as the first two paragraphs, V. 2–6 and 7–11, with which this "Mosaic Lawgiving" starts; since the basis of Torah law is human rights, how absurd it would be to commence the code with "When a man sells another man ... " or "When a man sells his daughter"!' Evidently, he writes, a mass of laws and principles—the Oral Law—must be assumed *before* these marginal cases can be stated.[30]

Hirsch's son-in-law, Rabbi Dr J. Gugenheimer, wrote a series of articles to demonstrate 'how Hirsch endeavoured to answer the arguments of the Bible critics in the course of his Commentary by explaining the Torah in such a way that these problems either did not arise or were implicitly answered by Hirsch's translation and exposition of the text', notwithstanding the fact that Hirsch does not refer explicitly to the Bible critics. 'The reason for this is obvious', writes Grunfeld, 'Hirsch did not wish to introduce *tumah* ['impurity'] into the sphere of *kedushah* ['holiness'].'[31] That is, Hirsch did not wish to introduce the 'impurity' of Bible criticism into the 'holiness' of his

[29] *Collected Writings*, i. 195–6.   [30] *Commentary on Exodus*, Exod. 20: 2.

[31] I. Grunfeld, in S. R. Hirsch, *Commentary on Genesis*, pp. xxii, xxiii; Gugenheimer, 'Die Hypothesen'.

own Bible commentary, but on the principle of 'know how to respond to an unbeliever'[32] interpreted scripture in such a way as to defeat the arguments of the critics. Examples of this are Hirsch's cosmogony, presented in such a way as to avoid contradictions between Genesis 1 and 2, and his explanation of the divine names (Gen. 2: 4; Exod. 6: 2, 3), intended to undermine one of the main arguments for different pentateuchal sources. His avoidance of explicit reference to Bible criticism in his commentary contrasts with the greater openness of S. D. Luzzatto, though the underlying attitudes are not dissimilar.

Hirsch must have had some familiarity with contemporary science, but wriggles uncomfortably. On Psalm 19 he writes:

David . . . talks in the language of men . . . His language is the same as that of Copernicus, of Keppler [sic] and Newton . . . This language will remain the same even when the assumption that the sun is static and that the earth revolves around it . . . will have been proven to be irrefutable certainty. For it is not the aim of the Holy Scriptures to teach us astronomy, cosmogony, or physics, but only to guide man in the fulfilment of his life's task.[33]

Robert Liberles has pointed out that in at least one instance Hirsch comments, if obliquely, on contemporary political events: 'A new king arose in Egypt who did not know Joseph . . . he said to his people, "Look, the Israelites are too many for us"' (Exod. 1: 8–9). Where traditional commentators held that a new dynasty had been established by a native house, Hirsch suggested that a foreign usurper had taken over and stirred anti-Israelite feeling among the otherwise friendly natives; the unstated parallel was the Prussian occupation of Frankfurt in 1866 leading to Frankfurt's subordination to Prussia, followed by anti-Jewish incidents on the part of Prussian officials.[34]

Hirsch is sensitive to aesthetics, though his notes on the Psalms put the emphasis elsewhere; many of his works show a deep appreciation of German literature, and he encouraged beautiful rendition of the liturgy, including choral singing. However, aesthetics was for him secondary to religion and morality. Noah's three sons, Ham, Shem, and Japheth, stand respectively for sensuality, spirituality, and beauty; Japheth, ancestor of the Greeks, must be subservient to Shem, ancestor of the Hebrews, and is needed to wean Ham from his sensuality:

This culture of beauty and grace, the *kalokagathon* of 'Japhet' schooling is a precursor of the semitic mission, a preparatory school for teaching people to reach

---

[32] Attributed to R. Eleazar ben Arakh in Mishnah *Avot* 2: 14.

[33] *The Hirsch Siddur*, 56–7.   [34] Liberles, *Religious Conflict*, 194–5.

the loftier concept of life, the still greater beauty which lies in a harmonious joining of all the aspects of life under the single idea of devotion to God.[35]

Hirsch interprets biblical language in accordance with neither Mendels-sohnian aesthetics nor conventional philology, but in terms of a remarkable scheme of his own devising, which he believes demonstrates the perfection of the Hebrew language. Since the time of the Hebrew grammarian Judah ben David Hayyuj (c.945–1000) most scholars had accepted the theory that Hebrew roots are triliteral (consist of three letters). Hirsch, however, believes that *each individual letter* of the Hebrew alphabet has a distinct meaning, and that roots are made up by using the individual letters as modifiers; he has invented a *mono*literal theory of the Hebrew language.

His notions of the interchangeability of consonants are remote from standard philology; he routinely proposes the interchangeability of *alef* and *ayin*, so that for instance he can relate אור, *or* 'light', which begins with an *alef*, to the root *ayin-vav-resh* 'to be awake, to become or to be receptive to external impression', and define light as 'the awakening element, that awakens all forces to development'.[36]

Hirsch's idiosyncratic interpretation of the Hebrew language, developed throughout his literary career and comprehensively summed up in *Jeschurun* in 1862, coincides neither with tradition nor with science; its purpose seems to be to discredit non-Jewish philology, and hence historical criticism, by supplying a superior, alternative 'science' for correct reading of scripture. It has been curtly dismissed by Barry Levy as a 'fanciful philology'.[37]

Malbim
(Meir Leibush ben Yehiel Michel Weiser, 1809–1879)

The surname Malbim is an acronym formed from Meir Leibush ben Jehiel Michel; the family name was Weiser. Malbim was born in Volochisk, Volhynia (Ukraine). After serving in various communities, he was inducted as chief rabbi of Rumania in the summer of 1858.

He was uncompromising in his opposition to Reform, which he believed undermined the foundation of Judaism by questioning rabbinic tradition and the doctrine of *torah min hashamayim*. His Hebrew Bible commentary, com-mencing with the volumes on Ruth (1835), Esther (1845), and Isaiah (1849), was designed to rebut the critical arguments adopted by Reformers by dem-

---

[35] *Commentary on Genesis* 9: 27; Levy trans., p. 193. *Kalokagathon* is a contraction of Greek *[to] kalon kai [to] agathon* ('the beautiful and the good').   [36] Ibid. 1: 1; p. 8.
[37] Levy, 'Our Torah, Your Torah, and Their Torah', 148–9.

onstrating the coherence and sublimity of the revealed Torah and traditional exegesis. He also published sermons, halakhic works, and writings on
language, poetry, and logic.

Reformers and assimilationists slandered him to the Rumanian government, alleging that by his insistence on the laws of kashrut 'this rabbi by his
conduct and prohibitions wishes to impede our progress'; the main charge
against him, though, was that in his commentary on Isaiah he had insulted
Christianity. He was imprisoned, then released on the intervention of Sir
Moses Montefiore and on condition that he leave Rumania and not return.
During his wanderings in the following years he was variously persecuted by
maskilim and hasidim as well as by Reformers. He died in Kiev.

In the preface to his commentary *Hatorah vehamitsvah* on *Sifra* (a halakhic
midrash on Leviticus), first published in Bucharest in 1860, Malbim states
that he felt impelled to write that work in consequence of the 1844 Braun-
schweig (Brunswick) Assembly of Reformers, which had challenged the
authority of the Talmud and the Oral Law:[38]

> In the year 5604 from the creation (1844) we heard the voice of the sick, [cries of]
> pain as of one who gives birth to her firstborn . . . some of the shepherds of
> Germany ran wild and provoked God, and they gathered to put an end to religion
> and law and took counsel against its secrets. Many were the shepherds who came to
> pasture but consumed the flock of their pasture, calling themselves rabbis and
> preachers and cantors yet slaying their congregations. All these men assembled in
> the city of Brunswick . . . and fire went forth . . . to destroy the tablets of stone . . . and
> the appointed places of God upon the earth.
>
> And at that time . . . I resolved . . . to stand in the breach . . . [and to defend both]
> the Written Torah which this evil assembly looked on as one of the stories of the
> ancient peoples, and its poems and expressions as the poetry of Homer and the
> Greeks . . . and the Oral Torah which they treated with scorn and as negligible and
> whose sages they reproached and accused of ignorance of the plain meaning and
> grammar of scripture . . .
>
> Then I girded my loins . . . and commenced my compositions on the Bible,
> according to the principles I formulated in the introduction to my commentary on
> Isaiah and in [my article in] *Hamevaser* which I published in 5608 [1848]. I prepared
> for the Oral Torah a protective covering and built her a strong tower and a mighty
> fortress.[39]

He robustly opposes the view that the scriptural quotations cited by the
sages in support of their halakhic exegesis are mnemonic devices to facilitate

[38] In the complete edition of his Bible commentaries, i. 227*a* (p. 453).

[39] Among the many who attacked the Brunswick Reformers with comparable vehemence
was Schiller-Szinessy, who in a later volte-face became rabbi of the Reform Congregation in
Manchester. See Loewe, 'Solomon Marcus Schiller-Szinessy', 150.

remembering laws that had been handed down orally from Sinai, and argues forcefully that the scriptural text itself, if only one penetrates into the proper spirit of the holy tongue as carefully phrased in the text of the Torah, provides a perfect medium from which to derive these interpretations and laws on a strictly philological basis. As he puts it, the exegesis of the sages is the *peshat*, the plain and straightforward meaning of the scriptural text.[40]

Malbim perceives the significance of *midrash halakhah*, in this case *Sifra*, in 'uniting the dual Torah',[41] that is, in presenting Bible text and rabbinic interpretation of the text as a seamless whole; in this, he is following in the steps of the Vilna Gaon and others. He does not comment directly on the 13 exegetical principles attributed to Rabbi Ishmael, nor does he include them, as some do, in his edition of *Sifra*. Clearly, he has done his own careful analysis of the ways in which the sages of *Sifra* relate to the biblical text, and this is set out in full detail in his introductory treatise *Ayelet hashahar*. He expresses his joyful astonishment that when he had completed the analysis and counted the total of exegetical procedures it came to precisely 613!

Although he stresses the conformity between the exegetical techniques of the sages and the principles of Hebrew grammar, his grammar is by no means that of the academy. His first two principles, for instance, lay down (*a*) that no Hebrew root has more than three letters, which is fine, but also (*b*) that verbs with medial *alef, heh, vav*, or *yod* have two-lettered roots. He was evidently unconvinced by Hayyuj, not to speak of Abraham Ibn Ezra and a whole line of grammarians, who held that all Hebrew roots were triliteral. On the other hand he is by no means insensitive to, though he does not openly cite, the 'modern' philology of Mendelssohn and his circle.[42]

In the fourth paragraph of his essay 'Heharash vehamasger' ('The Crafts-man and the Smith'—cf. 2 Kgs 24: 14) which forms the Afterword to his commentary on the Song of Songs, also published in 1860, he writes:

So if anyone should ask you, What is the basis of this poem according to its plain meaning, and what is the metaphor it conveys, take great heed and exceeding care not to tell him that its plain meaning is about a shepherd and a shepherdess, a young woman and her lover, words of love and desire, God forbid. But tell him this. The metaphor is its plain meaning, the story of what befell that holy shepherdess, the soul of King Solomon, peace be upon him, and her dispute with her lover in heaven on the five occasions when she came forth from the pit and removed the

[40] Malbim, *Hatorah vehamitsvah*, i. 226*a* (p. 451).

[41] I borrow the phrase from the title of a book by J. Neusner.

[42] Rosenbloom, *Malbim* (Heb.), 11–12 and ch. 2. On p. 12 Rosenbloom claims that Malbim occasionally assigns later dates than conventional to biblical chapters, but this does not appear to be substantiated in ch. 2.

garments of her captivity . . . for this holy story . . . differs from all others in scripture, for all of them tell of happenings in the lowly, material world, and of matters perceived by the senses . . . but this poem speaks of what happens to the divine soul [of man] . . . as it ascends and descends, when it dwells in the body and when it leaves it . . . concepts of the intellect and not of the senses.

The title pages of the complete Bible edition, which incorporates the Leviticus commentary and others, both earlier and later, bear the following claim:

The commentary is based on three fixed principles:
It explains the words of God in such a manner that there will never be found two expressions which say the same thing in different words.
Every word in a phrase (ma'amar) has to be just what it is in that phrase in accordance with the principles of language and differences in homonyms [shemot nirdafim.][43]
No phrase is devoid of a profound thought.

Malbim's attitude to kabbalah needs investigation. In his *Rimzei hamishkan* on the Torah portion 'Terumah' (Exod. 25) he draws on a range of sources from kabbalah to Maimonides' *Guide for the Perplexed*. Yet this work, in effect an independent monograph, is unannounced and unexplained. What is its history? How does it relate to the 'normal' commentary it accompanies? Elsewhere in his commentary, Malbim cites Zohar as he might cite any midrash; for instance, on Genesis 6: 15, 'This is how you shall make it', he writes: 'This hints that God would spread over the new world a tabernacle of peace, as is explained in the *Tikunei zohar*', and goes on to interpret the divine names in a zoharic manner. Yet the commentary as a whole is not kabbalistic; Malbim's exegesis of the narrative parts of scripture is far closer to the rationalist tradition of Ibn Ezra, Kimhi, and Abravanel.

Noah Rosenbloom claims that Malbim was acquainted with the views of Bayle and Leibniz and that he had some knowledge of Kant's epistemology and frequently relates explicitly to the *Critique of Pure Reason*: 'Malbim deals broadly with the concepts of space and time, phenomenon and noumenon, practical and theoretical reason, categories, a posteriori and a priori reasoning, the categorical imperative etc., though sometimes Malbim departs from Kant's position for reasons of religious faith, and he engages with metaphysical and theological issues, a realm that Kant had closed to human

[43] See above, Ch. 12 n. 22, for details of S. Z. Herr's work on the homonyms of the Vilna Gaon and Malbim; Grünbaum, *Hakarmel*, expounds Malbim's homonyms.

reason.'[44] 'Deals broadly' is an important qualification; anyone turning to Malbim for informed commentary on Bayle, Leibniz, or Kant is likely to be disappointed.

[44] Rosenbloom, *Malbim* (Heb.), 12.

FIFTEEN

IN THE STEPS OF THE GAON
Written and Oral Torah Are One

Naftali Tsevi Yehudah Berlin (1816–1893)

Naftali Tsevi Yehudah Berlin is known as 'the Netsiv', the Hebrew acronym for his name. He was born in Mir, Belarus, married a granddaughter of Hayim of Volozhin, and in 1854 became head of the yeshiva at Volozhin (Belarus, midway between Vilnius and Minsk); in almost forty years in this position he transformed the yeshiva into a major spiritual centre for non-hasidic Jewry. With a roll of around 400 students the yeshiva was large by standards of the time, though in the context of a Jewish population within the Pale of Settlement numbering millions it can have served no more than a tiny elite. The Hebrew poet Hayim Nahman Bialik (1873–1934), one of many of its distinguished alumni, recorded impressions of his student days there in his poem 'Hamatmid'; though reflecting on the failure of the yeshiva to hold students to its ideals, he writes with warmth and respect of the personality of the 'head of the yeshiva', generally identified as Berlin.

In the tradition of the Vilna Gaon Berlin taught the whole of the Babylonian Talmud in order, contrary to the general yeshiva practice of focusing on the half-dozen tractates that gave most opportunity for intellectual ingenuity. Like the Gaon, he ascribed great importance to the study of the Jerusalem Talmud and the halakhic midrashim, and also to geonic literature, on which he composed commentaries, including one on the *She'iltot* of Rabbi Aha of Shabha (eighth century).[1]

His commentary *Ha'amek davar* on the Pentateuch is the fruit of his regular weekly lectures to his students,[2] and he overlooks no opportunity to drive home the supreme value of Torah study and the uniqueness of the Jewish people. At the same time, he seeks to demonstrate the consonance of the interpretations transmitted in talmudic sources with the plain meaning of

---

[1] *Ha'amek she'elah.* The title derives from the phrase *ha'emek she'elah* 'Ask a deep question' (Isa. 7: 11).   [2] The title is an adaptation of the preceding.

the Written Torah and the rules of Hebrew grammar. He does not seem to be aware of scientific philology, or to have any interest in ancient versions and languages. For instance, though Ancient Egyptian had been deciphered by his time it does not occur to him that words such as *avrekh* (Gen. 41: 13) and *tsofenat pa'ane'ah* (Gen. 41: 45) might be Egyptian; he simply follows medieval commentators who relate them to Hebrew or supposed Aramaic roots.

In the introduction to *Ha'amek davar* on Leviticus he considers the *derashot* of the rabbis, that is, the way in which they derive *halakhot* from the precise wording of scripture, and which may appear at first sight arbitrary or philologically unsound. He accepts the theory that they are mnemonics; we could not derive *halakhot* directly from scripture if we were not already in possession of an oral tradition concerning those *halakhot*, but now that we possess the tradition we can see that the *halakhot* are hinted at in the careful wording of scripture.

On Deuteronomy 6: 4 he argues that many verses were composed and known before their inclusion under prophetic inspiration in scripture. This looks rather like a concession to source theory, but the intention is precisely the opposite. Midrash says that the words 'Hear, Israel' were originally addressed to Jacob by his sons, long before the Torah was given through Moses;[3] Berlin wants to explain that though the verse had a pre-Mosaic origin, it became Torah only when sanctioned at Sinai. It is a *rebuttal* of source theory, not a confirmation, but demonstrates sensitivity to questions that were being raised beyond the gates of the yeshiva and were doubtless transmitted through his students.

In a general introduction to *Ha'amek davar*, called *Kidmat ha'emek*, Berlin addresses some significant issues. Why, for instance, is the Torah referred to as *shirah* 'a poem'?[4] He says that poetry has two characteristics. First, its 'natural' mode of expression is non-literal—one who takes it literally misunderstands the author's intention, for the 'plain' meaning is not the literal one. Second, beyond that 'plain meaning' the poet may wish to convey something more, and this may lead to unusual or irregular constructions; for instance, if a poem is written as an acrostic this will affect the author's choice of words.

In sections 4 and 5 he pursues an analogy with natural science. Whereas natural science is allotted to the nations, the science through which Israel understands the universe is Torah. The natural scientist, understanding little of the workings of nature, sees many events as anomalies; as he progresses,

---

[3] *Gen. Rabbah* 98: 3 on Gen. 49: 2.

[4] *Kidmat ha'emek*, no. 3. The reference is to Deut. 31: 30; BT *Ned.* 38*a* interprets this with reference to the whole Torah, though the plain sense is that it refers to the poem in 32: 1–43.

he learns that these events are covered by more profound laws. Likewise, one who commences the study of Torah finds statements which appear strange or contradictory; deeper study reveals their coherence. The discovery of more general laws as one generation succeeds another applies to Torah science just as it applies in natural science. Ongoing research is required in both disciplines; rules (laws) are provisional.

In section 5 he writes about the composition of his commentary and pays tribute to his teachers and influences. He makes reference to Rabbi Hayim, disciple of the Vilna Gaon and founder of the Volozhin yeshiva, though curiously not to the Gaon himself; I have not noted any reference to the Gaon personally or to his work *Aderet eliyahu*. He claims to have based his work on the commentaries of Ramban, Rashbam, Sforno, and Ibn Ezra, but no others, 'for there is no end of multiplying books' (Eccles. 12: 12), though 'if occasionally I have found an opinion like mine in some other book, I have not in general refrained from indicating it'. He records explanations he heard in his youth from his father-in-law Isaac, son of Hayim of Volozhin, and from other *gedolim* ('great ones', i.e. leading talmudic scholars). Acknowledging that some of his explanations might have been written independently by others, though in a different style, he reflects that no two poets (or prophets) have the same style[5]—Judah Halevi is unlike Ibn Gabirol.

In sections 6 through 9 he deals with homonyms. In section 10, perhaps again alluding to scientific method, he notes that one should not be surprised if exceptions are found to rules which have been established by research; further enquiry will reveal some underlying reason.

He occasionally reinterprets a passage in the light of recent observations of nature. Two instances occur in his treatment of the story of Noah's Flood, which of course he takes to be a historical account. On 'The waters increased greatly over the earth' (Gen. 7: 20) he writes:

They uprooted a great quantity of earth and created new hills and mountains that had not existed before the flood. This must be so, as it would appear from scripture that the mountains of Ararat are the highest in the world; this is not the case [today], but those mountains [that are now higher than Ararat] were formed by the flood.

On Genesis 7: 23 'And all [creatures] that existed on the earth perished':

Only those on the surface of the earth [were obliterated], but there were many bodies on which much earth fell as a result of the flood, and those bodies remained. They are the bones that archaeologists find, and they find bones of creatures that no longer exist on earth. On this basis many have judged that there was another world before the creation of this one, and then there were different kinds of creatures.

---

[5] BT *San.* 89*a*.

Indeed we read in *Genesis Rabbah* on the verse 'Behold it was very good' (Genesis 1: 31) that the Holy One, blessed be He, created and destroyed worlds before this one, saying 'This satisfies Me' and 'That does not satisfy Me.' The same is [written] in the Zohar on the verse 'And if his sacrifice is a peace-offering' (Leviticus 3: 1).

But I find this problematic, since in *Exodus Rabbah* 30 [we read] ' "These are the generations of the heavens and the earth"—What did He reject? He was creating worlds and considering them and they were not pleasing to Him so He returned them to *tohu vavohu* [empty and void].' But if so, no trace remained of them. So it seems that these bones must be from before the Flood. Although they are found in a climate in which they could not live, this is because they changed their habits before the Flood and went to other places.[6] [The reason] that they find strange creatures [that do not exist today] is that they crossbred (two) different species and in this way strange creatures were born, just like the mule that comes from crossing a horse and a camel [*sic!*]. [God's] providence [ensured] that bones should remain, so that a later generation might come that would know the secrets of nature . . . Providence decreed that many generations should pass before the bones of those creatures [were found], so that they would not try to recreate them [by cross breeding].

Catastrophism, the theory that the differences in fossil forms encountered in successive stratigraphic levels were the product of repeated cataclysmic occurrences and represented new creations, is associated with the name of the great French anatomist Baron Georges Cuvier (1769–1832); it is far from clear that Cuvier thought his geological ideas were compatible with Genesis, and unlikely that he believed in a supernatural cause for the origin of new species,[7] though Christian theologians were quick to use his ideas in that way. Whether Berlin was aware of such developments is doubtful, though some of his students may have been; or he may independently have thought of the same way to reconcile the existence of fossils with the biblical narrative.

Genesis 9: 20–7 explains the curse on Ham, son of Noah, who is to be a slave to his brothers. Although Genesis is probably concerned to justify the Israelite conquest of the territory of Canaan, son of Ham, the narrative has been used to defend slavery, particularly of black people as progeny of Ham. Berlin, commenting on verse 25, notes that slavery has not in fact been confined to descendants of Ham, nor are all descendants of Ham slaves; the effect of the curse, he says, is that descendants of Ham are more likely to be enslaved and to acquiesce in their status, seeing they are descended from slaves, than descendants of Shem and Japheth, who if enslaved are more likely to strive for freedom. This is not a categorical rejection of the institution of slavery or of the racism implicit in the notion of the inferiority of black

---

[6] This is his interpretation of 'all creatures had corrupted their way' (Gen. 6: 12).

[7] Rudwick, *Georges Cuvier*, 81–4.

people, but it does show some sensitivity to social issues that were being widely discussed in the late nineteenth century.

Abram's subterfuge in Genesis 12 troubled Berlin's conscience. In time of famine, Abram went down to Egypt and asked his wife, Sarai, to say that she was his sister: 'When the Egyptians see you, and they say "This is his wife,",', they will kill me and keep you alive; please say you are my sister, so they will do good to me on your account, and I will save my life through you' (Gen. 12: 12–13). Berlin cannot believe evil of Abram, and rejects Nahmanides' admission that Abram did wrong on this occasion. So long as Abram remained in the Holy Land, says Berlin, he trusted that God would protect him, for God had promised 'those that curse you I will curse' (Gen. 12: 3). However, that promise had been made only in connection with the land, so Abram was not sure it would hold good in Egypt; if it was God's intention to save him, then God would certainly save Sarai from sin even if she said she was his sister. Moreover, says Berlin, the Zohar explains that an angel accompanied Sarai to protect her. If this is how things were, Sarai was not in danger; all Abram had to fear for was his own life, and to save his life he was justified in telling a lie.

On Genesis 12: 17 he develops a typological theory according to which the patriarchs correspond to the three values of Torah, *avodah* (work, or the service of God), and charity.[8] Abraham stands for Torah, hence the sword is mentioned in connection with several of his exploits, for the attainment of Torah learning is compared to waging war against the evil instinct. Isaac, who was himself a sacrifice, stands for *avodah*, for work brings sustenance, hence the stories of Isaac emphasize the prosperity afforded him through Providence. Jacob distinguished himself through charity, and Providence was manifested to him through peace.

In his introduction to Exodus Berlin comments on the fact that the *Halakhot gedolot* (a summary of talmudic law compiled by Simon Kayara in the first half of the ninth century) refers to this book as *Ḥomesh sheni*, the 'second fifth [of Torah]', though it does not use analogous names for the other four books. Exodus is designated *sheni* (second), says Berlin, because Genesis, as an account of creation, is incomplete in itself. Genesis tells how people of ethical disposition came into being; this had to happen before it was possible for anyone to receive the Torah and thus complete the creation. He continues:

This [the Torah] is to the people of God as human knowledge and ethical principles are to *torat ha'adam* [the law of humankind]. For even though the world in its entirety did not achieve this state until long after the creation of heaven and earth, and even today there are many people who have not attained it, it is obvious even to

---

[8] Simon the Righteous in Mishnah *Avot* 1: 2.

the gentiles that this alone is the purpose of man. So we should believe that even though the Torah and its laws were not given until after the Exodus, and even today there are many Jews who have not achieved knowledge of Torah, the Torah alone is the purpose of Israel.

In contrast with Mendelssohn, and notwithstanding his characterization of the Torah as a 'poem', Berlin ignores literary aesthetics. He is concerned, rather, to demonstrate the halakhic appropriateness of each statement. For instance, *az yashir*, '*then* he sang' (Exod. 15: 1), is related to a statement in the Jerusalem Talmud to the effect that only on the completion of deliverance should one offer thanks.[9] His commentary on Genesis 15: 27 offers a more extended example:

'There were twelve wells of water and seventy palm trees.' Scripture informs [us] how the Holy One, blessed be He, prepared that place in advance, as *Mekhilta* cited by Ramban teaches: Rabbi Eleazar Hamoda'i says, when the Holy One, blessed be He, created His world He created twelve wells corresponding to the twelve tribes, and seventy palms corresponding to the seventy elders. So what does 'they encamped there by the waters' teach? It teaches that they were occupying themselves with the Torah that had been given to them at Marah. This teaches us about a matter in connection with what they had been given to understand at Marah, namely that though Moses had made known to them that the way of Torah is to be satisfied with little, this is the 'way of Torah' only when one first approaches the power of Torah; once anyone has successfully reached the level of Torah he has the right to generous provision and to things that ensure comfort so that he might increase his understanding of Torah . . . Therefore, just as at Marah they were given the quality of restriction and austerity, so at Elim, when they had busied themselves with Torah, they were given twelve wells of water, a plentiful supply, and seventy palms, which [bear the fruit that] is specially apt for [learning] Torah, as it says in [BT] *Ta'anit* 9*b*, that Ulla said, 'A basketful of dates for a *zuz* and the Babylonians don't study Torah!'

Berlin is also concerned to demonstrate, contrary to Mendelssohn—who is never cited, but whose work would have been well known to many of Berlin's students—that every word has a precise meaning and that there is no repetition; for instance, the change of divine name in Exodus 6: 2 shows that God effected deliverance through both his attribute of justice and his attribute of mercy. This concern becomes evident when we contrast Berlin's interpretation of the words *lekh lekha* ('go'—Gen. 12: 1) with that in Mendelssohn's *Be'ur* on the same verse.

Rashi comments that the reflexive pronoun *lekha* 'to you' in these words addressed to Abram means 'for your benefit, and for your good'. Ramban rejected this on the grounds that the word *lekha* was a normal usage implying

[9] *JT Pes.* 10: 6 (37*d*).

nothing personal, as for instance in Song of Songs 2: 11, where it is said of the rain *halakh lo*, the word *lo*, 'to it', being equivalent to *lekha* in Genesis. The *Be'ur* cites these opinions, and then argues that the Song verse actually justifies Rashi, since it is a poetic metaphor which conjures up an image of the rain fleeing to another climate to fulfil its nature there. That is, the *Be'ur* interprets scripture *as literature*.

Berlin likewise cites Rashi and Ramban and comes down on the side of Rashi, but not on the basis of the literary qualities of the Song image. He argues that the precise meaning of the reflexive is to stress the loneliness or separateness of the subject, as in the identical words *lekh lekha* used in the story of the Akedah (Gen. 22: 2). In that case, though, Rashi has noted that Abraham's journey is intended to be public knowledge, hence *lekh lekha* cannot apply to the journey itself; it must apply to the private, personal benefits Abraham is to receive. Berlin, that is, has rejected the literary approach in favour of one which stresses verbal consistency, hence (as he understands it) the perfection of the Torah.

In sum Berlin, 'in the footsteps of the Gaon', skilfully forges scripture and a vast range of rabbinic sources into a self-consistent whole. Occasionally, he will make use of some scientific theory or information he has picked up, but not of the literary and philological techniques in vogue in his time. He reacts against the broad thrust of historical criticism rather than against any specific arguments; unlike his colleagues in the German and Italian schools he does not fight Bible criticism with its own tools, nor does he appear aware of the precise forms it takes.

Me'ir Simhah Hakohen of Dvinsk (1843–1926)

Me'ir Simhah Hakohen, a child prodigy, was rabbi of Dvinsk (Daugavpils, Latvia) for some forty years. His reputation as a halakhist was established through his novel interpretations (*hidushim*) in *Or same'ah* on Maimonides' *Mishneh torah* (1902–26); novel interpretations on some talmudic tractates were published posthumously. He was active in public affairs and devoted to his own community; during the First World War, when most of the Dvinsk community fled and only a few of the poorest inhabitants remained he stayed with them, declaring that as long as there were nine Jews in the city he would be the tenth.

His commentary on the Pentateuch, *Meshekh hokhmah* (1927), has much in common with Berlin's *Ha'amek davar*. Like Berlin, he aims to present Written and Oral Torah as a whole; like Berlin, he draws on his vast knowledge of Talmud and midrash; again like Berlin, he is resourceful in attaching halakhic implications to narrative as well as legal portions of scripture. On the other hand, he shows little concern with philological aspects of the text.

Sometimes they read a text in radically different ways. Me'ir Simhah affirms clearly and emphatically that when Genesis 1: 27 states that God made humans in the 'image of God', this means that he made them with free will, that is, not subject to fixed laws of nature. Berlin, on the other hand, makes great play of the fact that the divine name in this verse is Elohim, which signifies God in his relationship with Nature; when God created Adam 'in His image', this means that Adam was the summation of Nature; after the sin,[10] however, few men and even fewer women attain such a blessed state.

Me'ir Simhah often uses kabbalistic texts to elaborate a point made in Talmud or midrash. In his discussion on Pharaoh's dreams (Gen. 41) he first cites from the Talmud Rava's view that dreams in general are nonsense, but those mediated by an angel convey truth,[11] then elaborates by citing from the Zohar that Gabriel is in charge of valid dreams, whereas nonsensical ones are instigated by demons, an idea which (according to Me'ir Simhah) tallies well with the wording of Daniel and with certain aspects of rabbinic demonology. Like other non-hasidic writers, his interpretation of Zohar is non-Lurianic; he treats it as he would any other midrash.

Barukh Halevi Epstein (1860–1942)

Epstein was born in Bobruisk, Belarus, which was also the birthplace of his father, the renowned halakhist Jehiel Michel ben Aaron Isaac Halevi (1829–1908), rabbi of Novogrudok, Belarus, and author of the halakhic code *Arukh hashulḥan*.[12] Epstein senior's sister was the wife of Naftali Tsevi Yehudah Berlin, under whom Barukh studied at Volozhin.

Epstein was reluctant to enter the rabbinate, and until the Russian Revolution was a bank manager in Pinsk, where he found time to devote himself to Torah study and writing. His three-volume *Mekor barukh* (1928) is a history of Volozhin and of his own family; *Barukh she'amar* is a commentary on the prayer book; *Tosafot berakhah* is a midrashic work; and he published a short treatise on the importance of knowing the Hebrew language. In addition, he was joint author of a commentary on the Five Scrolls under the title *Avodat haleviyim*. He died as a victim of the Holocaust.

His reputation rests on his *Torah temimah*, a popular commentary on the Pentateuch, first published in 1902. O. Feuchtwanger wrote of this:

---

[10] Berlin assumes the kabbalistic (and Augustinian) concept of an original sin transmitted to Adam's progeny.

[11] BT *Ber.* 55b, citing Zech. 10: 2.   [12] See S. Fishbane, *Boldness of an Halakhist.*

The Torah Temimah is the first attempt to bring the Written and the Oral Law visually together and to explain their interdependence in the shortest and simplest, but also the most convincing terms. Voloshin had revealed to him the organic growth of the principles governing the Oral Law from the finer nuances of the Written Law. He did not have to be a doctrinaire laying down new and sometimes not fully substantiated linguistic principles as we find in the writings of the Malbim and S. R. Hirsch, in order to justify the cogency of the Oral Law, nor had he to accept Halevi's[13] halakhic fundamentalism which did not allow the Oral Law to be creative and looked upon its alleged derivation from the Written Law largely as a matter of apologetics aiming at the Sadducees. He showed how both Laws naturally dovetailed and complemented each other.[14]

Of course Epstein was not the first to attempt to bring Written and Oral Torah together; he was well acquainted with the work of his uncle Berlin, and of Malbim, who did just that and which was, after all, the purpose behind the composition of *midrash halakhah* 1,500 years earlier. The emphasis here must be on 'visually'. Unlike earlier commentaries, *Torah temimah* places all the essential rabbinic texts on the page, with Epstein's notes below; it is quite possible to read the former and to refer to the latter only on obscure points. The originality of Epstein's selection of texts and of his interpretation should not be underestimated.

He is certainly more relaxed than Berlin or Malbim; he achieves similar results without Berlin's insistent preaching and without Malbim's rigid rule system, and has a clarity and lightness of touch that demands less effort from the reader than either of them.

Like all who walk 'in the footsteps of the Gaon' he does not doubt that Torah is perfect, superior to all other sources of knowledge, and that our task is to expound it as coherently as possible; if we do this, only sheer wilfulness can lead people to stray after the detractors from Torah, with whose worthless arguments it is best we should not contaminate ourselves. Unfortunately, this attitude makes a virtue of ignorance, so that even the positive contribution that historical studies can make to the understanding of Bible and Talmud is ignored and traditional errors are perpetuated.

And so to Germany and the West, where it was more difficult to ignore the claims of historical criticism.

---

[13] *Sic.* Who does he mean?
[14] Feuchtwanger, *Righteous Lives*, 41–2. For a fuller biography see Tarshish, *Rabi barukh halevi epstein.*

SIXTEEN

HOFFMAN AND GERMAN ORTHODOXY

David Hoffman (1843–1921)

David Tsevi Hoffman, born in Vrbové (Werbau, Verbó), Slovakia, studied at Hungarian yeshivas, at Azriel Hildesheimer's modernizing seminary in Eisenstadt, and at the universities of Vienna, Berlin, and Tübingen. Hildesheimer moved his seminary to Berlin in 1873, where it became known as the Rabbiner-Seminar für das orthodoxe Judentum (Rabbinical Seminary for Orthodox Judaism). Following Hildesheimer's death in 1899 Hoffman was appointed rector, and at the same time head of the *beit din* (rabbinical court) of the Orthodox Adass Yisroel congregation in Berlin.

His responsa to the questions addressed to him as head of the *beit din* were published posthumously by his son under the title *Melamed leho'il* (Frankfurt, 1935); they offer a revealing insight into the concerns of Orthodox German Jewry in the early twentieth century. He was vigorous in opposition to Reform and in defence of the Talmud and *Shulḥan arukh* against both Jewish and antisemitic detractors.

Hoffman was prepared to use the tools of historical criticism in his studies of rabbinic works, even though as a young man he had endured severe criticism from rabbis Elhanan Wechsler,[1] S. R. Hirsch, and others for daring to treat the talmudic sage Shmuel, in his biography, as a 'mere' mortal. No doubt, as David Ellenson and Richard Jacobs claim, he hoped in this way 'to raise the dignity of contemporary Jewish life and to aid in the task of Jewish collective self-understanding'.[2] He laid foundations for the historical study

[1] Elhanan Pinhas Mosheh Hayim Wechsler (1843–94), generally known as 'Hile' or Henle Wechsler. Hoffman's wife, Zerline, was Wechsler's cousin; both Hoffman and Wechsler had studied in 1863 at the Pressburg (Bratislava) yeshiva under the Ketav Sofer (Abraham Benjamin Samuel Sofer, 1815–71, author of a traditional commentary on the Torah). See B. Strauss, *The Rosenbaums of Zell*, 40. Strauss's volume reproduces on pp. 61–138 Wechsler's anonymous tract *Yaschern Milo Debor* predicting the destruction of German Jewry and calling for a return to the Land of Israel.

[2] Ellenson and Jacobs, 'Scholarship and Faith', 30, 28; their more detailed study reaches similar conclusions to those presented briefly here.

of the Mishnah and other classical rabbinic texts, and many of his seminal studies appear in the *Magazin für die Wissenschaft des Judentums* that he edited from 1876 to 1893 together with Abraham Berliner. But he rejected the findings of historical criticism of the Bible, in particular Wellhausen's allotment of sections of the Pentateuch to different authors, and composed several works to uphold the traditional view.

In the introduction to his *Commentary* on Leviticus Hoffman reiterates his unwavering commitment to belief in the integrity and Mosaic origin of the received text of the Pentateuch and in the divine origin of the Oral Torah; though he consistently upholds the traditional view on the origin of the Pentateuch, his rabbinic studies support the notion of a divine origin for the Oral Torah only in the most attenuated form.

He did not reject historical criticism in principle, however, only what he regarded as the unwarranted conclusions drawn by some of its practitioners. He is familiar with the biblical scholarship of his time, including philology and archaeology, and with developments in science and the arts; unlike S. R. Hirsch, his arguments against Bible critics are openly expressed in his commentaries. In a dedicated monograph, as well as in commentaries on Leviticus and Deuteronomy, he pointed out weaknesses in the documentary hypothesis and drew attention to the relevance of rabbinic texts for understanding the Bible.

Hoffman did not propose a constructive alternative to the Wellhausen hypothesis, but fell back on the traditional doctrine of *torah min hashamayim*, assuming that if he had undermined the critics' arguments he had successfully defended the traditional standpoint. This is a common error in religious apologetics. Even if Wellhausen's proposal that the Pentateuch had been put together out of sources J, D, E, and P was demonstrably wrong, this would not prove that the Pentateuch was dictated by God to Moses in its present form, as innumerable alternatives remain; the arguments *against* the traditional view retain their cogency, and another proposal to account for the compilation of the Pentateuch, such as that put forward by Cassuto, might be more successful.[3]

Hayim Hirschensohn (1857–1935)

Both Hayim Hirschensohn and his brother Isaac (1845–96), sons of a Jacob Mordecai who emigrated from Pinsk to Palestine in 1848, were accused of heresy. Isaac distinguished himself through his work on variant readings in

[3] We will run up against a more subtle, recent instance of this error in Ch. 20, when we discuss Halivni's claim that a perfect Torah text once existed.

the text of the Talmud, then moved to London where he published a religious Zionist journal and died early. Hayim moved to the United States in 1904, and was for many years rabbi of the Orthodox communities of Hoboken, New Jersey. He wrote books on many Jewish subjects, including the relationship between the views of scientists and those of the talmudic aggadists, on biblical chronology, and a vast work in six volumes, ostensibly about the laws that should govern a Jewish state, but ranging widely. In the second of these six volumes Hirschensohn formulated his views on *torah min hashamayim*. Zvi Kurzweil writes of Hirschensohn:

In his halakhic treatise *Malki ba-Qodesh*, he establishes a graded scale of halakhically permitted or forbidden activities. To deny the Mosaic authorship of the Bible, or to admit it while maintaining that Moses was not divinely inspired, is tantamount to heresy . . . Any other relevant scholarly approach, be it archaeological, historical, philological, or exegetic in a general sense, as well as the suggestion of changes in the masoretic text of the Bible, is either unconditionally permitted or permitted within the framework of university studies, though not encouraged. The motive for leniency in this matter is 'in order to know what to answer the heretic'.[4]

This is comfortably close to Hoffman's view.

Benno Jacob (1862–1945) and A. S. Yahuda (1877–1951)

We return now to the German scholars. Benno Jacob, like Hoffman, attempted to refute Bible critics, especially Christians, on rational grounds; his best-known work is his commentary on Genesis.[5] He strongly emphasized the need to understand the Bible in its own terms and historical context, contrasting this approach with that of Christian Bible scholars who, he felt, read it in terms of its justification for Christian doctrine. He rejected source criticism as a futile exercise, though not because he believed in any dogma of literal inspiration or Mosaic authorship:

Although he was not a fundamentalist, his conclusions, as a result of his study of the text rather than on religious grounds, were a complete denial of modern Bible criticism—both textual criticism and Higher Criticism with its documentary hypothesis. He regarded the traditional text [as] more reliable than the ancient translations. He considered the arbitrary textual emendations of Higher Criticism to be unscientific because their only purpose was to validate the latter's own assumptions. Moreover, he accused the school of Higher Criticism of antisemitic trends and of prejudices against Judaism.[6]

[4] Kurzweil, *Modern Impulse*, 152 n. 9, citing Hirschenson, *Malki bakodesh*, pt. 2, pp. 243–50.   [5] Jacob, *Das erste Buch der Tora*.
[6] Jacob Rothschild, in *Encyclopaedia Judaica*, 1st edn., s.v. Jacob, Benno.

Abraham Shalom Yahuda, born in Jerusalem to an Iraqi family, studied Semitics under the German orientalist Theodor Nöldeke (1836–1930), and lectured from 1904 to 1914 at the Berlin Hochschule für die Wissenschaft des Judentums. He made extravagant claims for the influence of Egyptian on the Pentateuch, particularly in Genesis and Exodus;[7] though his claims have been dismissed by the experts as excessive, he helped bring to Jewish and popular attention the need to read the Bible in the context of the ancient world.

Isaac Breuer (1883–1946)

Isaac Breuer, a grandson of S. R. Hirsch, practised law in Frankfurt, but eventually settled in Jerusalem where he influenced the ideology of the religious political party, Agudat Yisra'el.[8] He was a philosopher of religion rather than a commentator, a member of the Kant Gesellschaft until he left Germany, but his ideas on *torah min hashamayim* mark a significant development in Orthodox thinking. His main philosophical work is *Der neue Kusari* (1934). Zvi Kurzweil sums up his ideas:

Isaac Breuer incorporated Kant's epistemological stance, in particular his fundamental distinction between phenomena and noumena . . . He uses this Kantian distinction skillfully in order to neutralize the danger to Orthodoxy lurking in higher biblical criticism. He does not see the need to enter into detailed polemics with these critics of the Bible, because, to use his nomenclature, they refer to the biblical text as 'phenomenon' without taking cognizance of the Bible as 'noumenon' . . .

It is quite clear that Breuer's ideas about Torah min haShamayim, which are laden with mystic allusions, represent a peculiar fusion of Kant's epistemology with ideas borrowed from Kabbalah, particularly the branch of it that he acquired from the study of The Two Tablets of Stone[9] by Rabbi Isaiah Horowitz (1555–1625). His philosophic stance at this stage may be summed up as follows: The written text merely represents the outer garb, hiding its true meaning from the reader. It has to be read with the help of the fundamental hermeneutic rules and other interpretations of the oral tradition. However, even when this procedure is followed, the Torah as 'noumenon' continues to be veiled in mystery. The truth of the Written Torah is vouchsafed by the Oral Torah, and that of the Oral Torah by Knesset Israel—a mystically charged concept—which stands for the people of Israel in their linkage to the Godhead. The underlying conception may be characterized as the mysterious triple identity of the Godhead with Knesset Israel and Torah . . .

---

[7] Yahuda, *Die Sprache des Pentateuch*.

[8] Mittleman, *Between Kant and Kabbalah*; I. Breuer, *Mein Weg*.

[9] Inaccurate translation; it should be 'Two Tablets of the Covenant'.

... Written Torah yields something of its innermost kernel if interpreted and accepted in the light of the Oral Torah ... In addition, the written text of the Torah admits a secret mystical interpretation accessible only to those initiated into its esoteric lore ... all these presuppositions are placed by Breuer into a framework of Kantian epistemology with its fundamental distinction between 'phenomena' and 'noumena'.

Once these assumptions are accepted, all the elaborations of modern Bible criticism become irrelevant, since modern biblical scholarship is based on entirely different presuppositions from Breuer's. The modern biblical scholar engages solely in the literary interpretation of the written text ... For Breuer higher criticism is so irrelevant to his way of thinking that he considers it completely unnecessary to disprove its conclusions.[10]

Since Kant held that noumena were unknowable it would follow that the 'real' Torah is unknowable, but at this point Breuer conveniently takes leave of Kant. His attitude may be compared with that of J. D. Soloveitchik, to be discussed in Chapter 18; both place the Torah beyond the reach of historical or textual criticism by transforming it into a metaphysical entity and detaching it from its socio-historical roots. This is all very well, but the question remains of the relationship of Torah to the world of phenomena in which we normally live and history is enacted. If they are really saying that history doesn't matter and maybe Moses didn't, historically speaking, lead the Israelites out of Egypt, and maybe the Bible was compiled as the critics say but that doesn't matter either seeing that what we are concerned with is a 'higher' metaphysical entity, why don't they say so openly?

Jehiel Jacob Weinberg (1884–1966)

Hoffman was succeeded as rector of the Hildesheimer Seminary by Joseph Wohlgemuth, who retired owing to ill health in 1932. The new rector, who remained at his post under Nazi rule until the institution closed in November 1938 following the Kristallnacht pogrom, was Jehiel Jacob Weinberg, a distinguished talmudic scholar and halakhist whose early training had been in the Lithuanian yeshivas.

Weinberg received his doctorate from the University of Giessen for a thesis on the Masorah, and while there met Paul Kahle, co-editor of the Kittel–Kahle edition of the Hebrew Bible, with whom he formed a lasting relationship. Marc Shapiro has documented the anguish of a scion of the Lithuanian yeshiva world attempting to adjust to Western scholarship without com-

---

[10] Kurzweil, *Modern Impulse*, 79–81. Isaac's nephew Mordecai Breuer developed his uncle's ideas in two essays, 'Faith and Science'.

promising his intellectual integrity;[11] nowhere could this have been more problematic than in the attempt to maintain something like traditional belief in *torah min hashamayim* in the light of new information about the history of the Masoretic and pre-Masoretic texts. Weinberg did concede, as we noted in Chapter 8, that there might be minor variants from the Masoretic texts which were not merely copyists' errors; but beyond that he was not prepared to go. The historical critical methods he so ably used in his *Meḥkarim batalmud* (talmudic researches) were simply too dangerous to apply to scripture.

Joseph Herman Hertz (1872–1946)

Born in Rebrény (now Zemplinska-Siroka, in Slovakia) in 1872 but taken to the USA as a boy, Joseph Herman Hertz became the first rabbinical graduate of the Jewish Theological Seminary of America, founded in 1886; the seminary had not yet fully articulated its Conservative identity, though it sought continuity with the 'positive-historical Judaism' of Zacharias Frankel. He obtained a series of posts as an Orthodox rabbi in the US and in South Africa, and in 1913 was appointed Chief Rabbi of the United Hebrew Congregations of the British Empire, a post in which he remained until his death, by which time the British empire had commenced its metamorphosis into the Commonwealth.

Hertz lacked the strong yeshiva background of the east Europeans, and under Sabato Morais and Alexander Kohut had imbibed a more scientific approach to the sources of Judaism. He was a forceful leader—the *Dictionary of National Biography* notes that it was said of him that he never despaired of finding a peaceful solution to any problem when all other possibilities had failed—and a vigorous advocate for traditional Judaism. He was dismayed by attacks on the authority, accuracy, authenticity, and morals of scripture made not only by Christian and 'free thinking' critics, but by liberal Jews such as Claude Montefiore, and produced *The Pentateuch and Haftorahs* to rebut their criticisms and thereby augment the faith of the Jewish people; in the original preface, dated 10 May 1936, Hertz refers to the work as 'a People's Commentary on the Pentateuch'.[12]

---

[11] Shapiro, *Between the Yeshiva World and Modern Orthodoxy*.

[12] The single-volume edition was first published in 1937 (London: Soncino Press); a second edition appeared in 1960, with additional *haftarot*. The challenges that prompted Hertz's commentary are examined in Meirovich, *Vindication*. Meirovich (p. 2) notes that the project of biblical commentary written under Jewish auspices had been mooted by Solomon Schechter before he left England to become President of the Jewish Theological Seminary of America in 1901; Schechter remained a profound influence on Hertz.

Hertz, who was assisted in his work by Joshua Abel, Abraham Cohen, and Gerald Friedlander, frequently cited and scathingly dismissed arguments against the integrity of the extant scriptures put forward by what he presented as a bizarre hotchpotch of men hell-bent on discrediting holy writ, perhaps (it was not so darkly hinted) for antisemitic motives. Yet when it suited his purposes Hertz could invoke their authority in support of tradition. Archaeology in particular was held to 'prove the truth of the Bible', and in a series of seemingly learned additional notes Hertz harmonized Genesis with the science of the 1930s, invoked archaeology to 'prove' Noah's Flood, contrasted the Code of Hammurabi with the superior legislation of the Torah, identified the Pharaoh of the Exodus, demonstrated the antiquity and Mosaic authorship of Leviticus, rejected christological interpretation of the Bible, and generally succeeded in making his Jewish readers proud of their unique heritage and at the same time aware of the challenges confronting them. He cites Mendelssohn, Luzzatto, Malbim, S. R. Hirsch, Hoffman, Cassuto, and other recent Jewish commentators, including men such as Abraham Geiger and Claude Montefiore, whose opinions he loathed, but makes no reference to the Vilna Gaon, Mecklenburg, Berlin, or others of that trend. Though ready to concede that the dual authorship of Isaiah 'touches no dogma, or any religious principle in Judaism', he argues for the unity of the book,[13] and on the antiquity and Mosaic authorship of Deuteronomy he is totally unyielding.[14]

Hertz was undoubtedly closer to Morais, Kohut, and the Jewish Theological Seminary of America Conservatives than to the neo-Orthodoxy of S. R. Hirsch and his followers, for he was quite willing to promote the notion of historical positivism in reconstructing the history of the oral tradition.[15] Moreover, while stressing the uniqueness of 'the moral theology of Israel' he used archaeological and philological evidence to present ancient Israel within the cultural context of Near Eastern antiquity, hoping thereby to demonstrate its moral superiority. For instance, Hertz argues robustly, adducing copious evidence, that treatment of slaves was far more humane in Israel than elsewhere in the ancient world, particularly Rome, though he conveniently forgets that it was Jewish rather than Roman law that objected to the freeing of alien slaves (Lev. 25: 46).[16]

Hertz was attacked by Moses Gaster, Ashkenazi head of the Sephardi community, for claiming that there was Jewish dogma and for confusing the public with controversial issues, and by Redcliffe Salaman, the great authority on the potato, for using the Bible to explain science rather than the other way

---

[13] Hertz, *Pentateuch and Haftorahs*, Additional Note H to Deuteronomy, pp. 941–2.

[14] Ibid., Additional Note G to Deuteronomy, pp. 937–41.

[15] Meirovich, *Vindication*, 15, 148–153   [16] Hertz, *Pentateuch and Haftorahs*, 537, 848.

around.[17] Nevertheless, the 'People's Commentary' proved enduringly successful, and for many decades was by far the most popular commentary
among English-speaking Jews, Orthodox, Conservative, and Reform. Only
towards the end of the twentieth century did it lose its pre-eminence, as
each of the denominations produced a distinctive commentary of its own, a
phenomenon to which I shall return in Chapter 21.

Summary of Part III

◆

Orthodox reaction to textual and historical criticism of the Bible, as it appears
in Bible commentaries from the late eighteenth century onwards, took two
distinct forms.

In Germany the reaction was based on acknowledgment of the basic
validity of the historical approach; the defence was that the critics had got it
wrong, perhaps from a theological motive to discredit the Old Testament
in favour of the New (though how this squares with an equally radical
New Testament criticism is unclear), perhaps through sheer antisemitism.
This trend stems from Mendelssohn, whose German Reform and Italian
mainstream followers eventually made peace with historical criticism. The
conservative/liberal split was formalized into Orthodox versus Reform, and
Orthodox commentators beginning with S. R. Hirsch (even though he does
not cite the critics in his commentary) combated historical criticism 'on its
own ground'; this is the trend exemplified by David Hoffman, and eventually
in England by J. H. Hertz in his popular *Commentary on the Pentateuch*.

In the course of the twentieth century this way of defence lost cogency.
Hoffman's arguments may to some extent undermine a particular form of
documentary hypothesis, but they leave intact the principle of historical
criticism. The imputation to Bible critics of antisemitism, though well on
target in some instances, carries less weight now, and in any case does not
address any valid arguments they may have put forward. Further research and
archaeological findings have cast ever more doubt on the traditional position.
By the onset of the Second World War, Weinberg was forced to concede
Masoretic variants, Cassuto proposed what is in effect an alternative documentary hypothesis, and Breuer transformed scripture into an unassailable
metaphysical entity.

People associated with this approach are often referred to as 'Modern
Orthodox', though this is not a precise designation. They identify with

---

[17] Meirovich, *Vindication*, 170–2.

tradition and commit themselves to *torah min hashamayim*, but at the same time acknowledge the validity of the historical method while living in hope that the two can somehow be reconciled. The inconsistency of this position surfaces in the difference of approach to Bible and Talmud; at an institute such as the Bar-Ilan University at Ramat Gan, Israel, generally regarded as in the Modern Orthodox camp, it was until recently acceptable to apply the methods of historical criticism to the study of Talmud and other rabbinic classics and even to some biblical books, but not to the Pentateuch.

The other approach stems from the Vilna Gaon and characterizes the world of *haredi* Judaism. It is fideist in outlook; its starting point is faith in Torah and in the sages. It denies the legitimacy of historical criticism as applied to Torah, and also the legitimacy of addressing the biblical text other than through the lens of the rabbinic tradition, together with which it forms the complete Torah as revealed by God to Moses at Sinai. Since the Gaon valued Hebrew grammar as essential to Torah, philology is respected, though only with Mecklenburg does this appear to be the sort of philology recognized in academic circles; since the Gaon had called attention to the need to study previously neglected rabbinic sources such as the Jerusalem Talmud and the halakhic midrashim, these and other sources are invoked, with the texts often re-edited. The objectives are (1) to demonstrate the unity of Written and Oral Torah, (2) to demonstrate that the Oral Torah is the most rational and consistent way to read the Written Torah, and (3) to demonstrate that the Torah as a whole so far exceeds human comprehension that its divine origin cannot be called into question.

This approach has two additional features. One is a tendency to read halakhah into narrative as well as legal sections of scripture; this is partly to justify the behaviour of the patriarchs and others who are held up as models of correct behaviour, but also because halakhah is more and more seen as the essence of Torah. The other is the use of kabbalistic sources, including the Zohar, in a manner distinct from that employed in hasidic writings; kabbalah is cited as midrash, not specially privileged, its texts read in a plain manner rather than through a hermeneutic imposed by Luria or a hasidic school.

Whichever approach is adopted, there is a determination to preserve at all costs the doctrines of the verbal inspiration of the Pentateuch and of the indissoluble unity of Written and Oral Torah.

PART IV

◆

NEW FOUNDATIONS

Torah from Heaven:
The Reconstruction of Belief

T HIS PART consists of five essays, all focusing on ways in which the concept of Torah from Heaven has been reconstructed in modern times.

The first (Chapter 17) is concerned with non-Orthodox constructions (Mendelssohn, Steinheim, Holdheim, Krochmal, Formstecher, Samuel Hirsch, Hermann Cohen, Baeck, Buber, Rosenzweig, Heschel, Levinas).

This is followed by a full-length essay (Chapter 18) on the Orthodox J. D. Soloveitchik.

In Chapter 19 I consider the feminist critique whose origins lie in the eighteenth century, though it took two centuries for its full impact to become evident in Jewish religious circles.

In Chapter 20 I appraise recent attempts by four scholars with Orthodox leanings (Jacobs, Halivni, Kellner, Ross) to rewrite the concept of 'Torah from Heaven' in the light of contemporary scholarship and concerns.

Chapter 21 looks at the same issue from an institutional point of view. What has been the response to modernity of Orthodox, Conservative, and Reform Jews respectively, as reflected in the way the Torah is read and interpreted in their schools and synagogues?

SEVENTEEN

NON-ORTHODOX
RECONSTRUCTIONS

JEFFREY BLUTINGER has fully described the emergence of the term 'Orthodox' as the designation of a Jewish denomination.[1] The German equivalent, *rechtglaubig*, had been used by Lutherans to refer to those 'right-believing' Christians who accepted the Reformer's doctrines. Moses Mendelssohn, in a letter he wrote to Lessing in 1755, is the first Jew known to have used the term in a Jewish context, when he expressed doubt as to whether Dr Baumgarten of Frankfurt was 'really orthodox or does he just pretend so'; 'orthodox', for Mendelssohn as for other German Enlightenment figures, was not a denominational label, but meant 'holding on to traditional beliefs and hence opposed to the Enlightenment'. Salomon Maimon, in the autobiography he published in 1792, similarly characterized as 'orthodox' the rabbis who rejected his Enlightenment ideas; Saul Ascher (1767–1822), who published his *Leviathan* in the same year, hinted that 'orthodox' concerned practice as well as belief, though he was still not thinking in denominational terms.

When a formal Reform movement emerged in Germany in the early 1800s, 'orthodox' gained currency as a label for those who resisted change in the *practice*, not only the beliefs, of Judaism. In 1980 Michael Meyer published an anonymous manuscript, most likely the work of Maimon's friend Dr Sabbatja Joseph Wolff (1757–1832);[2] the author, who began writing in 1812, was attempting to persuade the Prussian authorities to permit innovation in Jewish religious organization, and made perfectly clear that 'orthodox' and 'heterodox' covered differences in prayers and ceremonies as well as attitudes to enlightenment.

[1] Blutinger, '"So-Called Orthodoxy"'; detailed references should be sought there. Blutinger makes no reference to the London-born French–Jewish politician Abraham Furtado (1756–1816), who is conventionally credited with introducing 'orthodox' in a Jewish context, in the course of debates in 1806/7 occasioned by Napoleon's proposals for Jewish emancipation. See also Kochan, *Making of Western Jewry*, 300–8.

[2] Meyer, 'The Orthodox and the Enlightened'. The original German text, with Meyer's notes, is reproduced on pp. 111–30, with a facsimile specimen facing p. 116.

The liturgical changes instituted by the early Reformers, who at the time thought of themselves as a trend rather than a distinct denomination, were roundly condemned in 1819 by eighteen rabbis under the leadership of the Hatam Sofer, Rabbi Moses Schreiber (Sofer) of Pressburg (Bratislava, Slovakia) (1762–1839), in the tract *Eleh divrei haberit* (Altona, 1819). Condemnation produced the inevitable reaction, and in the 1840s the new Reform movement held a series of conferences at which its leaders engaged in a process of self-definition that served to confirm a formal denominational split within Jewry; 'Orthodox' and 'Reform' then settled into their still current meanings.

Though Reform and Orthodox crystallized as distinct denominations only in the early nineteenth century, broadly liberal and conservative tendencies have always been present in Judaism; the 'modern' reinterpretation of *torah min hashamayim* was under way well before the rise of Reform.

Harry Austryn Wolfson (1887–1974), in his monumental studies of Philo and medieval religious philosophy, argued that the Middle Ages began with Philo; Spinoza marks the turning point to modernity.[3] This simplifies a highly complex process, but it encapsulates a profound reality. For Philo, revelation as recorded in scripture is the ultimate arbiter of truth, and reason the means to interpret it; for Spinoza, reason is the ultimate arbiter of truth, and determines what is valid or authentic in scripture. Philo's position dominated Jewish and Christian thought until the early modern period, and still prevails in traditional circles; Spinoza set the agenda for the modern re-evaluation of scripture. The modern reinterpretation of *torah min hashamayim*, we may say, began with Spinoza, and in particular with his *Tractatus Theologico-Politicus*, first published in 1670.

In the *Tractatus* Spinoza defines not *Torah*, but *faith*. From his understanding of faith we infer his concept of Torah, bearing in mind that he does not distinguish between the Five Books and the rest of the Bible, or even between Old and New Testaments; for Spinoza, all alike are books that people claim record God's revelation.

Spinoza distinguishes between *lex divina* 'divine law', which is universal, arising *ex necessitatae naturae* 'from natural necessity', physical or ethical, and human decree, which he calls *jus* (ordinance) rather than *lex*, and which is relative to specific times and places, serving to render life and the state secure. True knowledge of God and Love constitutes the Divine Law for people, since it corresponds to the nature of the highest good, and is universal and absolute.[4]

---

[3] Wolfson, 'The Philonic God of Revelation'.
[4] Spinoza, *Tractatus Theologico-Politicus* IV.

[A] true knowledge of faith is above all things necessary to understand that the Bible was adapted to the intelligence, not only of the prophets, but also of the diverse and fickle multitude.[5]

. . . the aim and object of Scripture is only to teach obedience . . . the Bible teaches very clearly in a great many passages what everyone ought to do to obey God; the whole duty is summed up in love to one's neighbour . . . we are not bound by Scriptural command to believe anything beyond what is absolutely necessary for fulfilling its main precept.[6]

It does not matter, in Spinoza's view, that Moses did not write the Pentateuch, that certain narratives are demonstrably incorrect or inconsistent, and that the Bible contains statements that are immoral, superstitious, or betray ignorance of natural phenomena, for such things may be discarded as arising from the human failing of its writers or of the masses to whom it is addressed; the Divine Law of God and Love is plainly there for all to see, and constitutes the real essence of scripture.

Spinoza's concept of Torah, that is, of literature commonly regarded as sacred, is of an imperfect text, replete with narratives of dubious moral value, incorporating laws and rituals of limited relevance, but of supreme importance since it inculcates obedience to the Divine Law of God and Love. He has no time for 'Pharisees and Papists', that is, for the interpretations and traditions of synagogue and church, but insists that scripture must be read only in its own terms.

Christians and Jews of conservative outlook found this position outrageously heterodox; the British Chief Rabbi, Lord Sacks, like S. D. Luzzatto, has identified Spinoza as the *bête noire* of Judaism, for his political as well as his theological ideas.[7] But although Spinoza was incorrect in many of his detailed observations, his basic position on scripture came to be widely adopted; the evolution of modern non-Orthodox Jewish theologies is a triumph of Spinoza over medieval Jewish (and Christian) doctrine.

Moses Mendelssohn: Revealed Legislation

Non-traditional reconstructions of 'Torah from Heaven' from the eighteenth century onwards have to be seen against the background of European, especially German, philosophy and theology of the same period.

I remarked in Chapter 12 on the absence from Mendelssohn's *Be'ur* of engagement with issues of historical or textual criticism. Mendelssohn's religious philosophy was close to Deism, though, and this coloured his

---

[5] *Tractatus* XIV, in *Benedicti de Spinoza Opera*, vol. i, p. 243 (Elwes' trans., p. 182).
[6] Ibid. 244, 245 (Elwes' trans., pp. 183, 184).   [7] Sacks, *Crisis and Covenant*, 181–4.

attitude to Torah. Torah, he claims, is entirely in conformity with reason—by which we understand that God exists, and has revealed the ethical principles upon which all reasonable people would agree; God and ethics form the content of the Seven Commandments of Noah, addressed to all humankind. The Torah contains no irrational dogma, such as those which cause confusion and strife among Christians. Though it contains legislation, this is addressed specifically to the people of Israel and is binding on no one else.

Mendelssohn's purpose in such works as *Jerusalem* was to mount a robust defence of Judaism, and his work must be assessed in terms of the pressing needs of his time and public obligations. But two important questions remain without satisfactory answers. Can anyone plausibly claim that Judaism is 'free from dogma'? By no means all conflicts within Judaism were primarily concerned with religious ritual. The major conflict of Karaites and Rabbanites, for instance, concerned belief in the Oral Torah, and all Judaism depended on belief in the Written Torah, yet it is scarcely plausible to treat such beliefs as matters of pure reason.

The second problem, which Mendelssohn addressed unconvincingly, was that if the rules and rituals of Torah were 'revealed legislation' pertaining to the ancient or idealized Israelite state, why should Jews in modern Europe be obliged to follow them?[8]

Salomon Ludwig Steinheim (1789–1866): Empiricist of Revelation

The leading German Idealists—Fichte, Schelling, and Hegel—were university professors whose fathers were Protestant pastors or who had themselves studied theology. This circumstance gave German Idealism an intensely serious, quasi-religious, dedicated character. This was combined with the individualism of the liberal Enlightenment, with Rousseauesque romanticism, and with a critical attitude to the literary sources of religion. Something like the following consensus emerged:

- The focus of philosophy is the human self and its self-consciousness.

- The volitional and the moral take precedence over the scientific and intellectual.

- The world is essentially *geistlich* (this means 'mental', as well as 'spiritual' in the narrow English sense), a sort of cosmic Self.

[8] Compare Pierre Bayle's effort to defend ancient Israelite theocracy in *De la tolérance*, pt. 2 ch. 4.

In 1792 Johann Gottlieb Fichte (1762–1814), encouraged by Kant, published *Versuch einer Kritik aller Offenbarung* ('Attempt at a Critique of All Revelation'). In this work he sought to explain the conditions under which revealed religion was possible. Religion, he maintained, was belief in the moral law as divine. This belief was a practical postulate, necessary in order to add force to the law. In *Die Bestimmung des Menschen* ('The Vocation of Man', 1800) he defines God as the infinite moral will of the universe who becomes conscious of himself in individuals. Later, in *Die Grundzüge des gegenwärtigen Zeitalters* ('Characteristics of the Present Age', 1806), he defined the place of the Enlightenment in the historical evolution of the general human consciousness, looking forward to belief in the divine order of the universe as the highest aspect of the life of reason; and in *Die Anweisung zum seligen Leben, oder auch die Religionslehre* ('The Way to the Blessed Life, or the Philosophy of Religion', 1806) he writes of the union between the finite self-consciousness and the infinite ego, or God.

The non-traditional Jewish thinkers of nineteenth-century German Jewry might well be termed 'Protestant Jews', and those in the early part of the century were responding to the wave of Romantic religiosity which, under the inspiration of the philosopher Friedrich Schleiermacher (1768–1834), had made religion socially respectable once again in the aftermath of Enlightenment scepticism. Whether out of prudence or conviction, many Jews had converted to Christianity. Those Jewish intellectuals who remained within the fold felt compelled to defend Judaism in terms of current philosophies; often, they used those philosophies to undermine the specific claims of Christianity.

Salomon Ludwig Steinheim was a physician and polymath, not a rabbi. He studied theology at the newly opened University of Berlin in 1810–11, but most of his career was devoted to medicine and public health and only in 1833 did he commence his Jewish religious publications. Though at one time close to the Reform leadership he did not identify with either the Orthodox or Reform camp; he criticized the former for their ceremonialism and the latter for their shallowness.

The first of four parts of his *Die Offenbarung nach dem Lehrbegriff des Synagoge, ein Schibboleth* ('Revelation According to Jewish Doctrine: A Criterion')[9]—clearly a response to Fichte—appeared in Frankfurt am Main in 1835. Steinheim admired Kant, but felt that in making the idea of God dependent on the certainty of ethical judgements Kant had seriously undervalued the spiritual. To Kant's four antinomies he added a fifth, that between reason and experience. Reason (by which he meant a priori judgement) constantly found

---

[9] Selections from the work are translated in Haberman, *Philosopher of Revelation*.

itself at odds with experience, even in the realm of science. For instance, science assumed that everything had a cause, whereas experience demonstrated freedom.

The fundamental defect of reason, as Steinheim sees it, is that it operates with logical necessity. It binds even God to the laws of causality. It turns out to be at odds with empirical observation, in particular with the existential notion of freedom.

Revelation is therefore necessary, not to yield ethical principles, which reason could establish, and certainly not to provide legislation. It is needed precisely for that which reason cannot offer, the knowledge of God as totally free Creator.

Steinheim's focus is epistemological, hence he has little interest in historical criticism. The important question is, how are we to recognize a supernatural revelation? Responding to Fichte, he set six criteria for revelation:[10]

- It must be communicable.

- It must be comprehensible.

- It must allow the distinction between true and false.

- It must not rest on mere 'feeling'.

- It is not validated by coincidence with our own consciousness.

- It must have the character of novelty, that is, it should contradict previously held opinion, yet in the end logically compel acknowledgment of its truth.

It is not difficult to see how the revealed doctrine of God as totally free Creator fits these criteria. What is perhaps more interesting is to note what Steinheim has deliberately ruled out:

- He rejects any form of progressive revelation. This includes both theories like those of Schelling and Hegel about the workings of the spirit through religions in general,[11] and specific claims of the superiority of the New Testament over the Old.[12] Revelation, for Steinheim, was a unique event at Sinai.

- He rejects Mendelssohn's idea that the Torah was essentially 'revealed legislation'; indeed, he finds 'law' as a translation of *torah* repugnant.[13]

- He rejects Schleiermacher's 'reduction' of religion to feeling.[14]

---

[10] Selections from the work are translated in Haberman, *Philosopher of Revelation*.
[11] Ibid. 128 ff.   [12] Ibid. 149 ff.   [13] Ibid. 287.   [14] Ibid. 159 ff.

Steinheim, a scientist as well as a philosopher, prefers the inductive to the deductive method.[15] He therefore attempts to describe the content of revelation on the basis of induction from the biblical 'data'. Four principles emerge: the uniqueness of God; creation; freedom; the immortality of the soul.[16] The laws of Torah, however, do not constitute revelation. True, the *actual* Torah incorporates laws, for instance the sabbath and dietary laws, but these are of value only in so far as they symbolize the revealed doctrine of God.

Samuel Holdheim (1806–1860): Radical Reform

Samuel Holdheim, a leading Reform rabbi, was chief rabbi of Mecklenburg-Schwerin from 1840 and head of the Berlin Reform congregation from 1847. Though of traditional background, he eventually espoused radical reform, to the extent of opposing circumcision and advocating observance of the sabbath on Sunday; more constructively, he proposed that bride and groom should play equal parts in the wedding ceremony and that women should enjoy equal rights with men with regard to divorce. Meyer has described his theological progress as 'the protracted quest for an acceptable religious authority';[17] rejecting step by step the authority of the recent sages, the 'non-divine' element of the Talmud, the Talmud as a whole, he eventually adopted the position that even scripture was but the human reflection of divine illumination, and concluded that authority lay in reason and conscience, not in texts.

Progressive Revelation: Krochmal, Formstecher, Hirsch, Cohen

Several Jewish thinkers committed themselves to the idealistic notion of revelation as a universal, gradual process. The Galician Nachman Krochmal (1785–1840) translated Hegel's Absolute Spirit into Hebrew as *haruḥani hamuḥlat* and identified this with the concept of God in religious tradition. Such an identification was possible since the essential nature of the Absolute is pure, unqualified cognition (German *Geist* conveys the mental as well as the spiritual), and Maimonides had characterized God as the knower, the knowing, and the known. Revelation was the process of ever-increasing consciousness of this immanent Divine Spirit. Krochmal thought the transition

---

[15] Shear-Yashuv, *Theology of Salomon Ludwig Steinheim*, 28, has an impressive table of Steinheim's inductive/deductive vocabulary. [16] Ibid., ch. 4.

[17] Meyer, *Response to Modernity*, 81. For details of Holdheim's reforms, bibliography, and a recent assessment, see Meyer, '"Most of My Brethren Find Me Unacceptable"'.

from the Absolute Reality to the generated reality of finite things was similar to the Lurianic notion of the world as generated by God's act of self-
confinement (tsimtsum).[18] Though all religious faith was based upon the
Spirit, the biblical faith was unique in its purity and the universality of its
imagery. The unique relationship between the Jewish people and God, the
Absolute Spirit, was at its strongest in the revelation on Mount Sinai and in
Israelite prophecy.

The German Reformers Solomon Formstecher (1808–89) and Samuel
Hirsch (1815–89) wanted to present Judaism in a way which conformed with
German Protestant Idealism yet rejected its christological doctrines, and
which would affirm the place of Jews in 'modern' society. Formstecher presents Judaism as an idea whose full value is revealed through the gradual,
progressive development of mankind; the Enlightenment and Emancipation
were the intellectual and social-political manifestations of this internal, spiritual process. Revelation is the divine communication concerning the true
nature of good and evil. It is the identification of God as a pure moral being,
not the communication of philosophical concepts, and was manifested in its
purest form through the prophets of Israel. Judaism fulfils its mission among
the nations not directly, but through Christianity and Islam, which bridge the
gap between paganism and full spiritual enlightenment.

Hirsch, who emigrated to the United States in 1866, published his major
philosophical work, Die Religionsphilosophie der Juden, in 1842. He interpreted
Judaism as a dialectically evolving religious system, in which man comes to
know the freedom of his sovereign will by which he alone among all creatures
transcends the determinism of nature. Embarrassed like all other Jewish
Hegelians by the master's deprecation of Judaism, yet reluctant to claim
Jewish superiority, he argues that Judaism and Christianity are both equally
valid. Judaism is 'intensive' religiosity, hence restricted to the community of
Israel, while Christianity is 'extensive' religiosity, whose function is to proclaim God to the pagan world; both are destined to become perfected as
'absolute' religiosity in the messianic era.

His attitude to halakhah was ambivalent. He opposed the radical lay
groups who disavowed the authority of the Talmud, and he upheld the rite of
circumcision and the use of Hebrew in public worship; yet he proposed

---

[18]   These ideas are worked out in his Moreh nevukhei hazeman.
[19]   Krochmal, Moreh nevukhei hazeman, ch. 13.

holding Jewish services on Sunday instead of the traditional Jewish sabbath, and actually implemented this change as rabbi of Keneseth Israel in Philadelphia.

Hirsch undoubtedly influenced the formulation of the fifth postulate of the Pittsburgh Reform Platform of 1885:

We recognize in the modern era of universal culture of heart and intellect the approaching of the realization of Israel's great Messianic hope for the establishment of the kingdom of truth, justice and peace among all men. We consider ourselves no longer a nation, but a religious community, and therefore expect neither a return to Palestine, nor a sacrificial worship under the sons of Aaron, nor the restoration of any of the laws concerning the Jewish state.[20]

The identification of Judaism and of the messiah with universal human progress reached its apogee in the work of the last systematic Jewish philosopher, the neo-Kantian Hermann Cohen (1842–1918), whose major work on Jewish religious thought, *Die Religion der Vernunft aus den Quellen des Judentums* ('Religion of Reason from the Sources of Judaism') was published posthumously in 1919. God reveals his will by creating man as a rational creature who through his reason is capable of apprehending the laws of logic and ethics. Thus, revelation is not confined to any historical event nor even to any special mode of cognition; it characterizes a trait of man, who through the possession of his rational faculties becomes the bearer of divine revelation— there is *correlation* between the uniqueness of God on the one hand, and human reason, as God's creation, on the other.[21] Judaism is the revelation of an ever more perfect ethical monotheism, no more, no less; indeed, 'every philosophy, every spiritual-moral culture, requires the presupposition of the *eternal* as opposed to the transitoriness of all earthly institutions and human ideas'.[22]

Yet already in Cohen's time, long before the Holocaust, belief in the inevitability of human progress was wearing thin. Arthur Schopenhauer's (1788–1860) pessimistic counter-testimony to the Hegelians had been taken forward by Nietzsche (1844–1900), with his reading of religion as symptomatic of a declining life; he predicted that absoluteness would become attached to the nation-state and the slaughter of rivals and that the conquest of the earth would proceed under banners of universal brotherhood, democracy, and socialism. And Oswald Spengler (1880–1936) was already working on

---

[20] The text of the Pittsburgh Platform on the website of the Central Conference of American Rabbis (the Reform assembly) is authoritative; <http://ccarnet.org/Articles/index.cfm?id=39&pge_prg_id=3032&pge_id=1656>.

[21] Cohen, *Religion of Reason*, 71–84.   [22] Ibid. 83.

Der Untergang des Abendlandes ('The Decline of the West'), in which he would proclaim that the West had already passed through the creative stage of 'culture' into that of reflection and material comfort ('civilization' proper, in his terminology), and that the future could only be a period of irreversible decline.

In continental Europe, though not to the same extent in Britain or America, Jews had to depend more on wishful thinking than on social reality to continue believing in their own acceptance into the promised new universal utopia.

Moreover, confidence in systematic philosophy was at a low ebb, Kierkegaard had been 'discovered' in Germany, Edmund Husserl (himself of Jewish origin) had invented phenomenology,[23] existentialism was coming into vogue. Cohen's two most gifted disciples, Buber and Rosenzweig, inaugurated the Jewish revolt against the 'old' philosophies.

Leo Baeck (1873–1956): Essence of Judaism

Leo Baeck, a graduate of both the Conservative Breslau Seminary and the Liberal Berlin Hochschule, studied philosophy at Breslau (Wrocław, Poland, then incorporated in East Prussia) under J. Freudenthal and at Berlin under Wilhelm Dilthey (1833–1911). From 1933, as president of the Jewish representative body in Nazi Germany, he devoted himself to defending the few rights that remained for Jews. He survived Theresienstadt concentration camp, and in July 1945 moved to London, eventually becoming chairman of the World Union for Progressive Judaism. He visited the USA intermittently to teach at Hebrew Union College in Cincinnati.

Baeck was shocked by the Christian triumphalism (at the expense of Judaism) of the Protestant theologian Adolf von Harnack's *Wesen des Christentums* ('The Essence of Christianity'), published in 1901. His full response, *Wesen des Judentums* ('The Essence of Judaism'), appeared only in 1905 and was subsequently heavily revised.[24] Like Cohen, Baeck defined Judaism as ethical monotheism, but he allowed rather more space for ritual observances; in interpreting them as directed towards ethical improvement he was in line with Maimonides and S. R. Hirsch. However, he rejected the idea of halakhah as a system of commandments; specific *mitsvot* were more like flashes breaking through the cloud of divine 'mystery' which stood in a permanent dialectic relationship with 'command'.

[23] Husserl's *Ideen zu einer reinen Phänomenologie und phänomenologischen Philosophie* was first published in 1913.
[24] For an account of the debate see Homolka, *Jewish Identity*, chs. 3–6.

Martin Buber (1878–1965): All Life Is Meeting

Von Harnack's *Wesen des Christentums* was not the first attempt to define the 'essence' of Christianity. In 1841 Ludwig Feuerbach (1804–72) had published a highly anti-theological tract under that title in which he turned the language of Incarnation on its head to contend that the Christian concept of God derived from the concept of man. The being of man exists 'only in community, it is found only in the unity of man with man—a unity that is supported only by the reality of the difference between I and Thou'. 'Man with man—the unity of I and Thou is God.'[25] People can only realize themselves as human beings in relation with other beings: 'The *ego*, then, attains to the consciousness of the world through consciousness of the *thou*.'[26] Theology, that is, becomes anthropology; there is no 'science of God', only a science of man. Feuerbach strongly influenced D. F. Strauss and also the young Karl Marx,[27] but was reviled in theological circles; even so, his anthropological approach to theology came to dominate religious thought, especially in the twentieth century.

As Feuerbach had reacted against the metaphysics of his teacher, Hegel, Martin Buber rebelled against the philosophical idealism of his teacher, Hermann Cohen. Buber was influenced not only by Feuerbach, but by the emphasis placed by Wilhelm Dilthey, under whom he studied at the University of Berlin, on the distinction between the 'objective' natural sciences (*Naturwissenschaften*) and the 'subjective' humanities (*Geisteswissenschaften*); law, religion, art, and history, in Dilthey's view, should concentrate on a 'human-social-historical reality'. Another major influence on Buber was the Danish religious philosopher and critic of Hegelian rationalism, Søren Kierkegaard (1813–55), whose previously neglected work was making an impact in early twentieth-century Germany and spawned the existentialist movement.

In his best-known philosophical work, *Ich und Du* ('I and Thou'), published in 1923, Buber expounded the philosophy of dialogue in a rhapsodic rather than a systematic manner; Ronald Gregor Smith, the first edition of whose English translation appeared in 1937, aptly speaks of Buber as a poet, and of *Ich und Du* as a poem.[28] There are two 'primary words', says Buber, 'I-Thou' and 'I-It', and all relationships are subsumed under these terms.

---

[25] These two citations occur in Karl Barth's introductory essay to Feuerbach, *Essence of Christianity*, p. xiii. They are taken from Feuerbach, *Die Philosophie der Zukunft*, 41.

[26] Feuerbach, *Essence of Christianity*, 83.

[27] Marx's attack on Feuerbach's version of materialism in his 1845 *Thesen über Feuerbach* may be taken as a compliment.   [28] Buber, *I and Thou*, 3–4.

God, according to Buber, is the 'Eternal Thou', not known through propositions about him, but encountered through each true meeting between an
individual and a 'Thou', whether it be a person, animal, aspect of nature, work
of art, or God himself. 'All living is meeting' ('alles Leben ist Begegnung').[29]

Where does this leave Torah? Buber conceives revelation as an encounter
with the Presence of God, not as the communication of ideas or instructions.
A human response is indeed elicited, but never gives rise to a general law,
only to a unique, subjective deed or commitment; revelation has no content
beyond the 'presence'. Far from being restricted to a specific event at Sinai,
revelation is a subjective category into which innumerable personal experiences may fit. While Buber was able in this way to assign value to scripture,
and for that matter to the stories of Jesus or of Rabbi Nahman of Bratslav, as a
record of encounters with the divine, his conception leaves no room for the
traditional notion of a sacred revealed text containing commandments.
Historical criticism has become, for Buber, simply irrelevant; like the hasidic
masters he admires, he does not so much read the text of the Bible as play
with it.

Franz Rosenzweig (1886–1929): Creation, Revelation, Redemption

Rosenzweig posits three elements of reality—God, man, the world—rather
like Kant's a priori concepts of soul, world, God. He was apparently unaware
that all three of his 'elements' were constructs from manifold individual
experiences and perceptions; but in any case, according to his disciple Nahum
Glatzer, they were only 'auxiliary concepts', to be cast off at a more mature
stage.[30]

The dialogue involving the three 'elements' comprises another triad: 'God,
man and the world reveal themselves only in their relations to one another,
that is, in *creation, revelation,* and *redemption*.'[31] Rosenzweig thought that the
Bible acknowledged this dialogue of human, world, and God and thereby
differed from and was superior to Greek paganism, which saw the three
'elements' in detachment from one another. This is puzzling—even the most
cursory reading of, say, Homer, reveals the Greek gods in frequent conversation with people and interacting with the world in innumerable ways, as when
Zeus fires thunderbolts and Poseidon stirs up the sea, generally in response
to human activities.

[29] Buber, *I and Thou*, 25.   [30] W. E. Kaufman, *Contemporary Jewish Philosophies*, 38.
[31] Glatzer, *Franz Rosenzweig*, 198, from a supplementary note to Rosenzweig, *Stern der
Erlösung* (my emphasis).

Book Two of his *Der Stern der Erlösung* ('The Star of Redemption') is headed 'Revelation of the Ever-Renewed Birth of the Soul'.[32] After some embarrassingly awful remarks on gender differences ('A young woman can be as ready for eternity as a man only becomes when his threshold is crossed by Thanatos', and more of the same) Rosenzweig warms to his theme:

The keystone of the somber arch of creation becomes the cornerstone of the bright house of revelation. For the soul, revelation means the experience of a present which, while it rests on the presence of a past, nevertheless does not make its home in it but walks in the light of the divine countenance.

God undergoes a 'conversion' from the concealed to the manifest.

For God, creation is not merely creation of the world, it is also something which occurs within himself as the concealed one.

[O]ut of the darkness of his concealment there must emerge something other than bare creative power, something in which the broad infinity of the acts of creative power is captured in visible form lest God should once more be able to retreat behind these acts into the Concealed.

It is love which meets all the demands here made on the concept of the revealer, the love of the lover, not of the beloved. Only the love of a lover is such a continually renewed self-sacrifice.

(The Soul) ... man ... is the other pole of revelation.

There is ... no faithfulness without defiance. Not that there is still defiance within the beloved soul itself—this defiance has wholly turned to faithfulness within it— but the strength to hold fast ... is drawn by it from that defiance of the self which has integrated with it ... the attribute of faithfulness endows the soul with the strength to live permanently in the love of God.

The I discovers itself at the moment when it asserts the existence of the Thou by inquiring into its Where.

Here is the I, the individual human I, as yet wholly receptive ... The commandment is the first content to drop into this attentive hearing ... that one commandment which is not the highest, which is in truth the only commandment, the sum and substance of all commandments ever to leave God's mouth ... 'Thou shalt love the Lord thy God with all thy heart and with all thy soul and with all thy might.'

'I have sinned.' Thus speaks the soul and abolishes shame ... 'I have sinned' means I was a sinner. With this acknowledgement of having sinned, however, the soul clears the way for the acknowledgement 'I am a sinner.' And this acknowledgement is already the full admission of love.[33]

---

[32] Citations are from William Hallo's translation.
[33] Ibid. 157, 159, 160, 162, 167, 170, 175, 176, 180.

The language of revelation 'speaks'; revelation becomes, for Rosenzweig, an aesthetic category, powerfully expressed in the Song of Songs, which is more than a simile.[34]

Rosenzweig certainly did not believe, in any literal sense, in the traditional story of God dictating the Torah, Written and Oral, to Moses; nowhere does he question the findings of historical criticism. Yet, contrary to Buber,[35] he takes a positive attitude towards the law (halakhah) and its fulfilment. In a letter to Glatzer, who had said that only the election of Israel came from God, but the details of the law were from man alone, he questioned whether one could draw so rigid a boundary between what was divine and what was human.[36] True, observance of the law cannot be based, as S. R. Hirsch demanded, on historical claims about its revelation at Sinai.[37] Only in *doing* do we actually come to perceive the law as articulating the Revelation of God:

Just as a student of William James knows how to put every 'religious experience' into the correct cubbyhole of the psychology of religion, and a Freudian student can analyze the experience into its elements of the old yet ever new story, so a student of Wellhausen will trace every commandment back to its human, folkloristic origin, and a student of Max Weber derive it from the special structure of a people . . . We know it differently, not always and not in all things . . . For we know it only when—we do.

What do we know when we do? Certainly not that all of these historical and sociological explanations are false. But in the light of doing, of the right doing in which we experience the reality of the Law, the explanations are of superficial and subsidiary importance . . . Only in the commandment can the voice of him who commands be heard.[38]

Rosenzweig is saying that the normative content of Torah, that is, its specific *mitsvot*, harks back in the practice of the faithful to 'the commandment' of love which arises in the dialogue of God, man, world; the love that is experienced in 'doing', i.e. in the performance of the *mitsvot*, rather than any sociological or historical basis, is our justification for doing them.

Abraham Joshua Heschel (1907–1972): Passion of the Prophets

Heschel's most valuable contribution to the understanding of revelation was his interpretation of the writings of the Hebrew prophets in such a way as to present a picture of a living, concerned God in intimate relationship with a

---

[34] William Hallo's translation, 185, 191, 199 ff.
[35] See his letter to Buber on teaching and law, translated in Glatzer, *Franz Rosenzweig*, 234–42.   [36] Glatzer, *Franz Rosenzweig*, 242.   [37] Ibid. 238.   [38] Ibid. 245.

fragile but noble humanity. He was a 'personalist' philosopher, in conscious reaction against what he regarded as the excessive 'abstraction' of medieval Jewish philosophers such as Maimonides, or the systematic philosophy of Hermann Cohen. 'As a report about revelation, the Bible itself is Midrash', wrote Heschel.[39] Neil Gillman has explained:

To characterize the entire Torah as a midrash is to say that it is, in its entirety, a human understanding of a 'text' which, in its pristine, original form, is beyond human awareness . . . It is a 'cultural' document because it preserves a human community's understanding of God's presence and will for that community, and that perception inevitably reflects the cultural conditions in which it was originally formulated. But it remains 'divine' because it is God's presence and will that the community insists it is perceiving.[40]

Though in his work *The Prophets* Heschel chose to ignore, or rather sidestep, modern biblical scholarship, a statement such as the one just cited shows that he accepted the broad conclusions of historical criticism and abandoned the claim of verbal inspiration. Like his Protestant friend Paul Tillich, he defined religion as concern about 'ultimate' questions; 'involvement' in the experience under consideration was what mattered, not the historical investigation of texts; he writes as a theologian, not as a biblical scholar.

Even so, he agonized over the problem of how to reconcile his own convictions with the rabbinic understanding of *torah min hashamayim*, and he devoted three Hebrew volumes, the last not quite finished at the time of his death, to this topic. Gordon Tucker's felicitous and well-annotated English translation of much of the work captures the flavour of Heschel's passionate style, in which citations and allusions from the full range of rabbinic texts ancient and relatively modern are skilfully woven. Susannah Heschel has written,

For my father . . . *Torah min Hashamayim* was . . . a religious text . . . shaping the rabbinic sources to bring to the surface their often subtle and even concealed views on God, revelation, and the nature of interpretation, and at the same time responding to contemporary concerns that only a strict and uncompromising halakhic Judaism was authentic and legitimate. As always in his writings, he sought to demonstrate that a pluralism of religious views stands at the heart of rabbinic Judaism and was the source of Judaism's vitality and vigor.[41]

A Mormon philosopher wrote to Tucker that 'Heschel sings rather than argues'.[42] The song—or is it a symphony?—may be analysed in classical

---

[39] A. J. Heschel, *God in Search of Man*, 185. The whole of Part II of his work is dedicated to the theme of revelation.   [40] Gillman, *The Death of Death*, 32.
[41] A. J. Heschel, *Heavenly Torah*, p. xvii.   [42] Ibid., p. xxv.

sonata form: there is an exposition with contrasting first and second subjects, an extended development, and fulsome recapitulation. The contrasting subjects are the 'philosophies' of the second-century sages, Akiva and Ishmael, presented as prototypes not only of subsequent Jewish exegesis and theology but of theological debate in general. I attempt to distil from Heschel's prolix account the defining characteristics of each of these approaches:[43]

Rabbi Akiva could be credited with seeking out the wondrous (33); [his] teachings sought to penetrate to inner depths . . . He did not shrink from anthropomorphism, but rather he preserved the concrete in Scripture, cherished imaginative meanings, added metaphorical embellishments, and created images of the supernal world. Instead of a logic that was subservient to surface meaning, he championed free exegesis and intellectual flights. A poet at heart, and at the same time a razor-sharp genius, [he] combined . . . poetry and acuity, the esoteric and the analytic . . . [He was] a man of action, a spokesman for his people (34) inclined towards a mutual empathy with God . . . Israel's salvation is a divine need (35) . . . [his was] an outlook that denigrated this world (36); the Shekhinah has a dwelling-place (God is immanent) (36); [Akiva] often departed widely from the plain meaning of the text . . . every detail and every stylistic form has a deep significance and a hidden intent . . . the covert in the Torah is far greater than the overt (39); human language is unlike the language of Torah (40); every word of the Torah commands and imposes obligation (41).

[Rabbi Ishmael] inclined toward accommodation and adaptation and was opposed to rebellion and revolt against the Roman government (31); Rabbi Ishmael's path was that of the surface, plain meaning of the text (33); he sought the middle way . . . his emotional equilibrium and intellectual sobriety did not allow his feelings to sweep him off into extremism . . . paradox was anathema to him (33); Rabbi Ishmael could be credited with shunning out the wondrous (33); [he preferred] straightforward logic . . . simplicity of language, and was averse to intellectual games . . . the world is built on compassion, not heroism (35); he challenged the denigration of the here and now (36); the Shekhinah is present everywhere (God is transcendent) (36), i.e. his justice and righteousness are revealed in history (37); each verse's plain meaning, which emerges from our rules of logic, is firm and steady, and whoever expands such teachings seeks to restamp the Torah with a die that is foreign to it (39); the Torah speaks in human language (40); Torah sometimes teaches . . . things pertaining to culture in general . . . There are things in the Torah that are obligatory, and there are those that are optional (41).

Heschel himself sums up:

There were thus two points of views among the Sages: (1) a transcendent point of view, comprising a method of thought always open to the higher realms, striving to

---

[43] The distillation is based on A. J. Heschel, *Heavenly Torah*, especially pp. 32–64; citations are not all word for word. (Numbers in parentheses refer to the pages of the English version.)

understand matters of Torah through a supernal lens; and (2) an immanent point of view, comprising a method of thought modest and confined, satisfied to understand matters of Torah through an earthly lens defined by human experience.[44]

'Transcendent' in this summary is nothing to do with the transcendence of God, since it is Ishmael rather than Akiva who, in Heschel's view, regards God as transcendent. Rather, as he explains in chapter 14, the 'transcendent point of view' is the notion that the earthly Torah is a copy of the heavenly prototype, just as physical objects are, in Plato's view, mere copies of 'ideas'; the Ishmaelean view, in contrast, is labelled 'immanent' or 'terrestrial' to indicate that that the earthly Torah is the real one, and is the vehicle through which God's actual teaching has entered and is present in the material world. Am I alone in finding this terminological ambivalence confusing?

Scholars may well object that Heschel does nothing to establish the authenticity of his citations from Rabbis Ishmael and Akiva, taking the attributions in the Talmuds and midrashim at face value; though the application of form criticism to rabbinic texts was in its infancy when he was writing, many scholars, not least some of his colleagues at the Jewish Theological Seminary, had by that time amply demonstrated the need for caution in the historical evaluation of rabbinic source material. Even Tucker concedes that Heschel 'certainly does not set out to do meticulous history';[45] rather, 'For Heschel, Ishmael and Akiva were of interest . . . only as stand-ins for what are eternal paradigms of religious thought that sometimes war with one another, sometimes complement one another, and always challenge and refine one another'.[46]

This may be so, but Heschel surely undermines his own case by reading his preferred views into texts that by no means invariably support them, and which he sometimes seriously misrepresents. For instance, he argued that Abaye's statement that the curses in Deuteronomy were spoken by Moses 'on his own initiative' (*mipi atsmo*),[47] like other statements in similar vein, indicated that Abaye held that some parts of the Torah were not literally inspired.[48] This is simply a misunderstanding, since the *record* of what Moses said would, in Abaye's view, have been divinely dictated, just as the records of other actions performed by people of their own free will were divinely dictated; for instance, Joseph's brothers threw him into the pit on their own initiative, but the *record* of that event, as we have it in Genesis, would undoubt-

---

[44] Ibid. 42.   [45] A. J. Heschel, *Heavenly Torah*, p. xxviii.

[46] Ibid., p. xxix.   [47] BT *Meg.* 31b.

[48] A. J. Heschel, *Heavenly Torah*, chs. 22 and 24 (Heb. vol. ii, chs. 7 and 9). As there is considerable overlap and repetition in Heschel's work the topic frequently surfaces in other passages.

edly, in Abaye's view, have been divinely dictated. No one denies that on occasion Moses spoke his own words; what they deny is that he personally inserted them in the Torah without having been instructed by God to do so. A similar point arose in our discussion of Naftali Tsevi Yehudah Berlin in Chapter 15; Berlin, citing a midrash that the words 'Hear, Israel . . . ' (Deut. 6: 4) were addressed to Jacob by his sons long before the Torah was given through Moses, correctly (from the standpoint of tradition) argues that these words became Torah only when sanctioned at Sinai.

Heschel argued that the rabbis who maintained, like Ishmael, that 'the Torah speaks the language of men' believed that the divine revelation was modified by human beings.[49] Apart from the fact that this statement is occasionally attributed to Akiva and others as well as to Ishmael,[50] the interpretation is an unjustified extrapolation. All the phrase means is that where biblical Hebrew usage corresponds to normal Hebrew idiom it is not necessary to look for an interpretation beyond the plain meaning; it does *not* imply that Moses (or anyone else) modified what God told him. The confusion here arises from Heschel's assumption that the actual revelation transcended mere words, so that any attempt to confine it in human language necessarily imports the thoughts of the transcriber. This may be true, but it is not a point of view likely to have been shared by Rabbi Ishmael or any of his second-century colleagues, to whom the notion of God verbally dictating a text was not at all strange; indeed, they would most likely have assumed that God had devised the Hebrew language, so it was perfectly formed to articulate his 'thoughts'.

Perhaps even more serious is the notion, frequently repeated by apologists for non-Orthodox Judaism, that the Talmud encourages (to use Susannah Heschel's phraseology) a 'pluralism of religious views', as opposed to the alleged 'strict and uncompromising halakhic Judaism' of the Orthodox. There is an element of truth in this—the Talmud does not engage in doctrinal definition in the manner of the councils of the early church, and tolerates *some* latitude in the expression of religious belief. But on the other hand it offers no comfort to those who reject its fundamental premise that the Torah consists of God's words, faithfully transcribed (give or take the final verses) by Moses, or to those who decline to obey its commandments as formulated by the rabbis.

---

[49] A. J. Heschel, *Heavenly Torah*, 40, and chs. 21 and 22 (Heb. vol. i, p. 16 and vol. ii, chs. 6 and 7).

[50] For instance, in BT *Ber.* 31b it is attributed to Akiva, though the parallel passage in BT *Sot.* 26a attributes it to Ishmael. Contrary attributions in this and other contexts seriously worried the Tosafists, cf. Tosafot *Sot.* 24a s.v. *verabi yonatan.*

Nor does the fact that many talmudic debates remain undecided indicate a liberal stance on halakhah. Undecided debates are a simple consequence of the fact that the anonymous editors of the Talmud were recording debates, not making decisions; the ideal for the sage was *asokei shamata aliba dehilkhata* 'to settle the topic in accordance with the correct halakhah'.[51] *Hora'ah* (decision-making), says the 'Book of Adam', came to an end with Rav Ashi and Ravina, early in the fifth century,[52] though much of the material incorporated in the Talmud is obviously later. The *gaon* Sherira, our main source for the history of the tradition, does not list 'editors' among those responsible for its stewardship, but only those who possessed the capacity to make decisions; decision-making (not inconclusive debate), he states emphatically, is what defines a Torah scholar.[53]

Liberal-minded Jews may have good reason both to doubt the doctrinal assumptions of the Talmud and to seek to adjust its laws in the light of modern attitudes, as well as in calling for a 'pluralism of religious views', but they are not helped by spurious claims to continuity with talmudic models. Heschel is as inspiring a writer as he was an orator, and the values he promotes are sound; all the more pity that he fails to address the historical, scientific, and moral problems with which this book is primarily concerned. Religion—Judaism—is indeed concerned about 'ultimate' questions and 'involvement', but it is also concerned with truth and integrity, and this demands that we acknowledge the deficiencies as well as the many excellencies within our traditions.

Emmanuel Levinas (1905/6–1995): The Face of the Other

In February/March 1976 the French Jewish philosopher Emmanuel Levinas took part, together with Paul Ricoeur (1913–2005) and others, in a seminar on revelation at the School of Religion and Philosophy of the Saint-Louis University in Brussels; the five leading papers and a discussion were published the following year.[54] The novelty of this seminar lay in the broad interpretation of revelation as a phenomenon common to the major religions, and in the sympathetic rereading of 'revelation' in the light of phenomenology and hermeneutics. The question of the historical validity of the scriptures and

---

[51] BT *Yoma* 26a, *Sot.* 7b, *BK* 92a, *San.* 106b.   [52] BT *BM* 85b–86a.

[53] Schlüter, *Auf welche Weise*, 213. See also Solomon, *The Talmud: A Selection*, p. xxxvi.

[54] Ricoeur, *La Révélation*, 55–77, incorporated in Levinas, *Au-delà du verset*, 158–81. English trans. by Sarah Richmond in Hand (ed.), *The Levinas Reader*, 190–210, as 'Revelation in the Jewish Tradition'. References are to the English translation.

their received interpretation does not appear on the horizon, and there is an obvious distaste, expressed openly by Ricoeur,[55] for authoritarian forms of religion. The problem with which the participants grapple derives from the classical opposition of reason and revelation; how can a transcendent revelation produce truths that are not amenable to the all-encompassing faculty of reason?

Although it is difficult to detach Levinas's concept of revelation from his general philosophy, in which it plays a major role, and even more difficult to demonstrate the commonsense that surely underlies the philosophical jargon, a few paragraphs will give the flavour of his thought. He sees the basic problem clearly enough:

Our world lies before us, enabling us, in its coherence and constancy, to perceive it, to enjoy it . . . Within this world, it appears that the opening of certain books can cause the abrupt invasion of truths from outside—from where?—dated according to the 'chronology' of Sacred History . . . And, in the case of the Jews, this sacred history leads, without any break in its continuity, to the 'historian's history', which is profane history.[56]

In plain English (a similar 'translation' into plain French would be possible), how does 'religious truth' relate to the real world? Or, how does the mythical history of Israel relate to the existence of real people with a real history?

How can we make sense of the 'exteriority' of the truths and signs of the Revelation which strike the human faculty known as reason . . . how can these truths and signs strike our reason if they are not even of this world?

These questions are indeed urgent for us today, and they confront anyone . . . who is still troubled to some degree . . . by the news of the end of metaphysics, by the triumphs of psychoanalysis, sociology and political economy . . . The ontological status or régime of the Revelation is therefore a primordial concern for Jewish thought.[57]

To continue in plain English, the question posed in the previous paragraph arises today in acute form since the literal understanding of scripture as history has been discredited by modern philosophy and social sciences. It is interesting that neither Levinas nor the other contributors to the symposium seem greatly troubled by other problems we have discussed, such as textual history, moral lapses, and conflict with the 'hard' sciences.

Levinas answers his question:

---

[55] Ricoeur, *La Révélation*, 16. He writes of the 'doctrines imposés par le magistère comme règle d'orthodoxie' that he deplores them because 'il n'est pas seulement opaque, mais autoritaire'.   [56] Hand (ed.), *The Levinas Reader*, 191.   [57] Ibid. 192–3.

This exteriority . . . cannot be transformed into a content within interiority; it remains 'uncontainable', infinite (infinie), and yet the relation is maintained . . . we may find a model for this relation in the attitude of non-indifference to the Other, in the responsibility towards him . . . it is precisely through this relation that man becomes his 'self' (moi) . . . and—in this sense—free. Ethics provides the model worthy of transcendence and it is as an ethical kerygma that the Bible is Revelation . . . The Revelation, described in terms of the ethical relation or the relation with the Other, is a mode of the relation with God and discredits both the figure of the Same and knowledge in their claim to be the only site of meaning (signification).[58]

That is, the 'sacred history' cannot be captured in words or rational discourse, but it nevertheless impinges on real human beings in the ethical sphere.

Levinas is at pains to explain, against Ricoeur, that revelation is prescriptive rather than dogmatic; it confronts humans by stimulating commentary on its texts, a commentary which is never complete, hence the ongoing nature of rabbinic discourse through Oral Torah, or the 'oral revelation', as he calls it. Although every individual is summoned to 'obedience' by engaging in the commentary, its details are by no means subjective and arbitrary, but confined (though not precisely determined) by the 'continuity of readings through history'.[59]

Levinas is embarrassed by the Jewish claim of 'chosenness', so he emphasizes the *specificity* of revelation. Though the truths of revelation are absolute and universal, revelation has to appear in a specific setting: 'The revelation of morality, which discovers a human society, also discovers the place of election, which in this universal society, returns to the person who receives the revelation'.[60]

Has Levinas *reduced* Torah to ethics, as Cohen, Baeck, and others appeared to do? Probably not. Ethics may be the point at which the transcendent erupts into human reason, but the eruption does not stop there; in the specific instance of the Torah and the Jewish people it carries with it the full 'commentary' of the halakhic and aggadic tradition and the experience of the Jewish people.

♦

[58] Ibid. 207, 208.   [59] Ibid. 196.   [60] Levinas, *Difficult Freedom*, 21.

A bouquet garni of 'images' of Torah arises from the discussion in this chapter:

Non-Orthodox interpretations of 'Revelation'

Mendelssohn   Torah consists of revealed legislation.

Steinheim   Revelation yields knowledge of God as totally free Creator. Four principles constitute Torah: the uniqueness of God, Creation, freedom, and the immortality of the soul.

Holdheim   Scripture is the human reflection of divine illumination; authority lies in reason and conscience, not in texts.

Krochmal to Cohen   Revelation is progressive, not a single past event; ethics constitute its essence.

Baeck   Dialectic of mystery and command; ethical monotheism.

Buber   Revelation is a subjective category; the encounter with God does not communicate ideas, instructions, or laws, but leads rather to a unique, subjective deed or commitment.

Rosenzweig   Revelation is an aesthetic category; only in doing do we actually come to perceive the Law as articulating the revelation of God.

Heschel   'As a report about revelation, the Bible itself is Midrash.'

Levinas   Revelation is the transcendence of the ethical, demanding that each individual interpret his responsibility for the Other; yet it is specific, resulting in a constantly evolving 'commentary' of halakhah and aggadah.

Of these thinkers, all except Mendelssohn abandon the conventional conception of revelation as divine dictation. Yet they do not abandon Bible, Talmud, or Jewish tradition, preferring to reinterpret them as forms of encounter with God, as 'midrash', 'aesthetic category', 'human reflection of divine illumination', and the like, placing authority in reason and conscience rather than in texts.

Would it be possible, in the light of modern developments, to reassert the *absoluteness* of the received Torah, its texts and its laws? In the next chapter we will see how Soloveitchik attempted precisely this.

EIGHTEEN

JOSEPH DOV SOLOVEITCHIK
AND THE A PRIORI TORAH

I FIRST VISITED the United States early in 1981, and with my late wife spent each of five successive sabbaths in a different city; on each sabbath we visited a randomly chosen Orthodox synagogue. The rabbis of all five congregations turned out to be disciples of Joseph Dov[1] Soloveitchik (1903–93). At that time it was probably true that most Orthodox pulpit rabbis in North America had come under his influence during their training at Yeshiva University, New York; from 1941 until his final illness he had travelled there regularly from his home in Boston to teach Talmud to a generation of devoted students.

Born in Pruzhany, Belarus (then within the Russian empire), into a leading family of *mitnaged* rabbis,[2] Joseph Dov studied Talmud under his father, Moshe Soloveitchik. There were other influences, too; he was attracted by the warmth of hasidic prayer, and his mother read him Ibsen, Pushkin, Lermontov, and Bialik. By the time he left to study in Berlin in 1924 he had mastered talmudic dialectics, dabbled a little in hasidism despite the family's strong *mitnaged* tradition, and taken his first steps in general European culture. His teachers in Berlin included Tonya Lewit, whom he married; his friends included Alexander Altmann, with whom he studied the writings of Hermann Cohen, Edmund Husserl, and Max Scheler. Some of the rich diversity of Jewish cultural life he would have encountered in Weimar Germany is revealed in the memoirs of Gershom Scholem,[3] Hillel Goldberg,[4] and other contemporaries who profoundly influenced late twentieth-century Judaism.

Soloveitchik left Germany for the United States in 1931, after submitting his doctoral thesis on Hermann Cohen's epistemology to the philosophy

---

[1] He is often called 'Joseph Ber', the Yiddish form of 'Joseph Dov', and given the initials J. B. rather than J. D.

[2] *Mitnaged* 'opponent' is the term applied by hasidim to traditional Jews who reject their teachings.　　　　　　　　　　　　[3] Scholem, *From Berlin to Jerusalem*; id., *Walter Benjamin*.

[4] Goldberg, *Between Berlin and Slobodka*.

faculty of the Friedrich-Wilhelms University, Berlin.[5] After his father's death in 1941, he took over the teaching of Talmud at Yeshiva University in New York. He taught halakhah, wrote philosophy, and developed a thought-provoking homiletic style, most evident in his eulogies and in the lectures he gave annually on the anniversary of his father's death.

His main philosophical testament is the 1944 Hebrew essay *Halakhic Man* (*Ish hahalakhah*).[6] Influenced by Max Scheler's (1874–1928) typology of exemplary leaders as saint, sage, hero, and connoisseur, he created a threefold human typology:

- Scientific (cognitive, objective) Man, seeks to measure, discover, control.

- Religious (subjective) Man, seeks mystery and the preservation of the 'dynamic relationship between subject and object'.

- Halakhic Man bridges the divide between the two. Neither transcendent nor superficial, Halakhic Man 'comes with his Torah, given to him at Sinai . . . like a mathematician who forms an ideal world and uses it to establish a relationship between himself and the real world'.

Soloveitchik modelled 'Halakhic Man' on his grandfather, Hayim Soloveit-chik (1853–1917). 'Reb Hayim' had achieved note for his development of a form of talmudic dialectics, known as the 'Brisker *derekh* (way)',[7] which came to dominate talmudic study in the Lithuanian yeshivas.[8] One of its peculiarities is the reification of concepts; Reb Hayim talks of Torah laws and concepts as if they were metaphysical objects, enjoying an existence of their own seemingly independent of the world and of humanity—one of his characteristic expressions is *heftsa dedina*, literally 'the law-object'.[9] Reb Hayim himself may not have been aware of the philosophical implications of what to him was probably no more than a convenient way of talking, but his grandson absorbed the language, married it to Hermann Cohen's 'pure thought', and out of the blend devised a philosophy of halakhah as constitut-ing an independent a priori realm that confronts and bridges the opposing worlds of science and religion.

The Platonic notion of an 'absolute' realm of ideas was developed by Max Scheler, who attempted in his 1926 essay 'Problems of a Sociology of Know-

---

[5] The title of the thesis is 'Das reine Denken und die Seinskonstituierung bei Hermann Cohen'.   [6] Citations below are from Kaplan's English translation.

[7] Reb Hayim was for a time rabbi of Brest-Litovsk in Belarus.

[8] Solomon, *Analytic Movement*. The originator of the method was probably Jacob Isaac Reines (1839–1915), but the 'reification' is Reb Hayim's alone.

[9] Solomon, *Analytic Movement*, 177, 180, 184–8, 194–5.

ledge'[10] to set up what he called an a priori sociology of knowledge, rendering the science of sociology independent of history:

this science does not deal with individual facts and occurrences in history, but with rules, average and logical-ideal types, and, where possible, laws . . .

The main task of sociology is to characterize typologically and determine by specific rules a sociological event with reference to these two poles, to establish what in this event is conditioned by the autonomous self-development of spirit, such as the logical-rational development of law or the immanent logic of religious history, and what is conditioned by the relevant sociologically real factors, which have their own causality.[11]

in my view the highest goal of all nondescriptive and nonclassificatory sociology . . . is . . . a law governing the achievement of ideal and real factors in determining all life contents belonging to human groups.[12]

we avoid relativism, as Einstein's theory does on its own basis, by lifting up the absolute realm of ideas and values corresponding to the essential idea of humanity far above factual historical value systems.[13]

I have tried . . . not only to verify inductively . . . the above 'law of the order of causal factors' in the three phases of history, but also to make it understandable deductively according to a 'theory of the origins of human drives'.[14]

Scheler is wrong when he claims an analogy with Einstein. Mathematics, taken in itself, may be independent of 'factual historical value systems', but Einstein's theories were meant to stand or fall in the light of observation and experiment. The theory of relativity is a theory about the *real* world, and seeks to establish which mathematics best models it; it is *not* a mathematical theory that determines how the world *ought* to be. Einstein, and indeed the whole modern scientific enterprise, is at the furthest remove from the Platonic ideal of a priori science; modern science is a 'bottom up' rather than a 'top down' process. Scheler and Soloveitchik, however, like Hermann Cohen and other Idealist philosophers, prefer to work from the top down; theory, not empirical observation, determines their world view.

Soloveitchik's conception of halakhah as an a priori system renders it immune to history;[15] just as geometry is unaffected by the historical circumstances of its discovery, or by the empirical fact that no one can draw perfect circles, so halakhah remains unaffected by the history of how it came to be what it is, or by the problems of its implementation in the real world. But this

---

[10] Scheler, *On Feeling, Knowing and Valuing*, 166–200.   [11] Ibid. 168–9.

[12] Ibid. 169. On p. 171 he uses this idea to critique Hegel who 'holds that the course of cultural history is a purely spiritual process determined by its own logic'.

[13] Ibid. 174.   [14] Ibid. 193.   [15] Compare my remarks on Isaac Breuer in Ch. 16.

immunity comes at the price of wresting the texts of Torah and Talmud from the social and historical contexts in which they were formulated, and which determine their meaning, a point made by Rachel Shihor in a fine essay published in 1978.[16]

The Hermeneutics of 'Torah'

In Brisk, Berlin, and Boston Soloveitchik experienced three very different cultures, each of which, once absorbed, remained with him throughout his life. His works, halakhic, philosophical, and homiletic, the spoken word as much as the literary productions, are rich intertextual fields in which the Lithuanian rabbinic tradition with its internal intertextuality is interwoven with philosophy, science, general culture, and past and contemporary Jewish history. Hans-Georg Gadamer remarked, 'Hermeneutic reflection is limited to opening up new possibilities for knowledge which would not be perceived without it. Of itself it offers no criterion of truth.'[17] Soloveitchik used his German philosophical training as a hermeneutic key to understand the nature of Torah; what light does this throw on his concept of *torah min hashamayim?*

Gadamer comments on the awkwardness experienced by nineteenth- and early twentieth-century thinkers confronting the certainties of an earlier world:

As the foreignness [*Fremdheit*] which the age of mechanics felt towards nature and the world has its epistemological expression in the concept of self-consciousness and in the methodologically developed rule of certainty, of 'clear and distinct perception', so also the human sciences of the nineteenth century felt a comparable foreignness with respect to the historical world. The spiritual creations of the past, art and history, no longer belong to the self-evident domain of the present but rather are objects relinquished to research, data from which a past allows itself to be represented.[18]

The significant phrase here is 'foreignness with respect to the historical world'. Soloveitchik's 'new science'—that of the pure, self-validating halakhah —makes him a 'foreigner' in the actual historical world, so much so that the world of halakhah *confronts* the world of normal experience. However, he does not relinquish the world to research, as 'data from which a past allows itself to be represented', but rather asserts his 'Halakhic Man' as the vital bridge

[16] Shihor, 'On the Problems of Halakhah's Status', 30–1.

[17] H.-G. Gadamer, *Kleine Schriften* iv. 130, cited in Weinsheimer, *Gadamer's Hermeneutics*, 1.

[18] Gadamer, *Warheit und Methode* 4 (Tübingen: Mohr, 1975), 61, cited in Weinsheimer, *Gadamer's Hermeneutics*, 4.

between the world in which history is enacted and the world of transcendent religion.

The Jewish philosophers of ancient Alexandria interpreted Torah as *nomos* (law), and the rabbis carried the notion forward with their emphasis on halakhah. Soloveitchik takes the process to an extreme; *every* expression of Torah is for him an aspect of halakhah. When he addresses the perennial debate as to why bad things happen to good people, he builds his response on a 'simple halakhic solution', that 'suffering comes to exalt Man, to purify and sanctify his spirit'.[19] To classify this as a halakhic statement, and then to proceed to interpret Job as a halakhic manual, is to stretch the concept of halakhah to a point where it can no longer be distinguished from aggadah.

Presumably it is this extended concept of halakhah he had in mind when he penned his oft-cited words:

When halakhic man approaches reality, he comes with his Torah, given to him from Sinai, in hand. He orients himself to the world by means of fixed statutes and firm principles . . . furnished with rules, judgements, and fundamental principles, [he] draws near the world with an a priori relation. To whom may he be compared? To a mathematician who fashions an ideal world and then uses it for the purpose of establishing a relationship between it and the real world . . . The essence of the Halakhah, which was received from God, consists in creating an ideal world and cognizing the relationship between that ideal world and our concrete environment. . . . There is no phenomenon . . . which the a priori Halakhah does not approach with its ideal standard . . . When Halakhic Man comes across a spring bubbling . . . he already possesses a fixed, a priori relationship with this real phenomenon . . . he desires to coordinate the a priori concept with the a posteriori phenomenon.[20]

Perhaps, as some have suggested, the analogy with mathematics is only a metaphor; from a philosophical point of view, it is very difficult to see how the contingent propositions of halakhah can be regarded as a priori. But the intention is clear; Soloveitchik wishes to confer on the system of halakhah precisely the invulnerability to history that he thought was characteristic of logic and the mathematical sciences.

Rudolf Otto (1869–1937) succeeded Hermann Cohen as professor at Marburg in 1917. Otto, in his seminal *Das Heilige* ('The Holy'), sought to lay the foundations of a religious a priori, distinct from mere feelings. He claimed to identify in different religions a perception of 'creature-ness', a sense of absolute dependence on that which was 'wholly other', utterly

[19] Soloveitchik, 'Kol dodi dofek', 13.
[20] *Halakhic Man*, 19–20. 'When halakhic man comes across a spring bubbling . . .' is reminiscent of Buber's 'I consider a tree . . .' (*I and Thou*, 7).

transcending the mundane sphere. For this, the holy, he uses the term 'numinous', from the Latin *numen*, 'nodding', used to convey divine (or imperial) will, might, or majesty. The sense of the numinous, of the *mysterium tremendum*, is, for Otto, a supra-rational means of apprehension; it is not *irrational*, it does not *contradict* reason, but it yields knowledge which cannot be attained through the rational faculty. The Holy is for Otto an a priori category:

the 'holy', in the fullest sense of the word is a combined, complex category, the combining elements being its rational and non-rational components. But in both—and the assertion must be strictly maintained against all sensationalism and naturalism—it is a purely a priori category.[21]

Soloveitchik disapproved of Otto's characteristically Protestant antinomianism[22] but was attracted by his concept of holiness, even though he tried to distance himself from its 'religiosity':

Holiness consists of a life ordered and fixed in accordance with Halakhah and finds its fulfilment in observance of the laws regarding human biological existence, such as the laws concerning forbidden sexual relations, forbidden foods, and similar precepts. And it was not for naught that Maimonides included these prohibitions in his *Book of Holiness*. Holiness is created by man, by flesh and blood.[23]

He says that in the Jewish view the idea of holiness does not stand for a transcendence which is removed as far as possible from reality;[24] it is, rather, the constraint (*tsimtsum*) of the transcendent within the halakhah; halakhah, that is, is the channel through which the transcendent enters the 'real' world.

Otto seeks refuge in the a priori from the vulnerability of the religious concepts of holiness and transcendence to the charges of social and historical conditioning and relativity levelled against them by sociologists of religion such as Max Weber. In an analogous way Soloveitchik seeks refuge in the a priori from the vulnerability of halakhah both to the demonstration by historians that halakhah and its texts evolved in response to changing social, economic, and historical circumstances, and to the theological charge that it is not binding for all time and in all places.

Historical Criticism

During his years in Berlin, if not before, Soloveitchik must have become acquainted with the problems posed to traditional belief by historical criticism of the Bible. Certainly, as we saw in Chapter 16, these matters were

[21] Otto, *Idea of the Holy*, 129.   [22] *Halakhic Man*, 9.
[23] Ibid. 46–7. He instances the conquest of land, Jerusalem, etc.   [24] Ibid. 45.

widely discussed by Orthodox Jewish intellectuals, and leading figures such as Hoffman and Breuer at the (Orthodox) Berlin *Rabbinerseminar* openly attempted to rebut the 'Higher Criticism'; Jehiel Jacob Weinberg, the last head of the Berlin Seminary, was closely associated with the Christian masoretic scholar Paul Kahle, and Weinberg and Soloveitchik certainly met.[25] Soloveitchik, however, never engages with historical criticism, either because he found it too distasteful or because he felt that he had effectively sidestepped the issue through his interpretation of Torah as an a priori system; Torah for him is simply a 'given' that he can analyse and define but not question.

Of course, he has to concede that there is *some* human component to Torah, broadly conceived. In the beautiful essay he composed as a memorial for his wife Tonya, he distinguishes two types of allegory on the Song of Songs:[26]

- The metaphysical-historical allegory portrays the *actual* relationship between God and Israel as it has been (and will be) in history; this is the line taken in midrash, Targum, Rashi, Kuzari, Ibn Ezra.

- The metaphysical-universal allegory points to the *ideal* relationship between people and God; this is the approach of Rabbenu Bahya, Maimonides,[27] and kabbalah.

This is rather like the distinction he often makes between *goral* and *ye'ud*, Israel's (actual) lot in history, and its (ideal) destiny.[28] Like Plato, he conceives the ideal as the truly *real*, and the actual or historical as a transitory approximation. Since on this analysis the 'real' escapes history, it can be assimilated to the a priori framework.

The Oral Torah Problem

There comes a crucial point where riding above mundane historical reality is not merely unwise but impossible. If Torah is equated with halakhah, which in turn is conceived as a priori, what can be said about the 'Oral Torah' tradition, which undoubtedly includes not only biblical interpretation but legis-

[25] Weinberg was discussed in Chs. 8 and 16 above. Shapiro, *Between the Yeshiva World and Modern Orthodoxy*, 195, reports a conversation between Weinberg and Soloveitchik in Berlin.

[26] 'Uvikashtem misham', n. 1.

[27] Maimonides, *Mishneh torah*, 'Hilkhot teshuvah', 20: 3; id., *Guide* iii. 51.

[28] On pp. 10–12 of 'Kol dodi dofek' he distinguishes between the *kiyum gorali* (allotted existence, that is, existence as a normal people subject to the vicissitudes of history, a passive existence) of the Jewish people and their *kiyum ye'udi* (vocational existence, as a people designated by God for a certain task, an active existence).

lation initiated by the rabbis? How can what the rabbis *contingently* legislated be a priori?

Soloveitchik addressed this problem in a halakhic excursus that demonstrates even better than his philosophical works how he understands Torah, including Oral Torah. The topic is determination of the calendar. The 'law of Torah', as the rabbis interpret Exodus 12: 2, is that the Chief Court (Sanhedrin) in Jerusalem, as heirs to Moses, assess visual evidence as to the appearance of the new moon, and on this basis proclaim the new month; in addition, they assess the growth of crops and decide whether it is necessary to intercalate a month to ensure that Passover does not occur too early.

But what happens when there is no Chief Court in Jerusalem, or indeed when there is no court there at all?

Maimonides dealt with the problem at length in his early *Book of Commandments* and again in his great code, the *Mishneh torah*,[29] building on the Talmud's distinction between *kidush al pi re'iyah* (determination[30] on the basis of observation) and *kidush al pi heshbon* (determination by calculation).

Soloveitchik argues that, for Maimonides, the two ways of calendar fixation depend on two radically different *haluyot dinim*, ways in which a law may 'fall into place'.[31] Whether the month is fixed by observation or calculation, a formal court procedure is required; the new calendar month is never a mere automatic consequence of the position of the moon. The sanctity (*etsem kedushat hayom*) of festival days depends on the months being fixed by [the people of] Israel in the land [of Israel]. Calculation is merely, as Rambam expressly says, 'to reveal the matter', that is, to make known the dates fixed by the court in the land of Israel; it does not, in the absence of a formal procedure, establish when the month begins.

The High Court in Jerusalem functions in two ways. In respect of deciding Torah laws the court itself *is* the Oral Torah (*hem ikar torah shebe'al peh*); it is authorized by Deuteronomy 17: 8 to create *heftsah shel hora'ah* ('decision object'—note the reification of the law). However, in matters which need the consent of the people, the High Court *represents* the people of Israel. Soloveitchik adduces several proofs that the fixing of months falls in this latter category, in which the court represents the people of Israel as a whole; calendar fixation is a representative function authorized by Numbers 11: 16, 17, and to that extent a formal procedure, but it is not a legal decision.

Fixing by observation and fixing by calculation differ in two ways. Fixing by observation requires a formal decision; fixing by calculation works simply by all Israel observing the festivals.

[29] Maimonides, *Sefer hamitsvot*, positive commandment 153; id., *Mishneh torah*, 'Hilkhot kidush hahodesh' 5: 2.   [30] Literally, 'sanctification'.

Fixing by observation, being a formal decision, can only be carried out by an actual court, even though the court itself acts not on its own behalf, but on behalf of all Israel. Fixing by calculation is accomplished by the whole people of Israel observing the festivals on the basis of the calculated calendar.

Here Soloveitchik comes to the nub of his argument, and makes a point of some philosophical interest. It follows from what has already been established that a court which fixes the calendar is not doing so in its capacity as the Great Sanhedrin dispensing law to Israel, but rather as a body competent in legal decision-making (*hora'ah*) and qualified, through that competence, to act as if it were the whole of Israel; that is the basis on which the highest remaining court in the land of Israel continued to fix months after the demise of the Sanhedrin. They were indeed the continuation of the tradition leading back to Moses, and *constituted* that tradition; indeed, they actually *created* Oral Torah.[32]

This may sound as if Soloveitchik is adopting the historians' position that the sages adapted Torah to the needs of each generation, and is justifying the process as valid Torah, but in fact what he is driving at is something very different and thoroughly *ahistorical*, as becomes clear in his analysis of the concept of tradition (*masorah*) in the final section. Tradition, he says, is not a question of reliable transmission, of evidence as to what was handed down at Sinai; it is not a merely passive form of learning. For there are two aspects to Oral Torah:

First, the sages preserved the Oral Torah received at Sinai, so that we do indeed possess the Oral Torah received by Moses. (He offers no evidence, nor does he give details of what this Oral Torah comprises.)

Second, reception of the tradition is not merely a passive act of learning, but it 'brings into existence the category of tradition and receiving'.[33] Therefore, anyone who denies the authority of someone who is in the line of tradition, even though accepting the substance of the tradition, is a heretic.

This second aspect is a truly novel interpretation of the nature of Oral Torah. No longer is it merely authentic tradition in a historical sense; it is (at least in part) a new metaphysical object created by the sages in each generation.

Clearly, this issue is important to Soloveitchik, else he would not have developed it at such length or introduced the question of heresy. I suggest that

---

[31] Soloveitchik, 'Fixing the Date of Festivals' (Heb.). The essay comprises seven main sections, numbered from 1 to 6 and then, curiously, 9, though nothing appears to be missing.

[32] *Kulan mehavot ḥeftsah shel torah shebe'al peh* 'They all bring into existence an Oral Torah object'. Another instance of reification; law is treated as a metaphysical object.

[33] *Mehavah ḥalut sham bifnei atsmo shel masorah vekabalah*—more reification!

the strength of his feeling is an indication that he is plugging one of the most serious gaps in his general understanding of halakhah. His concept of halakhah as an a priori system may have some credibility if one views halakhah as a divine creation independent of human factors, riding above history. But if this is true of the revelation at Sinai, which may then be viewed as a 'quantification' of 'eternal truths', how can one apply it to the apparently very human process of rabbis interpreting the Torah in each generation? His answer seems to be that Oral Torah, as actively defined by the rabbis, is a further quantification of the halakhic 'realities' that constitute the essence of revealed Torah.

It is indeed a bold step on Soloveitchik's part to assimilate Oral as well as Written Torah to his a priori system. He was certainly aware of modern historical scholarship on the rabbinic period, and even more familiar with the reservations of medieval rabbis, not least Maimonides himself, as to the actual content of Oral Torah; yet he ignores all this in setting up as a vital doctrine of Judaism the belief that the Oral Torah we now possess is identical with, or at least a 'quantification of', that revealed to Moses at Sinai. His homiletics reveal further implications of this position, developed also in his later halakhic discourses.[34]

Philosophically, there is resonance here with Hermann Cohen. In his *Logik der reinen Erkentniss* Cohen expounded the concept of 'origin', which he used in *Religion der Vernunft aus den Quellen des Judentums* as the basis of his claim for the 'originality' (*Ursprünglichkeit*) of Judaism. Man's response to revelation from the Origin, i.e. God, constitutes the scientific process of cognizing the concepts of the Origin. For Cohen it was not difficult to visualize this as a historical process of revealing a priori truths which are themselves independent of history, but these are highly general truths, such as that you should love your fellow; the rest of traditional Torah was, in his view, culturebound and impermanent. For Soloveitchik, Origin becomes Torah, whose content is gradually revealed through the concept-based learning of Torah together with the creative activity of the legitimate guardians of Oral Torah, viz. the rabbis; the fundamental concepts of Torah are in themselves unchanging, and even if in some sense their cognition evolves through history, the received system of halakhah is thereby enhanced rather than invalidated. If at the theoretical level there is something in common between Cohen and Soloveitchik, at the practical level they remain poles apart.

[34] Soloveitchik, 'Two Types of Tradition' (Heb.). See in particular the definition of two types of *masoret* on p. 228 and the discussion of ways in which disputes could have arisen within Oral Torah.

Conclusion

Soloveitchik's concept of Torah as essentially halakhah, and of halakhah as a priori, articulates his reaction to historical criticism and relativism. It is an elegant recasting of Torah, and restores halakhah to a central position. However, it fails to address genuine historical questions, it does less than justice to the socio-historical setting of halakhah, and it ignores whole swathes of traditional material that resist confinement in the halakhic straitjacket.

From a philosophical standpoint, too, it is problematic. Just what *does* Soloveitchik mean by 'a priori'? He offers no definition, just an analogy with mathematics. Even if we ignore general philosophical critiques of the concept of 'a priori', we are left with Kant's problem of whether there can be synthetic a priori judgements. Even if we accept Kant's contention that ethics can be derived from a single synthetic a priori judgement, which he specifies, it would be difficult to find a comparable judgement from which to derive the system of halakhah, and Soloveitchik does not even attempt this; perhaps he wants us to regard each halakhic concept as an independent synthetic a priori judgement, but he doesn't say so, nor does he offer a list of halakhic concepts that he thinks *are* a priori; even if he did, how could the *actual* Written and Oral Torah be derived from them? Philosophically, his presupposition that Torah consists of a priori halakhah is simply incoherent.

When Mendelssohn (Chapter 17) argued that Torah was 'revealed legislation' we knew what he was talking about, and even to which passages in the Bible he referred; we could therefore pose the question, which he himself addressed, of whether that legislation was applicable today, to Jews or anyone else. But when Soloveitchik tells us that Torah consists of a priori halakhic concepts we can have no more than a vague notion of what he means, or of what concepts or texts he is referring to. He has cocooned his beloved Torah from the charge of historical relativism, but at the price of coherence.

At the end of the previous chapter we enquired whether it was possible, in the light of modern developments, to reassert the *absoluteness* of the received Torah, its texts and its laws. Soloveitchik undoubtedly made this assertion. However, it is no longer the open, verifiable historical assertion of Maimonides, but a transformation of the historical claim to a metaphysical, unverifiable, and therefore unfalsifiable one. This may be admirable piety, but it is fideism rather than philosophy, Hamann rather than Kant.[35]

[35] Immanuel Kant (1724–1804) sought to base religion on reason; Johann Georg Hamann (1730–88) extolled faith as the foundation for human thought. The contrast between these two German Enlightenment thinkers is less sharp than might appear, though; Hamann plays on an ambiguity in the German *Glaube*, which conveys both 'belief' in an epistemic sense and 'faith' in a religious sense, to argue that reason itself derives from faith.

NINETEEN

FEMINIST CRITIQUES

ECONOMIC AND SOCIAL CHANGES in the wake of the Enlightenment and the Industrial Revolution spawned the women's rights movement in late eighteenth-century Europe. Women's republican clubs in revolutionary France pleaded that 'liberty, equality, and fraternity' should apply to all, regardless of sex; subsequent movements sought to achieve equality for women with men with regard to control of property, opportunity in education and employment, suffrage, and sexual freedom. From Mary Wollstonecraft's *A Vindication of the Rights of Woman* (1792) through John Stuart Mill's *The Subjection of Women* (1869) to Simone de Beauvoir's contention in *Le Deuxième Sexe* (1949) that man is seen as subject, woman as other, arguments for change in women's role in society were formulated. At the same time, political activity achieved progress toward property, employment and educational rights, suffrage, and access to family planning.

Neither the Bible, nor its interpretation by church and synagogue, went unscathed in the process; traditionally, all of them have assumed a patriarchal, authoritarian model for society, just as until very recently they took for granted the existence of slavery. Slavery makes an apt comparison. Bible and tradition do not enjoin slavery but nor do they ban it; they merely regulate it. Freemen and slaves are, in the pre-modern view, a fact of nature, just as it is a fact of nature that people are of different races, colours, and genders. Laws are from time to time instituted to ameliorate the lot of slaves, but the existence of the state of slavery, and the social inferiority of those unfortunate enough to find themselves in that state, is not called into question. Likewise, the subordinate status of women is taken for granted, rationalized, regulated, now and then ameliorated, but never radically questioned. It is no coincidence that the women's movement came hard on the heels of progress towards the abolition of slavery; both are part of the modern impulse to the recognition of universal human rights. Two American pioneers of the women's movement, Lucretia Mott (1793–1880) and Elizabeth Cady Stanton (1815–1902), were redoubtable abolitionists.

So long as society at large did not question the subordination of slaves or women, few theologians were troubled either. But now that most societies do question the subordination of slaves, and most people in the liberal democracies question the subordination of women, theologians need to ask why the Bible did not take as radical a stance in these issues as it did with regard to, say, idolatry. The Bible uncompromisingly opposed idolatry even though it was a normal way of worship in the society of its time, so why did it not protest in equal measure against the oppression and subordination of women and slaves? It is not adequate to invoke the 'universal norms of pre-modern society' to explain away the Bible's acceptance of this injustice, since the Bible itself does not compromise with such norms in its polemic against what it castigates as the evil of idolatry.

Cynthia Ozick has expressed this graphically:

In creating the Sabbath, Torah came face to face with a nature that says, 'I make no difference among the days.' In giving the Commandment against idolatry, Torah came face to face with a society in competition with the Creator. In making the Commandment against dishonour of parents, Torah came face to face with the merciless usage of the old . . . In every instance Torah strives to teach No to unrestraint, No to victimization, No to dehumanization. The Covenant is a bond with the Creator, not with the practices of the world as they are found in actuality.

With one tragic exception. With regard to women, Torah does not say No to the practices of the world as they are found in actuality; here alone Torah reaffirms the world, denying the meaning of its own Covenant.[1]

Now it is not quite true that the Torah always teaches No; sometimes, it compromises. It compromises with slavery. And the rabbis suggest, for instance, that the limited permission granted by Deuteronomy 21: 10–14 for a soldier to cohabit with a captive woman is a compromise 'on account of the evil inclination';[2] better to regulate soldiers' behaviour in war than to place absolute restrictions on them that they would likely ignore. Other examples could be cited. Ultimately, it is a question of priorities. The Bible's priority is the elimination of idolatry. In order to secure that fundamental aim it compromises, at least on a transient basis, with other undesirable features of society; more troubling, it may fail to indicate clearly that those features are undesirable.

Nowadays few people would want to place the elimination of idolatry at the top of their agenda of social reform. Idolatry, at least as it is perceived in the Bible, no longer seems a major threat to society. Injustice, including discrimination on the grounds of race, colour or gender, is perceived as a far greater threat; whatever the situation may have been in Bible times, it is certainly not the case now that injustice arises primarily from idolatry. Quite a lot of injustice arises, indeed, from the uncritical application of religious norms to a

[1] Ozick, 'Notes toward Finding the Right Question', 149. [2] BT *Kid.* 21*b*.

society very different from that in which they were formulated; not least of the injustices supported in this way is discrimination against women.

Jewish feminism does not simply raise specific questions about women's rights in halakhah, it leads us to confront a fundamental theological question concerning the culture-boundedness of divine revelation. Tamar Ross has articulated this all the more effectively since she writes in defence of a Modern Orthodox position:

What makes the feminist analysis unique is that the ultimate question it raises does not concern any particular difficulty in the contents of the Torah (be it moral, scientific, or theological). Nor does it concern the accuracy of the historical account of its literary genesis. Highlighting an all-pervasive male bias in the Torah seems to display a more general skepticism regarding divine revelation that is much more profound. What it drives us to ask is, Can any verbal message claiming revelatory status really be divine? Because language itself is shaped by the cultural context in which it is formulated . . . is a divine and eternally valid message at all possible? Can a verbal message transcend its cultural framework? With these questions, the clash between Orthodoxy and historicism is transformed from a dispute over the facts of the matter to a debate over issues of general bias and the ubiquitous traces of cultural relativism . . . Allegorical interpretations of problematic passages in the Torah will not solve anything in this case. The male bias cannot be limited to specific terms or passages; it is all over the text.[3]

An analogous question was raised, of course, as soon as Bible-minded people began worrying about slavery, that is, as soon as Christians (who took the initiative in this matter) began to think that not just Christians should not be slaves, but that the very concept of slavery was contrary to God's teaching. Nowadays, both Jews and Christians abhor slavery and condemn it in the name of their traditions, but this is a quite revolutionary reading of scripture, since neither Hebrew Scripture nor New Testament opposes slavery in principle, even if they afford some basis for its limitation and amelioration. You can only read scripture as condemning slavery if you are prepared to acknowledge that scripture expresses itself in a culture-bound way, and that it is legitimate to reinterpret it in terms of our own culture.

Elizabeth Cady Stanton published *The Woman's Bible* in 1895 and 1898. It has often been described as an attack on the Bible, but that is misleading. Stanton does abandon the tradition of literal inspiration in favour of radical critical theory; however, her main thrust is not directed against the Bible but against the way she believes it has been falsified and read by Jewish and Christian men to justify the subjugation of women. In the opening pages, for instance, she comments on Genesis 1: 27:

[3] T. Ross, *Expanding the Palace of Torah*, 186.

we have in these texts a plain declaration of the existence of the feminine element in the Godhead, equal in power and glory with the masculine . . . Scripture, as well as science and philosophy, declares the eternity and equality of sex . . .

As to woman's subjugation, on which both the canon and the civil law delight to dwell, it is important to note that equal dominion is given to women over every living thing, but not one word is said giving man dominion over woman.

She then cites Astruc on the duality of the Genesis creation narratives, and continues: 'the second story was manipulated by some Jew, in an endeavor to give "heavenly authority" for requiring a woman to obey the man she married'.[4]

Clearly, Stanton reads scripture in terms of her world-view, rather than interpreting her world in the light of scripture; like Spinoza, she decides what constitutes 'authentic' scripture on the basis of what she regards as rational, scientific, philosophical ethics.

Much the same happens whenever people adduce proof-texts supporting equalization of the role of women in society with that of men; the proof-texts can only be read as supportive of gender equalization if you are prepared to admit that their original expression is culture-bound, and if you are prepared to select carefully which texts you will regard as constituting the essence of scripture.

Maybe one day Jews and Christians will be just as shocked at the suggestion that their sacred writings encourage the subordination of women as they now are at the suggestion that they support slavery. But that day has not yet dawned.

In the context of 'Torah from Heaven' the question is, can we affirm the divine origin of a Torah that appears to endorse a subordinate status for women, slaves, and non-Israelites? Put crudely, is there any justification for Orthodox men to continue to thank God each morning for having not made them (in ascending order of acceptability) a heathen (non-Israelite), a slave, a woman?[5]

The Sinai Covenant

Did women stand at the foot of Mount Sinai when the Torah was revealed? Were they party to the Sinai Covenant? I ask not as a historical exercise, but to clarify the foundational myth of Judaism, irrespective of whether the event took place in history; we need to know how to tell the story of the origin of Torah.

---

[4] Stanton, *The Woman's Bible*.
[5] Tosefta (Lieberman) *Ber.* 6: 18; BT *Men.* 43*b*. Readings vary, but all have *shelo asani ishah*, 'who has not made me a woman'.

According to Exodus, God revealed himself to *ha'am* 'the people', who were instructed, by way of preparation for the great event, to keep away from women for three days (Exod. 19: 15); evidently, 'people' here is men only. Perhaps this was simply a call to sexual abstinence, rather than an exclusion of women, though if so why segregate women from men rather than men from women? But even if the women were segregated at a decent distance from the men it is hardly likely that they could have failed to see and hear the lightning and thunder and the divine voice; it seems then that in the view of Exodus they were present but not 'visible', included by implication through their menfolk; men entered the covenant, that is, on behalf of their wives and children.

Deuteronomy 4, recalling the same event, has God address *hakahal* 'the congregation', and makes no reference to abstinence, segregation, or sexual differences. Just as Exodus explicitly includes women in certain legal contexts (e.g. Exod. 21: 20; 21: 28), Deuteronomy includes them in covenantal situations, for instance in the great covenant in the last days of Moses (Deut. 29: 10) and the septennial ceremony of *hakhel* (Deut. 31: 10 f.), when the king read the Torah to the assembled people. Perhaps Deuteronomy is telling us that men and women were equally present at Sinai; this inference is neither made nor denied in the classical texts.

In most of the world today, and in all of it until recent times, women were regarded as being in some sense subordinate to men, so perhaps it is historically inappropriate even to raise the question of whether women stood at the foot of Mount Sinai when the Torah was revealed, if by that we are asking whether they were included in the Great Covenant of Sinai; we are imposing our ways of thought on a culture to which they are alien. The traditional answer would always have been, 'Of course. They were included with the men.' But this is not really an answer to the question. It is not saying women were *included* in the sense that, for example, the tribe of Levi and the tribe of Dan were included, but rather that they were *not excluded*, it being assumed by default that any commitment made by their menfolk on their behalf was equally binding on them.

Moreover, the fact that women were included by implication does not imply that they were *equals* in the covenant; within the rabbinic tradition this possibility is rather discounted by the comment attributed to Eleazar ben Azariah (second century) that 'If the men came to learn, and the women to hear, why did the little children come? To earn reward for those who brought them';[6] he assumes, that is, that women did not come to learn, though he

---

[6]   BT Ḥag. 3a.

acknowledges that they were present; his older contemporary Eliezer ben Hirkanus had vehemently opposed the education of women.[7]

But though the question is not historically apposite, it must be faced today by anyone who wants to read the Bible as sacred, authoritative scripture. We cannot, of course, *rewrite* the Torah, and we should not falsify it by claiming it says things that it does not. But we can say that, speaking the language of its time to the people of its time, Torah tells of a Great Covenant between God and Israel at Sinai; *interpreting* that covenant in the language of our time for the people of our time, we understand the covenant as between God on the one hand, and each and every man, *woman*, and child of Israel on the other. But we should concede that this interpretation is at least as culture-bound as the original statement; a future generation might well want to interpret differently, possibly in the light of social attitudes that would seem very strange to us. Once we have accepted the culture-boundedness of scripture we must relinquish the right to claim universality for our own interpretations.

Language and Gender

Clifford Geertz pointed out in his essay 'Religion as a Cultural System' that religious symbols function both as models *of* the community's sense of reality and as models *for* its behaviour and social order.[8] So the question is not just whether we think of God as male or female, but of how the ways we talk about God influence male and female roles in society.

Language, by using the male gender for collective forms, is seen to perpetuate the 'invisibility', or 'otherness', of women and subordinate them to men.

Hebrew, like English, separates its pronouns by gender. As in Arabic and many other languages all nouns, pronouns, and adjectives have gender and most verb forms vary by gender. It is linguistically impossible to talk about God in Hebrew or Arabic without committing oneself on gender. Even the dodges, ugly but manageable in English, of using 'inclusive' language, avoiding pronouns, or coining neologisms such as 'godself', cannot work.

In mature languages grammatical gender, whatever its origin, is not to do with sex, so using masculine gender of God does not imply that he is in any way male. Even so, the constant and consistent use of masculine gender for God reinforces the concept of male superiority and male dominance in society. Even if it was desirable for all languages to become gender-neutral, it would be unrealistic to expect this to happen in the foreseeable future. And

---

[7] Mishnah *Sot.* 3: 4.   [8] Geertz, *Interpretation of Cultures*, 93.

even if current languages were changed, what could we do about older sources that are written in gender-rich language?

Rita M. Gross urged that familiar forms of addressing God in prayer should be transposed to the feminine.[9] For instance, *hakedoshah berukhah hi*—'the Holy One, blessed be She'—should be used in place of the current masculine form. This simply exacerbates the problem. If we don't want to speak about God as male, because God is beyond gender, we don't want to speak about God as female either, for the same reason. We want to *negate* gender, not to *balance* it; balancing gender would simply affirm it.

For the time being, therefore, we must resign ourselves to language as it is, pointing out its limitations, and constantly reiterating that it is nonsense to speak of God, who has no physical form, as intrinsically male or female.

Images of God

The principal target of biblical polemic is the pantheon of the Canaanites. Gods are reviled and their existence denied, and goddesses even more so, since they are associated with fertility cults, sexual excess, and temple prostitution.

It is forbidden to make graven images of God, but literary images are apparently acceptable; Bible and Talmud abound in them. Mostly, they are distinctly masculine, whether God is portrayed as a warrior (Exod. 15: 3), a shepherd (Ps. 23), or as the Ancient of Days (Dan. 7: 9). Occasionally, we find a feminine image: Psalm 123: 2 speaks of our relationship with God as that of a slave-girl to her mistress; Isaiah 66: 7–11 compares God's activity with that of a mother giving birth and nurturing her baby. No one objected to the psalm or to Isaiah on the grounds that God was *really* male.

'So God created humankind in His own image; in the image of God He created him; male and female He created them' (Gen. 1: 27). This implies that in using our concept of God to model human behaviour we should not distinguish between male and female. Consistent with this, the rabbinic formulation of the 'imitation of God' incorporates virtues associated with female as well as male roles. 'After the Lord your God shall you walk' (Deut. 13: 5) is interpreted as *imitatio dei*:

Said Rabbi Hama bar Hanina, 'How can a person walk after God? Is it not written "For the Lord your God is a consuming fire" (Deuteronomy 4: 24)? But follow God's attributes. As He clothes the naked ... as He visits the sick ... comforts the bereaved ... buries the dead ... so should you.'[10]

---

[9] Gross, 'Steps Toward Feminine Images of Deity'.   [10] BT *Sot.* 14a.

What is remarkable is the absence of distinctively male characteristics from those attributes of God we are called to emulate. It is God's care and compassion that we are exhorted to copy, not his vengeance and imposition of justice. (Though to characterize gender attributes in this way distorts reality.)

If the availability of distinctively feminine imagery of God within Jewish tradition is limited,[11] does it make sense to create new images? Images cannot, of course, be placed in the Bible or other founding texts if they are not there. But they can be used in telling or retelling stories and in theological discussion, and the non-Orthodox will feel free to introduce them into the liturgy.

Gross lists five basic 'goddess images' that need translating into Jewish terms: the 'coincidence of opposites' or 'ambiguity symbolism'; images of God the Mother; the goddess of motherhood and culture, twin aspects of creativity; goddess as giver of wisdom and patron of scholarship and learning; the assertion of sexuality as an aspect of divinity.[12] She sums up:

> Dimensions of deity that have been lost or severely attenuated during the long centuries when we spoke of God as if S/He were only a male are restored. They seem to have to do with acceptance of immanence, with nature and the cyclic round. Metaphors of enclosure, inner spaces and curved lines seem to predominate. What a relief from the partial truth of intervention and transcendence; of history and linear time; of going forth, exposure and straight lines!

Some of this imagery exists already within texts that are accepted by many Jews as traditional. Zoharic kabbalah, for instance, incorporates sexual imagery into the dynamic of the Ten Sefirot (emanations from God), though it regards God-in-godself—the *ein sof*, or unlimited—as utterly beyond language. There are masculine and feminine pairs of Sefirot, for instance the masculine (active) potency of *ḥokhmah* (knowledge) and the feminine (passive) potency of *binah* (understanding) that engender the second triad, but in the kabbalistic formulation the concept of male dominance is retained; male is always active, female passive.

The rabbis commonly used the term *shekhinah* in relation to God's presence. This noun, which means something like 'indwelling', certainly has feminine gender, but this is hardly significant, as all Hebrew abstract nouns of this grammatical form are feminine. Still, even if the rabbis were not thinking about the *shekhinah* in gender terms, it is clear that they thought of it as protecting and nurturing Israel; this is enough to afford a precedent for contemporary theologians who seek female imagery of God's relationship with people.

---

[11] Schäfer, *Mirror of his Beauty*, offers a judicious and comprehensive survey of the early material.   [12] Gross, 'Steps Toward Feminine Images of Deity'.

However, we should be on our guard against male and female stereotypes. Not all men are aggressive, or women nurturing; quite often the opposite is the case. Nor does there seem to be any compelling reason why 'immanence' should be regarded as feminine and 'transcendence' as masculine; the concept of immanence was, after all, devised by male theologians.

Equality before the Law

Equal in the eyes of God, yes; Genesis 1: 27 portrays male and female as equal creations of God. But the creation story of Genesis 2–3, with an Eve moulded from Adam's rib and yielding to temptation, shows the loss of the ideal and appears to justify placing Eve under Adam's authority.

Equality before the law has its limits, too. While women are equal persons in Jewish criminal law, in so far as its strictures and penalties are equally applicable to men and women, their testimony is unacceptable other than in specified instances; they are subordinate in matrimonial law, and differences apply in ritual obligations.

The situation has not been entirely static. The rabbis of the period of the Mishnah, for instance, enacted several measures to enhance women's rights in marriage and to increase the stability of marriage. They approved the *ketubah*,[13] ensuring that a woman's rights were safeguarded on divorce; to enable the re-marriage of a woman whose husband had disappeared they relaxed the normal legal requirement of two adult male witnesses for judicial procedures and accepted the testimony of one female.[14] Sympathy, yes; stretching and bending the law, yes, up to a point; but full equality, no!

Non-Orthodox Jews in recent times have introduced varying measures of gender equalization, such as ordaining women as rabbis and counting them in the prayer quorum. As they do not apply Jewish civil and criminal law, they have not needed to amend these laws. Certain aspects of marriage, divorce, and Jewish status remain problematic; some Reform groups recognize claims to Jewish parentage from individuals either of whose parents is Jewish, contrary to the traditional recognition only of those whose female parent was Jewish. New issues have arisen with regard to homosexual relationships.[15]

---

[13] The *ketubah* was actually a standard form of document in late antiquity, with Babylonian antecedents; the rabbis signified their approval by attributing its origin (BT *Shab.* 14b), or at least its major features, to Simon ben Shetah (BT *Ket.* 82b).

[14] Mishnah *Yev.* 16: 7; BT *Yev.* 88a.

[15] Rapoport, *Judaism and Homosexuality*, expounds and uncompromisingly upholds the biblical and rabbinic condemnation of homosexual practices by both males and females, but maintains that 'if we can be kind and understanding to all other people, irrespective of their

Among the Orthodox, the women's 'Rosh Hodesh' (New Moon) movement has made little headway in getting rabbis to take women's issues seriously, though several Orthodox rabbis have encouraged educational initiatives for women,[16] and some have grudgingly permitted women-only religious services. Yeshiva-type institutions for women have existed in Israel and the United States since the 1980s, and it seems inevitable that women's greater literacy in halakhah will lead to demands for a more active public role.[17] The 'private ordination' of 'Reb'[18] Mimi Feigelson in 1994 by Rabbi Shlomo Carlebach has attracted limited notice. It remains to be seen whether the more public action of Rabbi Avi Weiss, who in March 2009, at the Hebrew Institute of Riverdale, New York, conferred on Sara Hurwitz a kind of ordination that fell just short of conferring on her the title 'rabbi', will have greater impact within the general Orthodox community; the real test is not so much the title as whether Orthodox congregations will accept women as authoritative rabbis, not merely as educators and 'advisers'. Other women who have received Orthodox ordination include Haviva Ner-David (from Rabbi Arie Strikovsky) and Evelyn Goodman-Tau (from Rabbi Jonathan Chipman).

Despite the initiatives of Carlebach, Weiss, and others, the more common attitude among Orthodox rabbis remains that articulated by the late Rabbi Moshe Feinstein (1895–1986), who insisted that no deviation from traditional halakhah was to be allowed, since this would compromise belief in the eternal validity of the Torah that was revealed by God through Moses in the minutest detail. The Torah, Feinstein stressed, recognizes the equal *sanctity* of women with men—a female prophet, for instance, commands the same respect as a male one—while exempting women from certain more cumbersome duties to enable them to cope better with the sacred task of bearing and rearing children for Torah and *mitsvot*.[19] In line with this attitude, in April 2010 the Rabbinical Council of America rejected Weiss's initiative, resolving that women could not function in any way as rabbis, irrespective of title.

religious or moral shortcomings, then *a fortiori*, we must adopt the same attitude towards those who face the challenges, say, of an exclusive sexual orientation' (p. 120).

[16] Strong halakhah-based advocacy of women's Torah education is found in the opening responsum of Henkin, *Responsa on Contemporary Jewish Women's Issues*.

[17] The revolutionary potential of Orthodox women's learning is analysed by El-Or, *Next Year I Will Know More*.

[18] Her 'official' title is *mashpiah ruhanit*, roughly 'spiritual guide'. The constant use of quotation marks in this paragraph indicates lack of general recognition.

[19] Feinstein, *Igerot mosheh*, 'Orah hayim' 4:49; vol. vi, p. 80. The responsum is dated 18 Elul 5736 (13 Sept. 1976).

The Need for Change

Judith Plaskow writes: 'For me, then, feminism is not about attaining equal rights for women in religious or social structures that remain unchanged. But about the thoroughgoing transformation of religion and society.'[20]

The modern feminist critique obviously calls for rethinking biblical interpretation and for modification in the laws formulated by the rabbis. But what bearing has it on our theme, the fundamental notion of *torah min hashamayim*?

The ambivalence in the sources as to whether women actually 'stood at Sinai' indicates a deep problem. For the text of the Torah as we know it, both Written and Oral, is a male-dominated text. To claim that the Torah is eternally valid in all its details is therefore to proclaim the absolute rightness of male domination in society. On the other hand, to accept that the gender orientation of the Torah is *not* part of its eternal truth, but due to fallible human mediation of the divine message, is to concede that the text as we know it is imperfect in a major and pervasive respect.

The feminist movement, as part of the movement for universal human rights, poses a major challenge to the traditional concept of *torah min hashamayim*; no part of Judaism, whether its history, its law, its theology, can remain untouched by its justifiable claims.

[20] Plaskow, *Standing Again at Sinai*, p. xvii.

FOUR DEFENCES OF
TRADITIONAL BELIEF

BETWEEN 1997 and 1999 David Weiss Halivni, Louis Jacobs (1920–2006), and Menachem Kellner all published defences of traditional belief.[1]

All three hail from traditional Orthodox backgrounds. All three have strong emotional attachments to their origin. Each has achieved distinction in some field of Jewish study. They have in common that it is precisely their study of Judaism which has, in the first instance, led them to entertain doubts as to the authenticity and integrity of the way Judaism is currently presented in Orthodox circles, whether *ḥaredi* or Modern Orthodox. These doubts have been intensified by historical and scientific study and by philosophical reflection.

Beside the three I set Tamar Ross, whose *Expanding the Palace of Torah*, on Orthodoxy and feminism, appeared in 2004, and was cited in Chapter 19.

All four books display a wealth of scholarship, and each would be worth reading simply for its scholarly content. Yet more is at stake. Each of the first three authors has a strong interest in defending his personal religious commitment against the perceived charge that it is inconsistent with scholarship and reason on the one hand, and with traditional Judaism on the other. For Halivni and Jacobs the apologia has an institutional as well as a personal significance. Halivni taught Talmud for many years at the Jewish Theological Seminary where he exercised a leading role in the formulation of Conservative halakhah; in 1983 he broke with the Conservative movement over the ordination of women and was subsequently a co-founder of the Association for Traditional Judaism, which sees itself as the true torchbearer of Zacharias Frankel's 'positive-historical Judaism'. Jacobs was effectively excluded from the British (Orthodox) United Synagogue in 1963, and though he continued to consider himself 'modern Orthodox'[2] he not only worked closely with the

---

[1] Weiss Halivni, *Revelation Restored*; Jacobs, *Beyond Reasonable Doubt*; Kellner, *Must A Jew Believe Anything?* This chapter enlarges on my review article, 'Three Books on Jewish Faith'.

[2] He made this claim on pp. 241–2 of his autobiography *Helping with Inquiries*. He reviewed the events of his break with the United Synagogue in the introduction to *Beyond Reasonable Doubt*.

Rabbinical Assembly of the American Conservative movement, but came to be regarded as the spiritual mentor of a parallel movement in the UK. Kellner, professor of Jewish Religious Thought at the University of Haifa, has not formally broken with Orthodoxy; his situation is that of many Orthodox Jewish intellectuals who are alarmed by the aggressive yet naive fundamentalism of the *haredim*, which they perceive as a distortion, even a travesty, of tradition. Ross, a professor at the Orthodox Bar-Ilan University, sits firmly within the Modern Orthodox camp; she is concerned with challenges posed by the women's movement to acceptance of the Torah as divinely revealed and eternally valid.

The four address their problems with different emphasis and methods. Halivni, as befits the learned author of some of the most important text critical notes on the Talmud in recent years, worries about the imperfections of the received text, whether of scripture or of the Oral Torah which 'corrects' it. Jacobs is concerned with the nature of revelation: in what sense can the Bible, despite its apparent moral lapses and factual errors, be construed as the word of God? If we abandon the historical doctrine that the Oral and Written Torahs were received in their extant form by Moses from God and faithfully transmitted to us, why should we follow their teachings? What is the basis for the authority of scripture, or of the rabbis as its interpreters? Kellner doubts whether all the talk about correct belief and doctrine is appropriate within Judaism at all; Maimonides' formulation of the Thirteen Principles of the Faith was, in his view, an anomaly. Ross takes her stand on feminist critique; how can we accept as divinely inspired texts pervaded with the male bias of the societies in which they were formulated?

David Weiss Halivni: The Maculate Torah

Peter Ochs, introducing Halivni's volume, welcomes it as an exercise in 'post-critical theology', the purpose of which is 'to "rescue" foundational documents, i.e. to read them in such a way as to be meaningful and relevant in the present day'. This is a benevolent, if in some respects misleading, characterization of the attempts of theologians to retain a stable vocabulary while assigning different meanings to it. Halivni certainly wants to retain the traditional way of talking, which states that God revealed the Torah to Moses on Mount Sinai, but his acceptance of historical textual criticism means that he is not using the words to mean quite the same thing as they did in tradition. It is legitimate to do this, but it should be made clear that this is what he is doing, rather than endorsing the traditional reading.

It may seem strange that Halivni, who is so exercised about 'the imperfections of the received text', has little to say on the moral problems which so trouble Jacobs and others, such as how can a text which commends genocide of the Canaanite nations be regarded as holy? His autobiography provides a clue. In a letter composed before the vote on women's ordination in October 1983, he commented:

I realize that I might stand accused of willingness to follow reason against tradition in pursuing critical study, but unwillingness to follow morality against tradition . . . My only defense is that I have greater confidence in our sense of reason than in what we consider moral. I consider the former more objective.[3]

This is puzzling, not least because Halivni so sharply separates reason from morals. Does his lack of confidence in moral judgement stem from his reflection on the apparent failure of moral reasoning to stem the Holocaust? But surely most people, Halivni included, would be more confident to claim, for example, that genocide is evil than they would be to assert (to take one of Halivni's examples) that the 'original' text of Exodus did not say 'an eye for an eye'.[4] It is not easy to see how reason could demonstrate what the 'original' text of Exodus was, or indeed to see how any text-critical argument could yield greater certainty than the certainty we have on a moral issue such as the evil of genocide.

The question of 'original text' leads us to consider Halivni's basic position. It comprises four claims:

• God revealed a perfect Torah: 'God broke into human history to reveal his will once and for all—a real revelation'.[5]

• The Israelites, through their sins, 'maculated' it. ('Maculate' is technical jargon. Halivni does not explain why he uses this term instead of 'corrupt' or 'falsify', which is what he means, and what Muslims have often alleged was done by Jews and Christians to the revealed text. It is a seriously uncomfortable notion.)

• Ezra tried to restore the original revealed text, but didn't finish the job.

• Ezra's work is continued through the rabbinic tradition to the present day. Textual alterations may no longer be made, since Ezra's text has been accepted as sacrosanct. But where rabbinic tradition differs radically from

[3] Weiss Halivni, *The Book and the Sword*, 114.
[4] On pp. 7 and 8 of *Revelation Restored* he claims that the Oral Torah, substituting pecuniary compensation, 'restored the biblical commandment to its original state'.
[5] Weiss Halivni, *Revelation Restored*, 6.

the accepted text, as in the case of *lex talionis*, we have evidence of 'restoration' of the original meaning.[6]

The first pillar of this structure is that a 'correct' text was in fact revealed by God to Moses. This position differs from naïve fundamentalism as Halivni does not claim that we *possess* the actual text, only that it once existed. He supports his contention by an argument resting on two premises:

- Jewish tradition claims that the Torah was revealed by God to Moses.

- No critical theory of the Pentateuch's origins has been proven.

From these premises he derives a conclusion:

- The traditional account has not been ruled out, and therefore remains available.[7]

This argument has at least three weaknesses:

What is at issue is the *trustworthiness* of tradition, not its existence. The indubitable fact that a tradition exists does not demonstrate the reliability of the tradition. This is especially so here, where (*a*) there is no evidence (other than the tradition itself) that the tradition originated in the days of Moses, and (*b*) we are concerned with an event which, if it occurred, was supernatural, and which would therefore require even stronger evidence than a 'normal' historical event, a point emphatically made by David Hume in his famous chapter on miracles.[8]

It is true that no critical theory as a whole has been proven. Nevertheless, the traditional theory has been discredited. This might be compared with the evidence for Darwinian evolution. There are several competing theories about, for instance, the origin of *homo sapiens*. Any or all of them might be wrong. But the 'traditional' theory that humans suddenly came into being as the result of a supernatural event less than 6,000 years ago is certainly wrong.

Halivni himself admits that the text we have is 'maculate', a product of human fallibility, a document with a complex history, and not the 'original' Torah. This is obviously contrary to the tradition, which never concedes that more than minor changes may have occurred. But if it be admitted that the tradition is unreliable, why should we rely on it as evidence for a metaphysical event that resulted in the production of some unknown yet perfect text of

---

[6] Weiss Halivni deals with this at greater length in *Peshat and Derash*.

[7] Weiss Halivni, *Revelation Restored*, 6.

[8] Hume, *Enquiry*, section 10, 'Of Miracles'. The *Enquiry* was completed in 1748.

which we possess no more than the maculated remains? Surely there are much simpler ways to account for the texts we have!

Halivni draws a parallel with an argument of Maimonides, who rejected the theory of the eternity of the universe on the grounds that since the proofs of its eternity were inconclusive we should follow the plain meaning of scripture. This is not an apt parallel, since the issue facing Maimonides was not the veracity of scripture; he took for granted, in his discussion of the eternity of the universe, that scripture was authoritative and prima facie to be understood in its literal sense. His question was (a) whether rational arguments demonstrated the eternity of the universe and (b) whether, if so, scripture could be interpreted in accordance with that finding, rather than literally. Since, in his view, the rational arguments were balanced (there *are* some against), the literal interpretation of scripture could stand; however, should reason demonstrate the eternity of the universe, scripture might be interpreted accordingly. In Halivni's case, however, the issue at stake is whether the traditional account of the origin of the extant scriptures is *reliable*; to adduce tradition itself in support of this contention begs the question. Moreover, the universe undoubtedly *is* there, so the question as to its eternity is a real one. With regard to 'revelation' (whatever it means) the question is whether such an event ever took place; if it didn't, the question as to whether the traditional account is reliable doesn't arise.

Much of the book is devoted to the interpretation of rabbinic texts with the aim of demonstrating that the rabbis were engaging in a process of 'restoration' of the original Torah. One instructive example is the treatment of *shiurim*, quantities determined by the rabbis as minima and maxima in measurements of forbidden or unclean materials, lengths of time, and the like. Halivni maintains that three different ascriptions are offered for *shiurim*. According to Rav they are *halakhah lemosheh misinai*, laws given to Moses at Sinai;[9] the Gemara interprets this to mean they are traditional laws (*hilkhata*) with no foundation in scripture;[10] while a parallel source indicates that they are only *rabbinic* laws (as opposed to *hilkhata*).[11]

The discussion may by all means illustrate the tendency of the *amora'im*, stronger among Palestinians than Babylonians, to ascribe laws with no scriptural basis to the category of *halakhah lemosheh misinai*, a sort of independent Oral Torah; moreover, Halivni may be correct when he interprets this as a reaction to the tannaitic enterprise of reading everything into scripture and

---

[9] BT *Eruv.* 4a.

[10] BT *Suk.* 5b—Halivni counts this interpretation as a separate ascription.

[11] BT *Ber.* 41a–b. Note how the English 'only' by which Halivni translates *ela* ('but') implies a devaluation which is not demanded by the Hebrew.

views it as the foundation for the subsequent rabbinic flight from direct scriptural exegesis in the field of halakhah. Whether this reliance on independent Oral Torah rather than scriptural exegesis can be read as a way of restoring the original revelation is another matter, to which Halivni devotes his third chapter; I do not find his argument convincing.

One cannot fail to be impressed by the meticulous scholarship of this book, especially by the historically sensitive handling of talmudic passages. The theology is more questionable.

Louis Jacobs: Liberal Supernaturalism

Jacobs, in *Beyond Reasonable Doubt*, seeks not for the first time to defend the theological position of 'liberal supernaturalism', which he derives from Zacharias Frankel, on whom at one time he intended to write his Ph.D. thesis. He himself states that the purpose of the book is to 'prove' the position he took in *We Have Reason to Believe*;[12] the possible meanings of 'from' in 'Torah from heaven' give leeway for this 'fresh examination'.[13]

The liberal supernaturalist 'is liberal in that his reason compels him to adopt the critical historical approach . . . even though this involves a degree of rejection of the traditional view. He is supernaturalist because he sees no reason to deny the supernatural elements of his religion.'[14]

There are two major problems with liberal supernaturalism. On the one hand, it commits to belief in God and revelation, which is problematic for the sceptic; on the other hand, though it accepts the notion of divine revelation it is somewhat hazy about what actually constitutes this revelation, and this is a problem for the traditionalist. Jacobs makes clear his position 'that belief in God is entirely reasonable but that belief in the inerrancy of Scripture or the rabbinic tradition is not'.[15]

However, he is surprisingly perfunctory in his advocacy of belief in God, or the supernatural in general. He admits the weakness of traditional 'proofs' for the existence of God, including that from religious experience, but hopefully suggests that if they are not valid proofs they are at least 'arguments', with inductive rather than deductive validity,[16] and he cites with approval Richard Swinburne's dubious claim that several weak arguments can add up to a strong one. What he fails to observe is that for the 'scientific' or philosophical mind which he is trying to satisfy the major problem is not so much whether God exists as whether the term 'God' is coherent or meaningful. Swinburne has at least recognized this, and has been careful to include among his works a volume on *The Coherence of Theism*.

[12] *Beyond Reasonable Doubt*, 1.   [13] Ibid. 17.   [14] Ibid. 50.   [15] Ibid. 97.   [16] Ibid. 98.

Jacobs focuses rather on the *content* of revelation, which he believes includes halakhah. Ever since Sa'adiah took the Karaites to task for the arbitrariness of their biblical interpretation (an accusation that Karaites reciprocated in full measure),[17] Rabbanites and Orthodox have attacked reformist streams of Judaism on similar grounds. Jacobs is well aware that in abandoning the Orthodox perspective on the inerrancy of scripture and the perfection and immutability of halakhah he is laying himself open to a charge of arbitrariness, and of readiness to compromise with current fashions. If, for instance, he distinguishes on moral grounds between 'higher' and 'lower' parts of Torah,[18] where precisely does he draw the line? Of more practical concern, where is the line to be drawn with regard to religious observance? He concedes 'that the modern way of looking at the whole question of observance involves a strong degree of selectivity',[19] and that his criterion that 'a ritual should be observed if its observance enhances the spiritual life of the Jew' is ultimately rather subjective.

Subjectivity is indeed the key to this book. Not that it is in any way lacking in sound scholarship, but rather that it constitutes a very personal, and very mature and honest, statement of 'where I stand'. Jacobs writes with a deep nostalgia, nostalgia for the naive Orthodoxy he identified with in his youth, nostalgia for the Jewish mysticism he encountered in his early enthusiasm for Habad. He wants to hold on to these things, he values Jewish unity which might be fractured if he were to depart from the Orthodox over matters such as *gitin* (divorces), yet he cannot give his intellectual consent to the traditional edifice that he still loves.

In subjective mood he mulls yet again over the 'Jacobs affair'—perhaps a little self-indulgently, seeing that he has already written about it at length in his autobiography. If his chapters on Orthodoxy and Reform are occasionally impressionistic, they yield a precious insight into his own way of thinking and feeling, as does his surprisingly curt dismissal of Reconstructionist Judaism.[20]

Despite the essentially subjective approach there is hardly a page on which the reader is not illumined by the interpretation of some rabbinic passage or other. In chapter 10 ('Modernism and Interpretation'—there is no hint, by the way, of postmodernism) he tries 'to wed the theological approach to the historical critical one' by considering three significant Jewish themes, one of which is the enjoyment of life.[21] He carefully examines the oft-quoted statement in the name of Rav at the end of Jerusalem Talmud, *Kidushin* that 'A

---

[17] See above, Ch. 7.   [18] *Beyond Reasonable Doubt*, 51.   [19] Ibid. 118.
[20] Ibid. 175.   [21] Ibid. 214–25.

man will in future be called to account for everything his eyes saw and he did not eat', a statement used by Abba Hillel Silver among others to demonstrate Judaism's positive attitude to life. With learning and dexterity he places Rav's remark in its wider rabbinic context and demonstrates conclusively that it offers no basis for any kind of hedonism.

Jacobs sums up his work in the plain and honest words 'my dissent from fundamentalist Orthodoxy: that it is untrue to the facts'.[22]

Menachem Kellner: Rejection of the Dogmatic Approach

In the first six chapters of his book Kellner presents his understanding of what religious faith means in 'classical' Judaism. The title of the final, seventh chapter, 'How to Live with Other Jews', discloses his real agenda. He is troubled by the conflicts and divisions generated among Jews by the tendency of the ḥaredi religious leadership to define 'authentic' Judaism in credal terms.[23] As a specialist in medieval Jewish philosophy Kellner thinks he can lay much of the blame for the present discord on the shoulders of no less a figure than Maimonides, or at least on the way Maimonides is often interpreted.

In his *Dogma in Medieval Jewish Thought: From Maimonides to Abravanel*, as well as in several smaller studies, Kellner has pressed the view that the Maimonidean enterprise of defining Jewish belief was misguided, uncharacteristic of Jewish teaching as articulated in classical sources such as the Talmud. There is of course nothing novel about his view of Judaism as oriented around *praxis* rather than *pistis*, practice rather than belief; the problem is how to handle the numerous statements in the classical sources that imply and sometimes explicitly demand belief in some proposition or other. Notable among these is the Mishnah: 'All Israel have a portion in the World to Come . . . But these have no portion in the World to Come: one who denies that life after death is in the Torah, or says the Torah is not from heaven, or an Epicurean.'[24] Kellner distinguishes between vague and defined belief:

Judaism teaches that God exists and is one; it further teaches that God provides for all creatures. The Written Torah and the Talmud make no sense if we fail to affirm these teachings; they are absolutely central to the Jewish conception of the universe. That does not mean, as we have seen, that the tradition found it important to reach a normative, obligatory opinion concerning the actual, specific content of these

---

[22] *Beyond Reasonable Doubt*, 238.

[23] See the sections above on S. R. Hirsch and J. H. Hertz for comments on Judaism and dogma.   [24] Mishnah *San.* 10: 1.

teachings; it certainly made no effort to reach agreement on their implications and consequences.[25]

It would seem to follow from this that a Jew ought to go around ardently proclaiming God's existence, unity, and providence, but need entertain no clear notion as to what this means. Presumably the same applies to belief in revelation. No doubt the majority of 'ordinary' believers are every bit as hazy in their beliefs as Kellner would have them be. They are equally hazy about how their motorcars, their own bodies, or the laws of gravitation work, but bumble along reasonably well in normal circumstances. There are, however, other people around who make it their business to understand motorcars, medicine, and physics, and the rest of us depend on their expertise. It seems perfectly clear to me that at least from the time Jews first made contact with Greek culture, and far more so today when they are exposed to a more complex and mature intellectual culture, those who are capable of so doing need to formulate their convictions in a coherent manner, as Maimonides attempted to do in his time.

Whether people ought to *fight* each other about their beliefs, or exclude each other from their faith communities, is quite another matter, and this is where Kellner is right to castigate the *haredim* for their insistence on doctrinal correctness: 'Labelling non-Orthodox Jews and interpretations of Judaism as heretical is too exclusive, while true pluralism is too inclusive.'[26] But it would surely be far more to the point to argue the *incorrectness* of *haredi* doctrinal assertions than to insist on the vagueness of traditional Jewish teaching. Is Kellner perhaps reluctant to do this because he fears exclusion from the Orthodox ranks? Or, more charitably, because he fears for the future of Jewish unity, 'not whether Jews will have Jewish grandchildren, but how many different sorts of mutually exclusive Judaisms those grandchildren will face'?

Kellner's own solution is a little paradoxical, considering his firm rejection of the 'essentialist' notion of the Jewish people. He writes, 'God made a covenant with the Jewish people . . . I want to urge that we start with that notion of the Jewish people as basic.'[27] Since he believes that Jews are a people, not through sharing some metaphysical essence, but because they have a common legal system, viz. the halakhah, it is the only too definable halakhah which, for him, constitutes the basis for Jewishness.

I do not find the argument that the Torah ought to be interpreted in the way that best ensures the social cohesion of all Jews, loosely defined, at all convincing; it may be the case that lies are better than truth at ensuring social cohesion. But even if Kellner was right, and 'authentic' Judaism was to be

[25] Kellner, *Must A Jew Believe Anything?*, 22–3.   [26] Ibid. 110.   [27] Ibid. 111.

defined in national and halakhic rather than doctrinal terms, would this diminish controversy? Not very much, in all likelihood. The Modern Orthodox, including Kellner himself, might be happier, since in principle they regard themselves as bound by a divinely revealed halakhah, even though they interpret it in a more liberal fashion than the ḥaredim. But so far as other Jews are concerned, the imposition of halakhah as a criterion of their Jewishness is no less divisive than the imposition of credal criteria.

Few readers will be swayed by the thesis of this work, but many will be entertained and all will learn from the erudite yet accessible discussions of medieval Jewish thought. I particularly enjoyed the splendid discussion in chapter 1 of the 'God of Abraham versus God of Aristotle' debate which, contrary to the common assumption that it was sparked off by Blaise Pascal, was alive and well centuries earlier.

Tamar Ross: Cumulative Revelation

In Chapter 17 we reviewed the concept of progressive revelation as elaborated by Krochmal, Formstecher, Samuel Hirsch, and Hermann Cohen; most exponents of Reform Judaism have retained some notion of progressive revelation, even if they no longer express it as a naive Enlightenment belief in the inevitability of human progress.

Continuous revelation is not, however, the exclusive preserve of Reformers. J. D. Soloveitchik, we saw in Chapter 18, held that the content of Torah is gradually revealed through the creative activity of the 'legitimate guardians' of Oral Torah.

Though Ross rejects Soloveitchik's 'formalism', or 'positivism',[28] she adopts a position that might well be described as 'cognition evolves through history'. She calls her concept 'cumulative revelation', and claims it is a sort of 'theological restorativism'. The concept rests on three assumptions:

1. 'Revelation is a cumulative process: a dynamic unfolding of the original Torah transmitted at Sinai.'

2. God's voice is heard through the rabbinical exposition of texts.

3. 'Although successive hearings of God's Torah sometimes *appear* to contradict His original message, that message is never replaced.'[29]

These assumptions are not far distant from the exposition by many traditional authorities of the development of Oral Torah, and Ross aptly refers

---

[28] T. Ross, *Expanding the Palace of Torah*, ch. 5, pp. 71–99.   [29] Ibid. 197–8.

to Shalom Rosenberg's account of three ways in which they have understood how the Written Torah's meaning is gradually revealed: Torah as wellspring, acceptance by the nation, and halakhic process.[30] She cites the tradition of rabbinic commentary, stressing its innovative character.

What 'cumulative revelation' adds to this, she says, 'is merely the conviction that if these free-flung interpretations of the Torah have evolved in a certain way, there is likely something of significance to be derived from this particular evolvement'.[31]

Now, the authorities Ross cites would all have drawn fairly tight boundaries on halakhic innovation, and it would have been helpful had Ross been clearer on where she thinks the boundaries should be drawn. She accords revelatory status to feminism: 'A cumulativist view of revelation permits us to entertain the thought that some feminist understandings reflect more refined sensibilities that ought to accrue to the original religious model and even alter its meaning.'[32] But in practical terms what does this imply? Very little, it seems, in the here and now, though it opens up the *possibility* that more radical developments could occur, and that if they do, and are accepted within the community (which community?), they will be received as authentic Torah.

I was reminded of a Catholic cardinal who was asked, in my hearing, whether the Church would ever ordain women. He replied, 'I don't know; it seems unlikely at present. But if it ever does happen, the encyclical in which it is proclaimed will commence with the words, "As the Church has always taught . . . ".' And Ross actually writes, 'If feminist morality is more than a passing fad, it is likely that the interpretive tradition will discover that some of the values expressed by the feminists are indeed those of the Torah and should be pursued accordingly.'[33]

Then what is the difference between 'cumulative revelation' and 'progressive revelation' of the Reform kind, that permits wholesale revision of traditional norms in the light of new moral insights such as those of feminism, and permits it now? Ross, who feels herself greatly indebted to Abraham Isaac Kook (1865–1935), cites his correspondence with a student on the topic of slavery. When Kook suggested that the Torah's laws on slavery were an educational device to wean people away from the institution altogether, the student pointed out that this argument was akin to the Reformist position on progressive revelation. Kook insisted that there was an essential distinction between his concept and the arbitrary revisions of the Reformers. As Ross summarizes it:

[30] Rosenberg, 'Continuous Revelation: Three Directions' (Heb.).
[31] T. Ross, *Expanding the Palace of Torah*, 199. [32] Ibid. 210. [33] Ibid. 222.

By positing a supernal Torah and successive unfolding of that Torah as progressive revelations of a pre-existent ideal, R. Kook concludes that if certain unprecedented ideas or norms become absorbed within tradition, it is a fair indication of the workings of divine providence. Such providence is attuned . . . to our gradually maturing spiritual sensibilities.[34]

Now Formstecher and other early Reformers did not consider their revisions arbitrary, nor do Reform and Conservative Jews who today argue for gender equality accept that their revisions are arbitrary. From an intellectual point of view it is very difficult to draw a distinction between what is arbitrary and what is 'within the tradition'; the early Reformers, for instance, considered themselves very much within the Jewish tradition, though they defined that tradition as the prophetic tradition of Israel. Kook, and Ross in his wake, identify tradition as the Oral Torah developed by the rabbis; but if that is how 'tradition' is to be understood, the boundary question must be firmly addressed, since so much of what modern moral sensibilities demand runs directly counter to what the rabbis actually said.

It seems that for Ross the boundary is determined by what becomes accepted by the community and its halakhic authorities. This is a social rather than an intellectual process, and makes theological sense only on the assumption that the community of the faithful is guided by *ruah hakodesh*, the holy spirit. This idea has strong Jewish antecedents, and is akin to the Islamic doctrine of *ijma* (community consensus), or to Catholic teaching on guidance of the Church by the holy spirit. The problem is to identify which of many Jewish communities constitutes the 'community of the faithful'. It is easy to slip into circular arguments of the form: Which is the community of the faithful? It is the one that abides by the halakhic consensus. What is the halakhic consensus? It is the consensus arrived at by the community of the faithful.[35]

Finally, at the heart of 'cumulative revelation' lies a strong cultural relativism. We can talk of 'supernal Torah' just so long as we accept that in one society it is expressed in patriarchal terms and in another in feminist terms; in one society it is right to own slaves, in another it is the greatest sin to deprive another human being of his/her freedom. This may be correct; it is conceivable that there are 'eternal' values that transcend the particular ordering of society. But if it is true, it does suggest a quite radical revision of the system of *mitsvot* which Ross is not prepared to go along with. Surely it would be morally indefensible, in a society where individual freedom is

---

[34] T. Ross, *Expanding the Palace of Torah*, 205.
[35] In Ch. 25 I deal with 'authenticity' and with the survival potential of communities.

valued, to accept an interpretation of Torah that was 'right' in the slave-owning, male-dominated society of Bible and Talmud, while we wait indefinitely for some 'authority' to declare that after all that was not what Bible and Talmud really meant, and the law should be changed accordingly; yet this seems to be the situation we are in if we accept conventional rabbinic halakhah on a provisional basis, pending resolution by the community and its halakhic authorities of the latest cumulative revelation.

Strengths of the Four Approaches

None of the works reviewed gives an entirely satisfactory defence of Jewish belief as expressed in traditional sources. Their distinguished authors have nevertheless brought to light the history and development of Jewish belief and lent new impetus to the venture of reformulating traditional Judaism. Halivni has highlighted several rabbinic texts which might be taken as indicators of the possibility of a more flexible approach to the concept of 'sacred revealed text'; Jacobs has made clear what it is about the Orthodox vision that is of lasting value; Kellner has shown the relevance of the medieval debates; Ross has indicated lines along which Torah may 'accumulate' in response to new, divinely guided, insights. All this is a far cry from the contemporary *ḥaredi* hostility to modernity, and arguably closer to the reality of Jewish tradition.

Theologians safeguard the continuity of the faith community by enabling the faithful to use traditional forms of expression whilst at the same time subtly modifying their meaning in the light of changing social and intellectual perspectives. Some may regard this as progress, others as subversion. Whatever it is, all four authors have contributed to its achievement. In particular, we can carry forward the following ideas:

- From Halivni we take the stress on the concept of an imperfect text which is nevertheless sacrosanct.

- From Jacobs we learn the value of a rational presentation of Torah.

- From Kellner we discover that Torah need not be represented as a body of hard doctrine.

- From Ross we acquire the notion of a 'cumulative revelation' dependent on the consensus of the community and its halakhic authorities.

TWENTY-ONE

DIVIDED BY A COMMON SCRIPTURE

JEWS TODAY are commonly divided into religious and secular, and the religious are divided into three denominations, Orthodox, Conservative, and Reform. This glosses over smaller movements such as Reconstructionism, English Liberal Judaism, and the Association for Traditional Judaism, downgrades the major divisions within Orthodoxy to the status of mere trends, ignores the division into Ashkenazi, Sephardi, and Oriental, and pretends that you cannot be both religious and secular, or simply eclectic. My own camp, the Sceptical Orthodox, is not recognized at all, though I believe it is the most numerous.

Scripture might be expected to unite the Jewish denominations, but in fact it divides them.[1] The first Bible translation of the Jewish Publication Society (of America) was a joint project of Orthodox, Conservative, and Reform Jews. The revised translation ought likewise to have been a common project, and the committee set up in 1966 to prepare the section on *The Writings* (Ketuvim) worked 'in association with Rabbis Saul Leeman, Martin S. Rozenberg, and David Shapiro of the Conservative, Reform, and Orthodox movements',[2] but the excellent translation they produced has not been adopted by the Orthodox. This was an early symptom of the breakdown in cross-denominational consensus on Torah reading.

Orthodox, Conservative, and Reform Jews all read Torah publicly from a traditional parchment scroll, and there is no significant difference between the scrolls used by all three or in the Hebrew text of the books that congregants hold in their hands.[3] Differences lie in the translations, but even more in

---

[1] This is nothing new. Jews and Christians might be said to be 'divided by a common scripture', and Jewish sects in the Second Temple period were similarly divided by their selection and interpretation of holy texts; see Blenkinsopp, 'Interpretation and the Tendency to Sectarianism'.

[2] Preface to the first edition (1985), cited in *JPS Hebrew–English Tanakh*, p. xxiii.

[3] The Hebrew text in the Conservative *Etz Hayim* is based on the Leningrad Manuscript B19A (L) as presented in the Stuttgart *Biblia Hebraica*, but with four adjustments to the musical signs, and hence differs in a number of minor details from the common printed versions. See *Etz Hayim*, p. xviii.

the commentaries; each of the three denominations has fostered its own way of reading Torah, reinforced by an institutional, or quasi-institutional, version for synagogue use, just as each has developed its own liturgy complete with a full range of prayer books for all occasions. That is, all three groups read the same Torah, but they read it differently. Likewise, in principle they share the same rabbinic tradition, though their attitudes towards it differ greatly.

English-speaking Jews of all denominations used to favour the *Commentary on the Pentateuch and Haftorahs* of J. H. Hertz, discussed in Chapters 1 and 16 above. Other commentaries, such as A. Cohen's *Soncino Chumash*, consisting of a digest of the main 'classical' commentaries,[4] have enjoyed local popularity, but none has been as widely embraced and influential as the Hertz. In recent years Hertz's *Commentary* has lost ground, not just because some of its social attitudes (on race and imperialism, for instance) and much of the information it contains are out of date—after all, much the same could be said of Rashi himself—but because it no longer resonates with the self-understanding of the denominations. Reform and Conservative find Hertz too dismissive of historical criticism, while the more fundamentalist among the Orthodox regard him as heterodox.

The Hertz and Cohen commentaries were British productions; the works that have displaced them all originated in the USA. Reform pioneered the trend towards the new, single-volume, denominationally orientated commentaries. *The Torah: A Modern Commentary* appeared in 1981, and was supplemented in 1996 by *The Haftarah Commentary*, both published under the auspices of the umbrella Reform organization, the Union of American Hebrew Congregations.[5]

Hertz has been displaced in many Orthodox congregations by the 'Stone Chumash' compiled by Nosson Sherman, but financed by Irving I. Stone, from whom the popular name derives. The full title of this work is *The Torah: Haftaros and Five Megillos with a Commentary Anthologized from the Rabbinic Writings*. It is incorporated in the ArtScroll series, a library of fundamentalist publications by the Brooklyn, New York, company Mesorah Publications, which published commentaries on individual biblical books before the single-volume work.[6] The Stone Chumash was first published in 1993 and by

---

[4] A. Cohen (ed.), *The Soncino Chumash*.

[5] Plaut, *The Torah: A Modern Commentary*; Plaut and Stern, *The Haftarah Commentary*. Stolow, *Orthodox by Design*, has analysed the use by the ArtScroll publishers of design as a tool for mediating *haredi* religious authority. See also Finkelman, *Strictly Kosher Reading*.

[6] The series commenced publication in 1976. For an early critique, written 'from the perspective of the history of Jewish interpretation of the Bible', see Levy, 'Our Torah, Your Torah, and Their Torah'. In Levy's view (pp. 167–9), the series is a polemic directed against

1998 (the date of my own copy) had achieved its ninth edition, no small indication of the rapidity with which it penetrated the English-speaking Orthodox world. Modified editions have been produced with the imprimatur of organizations such as the Rabbinical Council of America; the Orthodox cannot share a single edition even among themselves.

Conservatives persisted for a long time with Hertz, but in recent years have developed their own distinctive commentary. This first saw light as a series of Torah commentaries on individual books by Nahum M. Sarna, Baruch A. Levine, Jacob Milgrom, and Jeffrey H. Tigay. In 2001 the Rabbinical Council of the United Synagogue of Conservative Judaism, through the Jewish Publication Society, produced a one-volume edition under the general editorship of David L. Lieber, with Jules Harlow as literary editor; it is called *Etz Hayim: Torah and Commentary*, and seems set to become the Conservative standard.

These are the three to be considered, though others have appeared. The Habad hasidim, for instance, commenced publication in 2003 of their own distinctive Torah, the 'Gutnick Edition', incorporating a commentary, *Toras Menachem*, based on the late Lubavitcher Rebbe's 'Rashi Sichos' (spoken discourses on Rashi's commentary) and writings.[7] Although this is clearly a response to the popularity of ArtScroll, and intended to illuminate the distinctiveness of Lubavitch teaching, it follows a trend established in the nineteenth century by such publications as *Mei hashilo'aḥ* of the 'Izbicer' (Mordechai Joseph Leiner, 1801–54) and *Sefat emet* of the 'Gerer Rebbe' (Judah Aryeh Leib Alter, 1847–1905), in which the teachings of hasidic rebbes were preserved for their hasidim in the form of discourses on the Torah.

I shall briefly review each of the three chosen commentaries, in order of their publication, to discover the distinctive way in which each denomination reads Torah—or rather, the way in which the leaders of the denominations encourage their followers to read Torah. To help draw a meaningful comparison I shall note how each addresses the Flood story (Gen. 6: 9–8: 22), the account of the birth of Jacob and Esau (Gen. 25: 19–34), and part of the 'Book of the Covenant' (Exod. 21: 1–37).

Hertz's *Pentateuch* and the Soncino Bible series edited by Abraham Cohen; his prediction (p. 160) 'Artscroll will not attain the popularity of Hertz as a companion to the weekly Torah reading' has been falsified by events.

[7] The edition, edited by Chaim Miller, was completed in 2008.

The Reform Torah

Since W. Gunther Plaut's *The Torah: A Modern Commentary* first appeared in 1981 several revisions have been produced. Plaut himself wrote the commentary on Genesis, Exodus, Numbers, and Deuteronomy; the commentary on Leviticus is that of his co-worker Bernard J. Bamberger. In his 'General Introduction to the Torah' Plaut distinguishes his approach from that of 'Orthodox Judaism, fundamentalist Christianity, and . . . most commentaries of the past'; the commentary, he says, 'proceeds from the assumption that the Torah is a book which had its origin in the hearts and minds of the Jewish people', contrary to the traditional notion that it is a work dictated in some form by God. But while 'God is not the author of the Torah in the fundamentalist sense, the Torah is a book about humanity's understanding of and experience with God'. Moreover:

The Torah is ancient Israel's distinctive record of its search for God. It attempts to record the meeting of the human and the Divine, the great moments of encounter. Therefore, the text is often touched by the ineffable Presence. The Torah tradition testifies to a people of extraordinary spiritual sensitivity. God is not the author of the text, the people are; but God's voice may be heard through theirs if we listen with open minds.[8]

However, this is not true of 'every verse and every story'. Judgement and learning must be exercised to distinguish that which is of permanent value from that which relates to a particular age, to distinguish legend from fact, and so that we should not 'gloss over those texts which represent God in anthropomorphic terms'. History alone is not sufficient; myth must be understood, and the way that the text has been received and read by Jews is as significant as its original meaning.

In sum, Plaut claims, the commentary poses three questions: 'What did the text mean originally?', 'What has it come to mean?', 'What can it mean to us today?'.[9]

Each book has a dedicated introduction, Bamberger's to Leviticus being especially noteworthy. William W. Hallo has contributed additional introductory essays to all five books, in which he aptly illustrates the value of ancient Near Eastern archaeology and documents for understanding the Bible in its literary and historical contexts, including philological detail such as the correct translation of the word *avrekh* (Gen. 41: 43), probably equivalent to the Akkadian *abarakku*, 'chief steward of a private or royal household'.[10]

---

[8] Plaut, *Torah: A Modern Commentary*, 4th edn., p. xix.   [9] Ibid., p. xxiv.

[10] Ibid. 10. As Hallo notes, the presence of an Assyrian title in the midst of the Joseph stories raises critical questions about its authorship.

The arrangement of the book is novel. Though the conventional *parashiyot* (weekly readings) and chapter and verse divisions are clearly indicated, the text has been divided into thematic units, of convenient length for liturgical use (not all Reform congregations read the full traditional *parashah* each week). Notes appear beneath the text to clarify its plain meaning. Each unit is followed by profounder reflections on the meaning and significance of the passage concerned, and occasionally by a tentative allocation of the text to 'original' sources. These are followed by 'Gleanings', a selection of related material from sources that range from ancient Near Eastern writings, through midrash and other rabbinic material, to modern Bible criticism, hasidic stories, and contemporary literature. Where appropriate there are focused sections, such as the summary of the Jewish dietary laws appended to Leviticus 11.

In his commentary on the Flood story Plaut distances himself from any sort of historical interpretation, emphasizing that it is 'a story with a moral. Its themes are sin, righteousness, and man's second opportunity to live in accordance with . . . the will of God'.[11] At the same time he gives full acknowledgement to the agreement between the Bible's story and other Near Eastern flood stories, extracts from which are in the 'Gleanings', bundled together with Qur'an 7: 37–62 and a paragraph each from Morris Adler, midrash, and Martin Buber—a truly eclectic mix. Following the text, and prior to the 'Gleanings', a thoughtful essay ponders how natural events can be understood as judgements of God. 'Most modern men' (presumably modern women too), it is alleged, reject the idea of an interventionist God, so they will find the relevance of the Noah story in its emphasis on God's moral judgement. Exactly how God exercises his moral judgement without intervening is not explained.

A section headed 'The Twins' places the birth of Jacob and Esau (Gen. 25: 19–34) in the context of the theme 'God watches over His chosen ones as they grow in understanding of the divine element in their lives.'[12] Rebecca 'went to inquire of the Lord' (Gen. 25: 22) means she consulted an oracle; a footnote cites, in quotation marks that presumably mean 'don't take this too seriously', a midrash that states she enquired at the teaching-house of Shem, the son of Noah. Other comments on the text note the resemblance of Esau to the shaggy Enkidu in the Gilgamesh epic, the occurrence of the name Yakub-El in ancient Syrian and Mesopotamian documents, and a comparison with the story of Parsifal. The essay that follows takes up the moral issue posed by Jacob's trickery in purchase of the birthright, and the 'Gleanings' range from

---

[11] Plaut, *Torah: A Modern Commentary*, 4th edn., p. 56.   [12] Ibid. 172.

Apocrypha through Rashi to a psychological interpretation by Henry E. Kagan, who opines that Rebecca preferred Jacob because she 'could not dominate the freer Esau as she dominated her husband and the younger twin'.

Exodus 20: 19(22)–21: 36, headed 'Law on Worship, Serfdom, Injuries', is placed, in line with historical-critical scholarship, in the context of the 'Covenant Code',[13] and there is much speculation as to its relationship with other law codes of the ancient Near East;[14] the textual notes draw attention to specific connections, a note on Exodus 21: 26, for instance, noting the long history of the concept of negligence in ancient Near Eastern law. The essay discusses the biblical treatment of slavery and its rabbinic interpretation, offering an apologetic that draws attention to the amelioration of slavery in the Bible relative to the practice in other societies. An apologetic line is taken also with regard to 'an eye for an eye', the non-literal interpretation of which is supported not only by rabbinic interpretation but by reference to the Near Eastern law codes; the argument shows a fine understanding of the origins of criminal law.

The commentary as a whole does not aim at consistency in detail; rather, the reader is provided with the informational tools to arrive at his/her own interpretation. Even so, the broadly liberal theology adopted by Plaut in his introduction shapes the programme. Historical criticism is accepted in principle; God figures as a non-interventionist Presence encountered as moral force, rather than as a commanding Person; a Jewish confessional reading, broadened with elements from modern 'universal' culture, is skilfully grafted on to the historical reading of the text.

The Orthodox Torah

Nosson Sherman (Scherman), in his introductory overview to *The Torah*, unreservedly endorses Maimonides' formulation of the principles that (*a*) the entire Torah now in our hands is letter for letter identical with that received by Moses and (*b*) no iota of it is subject to change. The Torah, he clarifies, 'was accompanied by an authoritative tradition that explained the meaning of obscure passages and provided the rules and methods of accurately interpreting the text'. Somewhat defensively, he rehearses several well-worn arguments to demonstrate the existence of this tradition, and concludes 'there is a companion to the Written Law, an Oral Law . . . without which the Written Torah can be twisted and misinterpreted beyond recognition, as indeed it has been by the ignorant down through the centuries'. Maimonides would have

---

[13] Ibid. 525.   [14] Ibid. 562 ff.

gone along with this—he did after all live in the twelfth century—but hardly with Sherman's deeply kabbalistic account of the Torah as 'Master Plan of Creation', and certainly not with the rather literal presentation of the statement that the Torah was originally written in black fire upon white.[15] In terms of the disagreement outlined in Chapter 6 between rationalists and kabbalists with regard to the nature of Torah, Sherman is firmly on the side of the kabbalists and does not so much as hint that there might be an alternative.

The Hebrew text is accompanied by an English translation that follows talmudic and midrashic exposition rather than academic biblical scholarship, or even the best medieval Jewish scholarship such as that of Abraham Ibn Ezra. Marginal notes supply headings for the contents. The Aramaic translation and Rashi's commentary are included for reference, but not translated.

One curious feature, common to the whole ArtScroll series, is the translation of the four-lettered name of God. Where most translations have 'Lord' or 'Eternal', ArtScroll uses 'Hashem' (the Name). Evidently the editors want something that sounds more personal than 'Lord' or 'Eternal', and something that can be perceived as distinctively, perhaps exclusively, Jewish. In context, the term conveys an impression of closeness and accessibility to Jews in particular—He is *our* God, powerful (since He commands, and one dare not pronounce the True Name), compassionate, and ready and able to intervene in human affairs. This understanding of God differs radically from the ethically upright, rather sanitized universal God of Conservative Judaism, and from the attenuated, non-interventionist God of Reform.

Modern philology is ignored, both in the translation and in the commentary. On the word *avrekh* (Gen. 41: 43), Rashi's comment that it is a compound of Hebrew *av* 'father' and Aramaic *rakh* 'king' is reproduced, with an equally implausible midrashic derivation; it is not noted that 'Aramaic *rakh*' is really Latin *rex*, nor is reference made to proposed Egyptian derivations or to the more likely Akkadian *abarakku* (see above).

The commentary itself makes no explicit reference to historical criticism, though there are often implicit rebuttals of the critical position.

Archaeological evidence is generally ignored. Often, the commentary flies in the face of well-known evidence. In a comment on the Tower of Babel, an event alleged to have taken place 1,996 years after Creation, or about 1760 BCE, it is stated that 'all the national families were concentrated in present-day Iraq'.[16] Really? The Chinese, too, and the Australian Aborigines?

ArtScroll's take on midrash is not entirely clear; is midrash sometimes to be understood as metaphor or symbol rather than as history, an approach for

[15] See above, p. 55.   [16] Sherman (ed.), *The Torah*, 48.

which there is ample precedent in traditional sources? ArtScroll seems reluctant to deny the literal truth of midrash, which it often presents without comment as historical fact. For instance, in connection with Rebecca's difficult pregnancy with Jacob and Esau (Gen. 25), we are told that Rebecca visited the Academy of Shem and Eber and was informed by Shem that 'the unborn infants represented two nations and two conflicting ideologies'. If we were left in doubt that this is to be taken literally, we read further that 'History has demonstrated this prophecy in practise. Two regimes, one espousing morality and justice and another standing for license and barbarity, cannot long coexist'. No illustrations or evidence are cited to support this contention, so one is left wondering what particular historical episode the editors had in mind. The story of the development of Jacob and Esau is amplified with midrashic detail emphasizing Jacob's conformity with Jewish teaching and Esau's evil ways, paving the way for the justification of Jacob's theft of the birthright. There is no hint of doubt as to the historical accuracy of the midrashim, which are even embellished with some dubious embryology demonstrating that Jacob was really the firstborn.[17]

Stories such as the Flood are read through the eyes of the rabbis; that is, the Flood is understood as an historical event, details of which are filled in by recourse to midrash. ArtScroll appears singularly untroubled by geological and palaeontological evidence. Perhaps they would like us to think it is all a plot by the *goyim* to discredit the Holy Torah, or else that God has planted fossils in the ground to test our faith. On the other hand, they may be more influenced than they care to admit by the 'creationist' notions of Evangelical Christians.

A similarly dismissive attitude to 'extraneous' sources of knowledge is evident in the commentary on the Code of Law in Exodus 21. There is some apologetic, as the commentators are evidently embarrassed by the Torah's acceptance of slavery, in particular by the right of a father to sell his daughter into slavery. The latter, we are told, is really for the daughter's benefit; it is a way of ensuring a good marriage for her. No one appears to have reflected what the daughter might think, whether she ought perhaps to be consulted, or whether there is something seriously wrong with a society in which the best way to secure your daughter's interests is to sell her into slavery.

ArtScroll solemnly declares: 'Western man differentiates between Church and State; the Torah knows no such distinction. To the contrary . . . holiness derives from halachically correct business dealings no less than from piety in matters of ritual.' But Torah most certainly *does* know a distinction between

[17] Ibid. 127.

church and state, as may be seen in its rigorous separation of the powers of king and priest; and if 'Western man' refers to Christians, they would certainly agree that holiness 'derives from . . . correct business dealings no less than from piety in details of ritual', and that 'Christian values' ought to influence state policy; it is not a viewpoint on which Judaism has a monopoly.

For the most part, however, ArtScroll on Exodus 21–23 engages in interpreting the text in line with the talmudic system of civil and criminal law, and this is something at which it excels. Contradictions between Exodus and Deuteronomy are deftly resolved in accordance with rabbinic tradition as expressed in the Talmud and halakhic midrashim, for instance by assigning some verses on slavery to the heathen slave and others to the Israelite slave; a comprehensive set of principles governing bailees is derived from the few instances in Exodus 22, and the laws of compensation for injury are drawn from the appropriate verses.

A rather disturbing aspect of the ArtScroll commentary series is its underlying world-view of Israel versus the Nations. This is often totally detached from reality, as in the introduction to the Esther commentary, where a graphic description is offered of the leaders of the nations in solemn conclave debating the correct interpretation and impending fulfilment of Jeremiah's prophecies. Nosson Sherman, in his 'Overview' of Esther, solemnly warns: 'Most of us have become indoctrinated with a non-Jewish, anti-Torah version of history.' The authentic history of the period (continues Sherman) tells us that 'For more than a generation, Jeremiah's prophecy haunted monarchs and their advisors . . . Belshazzar, grandson of and successor to the throne of Nebuchadnezzar, watched the days go by with trepidation.' More of the same follows, buttressed with demonstrably false historical 'information', such as that Nebuchadnezzar founded the 'then current Babylonian Empire . . . in the year 3318 (442 BCE)'.[18] This is rather surprising in view of the well-established date of Nebuchadnezzar II's death as 562/1 BCE, a full 120 years before the alleged (but erroneous) date of the foundation of the new Babylon, let alone of the fact that his father Nabopolassar commenced the rebuilding of Babylon, but it is an inevitable consequence of the paranoid ArtScroll view that any scholarship that does not derive from approved rabbinic sources is anti-Jewish and false.

The ArtScroll commentaries impart a mine of information not only from the classical midrash and mainstream medieval commentary but from more recent, often previously unrecorded, Orthodox commentary, not least that of twentieth-century *posekim* (halakhic authorities) and yeshiva worthies;

[18] Zlotowitz (ed.), *The Megillah*, pp. xx–xxiv.

Mendelssohn, Hertz, S. D. Luzzatto, and other Jewish commentators whom they regard as 'not kosher' are pointedly ignored. Information is there, but judgement is lacking. 'A little knowledge is a dangerous thing', but a lot of knowledge is even more dangerous if it is not allied to a capacity for judgement. The reader needs constantly to be on guard for tendentious selection and reading of the sources, and to resist the assumption that the traditional commentators shared some monolithic world-view, differing from one another only in detail; the full richness of tradition is obscured when the differences between rationalists and kabbalists, hasidim and mitnagedim, modernizers and traditionalists, are glossed over or obscured.

The Conservative Torah

Etz Hayim, a production overseen by the Rabbinical Assembly of the American United Synagogue, articulates the theology of Conservative Judaism. Conservative Judaism was conceived when Zacharias Frankel withdrew from the 1845 Frankfurt Conference of Reform Jews, and in 1854 founded the Jewish Theological Seminary in Breslau (Wrocław) to promote what was for long known as 'positive-historical Judaism'; it consolidated as a distinct movement only in the United States, in reaction to the radical 1885 Pittsburgh Platform of Reform. Conservative Jews affirmed Jewish emancipation, Western acculturation, and the separation of church and state; they endorsed such changes in religious life and ritual as they felt consistent with 'historical' interpretation of the sources; they were ready to accept the findings of historical criticism with regard to the composition of biblical and other source documents, and they accorded a central position to halakhah.

Etz Hayim comprises the Hebrew text based on the Biblia Hebraica Stuttgartensia, the most recent English translation of the Jewish Publication Society, a *peshat* (literal) commentary compiled by Chaim Potok, a *derash* (homiletic) commentary edited by Harold Kushner, and a halakhah commentary by Elliot Dorff and Susan Grossman; the commentary on the *haftarot* is the work of the eminent Bible scholar Michael Fishbane.

How does it compare with the Reform and Orthodox Torahs that preceded it? David Lieber opens his introduction to the volume in grandiloquent style:

The Torah is the foundational sacred text of Judaism; the study of its words and their meanings is at the core of Jewish religious experience ... Jews view the Torah as the teaching par excellence about God's relationship to the world and to the Jewish people, about God's covenant with the people Israel, and about the laws by which they are to live that they might be a 'holy people'.[19]

[19] *Etz Hayim*, p. xvii.

To this all of us, Reform and Orthodox too, will respond Amen! That is, until we read the subtext. 'At the core of Jewish religious experience' distances the work from the archetypal Orthodox; it means 'We are not fundamentalists. We will treat the text as indicating the profound experience of the Jewish people, not as a piece of divine dictation.' 'About the laws by which they are to live' establishes the boundary between Conservative and archetypal Reform; it means 'To us halakhah is sacred. We may interpret and modify it on the basis of historical contextualization, but it remains a quintessential and binding expression of Judaism.'

The functions of the three commentaries are spelled out consistently with this ideology. The *peshat* commentary is reverential rather than apologetic; it does not seek to rationalize institutions like slavery or to justify the extermination of the Canaanites; such passages must be 'reinterpreted by later generations in light of the principles of equity, justice, and compassion that are central to the Torah', a sentence that perhaps differentiates the Conservative approach from that of the Reformers, who would openly state that God does not speak through such verses. Archaeology, philology, and anthropology contribute to our understanding of the text.[20]

The *derash* commentary 'contains selected insights from more than 2000 years of Torah study'.[21] The emphasis here must be on 'selected', for 'in keeping with our commitment to Conservative Judaism, we have sought to learn from the Torah rather than to judge it'. But evidently we *do* pass judgement, for the commentary expresses disquiet about the treatment of non-Israelites and about the legal and social standing of women in ancient Israel; if, as Lieber claims, such disquiet arises from 'a conscience informed by Torah values', then surely we are selecting *which* Torah values should prevail. Fundamentalists, after all, regard the vilification of Amalekites and the secondary status of women as Torah values; if we are to privilege other Torah values over these, or even to reject them in the name of other Torah values, we are exercising judgement.

The *halakhah lema'aseh* (law in practice) commentary is 'not a code of Jewish law. Rather, it describes Jewish practice and demonstrates the role of Jewish practice in our quest for God.'[22] It is very difficult to understand how a comprehensive assemblage of normative statements differs from a code of law, other than in the trivial sense that it is not systematically arranged. If, on the other hand, the statements are merely descriptive, not normative, one wonders what is left of the binding quality which surely defines the nature of halakhah. This indecision reflects the problematic of Conservative Judaism's

---

[20] *Etz Hayim*, p. xix.   [21] Ibid., p. xx.   [22] Ibid.

attempt to define itself between Orthodoxy and Reform, and underlies Elliot Dorff's valiant if inconclusive attempt to establish what constitutes 'modern', i.e. Conservative halakhah: 'Although the Conservative Movement has not officially adopted many standards, many commonalities exist in how Conservative congregations observe Jewish law, most of which have grown out of the shared customs and perceptions of the movement.'[23] One wonders whether the 'shared customs and perceptions' stem from traditional halakhah, or rather from the bourgeois, politically correct professional circles with which American Conservative Jews for the most part identify.

The final section of the volume comprises a series of specialist essays, many of superb quality, on topics under the four heads 'Biblical Life and Perspectives', 'Biblical Religion and Law', 'Worship, Ritual and Halakhah' (this includes Dorff's essay), and 'Text and Context'. The whole is rounded off with useful maps, diagrams, tables, and an index, together with a list of the musical signs incorporated in the Torah text but no musical notation.

How do the objectives of the commentaries work out in connection with our selected topoi?

Introducing the Flood story, the *peshat* commentary promises to show how the Bible's story differs from other ancient Near Eastern flood stories. An instance of this would be the comment on Genesis 6: 14, where it is pointed out that Noah is instructed to make a boxlike vessel, lacking any navigational device, whereas in the Mesopotamian story the hero builds a regular ship. The opportunity is missed to follow up this observation by explaining the theological significance of the fact that Noah, in his floating box, had to entrust himself entirely to God, whereas Utnapishtim, in a ship with crew and navigational aids, was outwitting one god on the advice of another who favoured him. On the phrase 'The Lord shut him in' (Gen. 7: 16), however, the commentary does note that in contrast to the Mesopotamian survivors who battened the hatches and saved themselves, Noah's salvation is due entirely to the will of God. Several words and phrases are clarified by recourse to linguistic parallels, even when this results in a translation in conflict with tradition; *kinim* (Gen. 6: 14), generally understood as 'compartments', is interpreted on the basis of the Akkadian as 'reeds'. No comment is made on the historicity of the Flood; from Robert Wexler's essay on ancient Near Eastern mythology at the end of the book it would appear that we are to read it as a religious recasting of a myth that draws on the same literary tradition as the Epic of Gilgamesh.[24]

There is no *halakhah lema'aseh* commentary on the story. The *derash*

---

[23] Ibid. 1479.   [24] Ibid. 1344.

commentary moralizes on corruption, free will, and the ambivalence of Noah's character. Typical comments include: 'Noah had to decide what kind of person he really was' (on Gen. 6: 9); 'A corrupt, lawless society brings destruction on all of its citizens, innocent and guilty alike, and on the environment around it' (on Gen. 6: 17). Rather more imaginative is Aviva Zornberg's comment, cited on Genesis 8: 15, that Noah was 'eager to leave the ark and be relieved of the responsibility for so many people and animals'; but how does she know?

The *peshat* commentary on the birth of Jacob and Esau clearly articulates the plain meaning of the story within its ancient Near Eastern context. Rebekah's 'fetal movements are spasmodic and she has fears of miscarrying'; 'one would go [for divine guidance] to a specific sanctuary or to some charismatic personage of recognized authority' (the 'Academy of Shem and Eber' is not mentioned); 'In the ancient Near East, an heir could barter away his inheritance.' Philological details are clarified on the basis of recent scholarship; many readers will be surprised to learn that the Hebrew name *ya'akov* stems from a Semitic verb meaning 'to protect', so that 'the name Jacob is a plea for divine protection of the newly born'; the Bible's own derivation (Gen. 25: 26) is dismissed as 'folk etymology'.

The *derash* psychologizes and moralizes. 'Jacob represents the gentle, cerebral side of a person, reaching goals by persuasion or cleverness. Esau represents the active, physical side. When the Torah describes them as struggling within Rebekah's womb and continues to portray them as rivals growing up it may be telling us that these two sides of many people are struggling within each individual for dominance.' Maybe. Or maybe not.

Halakhah lema'aseh comments: 'The tragedy of infertility need not be borne alone. The Conservative Movement has created a ritual for coping with infertility . . . '. No reason is given for labelling infertility a 'tragedy' or for generating further anxiety by so labelling it. Nor is guidance offered, as surely would be done by an Orthodox halakhah commentary, as to what kinds of fertility treatment might be consistent with halakhic principles.

The 'Book of the Covenant' is analysed in the *peshat* commentary into four parts, the second of which (Exod. 22: 17–23: 19) places special emphasis on humanitarian considerations. Its superficial resemblance to 'other Near Eastern collections' is noted. Following Moshe Greenberg, the claim is made that its combination of civil, moral, and religious laws in one code is unique in the ancient Near East. Moreover, it is embedded in the Exodus narratives, and these are crucial to its meaning and significance. *Lex talionis* ('an eye for an eye') is explained, in accordance with biblical context as well as rabbinic teaching, to mean compensation. Hammurabi's categorization of assault and battery as criminal conduct to be prosecuted by the state is acknowledged as revolutionary; the Torah's innovations were the insistence on justice for all citizens regardless of social class and the outlawing of vicarious punishment. The *derash* commentary develops these themes, stressing the need for appropriate laws to ensure the ideal of a just society, and showing that if the Torah did not abolish slavery, it pointed the way to abolition by enacting laws that recognized the humanity of the slave.

One might have expected a great deal of *halakhah lema'aseh* on these chapters, since a large part of the Talmud is devoted to expounding them. However, the commentary limits itself to those matters considered of practical importance to Conservative Jews. 'Both husband and wife have the right to sexual satisfaction within marriage' is the first item; the extent of the right remains undefined, notwithstanding the comprehensive rabbinic literature on this. In the commentary on Exodus 21: 19 the five types of compensation for injury are listed, though no Conservative *beit din* handles such matters (nor do the Orthodox nowadays). Exodus 21: 22 elicits an important statement on abortion, and a less important one on mourning for a foetus; 21: 29 is the rabbinic source for laws on negligence; 22: 1 is interpreted to justify self-defence and the principle that saving life takes precedence over 'most other Jewish laws', the exceptions being elaborated in the commentaries on Leviticus 18: 5.

What concept of Torah does all this reflect? Elliott Dorff, in an essay on 'Medieval and Modern Theories of Revelation', outlines three concepts of revelation held by Conservative thinkers:[25]

- Joel Roth conceives of revelation as God communicating in actual words, and Jewish law as binding since it is the word of God, though he accepts the findings of historical criticism of the biblical text.

- Ben Zion Bokser and Robert Gordis held that God inspired certain individuals who then formulated their inspiration in human language; Jewish law remains binding for them since its original authors were inspired by God.

- Others, following Rosenzweig and Heschel, think of revelation as the human response to ineffable individual encounters with God. Dorff places David Lieber and himself in the 'rationalist' section of this camp: 'Rationalists affirm the importance of our personal encounters with God, but they also call attention to what we can learn about God from nature, history and human experience as a whole.'

[25] *Etz Hayim*, 1404.

Common to all three Conservative approaches is, first, that the authority of revelation derives from a combination of human and divine factors and, second, that revelation is an ongoing process.

Go Compare Denominations

The characteristics of the three commentaries are compared and contrasted in the table on page 287.

The ArtScroll commentary suppresses information from non-Jewish sources or from non-approved Jewish sources such as Hertz; presumed Jewish origin, traceable to Sinai, has become the criterion of truth. No clear or consistent attempt is made to distinguish between homiletic and historical statements; the distinction between *peshat* and *derash* tends to be glossed over, perhaps because the authors adopt the view expounded by Mecklenburg and Malbim that the *derash*, the exegesis of the sages, *is* the *peshat*, the plain and straightforward meaning of the scriptural text,[26] though it is unlikely that either Mecklenburg or Malbim intended this to apply to aggadah. Overall, however, what the commentary does is to consolidate and articulate the achievements of the Orthodox commentators of the eighteenth century onwards whose work we sketched in Part III. Likewise, the Conservative and Reform commentaries consolidate and articulate the positions of their respective communities.

Despite its modern-looking appearance the ArtScroll commentary, like much Evangelical Christian fundamentalist writing, constitutes a frontal attack on the underlying principles of modernity, and, in particular, of historical scholarship. The theology it articulates only superficially resembles that of the Middle Ages. Maimonides' principles on the integrity of the received biblical text and interpretative tradition were by no means implausible at the time they were formulated; to reiterate them nowadays, far from being reasonable, is an act of desperation that flies in the face of a large body of hard evidence. It is almost as though someone were to maintain that the earth is flat—surely a reasonable position to take before the demonstration in ancient Greece that it was spherical, but absurd now that people routinely fly around it in all directions.

Whether ArtScroll articulates the *actual* theology of Orthodox Jews is a moot point. In private conversation many educated Jews in Orthodox communities concede its absurdity. The *ḥaredi* leadership, however, though ready to adopt modern technology in communications and medicine, resists

---

[26] See above, Ch. 14.

Torah: Orthodox, Conservative, Reform

Orthodox	Conservative	Reform
Fideistic theology—belief in Torah and the rabbinic tradition —is the premise on which all else is based, and is the criterion of truth.	Tradition, generated by an encounter with God, is interpreted in the light of evidence and reason.	Tradition is interpreted in the light of evidence and the reason.
God is powerful, compassionate towards Israel, constantly present, and ready to intervene.	God is ethically demanding; halakhah is an expression of His will.	God is a non-interventionist Presence encountered as moral force, rather than a Commanding Person.
The Jewish people, since the Torah is entrusted to them, represent the purpose of Creation.	Jews have a universal mission.	Jews have a universal mission.
Torah laws, as the word of God, are eternally binding on Jews.	Accords a central position to halakhah, though this must be interpreted making due allowance for differences between the circumstances and world-view of the period in which it was originally formulated, and the present.	Rabbinic halakhah may be instructive, but is not binding.
Torah comprises Written Text, oral tradition of interpretation, and kabbalistic doctrines. Torah is the 'blue-print' of the world.	Bible (and a fortiori Oral Torah) to be understood as indicating the profound experience of the Jewish people, not as a piece of divine dictation. Reinterpretation is needed in the light of historical changes.	The Torah is ancient Israel's distinctive record of its search for God, a record of the encounter of human and Divine, not a piece of divine dictation. Judgement and learning must be exercised to distinguish that which is of permanent value from that which relates to a particular age.
Ignores historical criticism including modern philology and archaeology.	The results of historical criticism must be accepted.	The results of historical criticism must be accepted.
No clear or consistent attempt is made to distinguish between homiletic and historical statements.	*Peshat* and *derash* are consistently distinguished.	Legend must be distinguished from fact. However, history alone is not sufficient; myth must be understood, and the way that the text has been received and read by Jews is as significant as its original meaning.

the application of historical criticism and scientific method to matters of tradition.

In the days when Hertz ruled, an Orthodox Jew did not feel that he was stepping beyond the bounds of his community if he took a more relaxed view of rabbinic tradition, or accepted the findings of historical research. Now, however, this is a less comfortable position to take; the lines are drawn, and members of the communities feel pressured into denominational stereotypes.

It is sad that Bible study cannot unite Jews rather than divide them. The Oxford University Press *Jewish Study Bible* (2004)[27] could well take the place of denominational commentary; it is erudite, impartial, and clearly relates Tanakh to the interests of the Jewish people as a whole. But this will not happen since, as ever, sects define themselves in relation to a scripture on which they make an exclusive claim.

Is there a way out of the impasse? Is *torah min hashamayim* too dangerous a concept, now that it has been hijacked by fundamentalists, to be taught to children or preached from the pulpit? That is the problem to be faced in Part V.

Summary of Part IV

◆

We have seen how Jewish thinkers in modern times have attempted to reformulate their faith consistently with advances in science and socio-political thought, and how some of these reinterpretations crystallized in the form of biblical commentary.

Moses Mendelssohn recast Torah as 'revealed legislation', bypassing doctrinal problems but somewhat undermining his own arguments for the rigorous separation of church and state.

Salomon Ludwig Steinheim denied that revelation comprised formulations of ethics or law; the content of revelation was the four principles of the uniqueness of God, creation, freedom, and the immortality of the soul.

Samuel Holdheim, adopting the position that scripture was a human reflection of the divine, concluded that authority lay in reason and conscience, not in texts.

Several reformist thinkers (Krochmal, Formstecher, Samuel Hirsch, Hermann Cohen), stimulated by Enlightenment confidence in human progress, theologized this into the concept of progressive revelation.

[27] Berlin and Brettler (eds.), *The Jewish Study Bible*.

Martin Buber reduced the 'content' of revelation still further, to an 'encounter' between God and the individual, not captured in words; Franz Rosenzweig rescued halakhah, but not belief in divine dictation, by asserting that specific *mitsvot* hark back in the practice of the faithful to '*the* commandment', that is, the commandment of love which arises in the dialogue of God, Man, World.

Abraham Joshua Heschel understood religion as concern about 'ultimate' questions; 'involvement' in the experience under consideration was what mattered, not the historical investigation of texts.

For Emmanuel Levinas, to the contrary, texts *do* matter (though they are not 'revealed' in the traditional sense of being literally 'dictated' by God). Revelation is the transcendence of the ethical, demanding that each individual interpret his responsibility for the Other; yet it is specific, resulting in a constantly evolving 'commentary' of halakhah and aggadah.

On the traditionalist side, Soloveitchik's concept of Torah as essentially halakhah, and of halakhah as a priori, articulates his reaction to historical criticism and relativism; Torah is absolute, eternal, beyond history, bridging the gap between the world as perceived through science and the world as perceived by the mystic. We observed how his concept of Torah subordinated the historical to the metaphysical, sidestepping historical criticism.

I briefly reviewed Jewish feminist theology, and outlined a number of ways in which it has modified or challenged traditional understanding of Torah.

I examined the responses of four contemporary thinkers concerned to 'rescue' tradition. Halivni's notion of the 'maculate Torah' shifted the blame for the Torah's imperfections onto the sinful people; this left space for an 'original' perfect Torah, but was inherently implausible, and in any case undermined the traditional doctrine of reliable transmission. Jacobs' 'liberal supernaturalism' confirmed the notion of divine revelation but was vague as to what actually constituted this revelation, since he firmly rejected the doctrine of a divinely dictated text. Kellner sought to deflect the problem of right belief by focussing instead on the Jewish people and their covenant with God; Jews were a people because they had a common legal system, viz. the halakhah. Ross introduced the notion of a 'cumulative revelation' dependent on a consensus of the community and its halakhic authorities, making a fine (and to me unintelligible) distinction between this and the 'progressive revelation' of Reform.

We then saw how both the traditional and the new theologies have been articulated institutionally through English-language Bible commentaries favoured by each of the main denominations.

The conclusion seems inevitable that the only line of defence still available to those who want to uphold the rabbinic and medieval inter-pretations of *torah min hashamayim* is fideism, the acceptance of doctrines in pure faith.

This is no longer the fideism of Augustine, al-Ghazali, or Judah Halevi. *They* held that reason was inadequate either to establish or to refute religious truth, which could only be acquired through the 'mystery' of faith; they did not maintain that faith contradicted reason, but that it transcended and therefore *supplemented* reason. The modern fideist, to the contrary, assumes (even if openly denying it) that faith *contradicts* reason, that is, that it leads to beliefs that fly in the face of logic or of hard, empirical evidence. This is the fideism of the third-century Christian convert Lactantius (*c.*240–320) who, though well aware of Aristotle's three proofs for the sphericity of the earth, nevertheless maintained that it was flat; the wisdom of the ancients, he argued, was as nothing compared to the truth of God's word, and since Genesis states that the earth was flat, that is the end of the matter.[1] It is an absurd, dishonest faith.

But even if we can no longer uphold the rabbinic and medieval under-standing of *torah min hashamayim* as literal dictation by God, we may find an interpretation that is conformable with modern thought. That is what I shall attempt to do in Part V.

---

[1] Lactantius, *On the Divine Institutions*, book 3, ch. 24, pp. 426 ff.; Solomon, 'The Third Presence', 149.

PART V

◆

TORAH FROM HEAVEN

W̲E̲ ̲M̲U̲S̲T̲ now address the implications of the information and critiques assembled in the earlier parts. Five issues arise:

1. What options remain open for communities or individuals who want to follow traditional Judaism in some form? (Chapter 22)

2. Truth is preferable to falsehood, but what is truth? (Chapter 23)

3. What are the benefits and what the dangers of interpreting 'Torah from Heaven' as a myth of origin? (Chapter 24)

4. What is the future of the Jewish religion? (Chapter 25)

5. The futility of denial. (Chapter 26)

◆

TWENTY-TWO

OPTIONS

'Why people prefer quacks and charlatans to skilled physicians'

'Why some people leave a physician if he is intelligent'

Titles of tracts by the Persian philosopher and
physician AL-RAZI, c.854–923/932

THE CONVENTIONAL WAY of understanding *torah min hashamayim* generates acute moral, scientific, historical, and textual problems. Problems of this kind are not peculiar to Judaism, but affect all religions that base themselves on ancient texts they hold to be sacred and non-negotiable.

So why not simply abandon the whole idea, as many have done since the Enlightenment, and a few bold spirits even earlier? Why not abandon 'revealed truth' as a source of knowledge and guidance, and rely simply on a basic human sense of values ('humanism') and on scientifically verifiable sources of information? Do people simply 'prefer quacks and charlatans to skilled physicians'?

This is a question for you and me as individuals, and it is also a question for our leaders. As an individual I might ask 'Why should I commit myself to implausible beliefs and to inconvenient restrictions on my lifestyle?' Those who aspire to religious leadership should ask themselves, 'Why do we seek to impose implausible beliefs and inconvenient restrictions on people who turn to us for guidance?' Secular Jewish leaders may ask themselves, 'Should we continue to acquiesce in a situation in which most Jewish education, in school or religion classes, is conducted by rabbis and teachers who promote these beliefs and restrictions?'

Justifications

If *torah min hashamayim* could be demonstrated to be true in a *historical* sense, that is, if it could be demonstrated that it was a plain historical fact that God *literally* delivered to Moses the extant text of the Five Books plus the oral tradition as it has come down to us, this would constitute a justification both for the individual to believe and for educators to promote belief. God knows best.

Even if the *absolute* truth of *torah min hashamayim* could not be demonstrated, there might still be some justification for public policy to encourage people to *act* in accordance with traditional belief. Perhaps it could be shown that it conferred some benefit on the believer, or that it brought some advantage to the Jewish community or to society in general. Many psychologists claim that following a religion contributes to sounder health of body and mind for the individual and a more constructive attitude to society; encouraging belief at the communal level might be justified on the grounds that it made for sound mental health, a harmonious and co-operative society, and reduced criminality.

Torah min hashamayim would not have to be true in *all* respects to be worth holding on to, nor would it have to bring *only* advantages and not disadvantages. The justification would be that it possessed truth and/or personal or social benefit in sufficient measure to outweigh any misleading or disadvantageous aspects it might have.

Assessing whether *torah min hashamayim* is 'true' is complicated since both 'truth' and *torah min hashamayim* are open to a variety of interpretations, and have in fact been variously interpreted down the ages, so that the question of whether *torah min hashamayim* is true or false has to be met by 'it all depends on what you mean by . . . '.

Even if the conventional understanding of *torah min hashamayim* presents moral, scientific, historical, and textual problems, it may be possible and worthwhile to adopt some new interpretation, perhaps one of those described in earlier chapters, that will circumvent the problems.

In the next chapter I shall consider the tantalizing question, 'What is Truth?', and enquire whether people commit themselves to religious belief out of intellectual conviction or for quite different reasons. But first we must ask whether, irrespective of its truth or falsity, belief in *torah min hashamayim* offers any benefit to the community or the individual; even if it does, what is its 'cost', or potential downside?

The Community: Costs and Benefits of Belief

What are the possible benefits *to the Jewish community* of retaining an 'official' doctrine of *torah min hashamayim*, that is, of paying respect to a religious leadership that promotes the idea of *torah min hashamayim*, for instance by accepting their rulings on who is a Jew, or on who may marry whom, or by allowing them to educate our children? (Analogous questions might be put to the leaders of Christian, Muslim, and other religious communities and nations.)

Assume for this exercise that 'the Jewish community' is a homogeneous whole, though in reality it is divided along religious, political, and social lines.

The Jewish community collectively, or more precisely its de facto leadership, may convince itself that belief in the authority of scripture and tradition ensures the acceptance of important moral and ethical values. Rabbis, like their counterparts in other religions, often assert that religion is the basis of morality, hinting that without religion morality would break down. The conventional understanding of *torah min hashamayim* underpins this belief, so the leaders may come to believe that promoting belief in 'Torah from Heaven' will enhance the moral and ethical character of the community. They regard this as a desirable aim, whether disinterestedly or because they are jealous for the reputation of their community. (Of course, many individuals would question whether it is the business of community leaders to dictate moral and ethical values, or whether this constitutes unwarranted, authoritarian interference in private affairs. Moreover, many philosophers and sociologists robustly challenge the notion that morality depends on religious belief.)

Both Written and Oral Torah, according to rabbinic narrative, were revealed at Sinai to the whole people of Israel, born and yet to be born. The narrative binds Jews, through Torah, to the community, past and present and future, and fashions a powerful link ('covenant') between God and the people; it encourages social cohesion within the community, and confers transcendental value on that cohesion. A narrative of shared origin and destiny, especially one linked with God, enhances the sense of belonging together. This idea is powerfully expressed in *Midrash Rabbah* on Exodus 20: 1, introducing the Ten Commandments:

'And God spoke all these words, saying'. Rabbi Isaac said, Whatever prophets were to prophesy in generations to come, they received at Mount Sinai. For Moses said to Israel, 'Who is with us this day and who is not with us this day' (Deut. 29: 14)—He did not say, Who is *standing* with us this day, but [merely] Who is *with* us this day, [meaning] those souls yet to be created, that did not yet exist, of which it could not be said *they stood*. Even though they did not exist at that time, each one received its due . . . And not only did all the prophets receive their prophecy at Sinai, but even the Sages who were to arise in each generation each received his [wisdom] at Sinai. Likewise it is said, 'God spoke all these words to your whole congregation, in a loud voice that did not cease' (Deut. 5: 18): Rabbi Yohanan said, The one voice divided into seven, and they [in turn] separated into the seventy languages;[1] Resh Lakish said, This was the source from which all the prophets prophesied.

[1] It is assumed that there are seventy languages in the world, corresponding to the seventy ancestors who built the Tower of Babel (Gen. 10, 11: 1–9); the idea is that all the world's

Community leaders are generally of the opinion that the unity and cohesiveness of their community is a valuable asset, well worth preserving. Evidently, there are potential advantages from the point of view of the *religious* community, and the benefits devolve to the individual who wants to identify with that community. Whether a secular leadership would see things the same way is less certain; they might prefer another rallying point, such as Israel or the Holocaust, on which to focus Jewish identity, though neither of these is without its own problems.

Of course, what is beneficial to the community collectively may not be perceived as beneficial by the individual, so that under a government that guarantees freedom of religion the individual may decide that it is in his/her interest, or in accord with his/her conscience, to opt out of the community, or to remain on its margins.

Moreover, what is beneficial to a particular community—in this instance the Jewish community—may not be beneficial to society as a whole, and since the good of society as a whole affects the well-being of its parts, this would have to be taken into consideration in determining what is ultimately beneficial to the particular community.

There is a further cost. As I demonstrated in Chapter 21, the denominations differ in their understanding of *torah min hashamayim*; this introduces the possibility of interdenominational strife, which cannot be welcomed by community leaders. Nor should leaders welcome the possibility that religious extremism may cause strife with other faith communities.

Finally, there is the consideration that social utility alone is not adequate to justify religious belief. Unless belief can be justified in terms of its truth-claims as well as the moral qualities it endorses, the leaders who promote it are deceiving the public, telling what are at best 'noble lies' in order to control the ignorant masses. And the masses are not always ignorant, nor if they were would it be right for leaders to prey upon that ignorance.

The Individual: Costs and Benefits of Belief

In ages when the religious leadership held the reins of power, self-preservation depended on the stability and defence of the community whose protection you sought; if you stepped beyond the bounds of the community your life and that of your family were in danger. Not many people put the pursuit of 'truth

---

wisdom derives from Sinai. Though the midrash does not include proselytes among those who stood at Sinai, the Talmud (*Shab.* 146a) insists that their *mazal* (whatever this means—guardian angel?) was present.

wherever it might lead' before self-preservation and the well-being of their nearest and dearest; those who did often became martyrs.

In modern secular societies, where power is no longer in the hands of the religious leadership, there is still social pressure to conform to the ways and beliefs of the community into which you were born. Even without extraneous pressure, most people tend to conform to the norms of those around them; the instinct to conformity generally contributes to self-preservation, though sometimes it involves altruistic self-sacrifice in the interest of the group. But this is no longer sufficient reason to compromise significantly with the truth, if indeed it ever was. Nowadays, anyone who has some inkling of the difficulties faced by the conventional understanding of *torah min hashamayim* ought at least to examine the alternatives. What options does the individual have?

1. It would, in theory, be possible to substitute for the story of 'Torah from Heaven' an equivalent but more plausible story from another source, or to invent a new story about divine revelation. Anyone who attempted this, however, would have to decide whether he was (*i*) opting for another religion—problematic, since none of the major religions has a story of divine revelation that is less vulnerable to criticism than the Jewish one, or (*ii*) fabricating a new story. If he did fabricate a new story, his story might be perceived as a new interpretation of the traditional one, that is, as alternative (3) below. If it was seen as something radically different, it would undermine the sense of continuity needed for community identity, so he might well find that he was unwittingly starting a new religion or denomination. Something like this happened to Mordecai M. Kaplan (1881–1983), who retold the story of Sinai in non-supernatural terms; he intended to provide an inclusive 'umbrella' under which all Jewish denominations might shelter, but despite his best intentions set in motion a process that led to the formation of Reconstructionism as a separate denomination. Arguably, this is what happened to Jesus, who did not propose a new religion, Christianity, in opposition to his own, Judaism, but simply a new interpretation of Torah; within a generation or two his followers found they had become a new religious community at odds with the old one.

2. It is possible to abandon the notion of divine revelation altogether. Both deism and atheism follow this path. Deists acknowledge the existence of a supreme being, but not the authenticity of any specific communication; atheists deny both.

3. It is possible to retain the conventional story, abandoning only the hard version that entails divine dictation of a sacred text. This leaves the way open to reformulate or reinterpret along lines that will circumvent the objections raised.

If (1) is ruled out, the choice narrows between (2) and (3); that is, if you are not going to invent a new story, you must either abandon the old story or stick with it, reinterpreting if necessary. The choice does not hinge primarily on issues discussed in the present book. If you have already chosen a non-interventionist, 'deist' type of God, or if you are an atheist with no god at all, the problems generated by belief in a divinely revealed text do not concern you. Of course, some people are driven to deism, atheism, or simple agnosticism precisely because they reject the conventional account of divine revelation. All the more reason, then, that we should carefully examine option (3) to find out if, indeed, there is a way to reinterpret the conventional story in a manner free from the most serious objections.

My choice is option (3), so I shall stick with the old story and seek to reinterpret. That sets the agenda for the remaining chapters. Chapter 23 is about truth. What do we mean when we say that a particular doctrine, in our case Torah from Heaven, is 'true'? Once we know what *sort* of truth we are looking for in *torah min hashamayim*, we will have to ask, in Chapter 24, which of the many elements comprised in earlier accounts of *torah min hashamayim* are essential. If we abandon some of the historical and scientific claims, can we still retain enough of the original meaning to feel a sense of continuity with our forebears? If we reconstruct *torah min hashamayim* in the light of modern scientific knowledge and philosophical attitudes, can we still honestly claim that we stand in the tradition of the rabbis of the Talmud, of Maimonides, or of the Gaon of Vilna? Such matters carry implications for the future of Jewish society, and these will be spelled out in Chapter 25.

TWENTY THREE

WHAT IS TRUTH?

DEMOPHELES. Religion is no deception: it is true and is the most important of all truths. But because, as I have already said, its doctrines are of so lofty a kind that the multitude could not grasp them directly; because, I say, its light would blind the common eye; it appears veiled in allegory and teaches that which, while not strictly true in itself, is true in respect of the lofty meaning contained within it: and thus understood, religion is truth.

PHILALETHES. That would be fair enough—if it could only venture to present itself as true in a merely allegorical sense. But it comes forward claiming to be true in the strict and proper sense of the word: therein lies the deception, and here is the point at which the friend of truth must oppose it.

SCHOPENHAUER, 'On Religion: A Dialogue', 1851

IF IT IS CORRECT, as they say, that to the faithful no question is a question, while to the sceptic, no answer is an answer, then neither the faithful nor the sceptic exercises rational judgement. In that case, both positions deserve to be shunned. I shall adopt neither. My position is that plenty of questions *really are* questions. Some of the answers are answers, but others are not. Answers that are non-answers must be firmly rejected, however eminent or holy the person who has voiced them.

I take it as obvious that in most life situations truth is preferable to false-hood. There are proof-texts for this, too. Zechariah prophesied that Jerusalem would be called the City of Truth (Zech. 8: 3); Rabbi Hanina asserted that truth is God's signature;[1] at the New Year Jews pray: 'Purify our hearts to serve thee in truth; for thou, O God, art truth, and thy word is truth and endureth for ever.'[2]

Among Galileo's last recorded words was the observation, 'In questions of science, the authority of a thousand is not worth the humble reasoning of a single individual.' In religion, too, authority is not in itself an argument, though if authority derives from superior knowledge it may be a way to access

---

[1] BT *Shab.* 55a and parallels.   [2] *Service of the Synagogue for New Year*, 17.

truth. In general, we rely on authority for matters that we don't fully understand or lack time and motivation to study; life would be very difficult if we
could not rely on medical experts to prescribe medicines or on automotive
engineers to ensure that our cars worked. In practical matters, when we place
our trust in experts, we assume that, in principle, we could put what they tell
us to the test; but how does this work in religion?

The faithful assert that what God says is *absolutely* true. If God is the
authority, that would constitute an incontrovertible guarantee of truth, and we
need look no further; it would be futile as well as foolhardy to deny that what
God says is true.

But the problem is not whether or not what God said is true. The problem
is to know that it *was* indeed God who spoke, and to know just *what* he 'said'. *If
God said it* then surely it is true (granted there were no extraordinary circumstances such as those in 1 Kgs 22: 22–3, Jer. 4: 10 and 2 Chron. 18: 21–2), but
how can we be certain that he said it? Moreover, even if we could be sure that
God uttered certain words, how could we be sure we had understood them
correctly?

God does not routinely speak 'face to face' with ordinary followers of a
religion as he did with Moses (Exod. 33: 11), or with the Israelites at Mount
Horeb (Deut. 5: 4). He did not say to me personally, in so many words, 'do not
steal' (he may have *inspired* me not to steal, or, as a Quaker might express it, I
may be guided by an 'inner light' not to steal, but that is a different matter). If,
taking the position of an Orthodox Jew, I say, 'God told me not to steal', this is
shorthand for something like, 'The rabbi drew my attention to a statement in
the Book of Exodus claiming that God addressed the Ten Commandments to
the Israelites in the desert 3,000+ years ago, and one of the Ten was "do not
steal"; he claims, moreover, that his book is a correct transcript, by the prophet
Moses, of what God actually said to those people at that time, and that it is
binding on me as a result of that event.'[3]

All this leaves plenty of leeway for doubt, even if I accept the biblical
concept of God. This doesn't matter a great deal in the case of stealing,
because I believe stealing is wrong anyway (no theological underpinning
required); as regards theft, the ethical and the spiritual coincide. On the other
hand, it would matter very much were I ordered, like king Saul, to exterminate the Amalekites, or like Abraham, to sacrifice my only son; could it
really be the voice of God telling me to do something so morally repugnant?

The Christian theologian Søren Kierkegaard agonized at considerable

[3] In fact the situation is even more complicated; the Oral Torah maintains that 'do not
steal' in the Ten Commandments refers exclusively to kidnapping, since theft is already
covered by Lev. 19: 11 (*Mekhilta* 'Baḥodesh' 8; BT *San.* 86a).

length about why Abraham listened to the voice of God commanding him to sacrifice his son Isaac, surely a highly unethical thing to do, and contrary to God's earlier promise that Isaac would be Abraham's heir; he resolved the problem by inventing the 'teleological suspension of the ethical', i.e. Abraham suspended ethical judgement for a 'higher', spiritual or religious purpose—the fulfilment, through love, of God's command. This is a very dubious doctrine, to which Levinas opposed his reverse doctrine of the suspension of the religious before the ethical.[4] In Levinas' view the suspension of the ethical followed by a 'leap of faith' into the religious was a type of violence, and 'transcending' ethics was a pretext for injustice; God's transcendent command has been and is invoked with alarming frequency to justify the murder or persecution of those who refuse to acknowledge that God commanded whatever the aggressor claims he commanded. Whether it was the Israelites slaughtering the inhabitants of Canaan 3,000 years ago, the medieval Catholic Church hounding the Cathars, or the modern Al-Kaida committing atrocities against civilian populations, the justification has always been that they were doing what God said, and who would dare question the wisdom of God? Of course, no one would question the wisdom of God; but we would and should question anyone who claims to have superior, incontestable knowledge of what God said.

On a personal level, the conflict between the ethical and what God is alleged to have said matters profoundly to people who believe that homosexual activity within a loving relationship is morally acceptable, contrary to what the Bible (e.g. Lev. 18: 22) unequivocally states that God said. It matters less when it comes to ritual matters, such as restrictions on what I eat, my working days, the clothes I wear, or the company I keep, but if the restrictions become too irksome my resolution to abide by the ritual will be weaker than that of someone who believes that God really did issue precisely those instructions, and that obedience to God's instructions overrides considerations of ethics, let alone of mere convenience.

The only *possible* way for any individual to resolve conflicts between the ethical and the spiritual is by the exercise of personal judgement. People who refuse on grounds of conscience to do what a priest, speaking in the name of God, tells them they ought to do, are apt to be accused of arrogance; do they really think they know better than God what is right? However, the responsible exercise of personal judgement is not arrogant; it is quite simply inescapable, intrinsic to the human situation, a consequence of the ability to make decisions. The apparent alternative of delegating judgement to the

[4] Kierkegaard, *Fear and Trembling*. The contrasting views of Levinas and Kierkegaard are well set out in Westphal, *Levinas and Kierkegaard*, ch. 5.

priest, rabbi, guru, or other authority figure is itself an exercise in personal judgement, fraught with risk. Who is to say this rabbi/guru is better than some other with whom s/he is in total disagreement? By consenting to defer to him, I am exercising personal judgement.

We cannot be certain that God said this, that, or the other, that if he said it we know what it means, or that, if we know what it means and it appears unethical, whether or not we should suspend ethical judgement and do it anyway. This is already a problematic situation, but can we at least distinguish between truth and falsehood? That is our next topic of enquiry.

What Is Truth?

There are different kinds of truth, different situations in which we say that a sentence, proposition, or belief is 'true', and an extensive literature now exists in which philosophers have explored theories of truth and theories of justification.

Frank P. Ramsay (1903–30) denied that 'true' was a predicate at all, and a similar position was taken by others such as W. V. O. Quine (1908–2000), who adopted what is often called a 'disquotational' view of truth; according to this, saying for instance '"All swans are white" is true' is not saying more than 'All swans are white'; 'is true' is merely a device for removing the quotation marks.[5] (It is, by the way, not true that all swans are white.)

Discussion along these lines would not help the present enquiry, so I shall limit my comments to eight ways in which 'true' is or has been used by serious thinkers as a predicate. The first three are what might be called 'realist' or 'objective' concepts of truth; people who hold them believe that statements are true independently of person, place, or time, and that all reasonable and sufficiently well-informed people would agree with them (this begs the question of who counts as reasonable). The last four have a strong *subjective* content; they might also be regarded as metaphorical, so that it would be appropriate to place 'truth' in quotation marks. Moreover, what is 'true' in one of these senses for one person might not be 'true' for another. Between the two groups lies the 'truth' of moral judgements; some people regard them as objective, some as subjective (if, that is, they regard 'subjective' and 'objective' as meaningful categories at all, another philosophical conundrum in which we need not get involved).

---

[5]   Ramsay, 'Facts and Propositions'; Quine, *From a Logical Point of View*, 134–6. For truth theory in general, Kirkham, *Theories of Truth*, is a helpful guide; Williams, *Truth and Truthfulness*, is a more recent, original contribution.

1. **Correspondence.** Aristotle, defining truth and falsehood, wrote: 'To say that what is is not, or that what is not is, is false; and to say that what is is and that what is not is not, is true'.[6] This is the 'common sense', or 'realist', theory that a true statement (belief, proposition) is one that 'corresponds' with what is, i.e. with objective facts. If I say, 'there is a fire engine in the street', I expect an empirical fact, namely the presence of a fire engine in the street, to correspond with my statement. In science, and even more in historical investigation, there is always an element of interpretation, of 'loading', in reporting facts, but that is no justification for concluding that all statements are 'merely' subjective, or relative. Henry VIII *really did* marry Anne Boleyn (whether or not the ceremony was valid); hydrochloric acid *really does* react with sodium hydroxide in a predictable way (within defined ranges of temperature, pressure, etc.).

2. **Coherence.** Percy Brand Blanshard (1892–1987), an American disciple of the Oxford idealist philosopher F. H. Bradley, argued that coherence was not merely a criterion of truth, but defined the nature of truth: 'truth *is* coherence';[7] thought 'seeks its fulfilment . . . the satisfaction of coherent vision'.[8] Now a system of geometry, for instance, or the novels comprising Galsworthy's *Forsyte Saga*, may be internally coherent but nevertheless false, that is, they may not correspond to anything in the real world; perhaps the real world has a geometry of eleven rather than three or four dimensions, or perhaps the Forsytes never existed. The coherence theory of truth, however, 'holds that one system only is true, namely the system in which everything real and possible is coherently included'.[9] Moreover, in Blanshard's view, every item in the system entails all the others. Richard L. Kirkham has formally expressed the theory as one in which 'For each belief, *b*, *b* is purely true if and only if *b* is a member of a consistent set of beliefs that among them give a complete picture of the world and each of which entails each of the others.'[10]

This concept of truth applies to theories and generalizations rather than discrete statements, and depends on a peculiar view of the relationship between thought and reality; it appeals to ontological idealists, a rare and threatened breed that there would be little point in rescuing from the brink of extinction. A weaker form of coherence theory drops the requirement that every item in the system entails all the others; this has a much wider appeal. Coherence is undoubtedly important—bits ought to fit with other bits in a

---

[6] Aristotle, *Metaphysics* IV.vii.1 (1011b26). Compare V.vii.5–6 (1017a) and V.xxix (1024b).

[7] Blanshard, *Nature of Thought*, ii. 260—author's italics.

[8] Ibid. 262.   [9] Ibid. 273–4.

[10] Kirkham, 'Truth', 471. Kirkham, *Theories of Truth*, 106, offers a slightly more complex formula.

sensible way—though as soon as a philosopher concedes that the system has to give 'a picture of the world' we are back in the realm of correspondence theory.

3. Pragmatic. Truth is what works. Charles S. Peirce (1839–1914) wrote that 'any hypothesis . . . may be admissible, in the absence of any special reasons to the contrary, provided it be capable of experimental verification, and only insofar as it be capable of such verification'; likewise, 'the maxim of pragmatism is that a conception can have no effect or import differing from that of a second conception except so far as . . . it might conceivably modify our practical conduct differently from that second conception'.[11] Peirce later called his theory 'pragmaticism' to distinguish it from the 'radical empiricism' of his friend William James (1842–1910) (though James himself clearly distinguished the two), as well as from more popular uses of 'pragmatism'; he hoped that 'pragmaticism' was 'ugly enough to be safe from kidnappers', and so it has proved.

James, along with John Dewey and F. C. S. Schiller, took Peirce's idea and ran with it, but not always where Peirce would have liked them to run. James writes:

The truth of an idea is not a stagnant property inherent in it. Truth happens to an idea. It becomes true, is made true by events. Its verity is in fact an event, a process: the process namely of its verifying itself, its very-fication. Its validity is the process of its valid-ation.[12]

This begins to sound like the view later espoused by logical positivists such as A. J. Ayer (1910–89), who held that truth and verification were much the same thing. Verification, for them, is a general criterion of meaning; a statement only has meaning if it is in principle verifiable. However, pragmatists did not use the verifiability criterion to argue that unverifiable statements, such as those about God and the afterlife, were meaningless.

4. Moral. Moral and ethical convictions are said to be right or wrong, rather than true or false. If somebody asked me whether or not to steal I would answer, 'It is wrong to steal'; it would be obtuse to answer 'Stealing is not the truth.' But if somebody asked, 'Is it true that it is wrong to steal?' I would answer yes. Philosophers debate the logical status of moral judgements, including such questions as whether they are more like subjective feelings than like perceptions of objective reality, or whether they are expressions of attitude and emotion rather than statements about something outside and independent of actual people.

[11] Peirce, *Collected Papers*, 5:197; 5:196; 5:414.   [12] James, *Pragmatism*, 97.

Herodotus (484–420 BCE) observed that the Callatiae ate the bodies of their parents as a sign of respect and would be horrified at the suggestion that they should cremate them, whereas Greeks cremated their dead and would be horrified at the suggestion that they should eat them;[13] he drew from this the conclusion that moral judgements relate to specific societies. However, the view that moral judgements are culture-bound does not entail the conclusion that such judgements are subjective; Herodotus's illustration could be taken as proving the contrary: as demonstrating that respect for ancestors is a universal human virtue, common to all societies. Cultural relativism does not imply moral relativism; relativism arises when we ask how a universal value plays out in a particular society.

5. Spiritual 'depth'. Frequently, when confronted by a reasonable objection to some statement they have made, mystics, kabbalists, and the like will nod their heads sagely, saying 'Ah! But it has a *deep meaning*; it conceals a *deep truth!*' The appropriate response to such a claim is not yes or no, but Aaah! (or if one doesn't like it, Ugh! while screwing up the face).

6. Aesthetic truth. Wordsworth's 'To me the meanest flower that blows can give | Thoughts that do often lie too deep for tears',[14] or Keats's 'Beauty is truth, truth beauty'[15] illustrate this. Again, one cannot say yes or no, only sigh appreciatively or groan disapprovingly in response.

7. Psychological and social truth. Certain actions are emotionally satisfying even though not motivated by reason; they feel 'right'. Most often this happens when you have done some 'good deed', such as making a generous donation to charity, or paying respect to the dead at a funeral. The rabbis link both of these with 'truth'; charity is *tsedakah* 'rightness', from a root that also means 'truth', while the performance of funeral rites and obsequies is described as *hesed shel emet*, 'true kindness', ostensibly since it is done without expectation of reward from the one to whom respect is shown.[16]

The performance of rituals has a similar effect. Someone feels satisfied when he has recited the Kaddish or a memorial prayer for his deceased parent. 'I have done the right thing', he tells himself, though he would be hard put to it to explain why it was right, what good it had done, or even whether it was an authentic element of the Jewish tradition; he would say 'it rings true' or 'it was the right thing to do'.

---

[13] Herodotus, *Histories*, 3: 38. Herodotus may have got his facts wrong, but the argument stands.   [14] Wordsworth, 'Ode: Intimations of Immortality', section XI.

[15] Keats, 'Ode on a Grecian Urn', section V.

[16] Rashi on Gen. 47: 29, based on *Gen. Rabbah* 96: 5.

People repeat ritual acts even while conceding that they are not rational; doing again what was done before offers emotional stability in an inconstant world. The instinct to seek group approval, to copy what the group does, and to repeat it without questioning its rationality is deep-seated, though often misplaced.

8. **Mythological truth**. Stories, poems, and other literary artefacts are described as 'true' or even 'very true' if they convey understanding about human nature, about the way groups of people want to see themselves collectively, or about the universe, though we would say 'The story conveys truth' or 'How true it is!' rather than 'The story is true'. Shakespeare's *Macbeth* does not accurately recount the early history of Scotland, and you would be missing the point of the play if you read it purely for information on Scottish history, its power and its purpose lie in what it tells us about human nature, ambition, self-delusion, and conscience. If a story is referred to as a 'myth' many people jump to the conclusion that it is false and unworthy of serious consideration, but they are quite wrong. What we ask of a myth is not historical accuracy (though it may in fact be historically accurate), but the ability to articulate the human situation. A story can be both *mythos* and *logos*, myth and scientific or historical fact; the two are independent but entirely compatible. History is always story, but story is not always history.

Excursus: Consistency and 'Double Truth'

The coherence theory of truth depends more obviously than any other on consistency. However, too much emphasis on consistency can actually lead away from truth. Sometimes you have to put up with inconsistency in order to maintain a handle on truth.

Physicists debated for over two centuries whether light consisted of waves or particles. Some experiments fitted one model, some the other; no coherent explanation was forthcoming until the development of quantum mechanics in the twentieth century. What would have been wrong so long as the debate raged would have been to deny, in the name of consistency, the validity of the experimental data on either side; sometimes you just have to live with inconsistency. A Christian physicist remarked, 'On Mondays, Wednesdays, and Fridays we treat light as waves; on Tuesdays, Thursdays, and Saturdays we treat it as particles; on Sundays we just pray.' (Only the days need changing to make this a Jewish or Muslim story.)

Similar dilemmas occur in theology. On the one hand (it is claimed), God is infinitely powerful and good; on the other, evil exists. These two statements are prima facie incompatible. But this does not mean that it would be right to deny either in the name of consistency, even though many have taken this path. Atheists have denied God, and some theists have limited his powers, so leaving logical space for the existence of evil; religious thinkers such as Augustine and Maimonides have denied the existence of evil (evil is *privatio boni*, the absence of good, and appears to us as evil only because of our limited view—a position radically reversed by Schopenhauer[17]), thereby allowing logical space for an omnipotent and benevolent God. Both positions are ill-founded, since each denies a well-attested aspect of human experience.

Logical consistency is desirable, and it is characteristic of truth, but given the imperfection of human understanding it is not always available. In the real world we live with muddle; if the evidence points in contrary directions we should not arbitrarily reject half of it, but simply remain puzzled unless and until we can resolve the contradiction.

The struggle for consistency has often driven philosophers to attempt to circumvent the law of excluded middle, that is, the principle that every proposition is either true or not true. Together with the other two traditional laws of thought—the law of identity (whatever is, is) and the law of contradiction (nothing can both be and not be)—this law poses a serious obstacle to those who would like both 'to have their cake and eat it', for instance by asserting the truth of the claims of both science (in the Middle Ages, philosophy) and religion when they are in stark contradiction to each other. (Nowadays the fashion is to talk about 'going beyond binary logic'; multi-valued logics do indeed have their place, but this is not it.)

On 7 March 1277 Étienne Tempier, the bishop of Paris, issued a condemnation of 219 heterodox ideas. In his introduction he declared that Siger of Brabant, Boethius of Dacia, and other masters in the Parisian Arts Faculty 'hold that something is true according to philosophy but not according to the Catholic faith, as if there are two contrary truths, and as if in contradiction to the truth of Sacred Scripture there is a truth in the doctrines of the accursed pagans'.[18] This is the earliest clear reference to the doctrine of double truth, associated particularly with the name of Pietro Pomponazzi (1462–1525). The Muslim Ibn Rushd (Averroes; 1126–98) is sometimes said to be the originator of this doctrine, but it is not certain that he, his Christian follower John of Jandun (1285/9–1328), or others to whom such a doctrine has been attributed held that contraries were both true; they may have concealed their scepticism, or simply have preferred not to push matters to their logical conclusion.

[17] Schopenhauer, 'On the Suffering of the World', 41–3.
[18] Translated from *Chartularium universitatis pariensus*, 543.

Several scholars have attributed a 'double truth' theory to the thirteenth-century Spanish Jewish philosopher Isaac Albalag, who attempted to defend philosophy from the attacks of the traditionalists.[19] Albalag, who upheld the theory of the eternity of the universe, states that philosophy, far from being a threat to religion, shares its fundamental convictions.[20] God has rendered the truth palatable to ordinary people by conveying it in material terms that they can comprehend, but the truth is only fully expressible in philosophical terms; there are, also, prophetic truths concealed in the Torah which cannot be attained by speculation.[21] But it remains uncertain that Albalag, or Elijah del Medigo (c.1458–93) after him, actually held that contraries could be simultaneously true.[22]

No Jewish thinker appears more committed to a double truth theory than Maharal of Prague. Joshua 10 states that after the battle of Ai God caused the sun to stand still in the heavens until Joshua had completed the defeat of the Amorite coalition. For Maharal, in the wake of sixteenth-century progress in astronomy, this was problematic; surely the perfect motions of heavenly bodies were unchangeable? His solution is that there are two suns, one physical and the other spiritual. The physical sun continued on its course unhindered, for it is subject to the fixed laws of astronomy. Normally, the physical sun and the spiritual sun move in perfect synchrony. On this occasion, however, the spiritual sun stood still for the sake of Israel, a people who live on a spiritual plane. The Bible records the experience of Israel, the spiritual nation, for whom the sun stood still until they accomplished the defeat of their enemies; other people, who live only on the physical plane, would have seen no extraordinary event.[23]

But is this a theory about two accounts of the truth which are *logically* incompatible yet nevertheless both correct? Perhaps not. Maharal cannot be charged with ignoring logic by asserting that one and the same sun simultaneously followed and did not follow its normal trajectory; he is saying that there are two *realities*, two suns, not two contradictory descriptions of the identical event. The spiritual world need not, in his view, coincide with the material world, though mostly they are in synchrony.

Though Maharal's 'spiritual world' is not the mythic world implied in our eighth view of truth, it is not far removed from it. The consequences of understanding Torah from Heaven as myth are different from those that follow from interpreting it as independent spiritual reality, yet in both cases

[19] Albalag, introd. to *Tikun hade'ot*, his Hebrew translation and notes on al-Ghazzali, *Magasid al-falasifa*.   [20] Albalag, *Tikun hade'ot*, 2.
[21] Ibid. 4. See also Sirat, *History*, 238–43.   [22] See J. J. Ross, 'Elijah Delmedigo', no. 4.
[23] Judah Loew ben Bezalel (Maharal), *Gevurot hashem*, second introd.

there is a clear boundary between the world of the divine Torah and the world of history.

Benjamin Ish-Shalom says of Abraham Isaac Kook (1865–1935) that he 'rejected binary logic and asserts that a thing can be both itself and different from itself simultaneously'.[24] The context of this full-scale assault on logic is the nature of God—Kook was attempting to reconcile Spinoza's perception of the divine as unity and static completeness with Bergson's perception of the ultimate reality as continuous, free movement. But surely 'reconcile' is the operative word; Kook would have believed that the contradiction was ultimately resolved, if in a way inaccessible to human reason.

In What Sense Is 'Torah from Heaven' True?

In which of the senses of 'truth' outlined above can it be said that the doctrine of Torah from Heaven is true?

1. **Correspondence**. This, the traditional understanding of *torah min hashamayim*, is the weakest, for as we demonstrated earlier, especially in Chapter 9, there are numerous instances where hard historical or scientific evidence points to a conclusion at variance with the claims made in received texts. It is certainly not true, for instance, in any factual ('historical') sense, that two brothers, Jubal and Tubal-Cain, between them invented musical instruments and iron and brass forging (Gen. 4: 21, 22) or that, a little later, a huge deluge inundated the whole world and destroyed all living creatures on earth other than Noah, his family, and pairs or sevens of each species; abundant facts are now known that yield a much more nuanced and extensive account of ancient history.

2. **Coherence**. 'Torah from Heaven' brings together a large number of texts, stories, and laws, since it claims that they all emanate from 'one shepherd', namely God.[25] If they all emanate from God, and have been accurately transmitted, they should be mutually consistent, forming a coherent system. Everyone would admit that there are *apparent* inconsistencies, and that at least some of these might be attributed to imperfect transmission; the conventional view claims only that the tradition *as a whole* is coherent, it has a clear internal logic. But the system as mediated by the rabbis is self-sealing; apparent contradictions are resolved either in accordance with rules of interpretation or on an ad hoc basis. Everything *must* fit, since it all comes from one divine source; consequently, everything is *made* to fit. At its worst

[24] Ish-Shalom, *Rav Avraham Itzhak HaCohen Kook*, 46. [25] Eccles. 12: 11, cf. BT Ḥag. 3b.

this may lead to interpretations that disregard historical development or that are difficult to reconcile with normal linguistic usage, and at best it is a circular process.

Now I accept, say, the theory of plate tectonics as true because I believe that it gives a more coherent description of geological observations than any alternative that has been proposed, and because it fits into a coherent picture of scientific knowledge as a whole. 'Torah from Heaven' may likewise be a 'best fit' for a lot of religious stories and demands; it makes for a coherent system, which if not entirely consistent can perhaps be made so with suffici- ent perseverance and ingenuity. However, although 'Torah from Heaven' lends coherence to the system, it is seriously challenged from *outside* that system; it is not the 'best fit', for instance, when confronted with the evidence of textual variants or archaeology, since these suggest different origins and meanings for the texts. 'Torah from Heaven', that is, may be *internally* coherent, everything fitting to everything else, but it is not coherent within the wider body of available knowledge.

3. **Pragmatic**. James, Dewey, and Schiller held that a proposition would count as true if and only if behaviour based on belief in the proposition would lead, in the long run and all things considered, to beneficial results for the believers. What test of predictive value does 'Torah from Heaven' fulfil? Believers hold that beneficial results will accrue to the virtuous (as defined by them), but this may only become evident in life after death; although that is truly 'in the long run and all things considered', it is of no help in assessing a theory in the here and now. Moreover, if belief in life after death is derived from 'Torah from Heaven' the argument would constitute a vicious circle: '"Torah from Heaven" is demonstrated by the felicity of virtuous persons in the hereafter; we know the virtuous are happy in the hereafter because "Torah from Heaven" says so.'

4. **Moral**. 'Torah from Heaven' demands vigorous moral and ethical com- mitment. However, this commitment may resemble that of the driver who was told to drive furiously but was not sure he had been given the right direction. I am told to love my neighbour (Lev. 19: 18) and not to oppress my neighbour (Lev. 25: 14), but 'neighbour' is defined by a fourth-century Babylonian as 'one who is with you in Torah', a limitation that would rule out most people, including most Jews.[26] I am given lists of whom I shouldn't sleep with, and threatened with dire punishments if I do, but I find this very difficult to square with the recorded behaviour of biblical characters,

---

[26] BT *BM* 59a.

discordant with the respect for individual freedom of conscience which to me is at least as great a value as sexual correctness, and deficient in its casting of the role of women in society. 'Torah from Heaven' does indeed support a system of ethics and morality, and often this is on a high and inspirational level; but over time blemishes have become apparent or been introduced, and the system no longer rings entirely 'true'.

5. **Spiritual 'truth' or 'depth'.** The quotation marks surrounding 'truth' and 'depth' highlight the metaphorical use of those terms. Almost anything can be shown to contain a 'deep truth'. Robert the Bruce's spider remaking its web demonstrated, because he wanted it to, the 'deep truth' that it was worthwhile persevering in order to attain an objective. But there is no deep truth in a spider going about its normal business; the 'deep truth' lay entirely in Robert's *reading* of the event. Much the same is true of the 'deep' reading of traditional texts; it is not that they *contain* the wisdom attributed to them, but that they are sufficiently open for the wisdom (if such it be) to be read into them. Postmodern literary critics know this well; that is why they say that a text has no meaning until it is read, just as the third-century Babylonian Rava belatedly discovered of dreams that 'every dream goes by the mouth', that is, it has no meaning until it is interpreted.[27] So we may readily concede that every text has a 'deep' or 'spiritual' meaning; all this says is that we can, if we wish, read profound thoughts into it. We can do the same with spiders' webs, and even with tea leaves, if we are so minded. It is we ourselves who decide what the signifier signifies.

The alleged 'deep reading' not only puts things that are not there into texts, it may downgrade or abandon what *is* there. This is how Christian 'spiritual' reading of scripture bypassed the plain sense, abandoning the commandments; this is how the Zohar was able to claim that 'the stories of the Torah are just the garment of the Torah, and whoever thinks that garment is the Torah itself and not something else, may his spirit expire and he will have no portion in the world to come'.[28] This is what has happened recently in neo-hasidic movements of renewal, where the commandments are de-emphasized (though not abandoned in principle), and kabbalistic and other texts are read as psychology.[29]

'Torah from Heaven' exacerbates these dangers, since it claims that God issued the text (the Written Torah) *and* its interpretation (the Oral Torah). It is

---

[27] BT *Ber.* 56a.   [28] Zohar iii. 152a. See Ch. 3 above.

[29] These tendencies are manifest in movements such as those of Zalman Shachter and others operating under the umbrella of Aleph: the Alliance for Jewish Renewal; <www.aleph.org>.

legitimate to speculate as to what a human author meant when he composed his text, even if as postmodernists we don't care to 'privilege' the author's own reading. But with an omniscient divine author such speculation makes no sense; God knows everything, so if he issued the text he had everything, so to speak, 'in mind' at the time he issued it, and this could be taken to legitimate any interpretation of any text provided only that what was derived from the text was not intrinsically false.[30]

6. Aesthetic. Many passages in scripture are among the world's great literary treasures; if the rabbinic corpus does not match the grandeur and eloquence of Isaiah, it certainly contains some deeply moving narrative, especially in its aggadic sections, and the best Hebrew liturgical poetry has both elegance and spiritual power. Many people would say, moreover, that the fullest beauty of Judaism is expressed in its religious observances, such as the sabbath. What may be doubted is whether 'Torah from Heaven' as such contributes to the aesthetic value of Judaism. Probably not—I am moved by the music of Kol Nidrei or by the beauty of a Passover Seder irrespective of my doctrinal position. Whether or not I believe that the Torah came from heaven seems to make no difference; aesthetic appreciation depends on the suspension rather than the endorsement of doctrinal judgement. On the other hand, grand unification generates its own kind of beauty; just as there is aesthetic satisfaction in a mathematical theory that brings together diverse observations as an elegant unity, so there is aesthetic satisfaction in bringing together the manifold texts, teachings, and stories of tradition in the overarching grand vision of God revealing his Torah to Israel at Sinai.

7. Psychological and social. 'Torah from Heaven' certainly gives emotional satisfaction to many people. It relieves them from worry about problems of the sort we have been concerned with in this book and it makes them feel they are 'true to the faith of their ancestors', that they have 'done the right thing'. 'Torah from Heaven' points to a divine origin that proclaims the profound spiritual depth of our traditions, even those that at first sight appear superficial, erroneous, or immoral; it says that infinite wisdom lies behind them, and it calls us to search deeply for it, and when we discover it to utter an awestruck Aaaaah! But we do not always discover infinite wisdom, and often stumble over statements that confuse or disturb our emotions rather than enhance them.

[30] Rabbah (BT *BK* 20b/21a) states: *hekdesh shelo mida'at kehedyot mida'at dami* 'sacred unwittingly like lay wittingly' i.e. you cannot claim that 'sacred property' was unaware of trespass. As Rashi observes, this depends on the assumption that the Shekhinah itself has the required 'awareness', an analogous notion to that suggested here.

8. Mythical. The narrative of Torah from Heaven is powerful. It unifies Judaism, bringing together both Written and Oral Torah. It dissolves time, representing Torah as a timeless whole, revealed by God and managed by the rabbis. By introducing a divine point of origin for the whole it stakes a claim to perfection; as *mythos* rather than *logos* it renders itself immune from historical criticism. We may say 'Torah from Heaven' is 'true' in this sense, meaning that it effectively discharges its mythic function.

On 'Narrative Theology'

Is the mythic interpretation of 'Torah from Heaven' a kind of 'narrative theology', to use a term fashionable in 'post-liberal' Christian circles? Obviously, the 'narratives' central to Judaism exclude some of those that Christians regard as important, specifically those relating to Jesus; nor do Jews read scripture as primarily a story of salvation. On the other hand, there is no doubt that Bible stories, appropriately interpreted, are a major source for Jewish self-understanding, and they are amply supplemented by a vast tradition of story-telling. The Talmud has very little 'propositional' theology, preferring to convey religious truths in story form, and scarcely anything that might be described as 'systematic theology' is found in Jewish sources between Philo (to whom Christian theology is so heavily indebted) and the religious philosophy of the Middle Ages.

Highlighting the mythic function of *torah min hashamayim* is indeed an 'approach to theology that finds meaning in story', and in this respect it is not new to Judaism. However, we should not confuse the *story* of revelation ('Torah from Heaven') with the *content* of revelation. Telling the story of 'Torah from Heaven' does not carry salvific significance for Jews in the way that telling the story of Jesus carries salvific significance for Christians; no one is 'saved' by buying into the story of 'Torah from Heaven'. To the contrary, the story merely provides a context for the *content* of Torah, be that the commandments, halakhah, ethical monotheism, or whatever is deemed to be the true essence of Judaism.

Conclusion. 'Torah from Heaven': A Myth of Origin

The classical doctrine of 'Torah from Heaven', such as that of Maimonides, with its erroneous historical claims and occasionally questionable moral consequences, cannot be upheld by the serious historian, scientist, or philosopher. 'Torah from Heaven' is not 'true' in the sense that it gives a correct historical account of the origin of certain texts and traditions (correspondence theory of truth); it does not offer a coherent account of knowledge as a whole (coherence theory); nor does it possess verifiable predictive power (pragmatic theory).

On the other hand, it does offer a sanction for ethics and morality, though the answers it yields to ethical and moral questions are not always consonant with modern thought. If its answers clearly occupied the moral high ground, 'modern thought' might be dismissed. Sometimes this is the case, but there are also instances where it appears to fall short, and to encourage actions that are morally reprehensible, as we saw in Chapters 9 and 19. If someone invokes *torah min hashamayim* in support of an ethical or moral doctrine, great caution must be exercised to be sure that whatever it is that they claim was revealed by God through scripture as interpreted by the rabbis really is ethically or morally desirable; people have, after all, invoked scripture in defence of slavery, racism, the subjection of women, homophobia, and wars without number.

People who are committed to a belief in 'Torah from Heaven' may derive spiritual, aesthetic, and psychological benefits through their faith; it is reassuring to feel confident that you are doing what God wants, and doing it in the company and with the support and encouragement of like-minded people. Here again, though, caution is needed to avoid drawing conclusions which generate 'cognitive dissonance' with other sources of knowledge open to the believer; there is no reassurance in a belief system that remains vulnerable to contradiction from other things that you believe with equal or greater conviction.

Where *torah min hashamayim* really comes into its own is as a *myth of origin*. Myths of origin are important, even vital, to create a sense of identity. Poets, preachers, and politicians use them for this purpose. They encapsulate selected incidents of our past, together with the accumulated wisdom of the ages, and proclaim them in a succinct and accessible fashion. However, they are *interpretations* of that past, not scientific histories. 'God revealed the Torah to Israel at Sinai' is not a plain historical statement. For one thing, it is metaphysical and not open to any kind of scientific verification; also, its primary function is a religious one, not an historical one. It *interprets* our past, giving focus to episodes and developments which the historian sees as disparate events scattered over many centuries, but which from a Jewish religious perspective form a powerful, authoritative, timeless whole.

Myths serve as symbols, 'tangible formulations of notions, abstractions from experience fixed in perceptible forms, concrete embodiments of ideas, attitudes, judgments, longings, or beliefs'.[31] 'Torah from Heaven' as myth is

---

[31] Geertz, *Interpretation of Cultures*, 91.

part of the cultural pattern of Judaism, *any* form of Judaism. It is what Clifford Geertz called an 'extrinsic source of information', that is, it lies 'outside the boundaries of the individual organism . . . in that intersubjective world of common understandings into which all human individuals are born, in which they pursue their separate careers, and which they leave persisting behind them when they die. [It provides a] blueprint or template in terms of which processes external to themselves can be given a definite form.'[32] This is a vital function. It aids society and the individual to make sense of and so to face up to chaos and suffering. Whereas science and history proceed by empirical observation, and are guided by experience, religious myth *confronts* experience and transforms it in the light of prior authority; in this way it looks forward as well as backward.

'Torah from Heaven' is *mythos*, not *logos*; poetry, not prose; romance rather than history. This was a mode well known to the sages; their stories of Moses' 'ascent' to receive the Torah, cited in Chapter 2, were clearly *mythos* (though they would never have denied the historical accuracy of the Exodus narrative). Similarly, when kabbalists 'elevated' the Torah to mythical symbol (Chapter 3), in no way did they abandon belief in its perfection and historical accuracy. Maharal's 'spiritual' world of Israel (Chapter 23) and Soloveitchik's a priori Torah (Chapter 18) place Torah itself, or life on the spiritual plane, beyond the constraints of history, even though neither of them casts doubt on the historical accuracy of its content. It is not the *assertion* of the mythical nature of the story of Torah from Heaven that is disturbing to traditionalists, but the *denial* of its historical claims.

The religious poet may rhapsodize on God's love, expressed through his gift of Torah, and the preacher may preach. The historian does not participate in such discourse; his language is prose. The teacher who expounds the sacred text faces a dilemma, for the truth of *mythos* inspires, while the truth of history informs and instructs; the balance of inspiration and objective truth is delicate, and easily yields on the one hand to blind faith and fanaticism and on the other to a lack of sensitivity to spiritual issues.

[32] Ibid. 92.

TWENTY-FOUR

MYTH OF ORIGIN
Opportunities and Dangers

One myth is enough for one lifetime.

HARRISON BIRTWISTLE[1]

SOMEONE should invent another word to replace 'myth'. Until they do, I am stuck with it, even though in common English it has been debased into meaning, according to the *Concise Oxford Dictionary*, 'purely fictitious narrative, usually involving supernatural persons &c.'.

I protest. That is, emphatically, *not* what I mean, and it is certainly not how anthropologists use the word. I do not intend, when I call Torah from Heaven a myth, to denigrate it. Myths are among the most important symbols of our life; they say what *cannot be reduced to nameable facts*. To cite Clifford Geertz again, they are 'tangible formulations of notions, abstractions from experience fixed in perceptible forms, concrete embodiments of ideas, attitudes, judgements, longings, or beliefs . . . [they lie] in that intersubjective world of common understandings into which all human individuals are born . . . and which they leave persisting behind them when they die'[2] A story can be at one and the same time both myth and history, and it is certainly more persuasive if it is both, but even *without* the support of history it can function effectively as myth.

I want to articulate a way of understanding *torah min hashamayim* that will allow preachers and poets to enthuse people with a sense of continuity with the past and responsibility towards it, but that will not at the same time do violence to the findings of science and history or to current moral and philosophical consensus. Preachers and poets, but not historians and scientists,

---

[1] BBC Radio 3 broadcast 13 Aug. 2009 prior to a performance of his *Orpheus*, in reply to a question as to why he had spent so many years working on this myth and no other.

[2] Geertz, *Interpretation of Cultures*, 91–2. Ithamar Gruenwald, drawing on Mircea Eliade, has applied similar notions to the Passover Seder and the story of Torah from Heaven, e.g. 'when referring to the story of the giving of the Torah at Sinai as a myth, what is meant is determining the story as a functional factor in establishing the ritual history of ancient Israel'; Gruenwald, 'Relevance of Myth', 28.

since Torah from Heaven is neither history nor science, but of an entirely different genre. The historian and the scientist should, indeed, keep a jealous eye to ensure that the preacher does not stray into their territory; it is not for the preacher to declaim in the name of holy writ on matters that lie outside his/her range. Boundaries must be respected on both sides; *logos* and *mythos* should not be seen as jealous rivals for the same kingdom. You do not play cricket by the rules of football.

What 'Torah from Heaven' May Signify

A reconstruction of Torah from Heaven must incorporate several features.

As 'myth of origin' it seeks to present Torah as a unified whole; it must therefore be formulated so as to embrace the threefold Torah, that is, the written text of the Bible (with the Pentateuch privileged over other books), the Oral Torah as an ongoing tradition of interpretation, and customary Jewish law as defined by the practice of Israel (*minhag*). Within this context, the halakhah of Judaism may be seen as emanating from Sinai, and as reaching full expression through rabbinic interpretation and Jewish practice. This is not an historically tenable position, but an *interpretation* of history through faith; history can neither confirm nor disconfirm a non-physical origin, nor can it make a judgement as to what constitutes the full or 'authentic' expression of Torah.

Torah, as viewed through 'Torah from Heaven', is a unified whole—that is what 'Torah from Heaven' is about. But Torah is Torah, it is not something else; it should not be reduced to something else, such as halakhah or ethics or spirituality. Each is part of the vision of Sinai, but none constitutes the whole. Interpretations of Torah such as the early reformist reduction of Torah to 'ethical monotheism', or the reduction of Torah to halakhah, or popular modern presentations of Torah as spirituality, are inadequate; Torah comprises all those things, and others.

The received text of scripture is sacrosanct. *Torah min hashamayim* implies that any imperfections are due to failure of transmission, and indeed minor imperfections of transmission have always been acknowledged. Halivni argued that there had been substantial 'maculation' of both text and content, but that the text as 'recovered' by Ezra was now sacrosanct, even though rabbinic Judaism had taken and was taking the recovery process still further (Chapter 18). But this confuses history with myth. *Historically*, we may say that the text of Torah is imperfect, whether verbally or morally; *mythically*, however, perfection is of its essence, and cannot be denied or compromised.

History and Myth Do Not Conflict

From a logical point of view, history and myth do not conflict since their claims relate to independent realms. Shakespeare's play, as a mythical account of the history of Scotland, is not invalidated because the real Macbeth, contrary to Shakespeare's portrayal, was a powerful and successful monarch; it is only mildly enhanced by the fact, re-enacted in the play, that the historical Macbeth murdered Duncan I and was defeated by Malcolm III.

The story of the Flood in Genesis, taken as a myth expressing God's moral providence, does not conflict with the evidence of archaeology; the conquest of Canaan, as myth, may be related without implications being drawn from it as to correct modes of behaviour. We do not need to distinguish on moral or other grounds, as Louis Jacobs and others have done, between 'higher' and 'lower' parts of Torah.[3]

Conflict arises when people take myths literally and draw unwarranted conclusions from them. It may be avoided by careful selection of what to highlight and by the incorporation into preaching and teaching of interpretations that adjust text or content in the light of contemporary norms. Selectivity means, for instance, that we ignore texts calling for the genocide of the Canaanites. Such selectivity has always been practised, if not openly or even consciously; today the selection has to be conscious and deliberate, since knowledge and awareness both of traditional sources and of historical processes is far more widely available than in any previous era.

At the historical level, we must acknowledge the development of text and interpretation, and that the Torah was 'revealed' in a specific social/historical location reflecting, for instance (*pace* Ross, Chapter 20 above), male dominance and the acceptance of slavery. Being aware of such factors will inevitably affect our interpretation and application of its laws, particularly with regard to (a) the right to individual freedom, religious as well as social, (b) the rejection of slavery, (c) the rejection of discrimination against 'other nations', and (d) a significant measure of gender equality.

'Torah from Heaven': Uses and Abuses

'Torah from Heaven', in its classical form, made a number of assumptions that must be guarded against nowadays.

Authority and Power. Classical 'Torah from Heaven' entails authority for its 'guardians' (priests, rabbis, communal officials), in the name of God. It

---

[3] Above, p. 265.

empowers them to coerce people into doing and believing what they (i.e. the priests, the rabbis, and the communal officials) claim the Torah mandates. Pre-modern, autonomous Jewish communities imposed severe penalties on those who did not comply with the rulings of the rabbis, in religious as well as in civil and criminal matters. Jewish emancipation since the eighteenth century, combined with the modern commitment to representative government, means that religious leaders no longer have authority to define and impose civil and criminal law, though they may act as arbitrators with the consent of the litigants subject to the jurisdiction under which they live. Religious compulsion is incompatible with liberal democracy's respect for the autonomy of the individual conscience; religious leaders in liberal democratic societies have to accept that they are addressing congregations whose loyalty to religious demands is voluntary. Religious coercion, as Mendelssohn argued in *Jerusalem*, is not merely unethical but likely to be futile and counter-productive.[4]

Exclusivity. 'Torah from Heaven' is a metaphor in which God is portrayed as a man who hands a book (the Written Torah) together with instructions on how to use it (the Oral Torah) to his servant, Moses, to transmit to his people, Israel. A naïve application of this metaphor suggests exclusivity: this is *our* book, no one else has anything like it, and we are specially privileged because we have entered into a covenant with God on the terms of the book. This naïve reading, which confuses metaphor with historical fact, has in the past led Jews and Christians to engage in futile quarrels as to who now owns 'the covenant', as if it were some precious object like a diamond necklace over which people might squabble.

But 'covenant' is not an object; it is a metaphor. As one of several metaphors for God's relationship with Israel it can easily be adopted as a paradigm for his relationship with any people, a relationship that can be expressed through other cultures and religions, too; the Bible itself occasionally applies it to humanity or even to living creatures in general.[5] Such an interpretation permits Jewish theology to make space for other faiths, and so leads to acceptance of the idea that a political entity such as a nation-state may encompass different faith groups, and that members of all of these are called to co-operate, in mutual respect, for the advantage of society as a whole.

---

[4] See Kochan, *Jewish Renaissance*, 64–70, for a critical account of early Jewish reaction to the undermining of traditional *kehilah* authority.

[5] Notably in the story of Noah (Gen. 9: 9–17). I have explored this theme in my Spanish article, 'Alianza'.

Norms and Values. When we say 'The Torah comes from heaven' we may at one extreme be thinking of its 'essential principles', such as Spinoza's *lex divina* consisting of true knowledge of God and love;[6] at the other extreme, we may be thinking of Torah, as Elijah of Vilna did, as containing absolutely everything, in detail.[7] A balance must be established so that the high principles of Torah emerge clearly, some detail is preserved, but emphasis on minutiae is not allowed to submerge the underlying values. This requires a broad understanding of the 'threefold Torah'—scripture, oral tradition, and Jewish practice. Too narrow a focus on values rides roughshod over the details of practice; too narrow a focus on halakhic norms generates ever-decreasing circles of interpretation, harmonization, and explanations of explanations *ad infinitum*, losing contact with the social realities that the sources of halakhah originally addressed.

Benefits of Understanding 'Torah from Heaven' as *Mythos* rather than *Logos*

Several benefits accrue from acknowledging that the story of 'Torah from Heaven' is a foundational religious myth rather than an account of historical events.

Truth is better than falsehood, and valuable for its own sake. 'Torah from Heaven' fails as an historical account of the origins of Judaism, but it succeeds as a myth of origins that focuses the traditions of Judaism within a monotheistic theology where everything flows from the One God.

Many people live in an uncomfortable state of tension because they find themselves emotionally drawn to a traditional religious pattern even though their general educational and cultural background appears to contradict the beliefs that this implies. Beliefs were formulated in the Middle Ages in ways that are incompatible with the modern world-view; to insist on the same formulations now would be to commit oneself to the outmoded terms of philosophy and science in which Torah was previously formulated. Once the story of 'Torah from Heaven' is perceived as a foundational religious myth rather than as an account of historical events, the 'cognitive dissonance' is relieved; the important question becomes 'What do text and/or tradition actually tell me?' rather than, for instance, 'How did Maimonides formulate belief in Torah from heaven?'; Maimonides was, after all, addressing twelfth-century people, not twenty-first-century people.

Reading 'Torah from Heaven' as the precise report of an event that took place at a specific place and time in history leads to literalism in the appli-

---

[6] Above, Ch. 17.　　　　[7] Above, Ch. 12.

cation of biblical and rabbinic statements to contemporary situations, and so to various forms of biblical and rabbinic fundamentalism, potentially of an extreme sort, in politics as well as religion. Reading 'Torah from Heaven' as a myth of origin is less open to fundamentalist abuse, since it serves as a model for non-literal interpretation of sources generally. However, non-literal reading may 'spiritualize away' the practical content of tradition, notably the halakhah; the denominations of Judaism differ with regard to the extent to which they do this.

Understanding 'Torah from Heaven' as a myth of origin frees the believer to reappraise the *history* of origin, accessible through archaeology, through the study of ancient Near Eastern texts including the Bible, and through the study of the formation and development of rabbinic Judaism. Reflection on the *actual* history and culture of biblical Israel in its historical setting helps us to re-appropriate biblical theology and experience as part of our heritage and spiritual resource, and raises shrewd if sometimes disturbing questions about the relationship between biblical and later rabbinic teaching.

Dangers from Understanding 'Torah from Heaven' as *Logos* rather than *Mythos*

The refusal to acknowledge that the story of 'Torah from Heaven' is a foundational religious myth rather than an account of historical events causes confusion and harm.

Falsehood is intrinsically bad. Adopting 'Torah from Heaven' as an historical account of the origins of Judaism is wrong both because it promotes falsehood and because it fails to do justice to 'Torah from Heaven' as a powerful myth of origins.

Adopting *torah min hashamayim* as an historical account of the origins of Judaism leads, among people who have benefited from a modern education, to a frustrating and potentially damaging cognitive dissonance between the personal religious world of the believer and the assumptions on which the believer's everyday life is based.

It leads to extremes, in politics as well as religion. For instance, people may interpret Genesis' account of God's promise of the Land to Abraham and his descendants through Isaac in a very literal way, generating friction with those who happen to inhabit the land at any given time, but whose right to live there is denied since they are not recognized as descendants of Isaac.

Whether the biblical story is understood literally or read as myth of origin, the actual event of 'receiving the Torah' is described as a once-only irruption into history from beyond. But there is a difference. The literal reading leads to a failure to take the socio-historical contexts of halakhic development seriously; people begin to think of biblical and rabbinic texts as a textual resource that can be analysed logically to find answers to questions of law, without considering overarching moral values or changing social contexts; that is why the Orthodox tend to overemphasize minutiae of the law, and are slow to respond to social change or to modify interpretation in the light of general values. On the other hand 'Torah from Heaven' as myth of origin, though it frees Torah from historical constraint to the extent that it posits a transcendent event of enduring impact, is better able to accommodate the notion of historical development.

The dangers must not be exaggerated; few bad consequences of the wrong kind of reading are inevitable. Literal belief in 'Torah from Heaven' *tends*, for instance, to divert the believer away from considerations of socio-economic change, but it does not *necessarily* do this. It was, as we saw in Chapter 2, a third-century rabbi, Joshua ben Levi—undoubtedly a literal believer, though also a great story-teller—who said, 'Scripture, Mishnah, Talmud, aggadah—whatever a student would [one day] teach in the presence of his master, was already imparted to Moses at Sinai'—surely an acknowledgement that third-century Torah looked very different from that of the Bible or, as we would now put it, that Torah had responded to cultural and/or socio-economic change.

It is not illogical (though it may be incorrect) to maintain that God dictated the text of the whole Torah to Moses, from Genesis to Deuteronomy, and at the same time indicated to Moses how the laws should be modified in the light of social, economic, and historical changes to come. There are numerous instances where the authorities throughout the ages have modified a law in the light of changing circumstances; many books have been compiled to document this, sometimes with the agenda of justifying contemporary modification of the halakhah.[8] Orthodox and Progressive Jews differ on the extent to which such change has taken or ought to take place, but essentially the difference is one of degree rather than principle.

Things That Worry People

How do people react if they have been encouraged to believe literally that God dictated the Pentateuch to Moses in Sinai, together with its oral interpretation and secret meanings, and then they are told that this is not a factual history but a myth of origin? To some of them the news comes as a relief, because they were already troubled by the difficulties of reconciling traditional belief with their intellects and consciences. Others, though, feel destabilized; they

---

[8] For instance, Jacobs, *A Tree of Life*; Katz, *Divine Law in Human Hands*.

MYTH OF ORIGIN 323

become anxious and even angry, and denounce protagonists of the new interpretation as heretics and unbelievers.

Foremost among their worries is that sanction for the halakhah appears to be undermined. If God did not, as a matter of this-worldly historical fact, dictate Torah and commentary to Moses, why should anyone bother to follow its laws, which are often onerous and inconvenient? Surely the whole system of halakhah has been cut from its roots, and will fail to secure obedience?

There is some justification for this fear. If people obey the law of Torah out of an intellectual conviction that God dictated it, and evidence comes to light to weaken that conviction, their motivation for obeying the law will be undermined. However, very few people *do* follow the law primarily out of conviction that God dictated it, let alone out of pure fear or love of God. People follow laws—any laws—for much more complex reasons than that, such as identification with a particular social group, habit (inertia), a sense of joy, a sense of guilt, or because the law conforms with their own attitudes and aspirations. Motives are complex and often concealed deep within the unconscious. It might well be that some people *justify* their compliance with the laws of Torah by reference to the belief that God dictated the laws to Moses; if, however, someone convinces them that that is unhistorical, they will more often than not formulate another justification rather than abandon the law. They may well become a little less insistent on minutiae, more tolerant of those with whom they disagree, and more disposed to modify observance in the light of deeply held values; but this, it seems to me, is a good thing.

Perhaps those who are so fearful that the Torah will lose its hold on people should also ask themselves how they have come to adopt the attitude that the laws of Torah are onerous and inconvenient. It could be because they have failed to understand the joy of Torah; but it may also be because laws that in their original setting were truly joyful and inspiring continue to be implemented in settings where they no longer serve their original purpose, and they appear irrelevant and therefore irksome.

Another source of worry is the assumption that if you don't believe that *torah min hashamayim* is history, but you still support the halakhic system on which Jewish observance rests, you are a hypocrite who says one thing and believes another. For instance, in the classroom or from the pulpit you say that God gave the Torah, both oral and written, to Moses, but in the lecture hall you speculate whether Genesis was compiled in the Persian period, and what its source documents were.

This should not worry anybody. It is on a par with what happens in any other advanced discipline. If you try to present, say, physics or medicine to the general public, who are unfamiliar with the specialized discourse of the discipline, you have to find accessible illustrations and analogies to get the point across. You will talk about protons and electrons as if they were little billiard balls, because if you set the equations of quantum mechanics before the public they would not understand them, and might think you were trying to blind them with science, or talking nonsense; or you will talk about viruses as if they were nasty little animals out to get you, because the language and concepts of molecular biology are incomprehensible to the untrained. Likewise, in the case of religion, the traditional story of 'Torah from Heaven' makes an effective entry point into the system, focusing halakhah, aggadah, and other aspects of Judaism into one approachable whole in a way that scientific study of Bible and Talmud could not achieve without years of arduous study. No previous training or special aptitude is required on the part of the hearers, as would be the case with abstract theology or philosophy of religion.

Yet a third pretext for worry is that calling for modification of traditional belief will lead to friction with fundamentalist groups, leading in turn to the possibility of sectarian divisions and strife. This is a legitimate cause for concern, but not an excuse for yielding to falsehood; to the contrary, religious fundamentalism, in Judaism as in other faiths, must be confronted as a dangerous and subversive assault on truth, morality, and the social order.

Clearly, the proliferation of conflicting views about Torah from Heaven carries consequences for Jewish society; these will be addressed in the next chapter.

TWENTY-FIVE

DEMOGRAPHY
VERSUS REASON
The Future of Jewish Religion

HISTORIANS AND SOCIOLOGISTS have speculated about the future of the Jewish *people*; they range from pessimists like Bernard Wasserstein to optimists such as Calvin Goldschneider.[1] I am more concerned with religion than with demography. Can we determine what form the Jewish *religion* will take in, say, a hundred years' time?

It is tempting to assert that 'truth will out', that the form of belief that is closest to the truth will prevail. This has happened in the world of science; the cosmology of Copernicus prevailed over that of Ptolemy in the long run because it better fitted observations, so was presumably closer to the 'truth' (whether we understand this in terms of correspondence with external facts, coherence, or some other theory of truth).

In the world of the arts the situation is less clear. What survives? Beauty, dramatic power, insight into the human situation, creative imagination, all play some part in giving a work of art enduring worth. Correspondence to the facts of history is less relevant; it is inapplicable to music, unimportant in the visual arts (does it really matter who was the model for Mona Lisa, or whether the portrait resembles her?), and beside the point for non-documentary drama (*Hamlet* is not a documentary—it would be just as great had there never been a prince of Denmark).

What makes particular forms of religious ritual and belief endure? Certainly not the historical or scientific accuracy of statements made by religious leaders over the centuries. Beauty, dramatic power, insight into the human situation, creative imagination, usefulness—all have some part to play, but none of them is either necessary or sufficient on its own.

Something else is needed. Judith Plaskow has written:

The Jews of the past, drawing on the religious forms available to them, created and recreated a living Judaism . . . What determined the 'Jewishness' of their

---

[1] Wasserstein, *Vanishing Diaspora*; Goldschneider, *Studying the Jewish Future*.

formulations was not a set of predetermined criteria, but the 'workability' of such formulations for the Jewish people.[2]

It is not entirely clear what 'workability' is, but the point behind Plaskow's statement is well taken. The *social meaningfulness and practicality* of any form of religion is vital to its persistence, and involves both education and social welfare. Unless the community persists, the religion ceases to be, though much of its content may be absorbed into other religions or forms of culture. So, it must 'work' for the community. Religion affords space for the development of individual spirituality, but requires a community in relation to which that development can take place—not necessarily a community that constantly lives up to its most demanding requirements, but one that by and large endorses its ideals, follows its rituals, and speaks its language.

A theory in the 'hard' sciences is true or false independently of society; in the earth's gravitational field, an apple will fall from the tree whether or not there are humans who know or care. The arts, as forms of human expression and communication, need people to communicate and to be communicated with, and this presupposes some shared language and culture. Neither science nor arts will flourish unless there is a culture that provides opportunity for such activities, even though the most successful scientists and creative artists may break the bounds of the culture in which they were nurtured.

Science and the arts cross cultural boundaries. The geometry of Euclid is applicable to plane surfaces (if, in the real world, there are any) not only in Alexandria where he taught, but in any part of the world, or for that matter the universe; the poetry of Dante is appreciated in cultures very different from that of Renaissance Italy, even in cultures where the theological foundation on which it rests is rejected; the music of the German Protestant Bach has been rendered faithfully and superbly by non-Christian performers from Japan and Korea.

Religion is different. It depends on communities of people, faith communities, who *collectively* relate to its teachings and rituals. Every religion has core values that transcend its boundaries and may be shared and can certainly be appreciated by those outside the community. It also has elements, such as stories, forms of worship, and celebrations, that can be understood by others (often these elements pass from one religious community to another, with or without modification); religions can be and often are reformulated within the terms of reference of different cultures. But taken as a whole, a religion has definite boundaries, the boundaries that constitute the community of the

---

[2] Plaskow, *Standing Again at Sinai*, p. xix.

faithful. The boundaries do not have to be territorial, though they may be, as when national identity coincides with religious identity.

National leaders have often encouraged specific forms of religion in the belief that they enhance political loyalty by backing it with divine sanction. The Roman statesman Cicero wrote: 'I shall begin with soothsaying, which, according to my deliberate judgement, should be cultivated from reasons of political expediency and in order that we may have a state religion.'[3] That is, whatever Cicero's personal scepticism about soothsaying, he thought it was good for keeping control of the Roman populace by affording a focus for its culture. This may sound rather cynical, but it has been a common enough attitude among Christian and Muslim princes throughout the centuries. Freedom of religion has repeatedly been opposed on the grounds that it undermines the cohesion and therefore the security of the state; state religions have been imposed not because the prince was rationally convinced of their truth, but out of political expediency.

In the West, however, this attitude has largely disappeared. The multicultural nation-state may comprise citizens of different faiths; religion has become a private matter in which the state does not interfere other than when religion promotes civil or criminal wrongs, such as incitement to intercommunal violence.

To the religious leaders, however, religion is not private but a matter of group identification. When the Jewish community poses the question, 'Who is a Jew?', the answer cannot be given by a private decision, but only by a consensus within the community, often a consensus to follow the ruling of a specific *beit din* (rabbinic court). Definitions and recognized processes of conversion are urged, sometimes generating conflict between an individual's self-understanding and the category the community seeks to impose on him; for instance, someone whose self-understanding and general conduct are wholly in accordance with Jewish norms may be rejected by an Orthodox community because s/he did not have a Jewish mother and was not converted under Orthodox auspices, whereas another individual who happened to be born to a Jewish mother may have a Jewish identity imposed on him by the community despite lacking any personal sense of identity with the community or any commitment to Jewish beliefs and practices.

We can now reformulate our enquiry as to the future of the Jewish religion: what will be the predominant form of belief and/or practice (if any) by which Jewish communities orient themselves in time to come? Will this

---

[3] 'Ut ordiar ab haruspicina, quam ego rei publicae causa communisque religionis colendam censeo.' Cicero, *De divinatione*, II: xii, trans. W. W. Falconer.

form of belief be arrived at rationally, or by some other process? How will individuals within the community relate to it?

Does Reason Matter?

The intellectual seeks rational consistency, but this is not always available. The human intellect has so far proved unable to reduce all knowledge to a consistent framework. Philosophers have tried, and failed. Scientists have been more successful, but their success has been bought at the expense of ignoring many aspects of human experience; even in the hard physical sciences, where they are most successful, they have as yet failed to resolve major discrepancies such as that between general relativity and quantum mechanics at some scales.

Most people lack inclination, time, and ability to take arguments to their logical conclusion; if they sign up to the concept of 'Torah from Heaven' it is as part of a vocabulary of Jewish religious identity rather than as a logically coherent position. It is a heuristic, a 'rule-of-thumb' with which to approach the world in company with fellow-religionists, not a categorical statement about history or cosmology.

Much the same happened in the second and third centuries, when Christianity and rabbinic Judaism were in the process of formation. The Roman empire was home to an astonishing variety of philosophical schools and religious sects. How did people choose which lifestyle to adopt? Doubtless then as now most people did not actively choose, but by inertia remained in the pattern of their forbears. But some did choose, whether a mystery religion, Judaism, or Christianity (and if so which sect of either), or one of the many philosophical schools, such as the Academy or the Stoa. A midrash relates how Jethro, the father-in-law of Moses, tried all forms of idolatry before finally coming to accept the truth of Torah. Jethro, the midrash implies, acted rationally; he surveyed all the alternatives, and chose the best.[4]

But most people have neither the time nor the ability for a comprehensive and systematic examination of alternative philosophies and lifestyles. The Church Father Origen, reproached by philosophers for misleading the ignorant by teaching them Christian doctrine, took a sanguine view:

As this matter of faith is so much talked of, I have to reply that we accept it as useful for the multitude, and that we admittedly teach those who cannot abandon everything and pursue a study of rational argument to believe without thinking out

---

[4] *Mekhilta* on Exod. 18: 11. The midrash parallels Josephus' description, near the beginning of his autobiography, of his own investigation of the Jewish sects.

their reasons. But, even if they do not admit it, in practice others do the same. What man who is urged to study philosophy and throws himself at random into some school of philosophy, comes to do so for any reason except either that he has come across a particular teacher or that he believes some one school to be better than the rest? He does not wait to hear the arguments of all the philosophers, and refutation of one and the proof of another, when in this way he chooses to be a Stoic, or a Platonist, or a Peripatetic, or an Epicurean, or a follower of some such philosophical school. Even though they do not want to admit it, it is by an unreasoning impulse that people come to the practice of, say, Stoicism and abandon the rest.[5]

Origen goes on from this to extol the virtue of Christian faith, citing Plato (who of course was not talking about Christian faith at all, but about attaining the knowledge of Ideas): 'it does not at all admit of verbal expression like other studies, but, as a result of continued application to the subject itself and communion therewith, it is brought to birth in the soul on a sudden, as light that is kindled by a leaping spark, and thereafter it nourishes itself'.[6] If this sounds like regression into self-delusion it aptly sums up the process by which people become 'born again'—in Jewish terms, *ba'alei teshuvah*; it is not a rational process.

Then again, the influence of finance on religious affiliation should not be overlooked. Even the most spiritual depend ultimately on material resources, since otherwise they would die, so we have to ask who provides those resources, and whether they provide them selectively to favoured religious groups.[7] Within the Jewish community substantial funding is made available to such groups, often fundamentalist sects, by men (rarely women) who have been successful in commerce but are ill-equipped to discriminate among religious groups on a rational basis; rather, they tend to support those whose promotional skills are best, but whose religious teachings are naïve, close to the reassuring image of Judaism the donors formed in their childhood.

Does it matter that people adopt a belief system without submitting it to rational scrutiny, especially a belief system that carries far-reaching implications for human behaviour? The answer to this is complex.

First, we must acknowledge that many people simply lack the time or skill to engage in a process of rational scrutiny. Yet the human mind/brain, like a computer, has to operate on the basis of some assumptions, or 'defaults', even if it is ready to modify or abandon these in the light of experience. We cannot *avoid* adopting a belief system, even if it is a sceptical ('I believe that we cannot

---

[5]   Origen of Caesarea, *Origen contra Celsum* I: 10 (Chadwick, 13).
[6]   Plato, *Epistle* VII, 341c, trans. R. G. Bury.
[7]   The Rothschild family's backing for the Frankfurt group who appointed S. R. Hirsch was mentioned above, p. 185.

know') or provisional one. If we lack time and skill to choose well, our choice will be a gamble; most of us will gamble that our personal inheritance is the best for us, and follow the religion or philosophy of our parents or of some teacher who has impressed us favourably.

Then, we must ask what someone means by 'adopting the system'. Are they making questionable judgements on the basis of inadequate evidence, or are they simply identifying socially with a group with whom they feel in harmony? In the latter case, which seems common, they are most likely doing no more than adopting a vocabulary, a mode of discourse, which qualifies them as members of the group; they are not involving themselves in the business of making informed judgements about religious doctrines they do not properly understand, and of whose profounder implications they are quite unaware.

A minority have time, skill, and inclination to engage in a process of rational scrutiny. As truth is preferable to falsehood, this should be the preferred option. But there is a snag. *Nobody* has the time, Jethro-like, to investigate all the world's religions thoroughly. Even experts, whose names are bywords in the field of comparative religion, rarely have a deep knowledge of more than two or three religions, and none has mastered all the languages that are essential to a study of this kind, let alone the numerous other relevant disciplines. Even if they have read some of the source literature, it is impossible to experience within the span of a human lifetime what it is like to be a follower of each and every religion; Christianity alone is said to have 38,000 different sects,[8] and who is to say which, if any, is 'true' Christianity? Then, what skills (in addition to the linguistic ones) would be required to make rational judgements about the relative truths of the different religions and all their divisions and denominations, and on what criteria would such judgements be based?

In practice, judgement is usually made on the flimsiest of evidence, and in the light of some arbitrarily pre-adopted 'theology'. Surprise, surprise: when Christians write books comparing religions it generally emerges that trinitarian theology is really what best corresponds to the 'ultimate reality'; when Jews or Muslims write the books, it turns out that pure monotheism is the only rational path, and that trinitarian doctrine is a possibly idolatrous aberration. So although the process of rational scrutiny is the preferred option, it is not a realistic option; life is not long enough, nor does the human intellect measure up to the task.

These difficulties have been responsible for much speculation about the relationship between faith and reason. Philosophers of religion have always

---

[8]   Fairchild, 'Christianity Today'.

been divided on the question of whether unaided reason could reach the 'truths' of revelation. Even those who think it could do not recommend this as the path for the simple and the uneducated, so there must be other ways of enlightenment, whether through a personal 'inner light' of some sort, or through obedience to the superior wisdom of the holy and learned (rabbis, church, *ulema*).

The tenth-century *gaon* Sa'adiah is typical of those who held that reason, correctly used, would lead to the truths of Torah. God, being merciful, did not burden us unduly with the task of discovery, but revealed these truths to us, so that we need not remain in ignorance until such time as we could find proof, nor would we be besieged by doubt, and even women and children and those lacking intellect might benefit from the knowledge.[9]

Unfortunately this position understates the fact that learned and intelligent people disagree about such matters, and bypasses the question of why 'women, children, and those lacking intellect' should listen to one of the conflicting scholars rather than to another (this is not the place to dispute Sa'adiah's aspersions on women's intellects). Sa'adiah would, no doubt, have replied that people ought to listen to *his* interpretation of Torah since it was authentic. But what is 'authenticity' and how is it recognized? This is the next question.

'Authentic Judaism'

In Chapter 21 we described how each of the three main denominations of Judaism has its distinctive way of reading Torah, reinforced by an institutional, or quasi-institutional, version for synagogue use, just as each has developed its own liturgy complete with a full range of prayer books for all occasions.

People ask, 'Which denomination is right? Which kind of Judaism is *authentic?*'

One way to understand the question is to take it to mean 'Which denomination is most conformable to truth?' If 'authentic' is taken to mean 'true' in a strong sense, such as 'correspondence to the facts', we could immediately rule out of court as inauthentic those forms of religion that insist on the literal truth of texts that are demonstrably incorrect, such as statements giving the wrong age for the earth, or the wrong date for the flood. If we take 'true' to mean 'ethically and morally correct', we could also exclude those forms of

---

[9] Sa'adiah Gaon, *Book of Beliefs and Opinions*, introd. no. 6 (Rosenblatt, 32). See also Wolfson, 'Double Faith Theory' (not to be confused with the 'double truth theory' discussed above, in Ch. 23).

Judaism that insist on literal readings of texts that are manifestly immoral, such as those calling for genocide, discriminating against women, or inculcating false values such as the acceptance of slavery. If we follow this line, we will have to declare at least some forms of Orthodox Judaism inauthentic.

A more common use of 'authentic' is 'genuine'. Which form of Judaism is 'genuine'? Now, I know what it is to ask whether a portrait of Mona Lisa is 'genuine', and how to settle the question; all I have to do is to find out whether it was painted by Leonardo himself. But how do I settle what is the 'real' Judaism (or Christianity, etc.)? This involves a judgement of what Judaism is 'really' about, and we have already seen that there are divergent opinions on this. A Reform Jew might say, as Hermann Cohen and Leo Baeck did, that Judaism is about ethical monotheism, and not 'really' about laws and rituals, even though it incorporates them; authentic Judaism in this case would be a Judaism that focused on ethical monotheism. Orthodox Judaism, in so far as it focuses on halakhah rather than on ethics *per se*, would not be authentic on this understanding.

An Orthodox Jew, on the other hand, would hold precisely the opposite. While not denying that Torah embraces ethical monotheism, he would accord a focal position to the commandments, as he understands them. If a fundamentalist, he might claim authenticity in the strong sense that the rabbinic tradition accurately articulates what God told Moses at Mount Sinai. Reform Judaism would in his eyes be 'inauthentic' and Orthodoxy 'authentic'.

Authenticity can mean conformable to truth, and can mean genuine, but neither meaning exhausts the characteristic way the term is used by community leaders. Leaders, lay or religious, use 'authentic' to establish their authority by claiming the superiority of their interpretation of the foundational texts of their religion or political party. Authenticity, for them, represents a claim to time-honoured authority, such as the authority of scripture, so that 'authentic' justifies the acts or pronouncements of the leaders on the grounds that they are 'in accordance with what scripture really means'.

This ruse for justifying the exercise of authority is not new. During the Second Temple period several Jewish sects each claimed that they were the true, or as we might say authentic, form of Judaism on the strength of the claim that they alone interpreted the Bible correctly;[10] Christians picked up the idea and ran with it, claiming to be *verus Israel*, 'the true (i.e. authentic) Israel'. The ploy is common in political circles, where someone will lay claim to being a 'true', i.e. authentic, Marxist, Thatcherite, or whatever.

From the point of view of what is true or false, therefore, it seems that it makes no sense to enquire 'What is authentic Judaism?' as if this was a

[10] Blenkinsopp, 'Interpretation and the Tendency to Sectarianism'. See Ch. 21 above.

question that could, given adequate evidence, be settled objectively, like 'What is the authentic text of Shakespeare's *Hamlet*?' Authenticity, in the context of religious associations, is more about power than about truth. If the Pope states that Roman Catholicism is 'authentic' Christianity he implicitly rules out Orthodox and Protestant claims to authority. Likewise, if a chief rabbi refers to Jewish Orthodoxy as 'authentic Judaism' he is staking a claim that only the Orthodox possess the authority to interpret Judaism. Popes, chief rabbis, and their supporters may genuinely believe that what they teach is precisely the same as what Jesus taught his disciples, or God handed down through Moses and the rabbis, but the claim to 'authenticity' incorporates more than that, namely a denial of someone else's authority and an attempt to impose one's own.

This is disconcerting. It means that debates about which form of Judaism (Christianity, Islam, or whatever) is 'authentic', or more broadly, arguments about which prophecy or writing or tradition is the 'authentic' word of God, are likely to degenerate into power games, attempts to gain control of the masses of people who are insufficiently clever, knowledgeable, or motivated to engage in the debate.

Is our question as to what will be the predominant form of Jewish belief in time to come no more than a gamble as to which challenge for power will succeed?

Survival of the Fittest

Since Edward Wilson's ground-breaking *Sociobiology* first appeared in 1975, in the wake of his earlier studies on insect populations, people have tried to apply sociobiological principles to human populations. Wilson himself engaged in such speculation, endorsing the opinion of anthropologists that 'it is a reasonable hypothesis that magic and totemism constituted direct adaptations to the environment and preceded formal religion in social adaptation', and that the concept of an active, moral, high God was associated with the move from hunter-gathering to a pastoral way of life.[11]

Can modern group-selection theory help to predict the future of the Jewish community? So far as religion is concerned, this will depend on whether religion, in particular the subtle differences between different brands of Judaism, confers adaptive advantages on a society in the modern world. '*Deus vult* was the rallying cry of the First Crusade. God wills it, but the summed Darwinian fitness of the tribe was the ultimate if unrecognized beneficiary.'[12]

---

[11] Wilson, *Sociobiology*, 560.   [12] Ibid., 561.

Religious conformism may have been advantageous to groups or individuals in the pre-modern age, but is it still so? Moreover, what is adaptive for the group may be maladaptive for the individual and vice versa.

Donald T. Campbell, in 1972, published a brief but stimulating paper on the genetics of altruism. His main point was that the behavioural dispositions which produce complex social interdependence in human beings are products of *culturally* evolved indoctrination, unlike those in insects, which are *genetically* determined; in humans, genetic competition persists among co-operators, whereas in insects, such as bees, co-operators are infertile and therefore not in genetic competition.[13] As Campbell writes: 'Probably the overall adaptive advantage for indoctrinability, group identification, and fear of ostracism is strong enough to overcome the negative selection produced when the most indoctrinable incur greater fatality in wartime.'[14] People, that is, are easily indoctrinated into patterns of belief that prepare them to give up their self-interest or even their lives for the sake of an ethnic, religious, or national group, even though it is not in their individual interest to do so; they are more like sheep that follow a leader than like bees who sting and die to save the colony.

Much progress has been made since the 1970s in understanding the evolution of altruism (in which indoctrinability is an element), especially since the introduction of games theory into the discussion. However, there are significant differences between the *biological* evolution of indoctrinability, that is, of the *capacity* of the species to accept indoctrination, and the *cultural* evolution of the forms of indoctrination, whether religious, national, or other. Whereas *biological* evolution is genetically based and not subject to short-term or politically engineered change, *cultural* evolution is far less stable, and can be manipulated. Also, biological evolution is entirely dependent on species viability, which in turn depends on successful adaptation. The persistence of cultural groups, on the other hand, is only weakly linked to biological viability, since it is possible that all members of the group survive yet abandon the culture, or alternatively that all members of the group die but are replaced by recruits from outside the group, as is the case, for instance, with celibate monastic orders.

All this makes it very difficult to predict the forms that future Jewish religious identity might take. Obviously, whatever is the fittest form of Judaism will survive better than any other form; but this is a tautology since 'fittest', in the Darwinian sense, simply means 'fittest to survive'. Also, to enquire as to forms that future Jewish *religious* identity might take conceals an

[13] Campbell, 'On the Genetics of Altruism', 21 and 35.   [14] Ibid. 33–4.

assumption which may be incorrect, viz. that the 'fittest' Jewish community will be characterized by a specific form of Jewish religion. Perhaps it won't. Perhaps what will enable a Jewish community to survive in modern conditions is not its religious orientation, but the fact that it consists of tall people, or short ones, or black ones, or rich ones, or people who are resistant to some epidemic, or who have certain political views, or some combination of some or all of these factors with or without religion. Innumerable studies on Jewish identity have assessed factors currently seen as relevant, and among them Holocaust remembrance and loyalty to the State of Israel figure prominently; but neither of these necessarily has a religious dimension and it may well be, as Lionel Kochan argued, that both devalue the past, alienating Jews from the constructive elements in their heritage.[15]

Assuming that religion *will* be a factor in the continuation of Jewish identity, we can speculate *which* form of Judaism is fittest to survive, that is, to ensure the continuity of a group of people who regard themselves as Jews by religion. Important elements making for this type of fitness include conformity with what the faithful experience of the hard facts of life, emotional appeal, reproductive policy, and the internal coherence of the system.

Demographics is undoubtedly important, more so than reason. Rodney Stark explained the growth of Christianity from an obscure sect with just forty converts in the year 30 to a majority in the Roman empire in the fourth century, a growth rate of 40 per cent a decade for over two centuries, as due not merely to its appeal to Hellenistic pagans, but to lower mortality and higher fertility, including an emphasis on male fidelity and marriage which attracted a higher percentage of female converts who in turn raised more Christian children.[16]

If we look at the reproductive policies of the three main divisions of Jewry, we see that the Orthodox are the most vigorous in promoting reproduction as a religious virtue; among the Orthodox the *haredim* not only preach but earnestly practise what they see as the virtue of producing large families. Current demographics suggest that within the foreseeable future the bulk of the identifiably Jewish population will consist of Orthodox Jews, most of whom will be *haredi*.[17]

But this will not necessarily happen. Reproductive rates are not stable over several generations, nor can it be assumed that children of *haredi* parents will choose to remain within the *haredi* communities. Demography, like weather

---

[15] Kochan, *Jewish Renaissance*, especially ch. 4.

[16] Stark, *Rise of Christianity*. E. Kaufmann, 'Breeding for God', has reviewed evidence for a reversal of the securalizing trends of the past century and the impact of higher fertility among the religious.   [17] See for instance Graham, Schmool, and Waterman, *Jews in Britain*.

forecasting, is only a short-term guide, since the system is inherently chaotic, that is, it is extremely sensitive to variations in initial conditions which can never be determined with absolute precision, and predictions are unsafe since they can be upset both by feedback from within the system and by interference from outside. The *ḥaredi* population, or even the worldwide Jewish population, constitutes less than half of one percent of the global population, and is neither biologically nor culturally isolated from it in such a way that it could be treated as an independent evolutionary system.

The meteorological analogy can be taken further. Though detailed weather patterns cannot be forecast more than a few days ahead, the broad patterns of weather are more stable; we can be reasonably certain, for instance, that it will be hotter on average in summer than in winter in the northern hemisphere. Perhaps we can be just as certain that the *balance* of communities will follow a stable pattern; just as there are fairly predictable rainy seasons and dry seasons, so there are times when conservatives predominate over liberals and other times when liberals predominate over conservatives. But even that is uncertain; 'rainy' and 'dry' are far clearer concepts than 'conservative' and 'liberal', nor do 'conservative' and 'liberal' (with small c and l) correspond exactly with the gradation from Orthodox through Conservative to Reform; there are conservatives and liberals in all three camps.

William H. Durham has investigated the relationship between cultural and genetic evolution. He argues for three hypotheses on *coevolution*, that is, the way change is brought about through a combination of genetic and cultural factors:

1. Primary values are decision processes dependent on the structure of the nervous system; they are dominated by genetic evolution. Secondary values stem from collective experience and social history; they include languages, designs, and food processes, and are dominated by cultural evolution;[18] 'secondary value selection' is the main but not exclusive means of modification.

2. The gene–culture relationship operates in multiple modes.

3. Genes and culture evolve in co-operation.[19]

However, almost all the evidence that he adduces is based on observations of tribal societies that have limited contact with each other or the outside world, so that to some degree it is possible to isolate the factors that channel cultural development in a particular direction. Presumably selection of the 'secondary values' that characterize the separate branches of Judaism are dominated by

---

[18] Durham, *Coevolution*, 199–210, 451.   [19] Ibid. 433–44.

cultural rather than genetic factors, but this fact has little predictive value in a situation where the societies concerned are involved in constant complex interactions with the rest of the world.

Yet another avenue for hazarding predictions about societies was opened up by Clifford Brown and Walter Witschey. Brown and Witschey surveyed the geometry of the settlement patterns of the peoples of Mayapán, and related this to their sudden and almost complete demise well before the arrival of the Spanish *conquistadores*. They concluded that the 'fractal patterns of Maya settlement, some of which have the fractal dimensions of the same magnitude as those for forest fires and wars . . . and the historical patterns fulfil all of the criteria and expectations of a self-organized critical model', and speculated that 'analysis of the archaeological record will eventually show that early states were self-organized critical systems that were far from equilibrium'.[20] If Brown and Witschey are correct it should be possible to predict the future of the Jewish people or of any of its constituent parts from an analysis of the fractal dimensions of their settlement patterns. However, it has yet to be demonstrated that this method has greater predictive value than augury by entrails, or by demographic modelling.

Conclusion

No method is available to predict which, if any, of the current forms of Judaism will be the predominant form of Judaism in time to come. Differential rates of reproduction in different groups will certainly influence the outcome in the short to medium term, but in the long term may be outweighed by other factors.

There is no reason to suppose that future choices will be governed by evidence and logic, since few people make their life choices in that way. Nor, if we attach a definite meaning to the term 'authentic', can we suppose that 'authentic' (in any currently understood sense) Judaism will prevail, though undoubtedly whichever form does prevail will *proclaim* itself authentic, appropriating the authority of tradition and seeking to control the community.

Community leaders are primarily concerned with preservation of the community, whether to sustain their own positions or from altruistic motives. Either way, they will tend to encourage those forms of Judaism that appear to them to strengthen the sense of unity and encourage fertility; however, they will not necessarily be followed by the wealthy benefactors who, by distribution of their wealth, influence the growth or otherwise of religious trends.

---

[20] Brown and Witschey, 'Fractal Geometry of Ancient Maya Settlement', 1629.

Individuals may perceive their self-interest in the preservation of the community, and so follow the leaders. In a democratic and individualistic society well-meaning individuals will be more concerned with the pursuit of truth and what they perceive as virtue, and this may lead them away from community norms, or even away from the community altogether; at the other end of the scale, self-seeking individuals may be led away from the community by seeking their personal advantage.

I cannot predict what will happen, but for the sake of myself, my family, and like-minded people, I very much hope that the Jewish community will always welcome in its midst genuine seekers after truth, awkward and nonconforming though some of them may be.

TWENTY SIX

CONFRONTING CHANGE

On the first day of September 1730, the green plains and white villages of southwest Lanzarote were suddenly overwhelmed by the most spectacular eruption in memory, whether for duration of the phenomenon—six years—or for the immensity of the lava flow that buried ten villages and covered a quarter of the island with a mantle of incandescent magma.

ALBERT VASQUEZ FIGUERA, 'Océano', on the Lanzarote eruption of 1730

A Meditation at the Mountains of Fire (January 2004)

Montañas del Fuego, Lanzarote, Canary Islands

It is six years since I was last here. Little suspecting that it would be our last vacation together, I rode with my wife Devora (1932–98) through the tortured landscape of Timanfaya National Park. Guides explained its volcanic history, culminating in the devastating eruptions of 1730–6. We were located some 4,000 metres above a residual lava chamber, still causing geothermal anomalies at the surface with temperatures up to 610°C. Boiling steam erupted from fissures in the ground, and the Park Restaurant promised a meal cooked on stones just below where we stood. The ground beneath our feet felt ominously unstable.

Devora several times uttered the Hebrew words *oseh ma'aseh bereshit* ('[God] who performed the work of creation') that conclude the blessing we pronounce over stirring natural events. We experienced a strong sense of being present at a creative process, at the birth of a new thing. The world was not indeed being created *ex nihilo*, but it was certainly being re-formed.

Those of us who live far from areas of seismic disturbance easily delude ourselves into assuming that 'the earth abideth forever' (Ecclesiastes 1: 4), stable, as it was created. Even the inhabitants of such areas quickly forget the instability, rushing to replant the fertile slopes of an Etna or a Vesuvius.

In an age of faith we would attribute the occasional quake to a special act of divine intervention. Now we see earthquakes and volcanic eruptions as 'natural' events, no more acts of God than other manifestations of nature, yet no less acts of God than creation itself. Living with nature means living with change; only the brevity of the human lifespan relative to geological processes allows the illusion of stability.

What is true of nature is true of culture and of culture's artefact, religion. None of the world's major religions is more than a few thousand years old, a mere fragment of the known history of humanity; and if earth is a year old, the whole history of humanity packs into the final minute.

Priests strive to create an illusion of permanence and finality—'Torah is Eternal', 'Qur'an is the Final Revelation.' When we dared to ask in the context of Judaism, 'What is permanent?' we found that we were chasing shadows, grasping fine sand. We could not be absolutely sure of a basic Torah text, let alone of its interpretation. We found that theologians throughout the ages retained a vocabulary but constantly modified its meaning. 'Torah' did not mean the same to Maimonides as to his kabbalistic contemporaries, let alone to Rabbi Akiva and, say, Franz Rosenzweig, separated by 1,800 years.

Beneath the appearance of stability and of continuity lie the rumblings and eruptions of cultural change and the growth of human knowledge and skills. At no time was there a greater or more sustained disruption than that generated by the intellectual and social turmoils of the Renaissance and the modern (including 'postmodern') age. The tremors that have shaken the West in recent centuries have not yet subsided; they have spread to other civilizations across the globe, destabilizing societies and cultures.

Denial has been strong. People shrink from recognizing that change is taking place, since it undermines the certainties that make life comfortable and meaningful. Or if they do perceive change, they attribute it to wilful malevolence on the part of some enemy, real or imaginary; historical criticism, for instance, is attributed to atheists or secularists (if you are a Christian), to antisemites (if you are a Jew), or to Western decadence and imperialism (if you are a Muslim). The Catholic citizens of Timanfaya no doubt attributed the volcanic eruption to divine intervention visited on them for their sins, just as Jeremiah had attributed the Babylonian exile to the sins of Israel, and as people in earlier times might have blamed their misfortunes on malevolent deities. In no case do people easily accept that the status quo has radically changed, that the world has moved on and will never be exactly the same again.

Coming to Terms with Modernity

As soon as Timanfaya ceased erupting in 1736 nature began to re-establish itself. Lichens (there are now some 200 species on the island) were the first to establish, breaking the lava into fertile soil for colonization by higher plants; invertebrates paved the way for birds and mammals; the human population recovered, began to till the soil once again, and even to take advantage of the peculiar opportunities created by a new landscape. Normality returned to the island, though it was not the normality that had existed previously. To the new generations this was the definitive normality, to be accepted as if it had always been, and to be defended against the inveterate enemy, change.

Much the same happens in culture and religion. Though on the world scale the turbulence stirred up by modernity continues to wreak cultural havoc, in the West the new outlook has become normal. Apart from antiquarians and the religious, people have forgotten the world-view of the preceding age, and adapted to a new normality, centred on the political doctrine of the equality and right to personal freedom of the individual, irrespective of race, gender, or creed, and on the scientific attitude of doubt, experiment, and observation rather than reliance on authority.

We can no longer read the ancient texts as the ancients wrote them, or as our medieval forebears read them, because our normality is not their normality. When we read their texts, we make adjustments, wittingly or unwittingly.

We make *philosophical* adjustments. We interpret biblical anthropomorphisms ('the hand of God') as metaphors or symbols, or at the very least as possessing some 'deep meaning' other than the literal. This way of reading has ample precedent in rabbinic tradition, particularly in the Aramaic Targumim and in the medieval philosophical tradition, whereas Talmud, midrash, and kabbalah are less squeamish or consistent, and often quite blatantly anthropomorphic.

We make *scientific* adjustments. When we read the opening chapter of Genesis, we either attempt to harmonize the text with current cosmology, or we dismiss the ancient cosmology as simply part of the language of the time and draw attention instead to the 'underlying message' of the creation stories. When we read, in the story of Noah, that 'the windows of heaven were opened' (Gen. 7: 11), we take it as a metaphor, although there is little doubt that it was intended literally—as late as the Talmud the rabbis discourse with every appearance of seriousness about the seven heavens, of which the sixth (counting downwards), called *makhon*, houses stores of snow, hail, and assorted meteorological properties that God or his agents occasionally decant over us earthlings.[1]

We make *moral* adjustments. The genocide of the Canaanites is either condemned outright (for which there is no precedent in the early sources), or 'explained away' in accordance with rabbinic precedent as an act mandated by God on account of the peculiar needs of the time, but inapplicable 'in our day'. We argue (like the Talmud) that the permission in Deuteronomy 21: 10–14 to take a captive woman in war, or (unlike the Talmud) the condoning of slavery, were concessions to human weakness, discouraged though not forbidden by the Torah.[2]

We adjust to *outmoded metaphors*. If the Bible, or the rabbis, or the liturgy, portray God as an autocratic monarch who has to be propitiated, we are uncomfortable; the image doesn't work for us, since we no longer respect autocrats. We don't approach our own leaders with the self-abasement, propitiation with gifts, and appeal through influential intercessors that we associate with the court life of corrupt rulers; our leaders would probably despise us if we did, so why should such behaviour be pleasing to God? How do we explain to our democratic children that God is even greater than a 'king of kings', a powerful metaphor in its time but otiose and inept now? But we *do* explain, cautiously adjusting our image of kings.

We make *historical* adjustments, modifying our account of biblical and rabbinic history in the light of archaeological and literary evidence from external sources.

We make *practical* adjustments. Halakhah, even in the hands of the rabbis, was at some distance from biblical standards; for instance, the *prozbul* attributed to Hillel recognized the growing need for commercial credit, and effectively circumvented the cancellation of debts in the sabbatical year.[3] I commented, in Chapter 24, on the modification of halakhah in the light of social, economic, and historical changes, and noted that the difference between Orthodox, Conservative, and Reform was of degree rather than principle.

Some of us use midrashic precedent and 'postmodern' techniques to read text homiletically, abandoning all pretence of recovering the plain or original meaning, and even denying the legitimacy of such a concept as 'plain or original meaning'. In this, conservatives, such as those who adopt Malbim's contention (Chapter 14) that 'the exegesis of the sages *is* the *peshat*, the plain

---

[1] BT *Ḥag.* 12b. Later commentators interpret the whole passage in a mystical fashion, proving my point about the inevitability of 'adjustment'.

[2] BT *Kid.* 21b.   [3] Mishnah *Git.* 4: 3.

and straightforward meaning of the scriptural text', appear to join hands with the postmodernists in rejecting the notion that a text has a meaning of its own, independent of the reader; but where the traditionalists grant none but the sages authority to read, the postmodernists allow this privilege to each and every reader.

Because our world-view has been transformed and we have access to a far greater knowledge base, it is impossible for us to read as our predecessors did. *Impossible*, not merely undesirable. We might think we are reading in the same way, but we are not. Even if we use precisely the same words as those who preceded us, their meaning will have changed. Rashi, paraphrasing rabbinic comments on Exodus 14: 6, writes that Pharaoh sent officers to accompany the Israelites; when the officers reported after four days that the Israelites were not coming back, Pharaoh dispatched his army in pursuit of the Israelites; on the seventh night the Egyptians went down to the sea (and were drowned); the Israelites sang the Song of Praise (Exod. 15) in the morning, which is why we read it on the seventh day of Passover. No doubt Rashi meant exactly what he wrote, in the most literal fashion; in his time, the eleventh century, there was no reason to think it was other than a reasonable reconstruction of events. I might make the same comment today, but my *tone* would be different; I would not be engaging in historical discourse, but constructing an imaginary scene to link contemporary liturgical practice with biblical text. I might not even be committing myself to the belief that an Exodus actually took place. If I insisted on the same literal understanding as Rashi my words would not convey the same message to my hearers as Rashi's did to his; he was formulating a perfectly reasonable historical statement, given the information available to him, but I would be adopting a confrontational position, implying that the archaeological and ancient literary evidence should be ignored, and that history should be based exclusively on rabbinic homily.

This confirms Heraclitus' saying that you can't jump into the same river twice. The water has flowed on. The world has changed. You may repeat the words, but the message has altered; the form of the river is constant, but the water is new.

Intellectual Violence

In the light of the evidence assembled in this book, evidence readily available to anyone who seeks it and easy to understand, you may wonder why much of the Orthodox Jewish world is still committed to a rigorous, traditional interpretation of 'Torah from Heaven'. Not that they are exceptional in this:

similar beliefs in the *absolute* truth of scripture are common among the more conservative communities of Christians, Muslims, and people of other faiths, and secular groups too—for instance, political groups such as Marxists and Trotskyists—are equally resistant to evidence that casts doubts on their convictions. We are not dealing here with some weakness peculiar to Judaism, but with a universal human reluctance to relinquish an apparent guarantee of certainty.

Of course, it will not do to assess the extent of popular belief by listening to statements of the Orthodox religious leadership, nor are the numerous surveys of religious belief conducted by sociologists of much value, since religious belief is too nebulous to be subjected to statistical analysis like preferences for brands of soap powder. But undoubtedly a lot of people who consider themselves Orthodox react as if shocked or upset when doubts are cast on the historical value of biblical data or the wisdom of the great rabbis, and there is always a ready market for books that 'prove' the Bible is true and the tradition authentic.

Much popular belief stems from recollection of half-understood lessons in childhood. Ordinary Orthodox Jews, unable or unwilling to teach their children themselves, send them to religion classes staffed by fundamentalist groups, such as Lubavitch (Habad) hasidim, who engage in educational and social activities as a forum to promote their way of thinking. It does not seem to occur to parents that in handing their immature children into the care of religious extremists they are subjecting them to a form of intellectual violence possibly more damaging in the long run than physical abuse; or if they are confident that they can counteract what they regard as incorrect teaching, that they are exposing their children to a situation which will make Judaism, or at least Orthodox Judaism, ridiculous in their eyes.

Young men and women, full of the best intentions, enrol for a year or more in the numerous yeshivas and seminaries at which religious texts are intensively studied; the burgeoning numbers of students at such institutions in recent years guarantee a public familiarity and engagement with source texts which would have been the envy of previous generations. Many of the teachers are knowledgeable, open-minded, and accessible, but severe limits are placed on acceptable belief as well as behaviour, and there is considerable peer pressure to conform. The teachers themselves are usually under the sway of one or more of an invisible hierarchy of heads of traditional yeshivas, leading halakhists, or hasidic rebbes, who are of very conservative outlook. These *gedolei hatorah*, 'great ones of Torah', are less easily approachable, and have to be treated with a deference that does not make for light and easy conversation. It is generally impossible to engage in useful discussion with them on matters such as the significance of variant biblical manuscripts, or most other topics with which this book is concerned, since they make a virtue of ignoring anything suspected of being un-Jewish or heretical, that is, of anything other than the traditionally accepted rabbinic sources. It may well be that the situation will change, but for the time being conformity is expected, in such circles, with hardline beliefs adumbrated in reaction to the challenges of the Enlightenment. The Enlightenment and 'Western decadence' are as much the enemy in the traditional yeshiva as in the fundamentalist Christian seminary and Islamic madrasa.

Who Decides?

The reality of Orthodox society is that the invisible hierarchy, not any official rabbinical authority, defines acceptable belief and practice. But this is to simplify a complex social interaction where public mood, defensiveness, social and family pressures, and lack of a clearly defined leadership all have a part to play.

No one, indeed, is openly coerced into accepting dictates of the invisible hierarchy; they neither form a government nor are upheld by one. In principle, in Israel as well as elsewhere in the free world, the autonomous conscience of the individual reigns supreme in matters of religion. But social pressures are strong; family, society, nation, and the global ethos mould, if they do not entirely determine, the individual conscience.

These pressures do not all act in the same direction; society, nation, and the world at large may not concur with family, or there may be some other line of division. Sometimes an individual may break the mould; more commonly, he or she will live on different levels, paying respect to tradition in the home and synagogue, happily and even fervently endorsing a belief system which he or she blithely ignores in the lecture hall or at work. Only the few will have the motivation and perseverance to sort things out one way or another; most bumble haphazardly between two worlds, pulled in one direction by holy exemplars and in another by Enlightenment values. How do you choose between holiness and truth? (That which is false cannot be holy; on the other hand, that which is true is not necessarily holy.)

What I Have Dealt With

We have discussed the doctrine of 'Torah from Heaven', observed its development from the earliest times to the present, and examined attempts at reformulating it.

Our conclusion was not that the doctrine be abandoned, nor that it be radically modified, as for instance by requiring that certain sections of the Pentateuch be excluded from it. Our simple recommendation was that its logical status be changed from that of an historical statement to that of a foundational myth.

This is definitely not the traditional view expressed, for instance, by Maimonides. However, intellectual honesty in addressing new evidence and new moral perceptions force the abandonment of the straight historical interpretation. Among the advantages that accrue from treating *torah min hashamayim* as a foundational myth are (1) we are able to continue using traditional religious language, if with a modified interpretation, (2) the myth is easily extended to incorporate both written and oral Torah, as well as Jewish custom and later developments, and (3) since myth is impervious to historical evidence, moral questioning, and the like, we do not have to 'pick and choose' which bits of tradition to regard as 'Torah from Heaven'; we simply tell the story.

What I Have Not Dealt With

In the opening chapter, 'Orientation', I observed that Torah from Heaven is only one part of a bigger story, involving philosophical problems about the concepts of God and of Revelation, as well as general questions arising out of the clash between the scientific and religious world-views. In this book I have simply assumed that 'God' and 'Revelation' are coherent concepts, and I have not confronted head-on the conflicts between science and religion. Treating 'Torah from Heaven' as foundational myth in fact bypasses many of these profound issues, since it is compatible with almost any understanding of God and Revelation, from the traditional to the 'demythologized'.

Nevertheless, the topics remain important in their own right, and certainly deserve the serious attention of scholars and theologians. At the beginning of this book I recollected how, as a child, I sat in the synagogue and mused about the meaning of 'The Lord spoke to Moses saying'. I still don't understand it, though I am less worried than I was. Nor have the great scholars and theologians who debate such weighty matters enlightened me yet, so I must resign myself to continuing uncertainty and confusion.

I shall not therefore conclude *fortissimo*, with a paean of triumph, celebrating a Grand and Original New Theory to solve all problems, but rather, like the Fourth Symphony of Sibelius, in the *mezzo forte*, and with restraint. Many false claims have been rejected, and that is progress; if what I have put in their place is less loud and clamorous, it does at least stand on a firm foundation of evidence that is there for all to see. As Rabbi Tarfon said, 'The task is not yours to complete, but nor are you free to desist from it.'[4]

---

[4] Mishnah *Avot* 2: 16.

Bibliography

◆

ADANG, CAMILLA, *Muslim Writers on Judaism and the Hebrew Bible* (Leiden: E. J. Brill, 1996).

ALBALAG, ISAAC, *Sefer tikun hade'ot leyitsḥak albalag*, ed. G. Vajda (Jerusalem: Israel Academy of Sciences and Humanities, 1973).

ALEXANDER, PHILIP, 'Why No Textual Criticism in Rabbinic Midrash?', in George J. Brooke (ed.), *Jewish Ways of Reading the Bible* (Journal of Semitic Studies Supplement 11) (Oxford: Oxford University Press, 2000), 175–90.

ALTMANN, ALEXANDER, *Moses Mendelssohn* (London: Routledge & Kegan Paul, 1973).

—— (ed.), *Biblical and Other Studies* (Cambridge, Mass.: Harvard University Press, 1963).

—— (ed.), *Jewish Medieval and Renaissance Studies* (Cambridge, Mass.: Harvard University Press, 1967).

—— and S. M. STERN, *Isaac Israeli* (Oxford: Oxford University Press, 1958).

ARISTOTLE, *De caelo*.

—— *De generatione animalium*.

—— *De interpretatione*.

—— *Metaphysics*, trans. Hugh Tredennick (Loeb Classical Library, 271) (Cambridge, Mass.: Harvard University Press, 1933).

ARMSTRONG, A. HILARY (ed.), *Cambridge History of Later Greek and Early Medieval Philosophy* (Cambridge: Cambridge University Press, 1967).

ASTRUC, JEAN, *Conjectures sur les mémoires originaux dont il paroit que Moyse s'est servi pour composer le livre de la Genese* (1753).

ATHANASIUS, *Festal (Easter) Epistles*, in Philip Schaff and Henry Wace, *The Nicene and Post-Nicene Fathers*, 2nd edn., vol. iv (Grand Rapids, Mich: W. B. Eerdmans, 1971), 506–53.

AZRIEL OF GIRONA, *Commentary on the Aggadot* (Heb.), ed. I. Tishbi (Jerusalem: Mekitze Nirdamim with Mosad Harav Kook, 1945).

BADER, ROBERT, *Der alēthēs logos des Kelsos* (Tübinger Beiträge zur Altertumswissenschaft 33) (Stuttgart: Kohlhammer Verlag, 1940).

BAECK, LEO, *The Essence of Judaism*, trans. Victor Grubwieser and Leonard Pearl (London: Macmillan, 1936; based on the 6th German edn., 1932).

BANETH, D. H., 'Maimonides as Translator of his own Works' (Heb.), *Tarbiz*, 23 (1952), 170–91.

BAR-ILAN, MEIR, *Astrology and Other Sciences among the Jews in the Land of Israel during the Hellenistic–Roman and Byzantine Periods* [Astrologiyah umada'im aḥerim bein yehudei erets yisra'el batekufot hahelenistit–romit vehabizantit] (Jerusalem: Mosad Bialik, 2010).

BARKAI, GAVRIEL, 'The Priestly Benediction of the Ketef Hinnom Plaques' (Heb.), *Cathedra*, 52 (1989), 37–76.

BAR-KOCHVA, BEZALEL, *Pseudo-Hecataeus on the Jews: Legitimizing the Jewish Diaspora* (Hellenistic Culture and Society XXI) (Berkeley, Calif.: University of California Press, 1996).

BARTON, JOHN, *Holy Writings, Sacred Text* (Louisville, Ky.: Westminster John Knox Press, 1997).

BARUCH OF SHKLOV, *Euclid* (Heb.) (The Hague, 1780).

—— *Keneh hamidah* (Prague, 1784).

BAUER, GEORG LORENZ, *Biblische Theologie des Alten und Neuen Testaments* (Leipzig, 1796, 1802).

BAYLE, PIERRE, *De la tolérance: Commentaire philosophique*, ed. Jean-Michel Gros (Paris: H. Champion, 2006).

BEN-DOV, JONATHAN, 'The Initial Stages of Lunar Theory at Qumran', *Journal of Jewish Studies*, 44/1 (Spring 2003), 125–40.

BEN ISRAEL, MANASSEH, *see* Manasseh ben Israel

BEN-MENAHEM, N., 'Two Letters of Rabbi Jacob Tzvi Mecklenburg' (Heb.), *Sinai*, 65 (1969), 327–32.

Bereshit rabati, ed. Ch. Albeck (Jerusalem: Mekitze Nirdamim, 1940).

BERGER, MICHAEL S., *Rabbinic Authority* (New York: Oxford University Press, 1998).

BERLIN, ADELE, and MARC ZVI BRETTLER (eds.), *The Jewish Study Bible* (New York: Oxford University Press, 2004).

BERLIN, NAFTALI TSEVI YEHUDAH, *Ha'amek davar* (Vilna, 1879–80).

—— *Ha'amek she'elah*, 3 vols. (Vilna, 1861, 1864, 1867).

Bible *see* Berlin and Brettler (eds.), *Jewish Study Bible*; A. Cohen (ed.), *The Soncino Chumash*; *Etz Hayim*; Plaut, *The Torah: A Modern Commentary*; Sherman (ed.), *The Torah: Haftaros and Five Megillos*; Zlotowitz (ed.), *The Megillah*.

BLANSHARD, BRAND, *The Nature of Thought*, vol. ii (London: George Allen & Unwin, 1939; repr. London: Routledge, 2002).

BLENKINSOPP, JOSEPH, 'Interpretation and the Tendency to Sectarianism: An Aspect of Second Temple History', in E. P. Sanders (ed.), *Jewish and Christian Self-Definition*, vol. ii (London: SCM Press, 1981), 1–26.

BLUMENTHAL, DAVID, *Understanding Jewish Mysticism: The Merkabah Tradition and the Zoharic Tradition* (New York: Ktav, 1978).

BLUTINGER, JEFFREY C., '"So-Called Orthodoxy": The History of an Unwanted Label', *Modern Judaism*, 27/3 (2007), 310–28.

BREUER, E., 'Between Haskalah and Orthodoxy: The Writings of R. Jacob Zvi Mecklenburg', *Hebrew Union College Annual*, 66 (1995), 259–87.

BREUER, ISAAC, *Concepts of Judaism*, ed. Jacob S. Levinger (Jerusalem: Israel Universities Press, 1974).

—— *Mein Weg* (Jerusalem/Zürich: Morascha Verlag, 1988).

—— *Der Neue Kusari* (Frankfurt am Main: Verlag der Rabbiner-Hirsch-Gesellschaft, 1934).

BREUER, MORDECAI, 'Faith and Science in Biblical Interpretation' (Heb.), *De'ot*, 11 (1953), 18–25; 12 (1960), 12–27.

BRISSON, LUC, *Plato the Myth Maker* (Chicago, Ill.: University of Chicago Press, 1999).

BROOKE, GEORGE J., 'Some Remarks on 4Q252 and the Text of Genesis', *Textus*, 19 (1998), 1–25.

BROWN, CLIFFORD T. and WALTER R. T. WITSCHEY, 'The Fractal Geometry of Ancient Maya Settlement', *Journal of Archaeological Science*, 30 (2003), 1619–32.

BUBER, MARTIN, *I and Thou*, 2nd edn., trans. R. Gregor Smith (Edinburgh: T. & T. Clark, 1958).

BUXTORF, JOHANNES (II), *Tractatus de punctorum vocalium, et accentuum, in libris Veteris Testamenti Hebraicis, origine, antiquitate, & authoritate: oppositus Arcano punctationis revelato, Ludovici Cappelli* (Basle, 1648).

CAMPBELL, DONALD T., 'On the Genetics of Altruism and the Counter-Hedonic Components in Human Culture', *Journal of Social Issues*, 28(3), 21–37.

CAPPEL, LOUIS, *Hoc est arcanum punctationis revelatum* (1624).

CASAUBON, ISAAC, *De rebus sacris et ecclesiasticis* (1654).

CASSUTO, UMBERTO, *Biblical and Oriental Studies*, 2 vols., trans. Israel Abrahams (Jerusalem: Magnes Press, 1973, 1975).

—— *A Commentary on the Book of Exodus*, trans. Israel Abrahams (Jerusalem: Magnes Press, 1967).

—— *A Commentary on the Book of Genesis*, 2 vols., trans. Israel Abrahams (Jerusalem: Magnes Press, 1961, 1964).

—— *The Documentary Hypothesis and the Composition of the Pentateuch: Eight Lectures*, trans. Israel Abrahams (Jerusalem: Magnes Press, 1961).

—— *The Goddess Anath: Canaanite Epics of the Patriarchal Age*, trans. Israel Abrahams (Jerusalem: Magnes Press, 1971).

CHAMBERLAIN, H. S., *Grundlagen des XIX. Jahrhunderts*, 2 vols. (Munich, 1899); trans. J. Lees, *The Foundations of the Nineteenth Century*, 2 vols. (London: Bodley Head, 1911).

CHARLES, R. H., *The Apocrypha and Pseudepigrapha of the Old Testament in English*, 2 vols. (Oxford: Clarendon Press, 1913).

—— *The Assumption of Moses, Translated from the Latin Sixth Century MS.* (London: A. and C. Black, 1897).

CHARLESWORTH, JAMES H., *The Old Testament Pseudepigrapha*, 2 vols. (Garden City, NY: Doubleday, 1983–5).

Chartularium universitatis pariensus, ed. H. Denifle and A. Chatelain, vol. i (Paris, 1889).

CHLADENIUS, JOHANN MARTIN (CHLADNI), *Einleitung zur richtigen Auslegung vernünftiger Reden und Schriften* (Leipzig, 1742: repr., with introd. by Lutz Geldsetzer, Düsseldorf: Stern-Verlag Janssen, 1969).

CICERO, *De divinatione*, trans. W. A. Falconer (Loeb Classical Library 154) (Cambridge, Mass.: Harvard University Press, 1923).

—— *De legibus*.

CLEMENT OF ALEXANDRIA, *Stromata*, in Alain Le Boulluec (ed.), *Clémont d'Alexandre: Les Stromates: Stromate V* (Paris: Editions du Cerf, 2006).

COHEN, A. (ed.), *The Soncino Chumash: The Five Books of Moses with Haphtaroth: Hebrew Text and English Translation with an Exposition Based on the Classical Jewish Commentaries* (Hindhead: Soncino Press, 1947).

COHEN, HERMANN, *Religion of Reason out of the Sources of Judaism*, trans. Simon Kaplan (New York: Frederick Ungar, 1972).

CRAIG, EDWARD (ed.), *Routledge Encyclopaedia of Philosophy*, 10 vols. (London: Routledge, 1998).

DAUBE, D., 'Rabbinic Methods of Interpretation and Hellenistic Rhetoric', *Hebrew Union College Annual*, 22 (1949), 239–64.

DAVIDSON, ISRAEL, *Saadia's Polemic against Ḥiwi al-Balchi* (New York: Jewish Theological Seminary of America, 1915).

—— (ed.), *Book of the Wars of the Lord* (New York: Jewish Theological Seminary of America, 1934).

DE BEAUVOIR, SIMONE, *Le Deuxième Sexe* (Paris: Gallimard, 1949).

DELITZSCH, FRIEDRICH, *Die grosse Täuschung*, 2 vols. (Stuttgart: Deutsche Verlags-Anstalt, 1921–2).

DE' ROSSI, AZARIAH, *The Light of the Eyes by Azariah de' Rossi*, trans. with introd. and notes by J. Weinberg (New Haven: Yale University Press, 2001).

DE' ROSSI, SALOMONE, *Hashirim asher lishelomoh* (Venice, 1622/3).

DILLER, HANS, Review of *Galeni in Hippocratis Epidemiarum Libr. VI Comm. I–VIII*, ed. E. Wenkebach and F. Pfaff (Leipzig: Teubner, 1940), *Gnomon*, 22 (1950), 226–35.

DIODORUS SICULUS, *Bibliotheca historica*.

DOTAN, ARON, *Ben Asher's Creed: A Study of the History of the Controversy* (Missoula, Mont.: Scholars Press, 1977).

DROSNIN, MICHAEL, *The Bible Code* (London: Orion Books, 1997).

DRUCK, DAVID, 'The Gaon Rabbi Jacob Tsevi Mecklenberg' (Heb.), *Horeb*, 4 (1937), 171–9.

DUNHAM, WILLIAM, *Journey through Genius* (New York: Penguin, 1991).

DURHAM, WILLIAM H., *Coevolution: Genes, Culture, and Human Diversity* (Palo Alto, Calif.: Stanford University Press, 1991).

ELIACH, YAFFA, 'The Russian Dissenting Sects and their Influence on Israel Baal Shem Tov, Founder of Hasidism', *Proceedings of the American Academy for Jewish Research*, 36 (1968), 57–83.

ELIJAH OF VILNA, *Aderet eliyahu*, ed. Isaac Eisik Wildmann, 2 vols. (Jerusalem: 1988).

—— *Be'ur hagra*, commentary on Joseph Karo, *Shulḥan arukh*, 'Yoreh de'ah', 3 vols. (New York: Schulsinger Bros., 1953) .

—— *Pe'at hashulḥan* (Safed, 1836).

—— *Sifra ditsniuta im be'ur hagra* (Jerusalem: Hamesorah, 1985/6).

ELLENSON, DAVID, and RICHARD JACOBS, 'Scholarship and Faith: David Hoffman and his Relationship to Wissenschaft des Judentums', *Modern Judaism*, 8 (1988), 27–40.

EL-OR, TAMAR, *Next Year I Will Know More: Literacy and Identity among Young*

Orthodox Women in Israel, trans. Haim Watzman (Detroit: Wayne State University Press, 2002). Original Hebrew edn.: *Befesaḥ haba* (Tel Aviv: Am Oved, 1998).

Encyclopedia Judaica, 16 vols. (Jerusalem: Keter, 1972).

ENELOW, H. G., *Mishnat rabi eli'ezer* (New York, 1933).

Entsiklopediyah mikra'it, 9 vols. (Jerusalem: Mosad Bialik, 1965–88).

EPIPHANIUS, *Treatise on Weights and Measures: The Syriac Version*, ed. J. E. Dean (Chicago, Ill.: University of Chicago Press, 1935).

EPSTEIN, JACOB N., *Introduction to Tannaitic Literature* [Mevo'ot lesifrut hatana'im] (Jerusalem: Magnes Press, 1957).

ETKES, IMMANUEL, *The Gaon of Vilna: The Man and his Image*, trans. Jeffrey M. Green (Berkeley, Ca.: University of California Press, 2002). Original Hebrew edn. *Yaḥid bedoro* (Jerusalem: Merkaz Zalman Shazar, 1998).

Etz Hayim: Torah and Commentary, ed. David L. Lieber (Philadelphia, Pa.: Jewish Publication Society, 2001).

EUSEBIUS OF CAESAREA, *Ecclesiastical History*, vol. i, trans. Kirsopp Lake; vol. ii, trans. J. E. L. Oulton (Loeb Classical Library, 153, 265) (Cambridge, Mass.: Harvard University Press, 1926, 1932).

—— *Praeparatio Evangelica*, trans. E. H. Gifford (Oxford: Oxford University Press, 1903).

FACKENHEIM, EMIL L., *The Jewish Bible after the Holocaust: A Re-reading* (Manchester: Manchester University Press, 1990).

FAIERSTEIN, MORRIS M., *All Is in the Hands of Heaven: The Teachings of Rabbi Mordecai Joseph Leiner of Izbica* (New York: Yeshiva University, 1989).

FAIRCHILD, MARY, 'Christianity Today—General Statistics and Facts of Christianity', About.com Guide; <http://christianity.about.com/od/denominations/p/christian today.htm>.

FEINSTEIN, MOSHE, *Igerot mosheh*, 7 vols. (vols. i–v: New York, 1959–73; vols. vi–vii: Benei Berak, 1982–5).

FELDMAN, LOUIS H., *Jew and Gentile in the Ancient World: Attitudes and Interactions from Alexander to Justinian* (Princeton: Princeton University Press, 1993).

FELDMAN, W. H., *Rabbinic Mathematics and Astronomy* (London, 1931; repr. New York: Hermon Press, n.d.).

FEUCHTWANGER, O., *Righteous Lives: Forty-Two Leaders of Jewish Thought in the Last Ten Centuries* (Letchworth: Lehmann, 1965).

FEUERBACH, LUDWIG, *The Essence of Christianity*, trans. George Eliot (New York: Harper & Row, 1957).

—— *Die Philosophie der Zukunft* (1843; repr. Stuttgart: Frommann's Philosophische Taschenbücher, 1922).

FICHTE, JOHANN GOTTLIEB, *Die Anweisung zum seligen Leben, oder auch die Religionslehre* (1806).

—— *Die Bestimmung des Menschen* (1800).

—— *Die Grundzüge des gegenwärtigen Zeitalters* (1806).

—— *Versuch einer Kritik aller Offenbarung* (1792).

FILORAMO, GIOVANNI, *A History of Gnosticism*, trans. Anthony Alcock (Oxford: Basil Blackwell, 1990).

FINKELMAN, YOEL, *Strictly Kosher Reading: Popular Literature, ArtScroll and the Construction of Ultra-Orthodox Identity* (Brighton, Mass.: Academic Studies Press, 2011).

FINKELSTEIN, LOUIS, *Akiba: Scholar, Saint and Martyr*, 2nd edn. (Philadelphia, Pa.: Jewish Publication Society of America, 1962).

FISHBANE, MICHAEL, 'Accusations of Adultery: A Study of Law and Scribal Practice in Numbers 5: 11–31', *Hebrew Union College Annual*, 45 (1974), 25–45.

—— *Biblical Interpretation in Ancient Israel* (Oxford: Clarendon Press, 1985).

—— 'Torah' (Heb.), *Entsiklopediyah mikra'it*, vol. viii (Jerusalem, 1982).

FISHBANE, SIMCHA, *Boldness of an Halakhist: An Analysis of the Writings of Rabbi Yechiel Mechel Halevi Epstein the Arukh Hashulchan* (Brighton, Mass.: Academic Studies Press, 2008).

FISHMAN, TALYA, *Shaking the Pillars of Exile: 'Voice of a Fool', an Early Modern Jewish Critique of Rabbinic Culture* (Palo Alto, Calif.: Stanford University Press, 1997).

FORMSTECHER, SOLOMON, *Religion des Geistes* (Frankfurt am Main, 1841).

FÖRSTER, NICLAS, 'The Exegesis of Homer and Numerology as a Method for Interpreting the Bible in the Writings of Philo of Alexandria', in George J. Brooke (ed.), *Jewish Ways of Reading the Bible*, Journal of Semitic Studies Supplement 11 (Oxford: Oxford University Press, 2000), 91–8.

FRANK, DANIEL, *Search Scripture Well: Karaite Exegetes and the Origins of the Jewish Bible Commentary in the Islamic East* (Leiden: Brill, 2004).

FRANK, DANIEL H., OLIVER LEAMAN, and CHARLES H. MANEKIN (eds.), *The Jewish Philosophy Reader* (London: Routledge, 2000).

FRANK, EDGAR, *Talmudic and Rabbinical Chronology* (New York: Feldheim, 1956).

FRIMER, DOV I., 'Jewish Law and Science in the Writings of Rabbi Isaac Halevy Herzog', in B. Jackson (ed.), *The Halakhic Thought of R. Isaac Herzog* (Jewish Law Association Studies 5) (Atlanta, Ga.: Scholars Press, 1991), 33–48.

FRISCH, AMOS, 'R. Jacob Mecklenburg's Method in the Issue of the Patriarchs' Sins', *Jewish Studies Quarterly*, 10 (2003), 258–73.

GADAMER, HANS-GEORG, *Kleine Schriften*, 4 vols. (Tübingen: Mohr, 1967–77).

—— *Warheit und Methode*, 4th edn. (Tübingen: Mohr, 1975); trans. and ed. G. Barden and J. Cummin, *Truth and Method*, 2nd edn. (London: Sheed & Ward, 1979).

GALEN, *De usu partium*.

—— *On the Natural Faculties*.

GALIL, GERSHON, *The Chronology of the Kings of Judah and Israel* (Leiden: Brill, 1996).

GEERTZ, CLIFFORD, *The Interpretation of Cultures* (London: Fontana Press, 1993).

—— 'Religion as a Cultural System', in M. Bainton (ed.), *Anthropological Approaches to the Study of Religion* (London: Tavistock Publications, 1966), 1–46, repr. in Clifford Geertz, *The Interpretation of Cultures* (London: Fontana Press, 1993), 87–125.

GEIGER, ABRAHAM, *Urschrift und Übersetzungen der Bibel in ihrer Abhängigkeit der innern Entwickelung des Judenthums* (Breslau: Verlag Julius Hainauer, 1857).

GILLMAN, NEIL, *The Death of Death: Resurrection and Immortality in Jewish Thought* (Woodstock, Vt.: Jewish Publishing, 1997).

GLATZER, NAHUM N., *Franz Rosenzweig: His Life and Thought* (New York: Schocken, 1961).

GOLDBERG, HILLEL, *Between Berlin and Slobodka: Jewish Transition Figures from Eastern Europe* (Hoboken, NJ: Ktav, 1989).

GOLDSCHNEIDER, CALVIN, *Studying the Jewish Future* (Seattle, Wash.: University of Washington Press, 2004).

GOODMAN, LENN E. (ed.), *Neoplatonism and Jewish Thought* (Albany: SUNY Press, 1992).

GOODMAN, MARTIN, *State and Society in Roman Galilee. A.D. 132–212* (Totowa, NJ: Rowman & Allanheld, 1983; 2nd edn. London: Vallentine Mitchell, 2000).

GORDIS, ROBERT, *Kohelet, the Man and his World*, 3rd edn. (New York: Schocken Books, 1968).

GOSHEN-GOTTSTEIN, M. H., *The Aleppo Codex* [Keter aram tsova] (Jerusalem: Magnes Press, 1976).

GRAETZ, HEINRICH, *History of the Jews*, trans. Bella Löwy, vol. iii (London: David Nutt, 1892).

GRAF, K. H., *Die geschichtlichen Buecher des Alten Testaments* (Leipzig: T. O. Weigel, 1866).

GRAHAM, DAVID, MARLENA SCHMOOL, and STANLEY WATERMAN, *Jews in Britain: A Snapshot from the 2001 Census* (London: Institute for Jewish Policy Research, 2007); <http://www.jpr.org.uk/downloads/2001_census.pdf>.

GRAUPE, HEINZ MOSHE, *The Rise of Modern Judaism: An Intellectual History of German Jewry 1650–1942*, trans. John Robinson (Huntington, NY: Robert E. Krieger, 1979).

GRAYSON, A. KIRK, 'The Babylonian Origin of Apocalyptic Literature', *Atti dell'Istituto Veneto di Scienze, Lettere ed Arti*, 148 (1989–90), 203–19.

GREEN, ARTHUR, *The Language of Truth: The Torah Commentary of the Sefat Emet, Rabbi Yehudah Leib Alter of Ger* (Philadelphia, Pa.: Jewish Publication Society, 1998).

GROSS, RITA M., 'Steps Toward Feminine Images of Deity in Jewish Theology', in Susannah Heschel (ed.), *On Being a Jewish Feminist*, 2nd edn. (New York: Schocken Books, 1995), 234–47; repr. from *Judaism*, 30/2 (Spring 1981), 183–93.

GRUENWALD, ITHAMAR, 'The Relevance of Myth for Understanding Ritual in Ancient Judaism', *Annual of Rabbinic Judaism*, 3 (2000), 3–31.

GRÜNBAUM, YOSEF, *Hakarmel* (Szeged, 1899/1900).

GUETTA, ALESSANDRO, 'The Last Debate on Kabbalah in Italian Judaism', in Barbara Garvin and Bernard Cooperman (eds.), *The Jews of Italy: Memory and Identity* (Bethesda, Md.: University Press of Maryland, 2000), 256–75.

GUGENHEIMER, J., 'Die Hypothesen der Bibelkritik und der Commentar zur Genesis von Rabbiner S. R. Hirsch', *Jeschurun*, 13 (1867), 293–313, 397–409; 14 (1868), 1–18, 173–91, 312–25; 15 (1869), 81–100.

HABERMAN, JOSHUA O., *Philosopher of Revelation: The Life and Thought of S. L. Steinheim* (Philadelphia, Pa.: Jewish Publication Society, 1990).

HALAHMI, DAVID, *The Sages of Israel* [Ḥakhmei yisra'el] (Tel Aviv: Avraham Tsiyoni, 1957/8).

HALEVI, JUDAH, *Kuzari*.

HALKIN, A. S., 'Yedaiah Bedershi's Apology', in Alexander Altmann (ed.), *Jewish Medieval and Renaissance Studies* (Cambridge, Mass.: Harvard University Press, 1967), 165–84.

HALLO, WILLIAM W., 'The Concept of Canonicity in Cuneiform and Biblical Literature: A Comparative Appraisal', in K. Lawson Younger, Jr., William W. Hallo, and Bernard F. Batto (eds.), *The Bible and Canon in Comparative Perspective* (Scripture in Contact 4) (Lewiston, NY: Edwin Mellen Press, 1991), 1–17.

HAND, SEÁN (ed.), *The Levinas Reader* (Oxford: Blackwell, 1989).

HARVEY, ZEEV, 'The Halakhic Philosophy of the Ran' (Heb.), in Aviezer Ravitzky and Avinoam Rosenak (eds.), *New Streams in Philosophy of Halakhah* [Iyunim ḥadashim befilosofiyah shel hahalakhah] (Jerusalem: Magnes Press, 2008), 171–80.

HAYM, RUDOLF, *Herder* (Berlin, 1954).

HECHT, N. S. et al., *An Introduction to the History and Sources of Jewish Law* (Oxford: Clarendon Press, 1996).

HEINEMANN, ISAAC, *The Reasons for the Commandments in Jewish Thought: From the Bible to the Renaissance*, trans. Leonard Levin (Brighton, Mass.: Academic Studies Press, 2008). Original edn.: *Ta'amei hamitsvot besifrut yisra'el* (Jerusalem: World Zionist Organization, 1953).

HENKIN, YEHUDAH HERZL, *Responsa on Contemporary Jewish Women's Issues* (Jersey, NJ: Ktav, 2002).

HERBERT, EDWARD LORD, OF CHERBURY, *De Veritate*, trans. Meyrick H. Carré (Bristol: J. W. Arrowsmith, 1937).

HERDER, JOHANN GOTTFRIED, *Vom Geist der Ebräischen Poesie*, 2 vols. (Dessau: 1782, 1783).

HERODOTUS, *Histories*.

HERR, SOLOMON ZE'EV, *Likutei shoshanim* (Vilna, 1874/5).

HERTZ, J. H., *The Pentateuch and Haftorahs*, 5 vols. (London: Oxford University Press, 1929).

HESCHEL, ABRAHAM JOSHUA, *God in Search of Man* (Philadelphia, Pa.: Jewish Publication Society of America, 1965).

—— *Heavenly Torah: As Refracted Through the Generations*, ed. and trans. with commentary, Gordon Tucker with Leonard Levin (New York: Continuum, 2005). Original edn.: *Torah min hashamayim ba'aspaklariyah shel hadorot*, 3 vols. (London: Soncino, 1962–90).

HESCHEL, SUSANNAH, *Abraham Geiger and the Jewish Jesus* (Chicago, Ill.: University of Chicago Press, 1998).

—— *The Aryan Jesus: Christian Theologians and the Bible in Nazi Germany* (Princeton: Princeton University Press, 2008).

HIRSCH, SAMSON RAPHAEL, *Commentary on Exodus*, trans. Isaac Levy (London: privately published, 1959).

—— *Commentary on Genesis*, trans. Isaac Levy (London: privately published, 1959).

—— *Collected Writings of Rabbi Samson Raphael Hirsch*, trans. Jacob Breuer, 8 vols., 2nd edn. (New York: Feldheim, 1997). Original edn.: *Gesammelte Schriften von Rabbiner Samson Raphael Hirsch*, ed. Naphtali Hirsch, 6 vols. (Frankfurt am Main: J. Kauffmann, 1902–12).

—— 'Hellenism and Judaism', in S. R. Hirsch, *Collected Writings*, ii. 199–211.

—— *The Hirsch Siddur*, trans. Y. Feldheim (Jerusalem: Feldheim, 1978).

—— *Horeb: A Philosophy of Jewish Laws and Observances*, trans. I Grunfeld (New York: Soncino Press, 1981).

—— *The Nineteen Letters*, trans. Karin Paritzky with introd. and commentary by Joseph Elias, 2nd edn. (Jerusalem: Feldheim, 1995).

HIRSCH, SAMUEL, *Die Religionsphilosophie der Juden* (Leipzig, 1842).

HIRSCHENSOHN, HAYIM, *Malki bakodesh*, 6 vols. (New York: Moinester Printing Co., 1919–28).

HOFFMAN, DAVID, *Das Buch Deuteronomium uebersetzt und erklaert*, 2 vols. (Berlin: M. Poppelauer, 1913, 1922).

—— *Das Buch Leviticus uebersetzt und erklaert*, 2 vols. (Berlin: H. Itzkowski, 1905, 1906).

—— *Mar Samuel* (Leipzig, 1873).

—— *Melamed leho'il* [responsa] (Frankfurt: Hermon, 1935).

—— *Die wichtigsten Instanzen gegen die Graf-Wellhausensche Hypothese*, 2 vols. (Berlin: H. Itzkowski, 1903, 1916).

HOFFMAN, R. JOSEPH, *Celsus: On the True Doctrine: A Discourse Against the Christians* (New York: Oxford University Press, 1987).

HOLLADAY, CARL R., *Fragments from Hellenistic Jewish Authors*, 4 vols. (Chico, Calif.: Scholars Press, 1983–6).

HOMOLKA, WALTER, *Jewish Identity in Modern Times: Leo Baeck and German Protestantism* (Providence, RI: Berghahn Books, 1995).

HORNER, TIMOTHY J., *Listening to Trypho: Justin Martyr's Dialogue Reconsidered* (Leuven: Peeters, 2001).

HUME, DAVID, *An Enquiry Concerning Human Understanding* (1748).

HYMAN, AARON, *History of the Mishnaic and Talmudic Sages*, 3 vols. [Toldot tana'im ve'amoraim] (London, 1910).

IBN ABI ZIMRA, DAVID BEN SOLOMON, *Responsa* [She'elot uteshuvot haridbaz], 7 vols. (New York: Otsar Hasefarim, 1967).

IBN EZRA, ABRAHAM, *Commentary on the Torah* [Perush al hatorah].

IBN GABIROL, SOLOMON (AVICEBRON), *Avencebrolis Fons Vitae ex Arabico in Latinum translatus ab Iohanne Hispano et Domenico Gundissalino ed. Clemens Baeumker* (Münster: Aschendorff, 1892–5).

IDEL, MOSHE, 'Jacques Derrida and Kabbalistic Sources', in Bettina Bergo, Joseph Cohen, and Raphael Zagury-Orly (eds.), *Judeities: Questions for Jacques Derrida*, trans. Bettina Bergo and Michael B. Smith (New York: Fordham University Press, 2007), 111–30.

358   BIBLIOGRAPHY

IDEL, MOSHE, Jewish Kabbalah and Platonism in the Middle Ages and Renaissance',
    in Lenn E. Goodman, (ed.), *Neoplatonism and Jewish Thought* (Albany, NY: SUNY
    Press, 1992), 319–51.
—— *Kabbalah: New Perspectives* (New Haven, Conn.: Yale University Press, 1988).
—— *The Mystical Experience in Abraham Abulafia*, trans. Jonathan Chipman (Albany,
    NY: SUNY Press, 1988).
ISH-SHALOM, BENJAMIN, *Rav Avraham Itzhak HaCohen Kook: Between Rationalism
    and Mysticism* (Albany, NY: SUNY Press, 1993).
IVRY, ALFRED L., 'Maimonides and Neoplatonism: Challenge and Response', in Lenn
    E. Goodman (ed.), *Neoplatonism and Jewish Thought* (Albany, NY: SUNY Press,
    1992), 137–56.
JACKSON, BERNARD, 'On the Problem of Roman Influence on the Halakah and
    Normative Self-Definition in Judaism', in E. P. Sanders (ed.), *Jewish and Christian
    Self-Definition*, vol. ii (London: SCM Press, 1981), 157–203.
—— Review of David Novak, *Natural Law* (Cambridge: Cambridge University Press,
    1998), *Journal of Jewish Studies*, 52/2 (2001), 136–45.
JACOB, BENNO, *Das erste Buch der Tora, Genesis, übersetzt und erklärt* (Berlin:
    Schocken, 1934).
JACOB JOSEPH KATZ OF POLONNOYE, *Toledot ya'akov yosef* (Medzhybizh and Korets,
    1780).
JACOB OF MARVÈGE, *She'elot uteshuvot min hashamayim*, ed. Reuven Margalit
    (Jerusalem: Mosad Harav Kook, 1956/7).
JACOBS, LOUIS, *Beyond Reasonable Doubt* (London: Littman Library of Jewish
    Civilization, 1999).
—— *Helping with Inquiries* (London: Vallentine Mitchell, 1989).
—— *Structure and Form in the Babylonian Talmud* (Cambridge: Cambridge University
    Press, 1991).
—— *A Tree of Life: Diversity, Flexibility, and Creativity in Jewish Law* (Oxford: Littman
    Library of Jewish Civilization, 1984).
—— *We Have Reason to Believe: Some Aspects of Jewish Theology Examined in the Light of
    Modern Thought* (London: Vallentine Mitchell, 1957).
JAMES, WILLIAM, *Pragmatism: A New Name for Some Old Ways of Thinking* (1907;
    Cambridge, Mass. and London: Harvard University Press, 1978).
JEROME, *Preface to the Books of Samuel and Kings*, in Philip Schaff and Henry Wace, *The
    Nicene and Post-Nicene Fathers*, 2nd edn., vol. vi (Grand Rapids, Mich: W. B.
    Eerdmans, 1977), 489–90.
Jewish Encyclopedia, 12 vols. (New York: Funk and Wagnalls, 1901–06).
Jewish Study Bible see Berlin and Brettler (eds.), *Jewish Study Bible*
JONAS, HANS, *The Gnostic Religion: The Message of the Alien God and the Beginnings of
    Christianity* (Boston: Beacon Press, 1963).
JOSEPHUS FLAVIUS, *Contra Apionem*, trans. H. St J. Thackeray (Loeb Classical Library
    186) (Cambridge, Mass.: Harvard University Press, 1926).
—— *Antiquities of the Jews*.

JPS Hebrew–English Tanakh, 2nd edn. (Philadelphia, Pa.: Jewish Publication Society, 1999).

JUDAH LOEW BEN BEZALEL (MAHARAL), *Be'er hagolah* (Prague, 1600).

—— *Gevurot hashem* (Kraków, 1582).

—— *Tiferet yisra'el* (Prague, 1593).

JUSTIN MARTYR, *Dialogue with Trypho*, trans. Thomas B. Falls, ed. Michael Slusser (Washington, DC: Catholic University of America Press, 2003).

JUVENAL, *Satires*.

KADUSHIN, MAX, *Organic Thinking: A Study in Rabbinic Thought* (New York: Jewish Theological Seminary of America, 1938).

KALISCH, M. M., *A Historical and Critical Commentary on the Old Testament: Leviticus* (London: Longmans, Green, Reader, Dyer, part 1, 1867; part 2, 1872).

KAPLAN, ARYEH, *The Bahir* (Northvale, NJ: Jason Aronson, 1995).

—— *Sefer Yetzira: The Book of Creation* (York Beach, Me.: Samuel Weiser, 1997).

KARO, JOSEPH, *Beit yosef*.

KATZ, JACOB, *Divine Law in Human Hands: Case Studies in Halakhic Flexibility* (Jerusalem: Magnes Press, 1998).

KAUFMAN, WILLIAM E., *Contemporary Jewish Philosophies*, 2nd edn. (Detroit, Mich.: Wayne State University Press, 1992).

KAUFMANN, ERIC, 'Breeding for God', *Prospect Magazine*, 128 (19 Nov. 2006); <http://www.prospectmagazine.co.uk/2006/11/breedingforgod/>.

KELLNER, MENACHEM, *Dogma in Medieval Jewish Thought: From Maimonides to Abravanel* (Oxford: Oxford University Press, 1986).

—— *Must A Jew Believe Anything?* (London: Littman Library of Jewish Civilization, 1999).

KEYNES, J. M., 'Newton the Man', in *Newton Tercentenary Celebrations* (Cambridge: Cambridge University Press for the Royal Society, 1947).

KIERKEGAARD, SØREN, *Fear and Trembling*, ed. and trans. Howard V. Hong and Edna H. Hong (Princeton, NJ: Princeton University Press, 1983).

KIRKHAM, RICHARD L., *Theories of Truth: A Critical Introduction* (Cambridge, Mass.: MIT Press, 1992).

—— 'Truth, Coherence Theories of', in E. Craig (ed.), *Routledge Encyclopaedia of Philosophy*, vol. ix (London: Routledge, 1998), 470–2.

KNIGHT, DOUGLAS A., *Rediscovering the Traditions of Israel* (Missoula, Mont.: Scholars Press, 1975).

KNOPPERS, GARY N., and BERNARD M. LEVINSOHN (eds.), *The Pentateuch as Torah: New Models for Understanding its Promulgation and Acceptance* (Winona Lake, Ind.: Eisenbrauns, 2007).

KOCHAN, LIONEL, *The Jewish Renaissance and Some of its Discontents* (Manchester: Manchester University Press, 1992).

—— *The Making of Western Jewry, 1600–1819* (Basingstoke: Palgrave Macmillan, 2004).

KOTTEK, SAMUEL S., '*Amra li em*: La transmission de la médecine populaire par les femmes dans le Talmud', *Revue des Etudes Juives*, 169 (2010), 419–37.

KROCHMAL, NACHMAN, *Moreh nevukhei hazeman*, ed. L. Zunz (Lemberg: Schnayder, 1851); critical edn. by S. Rawidowicz (Berlin: Ayanot, 1924); rev. edn. (London: Ararat Publishing Society, 1961).

KURZWEIL, ZVI, *The Modern Impulse of Traditional Judaism* (Hoboken, NJ: Ktav, 1985).

LACTANTIUS, *On the Divine Institutions*, in *Patrologia Latina* 6, ed. J.-P. Migne (Paris, 1844).

LAMBERT, W. G., *The Background of Jewish Apocalyptic* (London: Athlone Press, 1978).

LAMBERTON, ROBERT, *Homer the Theologian: Neoplatonist Allegorical Reading and the Growth of the Epic Tradition* (Berkeley, Calif.: University of California Press, 1986).

LANGERMANN, Y. T., 'Maimonides' Repudiation of Astrology', *Maimonidean Studies*, 2 (1991), 123–58.

LASKER, DANIEL, 'Longevity of the Ancients: Religion and Science in Mediaeval Jewish Thought' (Heb.), *Dinei yisra'el*, 26–7 (2009), 49–65.

LAZARUS-YAFFE, HAVA, *Intertwined Worlds: Medieval Islam and Bible Criticism* (Princeton, NJ: Princeton University Press, 1992).

——, MARK R. COHEN, SASSON SOMEKH, and SIDNEY H. GRIFFITH (eds.), *The Majlis* (Wiesbaden: Harrassowitz Verlag, 1999).

LEIMAN, SID J., *The Canonization of Hebrew Scripture: The Talmudic and Midrashic Evidence*, 2nd edn. (Hamden, Conn.: Archon, 1991).

LESSER, HARRY, '"It is difficult to understand": Dealing with Morally Difficult Passages in the Hebrew Bible', in George J. Brooke (ed.), *Jewish Ways of Reading the Bible* (Journal of Semitic Studies Supplement 11) (Oxford: Oxford University Press, 2000), 292–320.

LEVINAS, EMANUEL, *Au-delà du verset: Lectures et discours talmudiques* (Paris: Editions de Minuit, 1982).

—— *Difficult Freedom: Essays on Judaism*, trans. Seán Hand (London: Athlone Press, 1990).

LEVITA, ELIJAH, *Masoret hamasoret* (Venice, 1538).

LEVY, B. BARRY, *Fixing God's Torah: The Accuracy of the Hebrew Bible Text in Jewish Law* (Oxford: Oxford University Press, 2001).

—— 'Our Torah, Your Torah, and Their Torah: An Evaluation of the Artscroll Phenomenon', in Howard Joseph, Jack N. Lightstone, and Michael D. Oppenheim (eds.), *Truth and Compassion: Essays on Judaism and Religion in Memory of Rabbi Dr. Solomon Frank* (Waterloo, Ont.: Wilfred Laurier University Press, 1983), 137–89.

LEWIN (LEVINE), B. M., *Otsar hage'onim: Thesaurus of the Geonic Responsa and Commentaries* (Heb.), 13 vols. (Jerusalem, 1928–62).

LEWYSOHN, LUDWIG, *Zoologie des Talmuds* (Frankfurt am Main, 1858).

LIBER, MAURICE, *Rashi*, trans. Adele Szold (1906; 2nd edn. Philadelphia, Pa.: Jewish Publication Society of America, 1945; French original probably 1905).

LIBERLES, ROBERT, *Religious Conflict in a Social Context: The Resurgence of Orthodox Judaism in Frankfurt am Main, 1838–1877* (Westport, Conn.: Greenwood, 1985).

LICHTHEIM, MIRIAM, *Ancient Egyptian Literature: A Book of Readings*, 3 vols. (Berkeley, Calif.: University of California Press, 1973, 1976, 1980; 2nd rev. edn. 2006).

LIEBERMAN, SAUL, *Greek in Jewish Palestine: Studies in the Life and Manners of Jewish Palestine in the II–IV Centuries C.E.* (New York: Jewish Theological Seminary of America, 1942; 2nd edn. 1965).

—— *Hellenism in Jewish Palestine: Studies in the Literary Transmission, Beliefs and Manners of Palestine in the I Century B.C.E.–IV Century C.E.* (New York: Jewish Theological Seminary of America, 1950; 2nd edn. 1962).

—— 'How Much Greek in Jewish Palestine?', in A. Altmann (ed.), *Biblical and Other Studies* (Cambridge, Mass.: Harvard University Press, 1963), 123–41.

LOEWE, RAPHAEL, 'Solomon Marcus Schiller-Szinessy, 1820–1890: First Reader in Talmudic and Rabbinic Literature at Cambridge', *Transactions of the Jewish Historical Society of England*, 21 (1962–7), 148–89.

LÖW, I., *Flora der Juden*, 4 vols. (Vienna: R. Löwit, 1926–34).

LURIA, SOLOMON, *Yam shel shelomoh* (Lublin, 1636).

LUZZATTO, SAMUELE DAVIDE, *Dialogues sur la kabbale et le Zohar et sur l'antiquité de la ponctuation et de l'accentuation dans la langue hébraïque* (Gorizia, 1852).

—— *Grammatica della lingua ebraica*, 4 vols. (Padua, 1853–67).

—— *Igerot shadal* (Przemysl, 1882).

—— *Il profeta Isaia volgarizzato e commentato ad uso degl'Israeliti da Samuel Davide Luzzatto* (Padua, 1867).

—— *Prolegomena to a Grammar of the Hebrew Language*, trans. Aaron D. Rubin (Piscataway, NJ: Gorgias Press, 2005; original Italian edn.: Padua, 1836).

MAHARAL OF PRAGUE, *see* Judah Loew ben Bezalel

MAIMONIDES, MOSES, *Guide of the Perplexed*, trans. S. Pines (Chicago, Ill.: University of Chicago Press, 1963).

—— *Igerot harambam*, vol. ii, ed. Isaac Shailat (Heb.) (Jerusalem: Ma'aliyot, 1987/8); trans. with notes by Leon D. Stitskin, *Letters of Maimonides* (New York: Yeshiva University Press, 1977).

—— *Maimonides' Responsa* [Teshuvot harambam] ed. J. Blau, 4 vols. (Jerusalem: Mekitze Nirdamim, 1957–86).

—— *Mishneh torah.*

MALBIM (ME'IR LEIBUSH BEN JEHIEL MICHEL WEISER), *Hatorah vehamitsvah*, 2 vols. (Jerusalem: Hapardes, 1956).

MALKIEL, DAVID, 'New Light on the Career of Isaac Samuel Reggio', in Barbara Garvin and Bernard Cooperman (eds.), *The Jews of Italy: Memory and Identity* (Bethesda, Md.: University Press of Maryland, 2000), 407–13.

MANASSEH BEN ISRAEL, *The Conciliator, a Reconcilement of the Apparent Contradictions in Holy Scripture. To which are added notes by E. H. Lindo* (London, 1842, repr. New York: Hermon Press, 1972).

MARX, ALEXANDER, 'The Correspondence between the Rabbis of Southern France and Maimonides about Astrology', *Hebrew Union College Annual*, 3 (1926), 311–58.

MARX, KARL, Critique of Hegel's 'Philosophy of Right', trans. Annette Jolin and Joseph O'Malley; ed. with introd. and notes Joseph O'Malley (Cambridge: Cambridge University Press, 1970).

MCGINN, BERNARD, 'Ibn Gabirol: The Sage among the Schoolmen', in L. E. Goodman (ed.), Neoplatonism and Jewish Thought (Albany: SUNY Press, 1992), 77–109.

MEIROVICH, HARVEY WARREN, A Vindication of Judaism: The Polemics of the Pentateuch (New York: Jewish Theological Seminary of America, 1998).

MENDELSSOHN, MOSES, Jerusalem, or, On Religious Power and Judaism, trans. A. Arkush (Hanover, NH: University Press of New England, 1983).

MEYER, MICHAEL A., '"Most of My Brethren Find Me Unacceptable": The Controversial Career of Rabbi Samuel Holdheim', Jewish Social Studies, 9/3 (Spring/Summer 2003), 1–19.

——— 'The Orthodox and the Enlightened', Leo Baeck Institute Yearbook, 25 (1980), 101–30.

——— Response to Modernity: A History of the Reform Movement in Judaism (New York: Oxford University Press, 1988).

MICHAEL, REUVEN, Heinrich Graetz: The Historian of the Jewish People [Heinrikh grets: hahistoriyon shel ha'am hayehudi] (Jerusalem: Mosad Bialik, 2003).

Midrash Rabbah.

Mikraot gedolot haketer, ed. Menachem Cohen, 10 vols. (Ramat Gan: Bar-Ilan University Press, 1992–).

MISHAEL BEN UZZIEL, Kitāb al-khilaf, ed. and trans. Lazar Lipschütz (Jerusalem: Magnes Press, 1965).

MILIKOWSKY, CHAIM, 'Seder Olam', in Shmuel Safrai, Zeev Safrai, Joshua Schwartz, and Peter J. Tomson (eds.), The Literature of the Sages: Second Part (Assen: Van Gorcum, 2006), 231–7.

MILL, JOHN STUART, The Subjection of Women (1869) in The Rights of Woman, by Mary Wollstonecraft, with The Subjection of Women, by John Stuart Mill, introd. Pamela Fraukau (Everyman's Library 825) (London: Dent, 1959).

MILLER, CHAIM (ed.), Chumash: The Gutnick Edition: All in One (New York: Kol Menachem, 2008).

MITTLEMAN, ALAN L., Between Kant and Kabbalah: An Introduction to Isaac Breuer's Philosophy of Judaism (Albany, NY: SUNY Press, 1990).

MODENA, JUDAH ARYEH (LEONE) OF, Ziknei yehudah, ed. Shlomo Simonsohn (Jerusalem: Mosad Harav Kook, 1957).

NACHMANIDES, Commentary on Genesis (Heb.).

NAVEH, JOSEPH, Early History of the Alphabet: An Introduction to West Semitic Epigraphy and Palaeography (Jerusalem: Hebrew University, 1982; 2nd edn. 1987).

——— On Sherd and Papyrus: Aramaic and Hebrew Inscriptions from the Second Temple, Mishnaic, and Talmudic Periods [Al ḥeres vegome: ketuvot aramiyot ve'ivriyot mimei bayit sheni, hamishnah vehatalmud] (Jerusalem: Magnes Press, 1992).

——— and SAUL SHAKED, Amulets and Magic Bowls: Aramaic Incantations of Late Antiquity (Jerusalem: Magnes Press, 1985).

NEMOY, LEON, 'Al-Qirqisāni's Account of the Jewish Sects and Christianity', *Hebrew Union College Annual*, 7 (1931), 317–97. Repr. in J. Neusner (ed.), *Origins of Judaism*, iii: 2 (New York: Garland, 1990), 111–91.

NEUSNER, J., *Genesis Rabbah: The Judaic Commentary to the Book of Genesis* (Atlanta, Ga.: Scholars Press, 1985).

—— 'A Zoroastrian Critique of Judaism: (Škand Gumanik Vičar, Chapters Thirteen and Fourteen: A New Translation and Exposition)', *Journal of the American Oriental Society*, 83/3 (Aug.–Sept. 1963), 283–94.

——, ERNEST S. FRERICHS, and PAUL VIRGIL MCCRACKEN FLESHER (eds.), *Religion, Science and Magic: In Concert and in Conflict* (Oxford: Oxford University Press, 1989).

NEWTON, SIR ISAAC, *Observations upon the Prophecies of Daniel, and the Apocalypse of St. John*, ed. Benjamin Smith (London, 1733).

NICKELSBURG, GEORGE W. E., JR. (ed.), *Studies on the Testament of Moses* (Cambridge, Mass.: Society of Biblical Literature, 1972).

NOVAK, DAVID, *Natural Law* (Cambridge: Cambridge University Press, 1998).

OPPENHEIMER, AHARON, 'Jewish Penal Authority in Roman Judaea', in Martin Goodman (ed.), *Jews in a Graeco-Roman World* (Oxford: Clarendon Press, 1998), 181–91.

ORIGEN OF CAESAREA, *Origen contra Celsum*, ed. Henry Chadwick (Cambridge: Cambridge University Press, 1953).

—— *Origène contre Celse*, introd., Greek text, French trans., and notes Marcel Borret SJ (Paris: Éditions du Cerf, 1968).

ÖSTBORN, G., *Tōrā in the Old Testament: A Semantic Study* (Lund: Håken Ohlssoms Boktryckeri, 1945).

OTTO, RUDOLF, *The Idea of the Holy*, trans. J. W. Harvey (London: H. Milford, Oxford University Press, 1923). Original edn.: *Das Heilige* (Breslau, 1917).

OVID, *Metamorphoses*.

OZICK, CYNTHIA, 'Notes toward Finding the Right Question', in Susannah Heschel (ed.), *On Being a Jewish Feminist* (New York: Schocken Books, 1983), 120–51.

PAPPENHEIM, SALOMON, *Yeriot shelomoh*, 3 vols. (Dyhernfurth, 1784, 1811, 1831).

PEIRCE, CHARLES S., *Collected Papers*, vol. v, ed. Charles Hartshorne and Paul Weiss (Cambridge, Mass.: Harvard University Press, 1934).

PENKOWER, JORDAN S., 'Maimonides and the Aleppo Codex', *Textus*, 9 (1981), 39–128.

PERLES, J., *R. Salomo b. Abraham b. Adereth: Sein Leben und seine Schriften nebst handschriflichen Beilagen* (Breslau: Schletter, 1863), repr. in *Teshuvot harashba*, ed. Hayim Z. Dimitrowsky, vol. i (Jerusalem: Mosad Harav Kook, 1990), 115–58.

PERLMANN, MOSHE, 'Eleventh-Century Andalusian Authors on the Jews of Granada', *Proceedings of the American Academy for Jewish Research*, 18 (1948/9), 269–90; repr. in Robert Chazan (ed.), *Medieval Jewish Life* (New York: Ktav, 1976), 147–68.

PFAFF, FRANZ, 'Rufus aus Samaria. Hippokrateskommentator und Quelle Galens', *Hermes*, 67 (1932), 356–9.

PHILO JUDAEUS, *De Vita Mosis*, trans. F. H. Colson (Loeb Classical Library, 289) (Cambridge, Mass.: Harvard University Press, 1935).

—— *Questions on Genesis.*

PHOTIUS, *Photius muriobiblion*, ed. D. Hoeschelius, Latin trans. A. Schottus (Geneva, 1611).

PLASKOW, JUDITH, *Standing Again at Sinai: Judaism from a Feminist Perspective* (San Francisco, Calif.: HarperCollins, 1991).

PLATO, *The Republic.*

—— *Epistle VII*, trans. R. G. Bury (Loeb Classical Library, 234) (Cambridge, Mass.: Harvard University Press, 1929).

PLAUT, W. GUNTHER, *The Torah: A Modern Commentary* (New York: Union of American Hebrew Congregations, 1981; 4th edn. 1985).

—— and CHAIM STERN, *The Haftarah Commentary* (New York: Union of American Hebrew Congregations, 1996).

PLINY, *Natural History.*

PLOTINUS, *Enneads.*

PLUTARCH, *Moralia*, vol. ii: *On Superstition (Peri Deisidaimonias)*, trans. F. C. Babitt (Loeb Classical Library, 222) (Cambridge, Mass.: Harvard University Press, 1928).

PODRO, J., *The Last Pharisee: The Life and Times of Rabbi Joshua ben Hananiah* (London: Vallentine Mitchell, 1959).

POLLIACK, MEIRA, *Karaite Judaism: A Guide to its History and Literary Sources* (Leiden: Brill, 2004).

POPKIN, RICHARD H., *The History of Scepticism from Erasmus to Descartes* (Assen: Van Gorcum, 1960).

—— and A. J. VANDERJAGT (eds.), *Skepticism and Irreligion in the Seventeenth and Eighteenth Centuries* (Leiden: Brill, 1993).

PORTON, GARY, *The Traditions of Rabbi Ishmael*, 4 vols. (Leiden: Brill, 1976–82).

POZNAŃSKI, SAMUEL, *Mose b. Samuel hakohen Ibn Chiquitilla, nebst den fragmenten seiner schriften* (Leipzig: J. C. Hinrichs, 1895).

PREUSS, JULIUS, *Biblisch-talmudisch Medizin* (Berlin: S. Karger, 1911).

PROCLUS DIADOCHUS, *Commentary on the First Alcibiades of Plato*, ed. L. G. Westerinck (Amsterdam: North-Holland, 1954).

PSEUDO-BAHYA, *Kitab al-ma'ani al-nafs* [On the Essence of the Soul], ed. I. Goldziher (Berlin: Weidmannsche, 1907).

QUINE, W. V. O. *From a Logical Point of View* (Cambridge, Mass.: Harvard University Press, 1953).

RADBAZ *see* Ibn Abi Zimra, David ben Solomon

RAMSAY, F. P., 'Facts and Propositions', *Proceedings of the Aristotelian Society*, supplementary vol. 7 (1927), 153–70.

RAPOPORT, CHAIM, *Judaism and Homosexuality: An Authentic Orthodox View* (London: Vallentine Mitchell, 2004).

RECANATI, MENAHEM OF, *Sefer ta'amei hamitsvot hashalem*, ed. S. B. Lieberman (London, 1962).

REGGIO, ISAAC SAMUEL, *Igerot yashar*, 2 vols. (Vienna, 1834, 1836).

REVENTLOW, HENNING GRAF, *The Authority of the Bible and the Rise of the Modern World*, trans. John Bowden (Philadelphia, Pa.: Fortress Press, 1984).

—— *The Problems of Old Testament Theology in the Twentieth Century*, trans. John Bowden (London: SCM, 1985); German original 1982.

RICOEUR, PAUL, ET AL., *La Révélation*, 2nd edn. (Brussels: Editions des Facultés Universitaires Saint-Louis, 1984).

ROKEAH, DAVID, *Justin Martyr and the Jews* (Leiden: Brill, 2002).

ROSENBERG, SHALOM, 'Continuous Revelation: Three Directions' (Heb.), in Moshe Halamish and Moshe Schwartz (eds.), *Hitgalut, emunah, tevunah* (Ramat Gan: Bar-Ilan University, 1976), 131–43.

ROSENBLOOM, NOAH H., *Luzzatto's Ethico-Psychological Interpretation of Judaism* (New York: Yeshiva University, 1965).

—— *Tradition in an Age of Emancipation: The Religious Philosophy of Samson Raphael Hirsch* (Philadelphia, Pa.: Jewish Publication Society of America, 1976).

—— *Malbim: Exegesis, Philosophy, Science, and Mysticism in the Writings of Rabbi Meir Leibush Malbim* [Hamalbim: parshanut, filosofiyah, mada, umistorin bekhitvei harav me'ir lebush malbim] (Jerusalem: Mosad Harav Kook, 1988).

ROSENTAL, DAVID, 'On the Sages' Treatment of Alternative Readings in the Bible' (Heb.), in Y. Zakovitz and A. Rofé (eds.), *Sefer yitsḥak aryeh seligman*, vol. ii (Jerusalem: Rubinstein, 1983), 395–417.

ROSENZWEIG, FRANZ, *The Star of Redemption*, trans. William Hallo (Boston, Mass.: Beacon Press, 1972). Original edn.: *Der Stern der Erlösung* (1921).

ROSMAN, M., *A Quest for the Historical Ba'al Shem Tov* (Berkeley, Calif.: University of California Press, 1996).

ROSS, JACOB JOSHUA, 'Elijah Delmedigo', *Stanford Encyclopedia of Philosophy*; <http://plato.stanford.edu/entries/delmedigo/>.

ROSS, TAMAR, *Expanding the Palace of Torah* (Waltham, Mass.: Brandeis University Press, 2004).

RUDERMAN, DAVID B., *Jewish Thought and Scientific Discovery in Early Modern Europe* (New Haven: Yale University Press, 1995).

RUDWICK, MARTIN J. S., *Georges Cuvier, Fossil Bones and Geological Catastrophes: New Translations and Interpretations of the Primary Texts* (Chicago, Ill.: University of Chicago Press, 1997).

SA'ADIAH GAON, *The Book of Beliefs and Opinions*, trans. Samuel Rosenblatt (New Haven: Yale University Press, 1948).

—— *Esa meshali*, ed. B. M. Lewin (Jerusalem: Mosad Harav Kook, 1942/3).

SACKS, JONATHAN, *Crisis and Covenant: Jewish Thought after the Holocaust* (Manchester: Manchester University Press, 1992).

SÆBO, MAGNE (ed.), *Hebrew Bible/Old Testament: The History of its Interpretation*, i: *From the Beginning to the Middle Ages (until 1300)* (Göttingen: Vanderhoeck & Ruprecht, 1996).

SAFRAI, SHMUEL, ZEEV SAFRAI, JOSHUA SCHWARTZ, and PETER J. TOMSON (eds.), *The Literature of the Sages: Second Part: Midrash and Targum, Liturgy, Poetry,*

Mysticism, Contracts, Inscriptions, Ancient Science and the Languages of Rabbinic Literature (Assen: Van Gorcum, 2006).

SAMUEL HANAGID, *Introduction to the Talmud* [Mevo hatalmud], in Babylonian Talmud (Vilna: Romm, 1886), *Berakhot*, addenda 42a–47a.

SANDLER, PEREZ, *Mendelssohn's Edition of the Pentateuch* [Habe'ur al hatorah shel mendelson vesiyato: hithavuto vehashpa'ato], introd. J. Klausner (Heb.) (Jerusalem: Rubin Mass, 1940).

SARNA, N. M., 'The Order of the Books', in Charles Berlin (ed.), *Studies in Jewish Bibliography, History and Literature in Honor of J. Edward Kiev* (New York: Ktav, 1971), 407–13.

SAWYER, JOHN F. A., *Sacred Languages and Sacred Texts* (London: Routledge, 1999).

SCHÄFER, PETER, 'Jewish Magic Literature in Late Antiquity and Early Middle Ages', *Journal of Jewish Studies*, 41 (1990), 75–91.

—— *Judeophobia: Attitudes toward the Jews in the Ancient World* (Cambridge, Mass.: Harvard University Press, 1997).

—— *Mirror of his Beauty: Feminine Images of God from the Bible to the Early Kabbalah* (Princeton, NJ: Princeton University Press, 2002).

SCHAFF, PHILIP, and HENRY WACE (eds.), *The Nicene and Post-Nicene Fathers*, 2nd edn., 14 vols. (Grand Rapids, Mich.: W. B. Eerdmans, 1975–9).

SCHARFSTEIN, BEN-AMI, *Mystical Experience* (Oxford: Blackwell, 1973).

SCHECHTER, SOLOMON, 'Geniza Specimens', *Jewish Quarterly Review*, 13 (1901), 345–57.

SCHELER, MAX, *On Feeling, Knowing, and Valuing*, ed. H. J. Bershady (Chicago, Ill.: University of Chicago Press, 1992).

SCHIFFMAN, L., and M. SWARTZ, *Hebrew and Aramaic Incantation Texts from the Cairo Geniza* (Sheffield: Sheffield Academic Press, 1992).

SCHLEIERMACHER, F., *On Religion: Speeches to its Cultured Despisers*, introd., trans., and notes Richard Crouter (Cambridge: Cambridge University Press, 1988). Original edn.: *Über die Religion. Reden an die Gebildeten unter ihren Verächtern*, 1799.

SCHLÜTER, MARGARET, *Auf welche Weise wurde die Mishnah geschrieben? Das Antwortschreiben des Rav Sherira Gaon: mit einem Faksimile der Handschrift Berlin Qu. 685 (Or.160) und des Erstdruckes Konstantinopel 1566* (Tübingen: Mohr, 1993).

SCHOLEM, GERSHOM G., *From Berlin to Jerusalem*, trans. Harry Zohn (New York: Schocken Books, 1980). Original edn.: *Von Berlin nach Jerusalem* (Frankfurt am Main: Bibliotek Suhrkamp, 1978).

—— *The Kabbalah in Girona* [Hakabalah begironah], ed. I. Ben Shlomo (Jerusalem: Hebrew University, 1964).

—— *Major Trends in Jewish Mysticism* (Jerusalem: Schocken, 1941).

—— *Ursprung und Anfaenge der Kabbalah* (Berlin: Walter de Gruyter, 1962). English: *Origins of the Kabbalah*, rev. by R. J. Zvi Werblowsky and trans. Allan Arkush (Philadelphia, Pa.: Jewish Publication Society, 1987).

—— *Walter Benjamin: The Story of a Friendship*, trans. Harry Zohn (Philadelphia, Pa.: Jewish Publication Society of America, 1981).

SCHOPENHAUER, ARTHUR, 'On Religion: A Dialogue', in id., *Essays and Aphorisms*, trans. R. J. Hollingdale, 2nd edn. (London: Penguin Classics, 2004), 95–114.

—— 'On the Suffering of the World', in id., *Essays and Aphorisms*, trans. R. J. Hollingdale, 2nd edn. (London: Penguin Classics, 2004), 41–3.

SCHORSCH, JONATHAN, *Jews and Blacks in the Early Modern World* (Cambridge: Cambridge University Press, 2004).

SCHWARZ, ADOLF, *Der Hermeneutische Syllogismus in der Talmudischen Literatur* (Karlsruhe: Bielefeld Verlag, 1901).

SEGREFF, KLAUS-WERNER, *Moses Mendelssohn und die Aufklärungsästhetik im 18. Jahrhundert* (Bonn: Bouvier Verlag Herbert Grundmann, 1984).

Service of the Synagogue for New Year (London: Routledge & Kegan Paul, n.d.).

SEXTUS EMPIRICUS, *Outlines of Pyrrhonism*, trans. R. G. Bury (Loeb Classical Library, 273) (Cambridge, Mass.: Harvard University Press, 1933).

—— *Against Physicists, Against Empiricists*, trans. R. G. Bury (Loeb Classical Library, 311) (Cambridge, Mass.: Harvard University Press, 1936).

SHAPIRO, MARC B., *Between the Yeshiva World and Modern Orthodoxy: The Life and Works of Rabbi Jacob Jehiel Weinberg 1884–1966* (London: Littman Library of Jewish Civilization, 1999).

—— *The Limits of Orthodox Theology: Maimonides' Thirteen Principles Reappraised* (Oxford: Littman Library of Jewish Civilization, 2004).

SHEAR-YASHUV, AHARON, *The Theology of Salomon Ludwig Steinheim* (Leiden: E. J. Brill, 1986).

SHERMAN, NOSSON (ed.), *The Torah: Haftaros and Five Megillos with a Commentary Anthologized from the Rabbinic Writings* (New York: Mesorah Publications, 1993).

SHIHOR, RACHEL, 'On the Problems of Halakhah's Status in Judaism', *Forum* (WZO, Jerusalem) 30–1 (Spring/Summer 1978), 146–54.

SIEGEL, J. P., *The Severus Scroll and 1QIs^a*, Society of Biblical Literature Masoretic Series 1 (Missoula, Mont.: Scholars Press, 1974), 159–65.

SILVER, D. J., *The Story of Scripture: From Oral Tradition to the Written Word* (New York: Basic Books, 1990).

SIMON, RICHARD, *Histoire critique du Vieux Testament* (Paris, 1678; rev. 5th edn. Rotterdam, 1685, repr. Frankfurt, 1967).

SIRAT, COLETTE, *A History of Jewish Philosophy in the Middle Ages* (Cambridge: Cambridge University Press, 1990).

SMITH, WESLEY D., *The Hippocratic Tradition* (Ithaca, NY: Cornell University Press, 1979; rev. electronic edn. 2002).

SOLOMON BEN ADRET, *Responsa* [She'elot uteshuvot harashba], 7 vols. (Benei Berak: Sifriyati, 1958).

SOLOMON, NORMAN, 'Alianza' (Spanish), *El Olivo*, 27/57 (Jan.–June 2003), 25–55.

—— *The Analytic Movement: Hayyim Soloveitchik and his Circle* (Atlanta, Ga.: Scholars Press, 1993).

—— 'The Evolution of Talmudic Reasoning', *Journal of the History and Philosophy of Logic*, 32 (2011), 9–28.

SOLOMON, NORMAN, 'Extensive and Restrictive Interpretation of Terms in Rabbinic Hermeneutic', in N. Rakover (ed.), *Jewish Law and Current Legal Problems* (Jerusalem, 1984), 37–54; also in *Jewish Law Association Studies*, 1 (1985), Touro Conference Volume, 125–39.

—— 'Judaism and Natural Science', in J. Neusner, Alan J. Avery-Peck, and W. S. Green (eds.), *The Encyclopaedia of Judaism*, vol. ii (Leiden: E. J. Brill, 2000), 960–76.

—— 'Reading Intolerant Texts in a Tolerant Society', in Tony Kushner, Sarah Pearce, and Nadia Valman (eds.), *Philosemitism, Antisemitism and the Jews* (Aldershot: Ashgate, 2005), 49–68.

—— *The Talmud: A Selection* (London: Penguin Books, 2009).

—— 'The Third Presence: Reflections on the Dialogue', in J. Bowden and A. Bayfield (eds.), *Dialogue with a Difference* (London: SCM Press, 1992), 147–62, 175–7.

—— 'Three Books on Jewish Faith', *Journal of Jewish Studies*, 52/1 (Spring 2001), 146–54.

SOLOVEITCHIK, JOSEPH DOV (BER), 'Fixing the Date of Festivals on the Basis of Observation versus by Calculation' (Heb.), in anon., *Kovets ḥidushei torah* (Jerusalem, n.d.), 47–65.

—— *Halakhic Man*, trans. Lawrence Kaplan (Philadelphia, Pa.: Jewish Publication Society of America, 1983). Original edn.: *Ish hahalakhah* (Jerusalem: World Zionist Organization, 1979).

—— 'Kol dodi dofek', in Shelomoh Schmidt (ed.), *Divrei hagut veha'arakhah* (Jerusalem: World Zionist Organization, 1982), 9–56.

—— 'Two Types of Tradition' (Heb.), in *Shiurim lezekher aba mari z'l*, vol. i (Jerusalem, 1983), 220–39.

—— 'Uvikashtem misham', in id., *Ish hahalakhah* (Jerusalem: World Zionist Organization, 1979), 119–21.

SOLOWEITSCHIK, MENACHEM [MAX, or MORDECAI, SOLIELI], and S. RUBASCHEFF [ZALMAN SHAZAR], *History of Biblical Criticism* [Toledot bikoret hamikra] (Berlin: Dwir-Mikra, 1925).

SPALDING, PAUL, 'Toward a Modern Torah: Moses Mendelssohn's Use of a Banned Bible', *Modern Judaism*, 19/1 (Feb. 1999), 67–82.

SPENGLER, OTTO, *Der Untergang des Abendlandes*, 2 vols. (Vienna: Braumüller, Beck, 1918–22).

SPERBER, DANIEL, *Magic and Folklore in Rabbinic Literature* (Ramat Gan: Bar Ilan University Press, 1994).

SPINOZA, BARUCH, *Benedicti de Spinoza Opera*, ed. J. van Vloten and J. P. N. Land, 2 vols., 3rd edn. (The Hague: Martinus Nijhoff, 1913).

—— *Benedict de Spinoza: A Theologico-Political Treatise*, trans. R. H. M. Elwes (London: G. Bell & Son, 1883; New York: Dover Publications, 1951).

STANTON, ELIZABETH CADY, *The Woman's Bible* (1895–8; Amherst, NY: Prometheus Books, 1999).

STARK, RODNEY, *The Rise of Christianity: How the Obscure, Marginal Jesus Movement Became the Dominant Religious Force in the Western World in a Few Centuries* (San Francisco, Calif.: Harper, 1997).

STEINHEIM, SALOMON LUDWIG, *Die Offenbarung nach dem Lehrbegriff des Synagoge, ein Schibboleth* (Frankfurt am Main, 1835).

STERN, MENACHEM (ed.), *Greek and Latin Authors on Jews and Judaism*, 3 vols. (Jerusalem: Israel Academy of Sciences and Humanities, 1974–84).

STERN, SACHA, *Calendar and Community: A History of the Jewish Calendar, 2nd cent. BCE–10th cent. CE.* (Oxford: Oxford University Press, 2001).

STOLOW, JEREMY, *Orthodox by Design: Judaism, Print Politics, and the Artscroll Revolution* (Berkeley, Calif.: University of California Press, 2010).

STRAUSS, BERTHOLD, *The Rosenbaums of Zell: A Study of a Family* (London: Hamakrik, 1962).

STRAUSS, DAVID FRIEDRICH, *The Life of Jesus Critically Examined*, trans. George Eliot (London: SCM Press, 1973).

STROUMSA, GUY G., 'Jewish Myth and Ritual and the Beginnings of Comparative Religion: The Case of Richard Simon', *Journal of Jewish Thought and Philosophy*, 6/1 (1997), 19–35.

SUNDBERG, A. C., *The Old Testament of the Early Church* (Cambridge, Mass.: Harvard University Press, 1964).

SWINBURNE, RICHARD, *The Coherence of Theism* (Oxford: Clarendon Press, 1977).

TACITUS, *Histories*.

TALMON, S., 'The Three Scrolls of the Law That Were Found in the Temple Court', *Textus*, 2 (1962), 14–27.

TARSHISH, A. Z., *R. barukh halevi epstein* (Heb.) (Jerusalem: Mosad Harav Kook, 1967).

TA-SHMA, ISRAEL, 'An Anonymous Critical Commentary on Psalms' (Heb.), *Tarbiz*, 66/3 (Apr.–June 1997), 417–23.

—— 'A Note on Biblical Criticism in Mediaeval Ashkenaz' (Heb.) in S. Yeft (ed.), *Memorial Book to Sarah Kamin* (Heb.) (Jerusalem, 1994), 453–9.

TASSO, *Gerusalemme liberata*.

TERTULLIAN, *Apology*.

TIGAY, JEFFREY H. (ed.), *Empirical Models for Biblical Criticism* (Philadelphia, Pa.: University of Philadelphia Press, 1985).

TISHBY, I., *see* Azriel of Girona

TOV, EMANUEL, *Scribal Practices and Approaches Reflected in the Texts Found in the Judean Desert* (Leiden: E. J. Brill, 2004).

—— *Textual Criticism of the Hebrew Bible* (Minneapolis, Minn.: Fortress Press, 1992; 2nd, rev. edn., 2001).

TRACHTENBERG, J., *Jewish Magic and Superstition: A Study in Folk Religion* (1939; Philadelphia, Pa.: Jewish Publication Society of America, 1961).

TRIVISH, DOV BER BEN YEHUDAH L., *Revid hazahav* (Grodno, 1797).

TROPPER, AMRAM D., *Wisdom, Politics and Historiography: Tractate Avot in the Context of the Graeco-Roman Near East* (Oxford: Oxford University Press, 2004).

TWERSKY, ISADORE, *Rabad of Posquières* (Cambridge, Mass.: Harvard University Press, 1962).

ULRICH, E., 'Jewish, Christian and Empirical Perspectives on the Text of Our Scriptures', in E. Brooks and J. J. Collins (eds.), *Hebrew Bible or Old Testament?* (Notre Dame, Ind.: University of Notre Dame Press, 1990), 69–85.

UNTERMAN, ALAN, *The Kabbalistic Tradition: An Anthology of Jewish Mysticism* (London: Penguin Classics, 2008).

UZZIEL, BEN-ZION, *Sha'arei uzi'el*, 2 vols. (Jerusalem, 1944–6).

VARGON, SHMUEL, 'The Controversy between I. S. Reggio and S. D. Luzzatto on the Date of Writing of the Pentateuch', *Hebrew Union College Annual*, 72 (2001), 139–54.

WALZER, RICHARD, *Galen on Jews and Christians* (Oxford: Oxford University Press, 1949).

WASSERSTEIN, BERNARD, *Vanishing Diaspora: The Jews of Europe since 1945*, rev. edn. (London: Penguin, 1997).

WEINBERG, JEHIEL JACOB, *Meḥkarim batalmud* (Berlin: Rabbinerseminar, 1937–8).

WEINSHEIMER, JOEL C., *Gadamer's Hermeneutics* (New Haven, Conn.: Yale University Press, 1985).

WEISS HALIVNI, DAVID, *The Book and the Sword* (Boulder, Colo.: Westview, 1998).

—— *Peshat and Derash* (Oxford: Oxford University Press, 1991).

—— *Revelation Restored: Divine Writ and Critical Responses* (Boulder, Colo.: Westview Press, 1997).

WELLHAUSEN, JULIUS, *Die Composition des Hexateuchs* (Berlin: G. Reimer, 1889).

WERBLOWSKY, R. J. Z., *Joseph Karo, Lawyer and Mystic* (London: Oxford University Press, 1962).

WESTPHAL, MEROLD, *Levinas and Kierkegaard in Dialogue* (Bloomington, Ind.: Indiana University Press, 2008).

WHITE, MICHAEL, *Isaac Newton: The Last Sorcerer* (London: Fourth Estate, 1997).

WILLIAMS, BERNARD, *Truth and Truthfulness: An Essay in Genealogy* (Princeton, NJ: Princeton University Press, 2002).

WILSON, EDWARD O., *Sociobiology: The New Synthesis*, 25th anniversary edn. (Cambridge, Mass.: Harvard University Press, 2000).

WOLFSON, H. A., 'The Double Faith Theory in Saadia, Averroes and St. Thomas', *Jewish Quarterly Review*, NS 33 (1942), 231–64.

—— 'The Philonic God of Revelation and his Latter-day Deniers', in H. A. Wolfson, *Religious Philosophy* (Cambridge, Mass.: Belknap Press, 1961), 1–26.

WOLLSTONECRAFT, MARY, *A Vindication of the Rights of Woman* (1792), in *The Rights of Woman, by Mary Wollstonecraft, with The Subjection of Women, by John Stuart Mill*, introd. Pamela Fraukau (Everyman's Library 825) (London: Dent, 1959).

YAHUDA, ABRAHAM SHALOM, *Die Sprache des Pentateuch in ihren Beziehungen zum Aegyptischen* (Berlin: W. de Gruyter, 1929).

YATES, FRANCES A., *Giordano Bruno and the Hermetic Tradition* (London: Routledge & Kegan Paul, 1964).

YEIVIN, ISRAEL, *A Collection of Mishnaic Geniza Fragments with Babylonian Vocalization* (Jerusalem: Makor, 1974).

—— *Introduction to the Tiberian Masorah*, trans. E. J. Revell (Missoula, Mont.: Scholars Press, 1980).

ZIMMERLI, W., *Das alte Testament in der Verkündigung der christlichen Kirche* (Munich, 1956).

ZLOTOWITZ, MEIR (ed.), *The Megillah. The Book of Esther. A New Translation with a Commentary Anthologized from Talmudic, Midrashic and Rabbinic Sources, Translated and Compiled by Rabbi Meir Zlotowitz*, 2nd edn. (New York: Mesorah Publications, 1976).

ZUCKER [TSUKER], MOSHE (ed.), *A Critique against the Writings of R. Saadya Gaon by R. Mubashshir Halevi* (New York: P. Feldheim, 1955).

ZUNZ, LEOPOLD, *Die gottesdienstlichen Vorträge der Juden, historisch entwickelt* (Berlin, 1832).

Index of Scriptural References

◆

Index of Rabbinic References

◆

General Index

◆

Printed and bound by CPI Group (UK) Ltd, Croydon, CR0 4YY